T0305706

This is a study of the development of Barcelona's cotton industry from its origins in calico-printing in 1728 to its introduction of steam-power in 1832. It thus describes the experiences of the leading industry of the city which provides the one Mediterranean exception to the tendency of early industrialization to be concentrated in northern Europe. Although it serves as an industrial history, a principal aim is to throw light on wider issues. It bridges the 'pre-industrial' and early 'industrial' periods, offering answers to such questions as: What caused 'merchant capital' to move into industrial investment? What were the links between 'pre-industrial' industrial activity and industrialization proper? Is it apt to refer to the economic changes of these years as an 'Industrial Revolution'? Should industrialization be studied on a regional or a national basis?

A further purpose is to provide an interpretation of the characteristics of the Catalan economy and of its relationship to that of Spain as a whole thereby contributing to the understanding of the 'Catalan question'. This it attempts by an analysis of Catalonia's industrial development over the very long term in which a dualism occasioned by the alternating dominance of 'commercial' and 'industrial' capital is demonstrated and by a focus on the links between the area's industrial growth and, on the one hand, the economic policies of the Spanish State and, on the other, developments in national and colonial markets.

A DISTINCTIVE INDUSTRIALIZATION

A DISTINCTIVE INDUSTRIALIZATION

Cotton in Barcelona, 1728–1832

J. K. J. THOMSON
University of Sussex

CAMBRIDGE
UNIVERSITY PRESS

PUBLISHED BY THE PRESS SYNDICATE OF THE UNIVERSITY OF CAMBRIDGE
The Pitt Building, Trumpington Street, Cambridge, United Kingdom

CAMBRIDGE UNIVERSITY PRESS
The Edinburgh Building, Cambridge CB2 2RU, UK
40 West 20th Street, New York NY 10011–4211, USA
477 Williamstown Road, Port Melbourne, VIC 3207, Australia
Ruiz de Alarcón 13, 28014 Madrid, Spain
Dock House, The Waterfront, Cape Town 8001, South Africa

http://www.cambridge.org

First published 1992
First paperback edition 2002

A catalogue record for this book is available from the British Library

Library of Congress Cataloguing in Publication data
Thomson, J. K. J.
A distinctive industrialization: cotton in Barcelona, 1728–1832 / J. K. J. Thomson.
p.   cm.
Includes bibliographical references.
ISBN 0 521 39482 1
1. Cotton textile industry – Spain – Barcelona – History – 18th
century.   2. Cotton textile industry – Spain – Barcelona –
History – 19th century.   3. Barcelona (Spain) – Industries –
History – 18th century.   4. Barcelona (Spain) – Industries –
History – 19th century.
I. Title.
HD9885.S72B378   1992
338.4'767721'094672–dc20   91-27092   CIP

ISBN 0 521 39482 1 hardback
ISBN 0 521 52262 5 paperback

For Verónica

Contents

ix

Contents   xi

Maps

xii

Tables

xiii

Acknowledgements

The researching and writing of this book were made possible by grants of leave of absence from the University of Sussex in 1984, 1989 and 1990 and the receipt of two research fellowships from the Nuffield Foundation in 1984 and 1990. Additional financial support for the project was provided by the University of Sussex's Arts Research Support Fund.

While I have been involved in this work I have received support from many sources. Colleagues both at my own and other universities in Britain have collaborated in a variety of ways and I would like in particular to acknowledge the support of John Harris (Birmingham), Colin Brooks, Michael Hawkins, Maurice Hutt, Willie Lamont and Keith Middlemas (Sussex), Maxine Berg and Guy Thomson (Warwick), Pat Hudson (Liverpool) and Stuart Woolf (Essex and Florence).

Serge Chassagne of Rouen University has been a source of encouragement as he was to my earlier work on Languedoc. In Catalonia my debts are multiple. The following historians have been generous in their provision of advice and in the communication of their enthusiasm – Rafel Aracil, Manuel Arranz, Josep-Maria Delgado, Montserrat Duran, Roberto Fernández, Ramon Grau, Miquel Izard, Marina López, Carlos Martínez Shaw, Pere Molas Ribalta, Jordi Nadal, Isona Passola, Elisa Rosa, Alejandro Sánchez and Jaume Torras. In particular I would like to express my gratitude to Montserrat Duran, for her role in organizing in 1988 a seminar on the Catalan manufacture in the eighteenth century in which I participated and which proved a great stimulus to my work and Jaume Torras who has been a constant and patient source of both encouragement and, by means of his own work on the Catalan economy in the eighteenth century, inspiration.

The personnel of the various libraries and archives which I have consulted in the research for this book has invariably been welcoming and cooperative. In particular I would like to express my gratitude for the assistance provided by Jaume Sobrequés, director of the Arxiu Històric de la Ciutat de Barcelona, Laureà Pagarolas, director of Barcelona's notarial archive, and the staffs of the archive of the Biblioteca de Catalunya and of the University Library at Sussex.

Cambridge University Press has been most supportive throughout the publishing process and my thanks are due in particular to William Davies for advice and encouragement and Linda Randall for her painstaking copyediting.

The book is dedicated to my wife. She in 1971 gave me a copy of the first volume of Pierre Vilar's superb history of Catalonia to help me, she said, to understand her country – in the long process of my achieving this she has been patient and supportive. Her family has since my marriage exemplified in my respect the Catalan qualities of hospitality and openness.

My own parents have throughout shown interest in, and provided maximal support for, this project – to them, too, I record my gratitude.

Abbreviations, languages, measures and monetary exchanges

Catalan, Castilian and English

Place-names
I have used Catalan versions of place-names in Catalonia (e.g. Banyoles rather than Bañolas) except when the Castilian version would be the more familiar to an English reader (e.g. Lérida rather than Lleida). In addition, I have used English versions of other Spanish place-names where they exist (e.g. Andalusia rather than Andalucía).

People's names
For the sake of consistency I have used Catalan versions of names throughout the text for Catalans even though usage in fact varies in different types of sources (e.g. Bernat rather than Bernardo).

Quotations
I have translated French, Catalan and Castilian quotations into English.

Use of Catalan, Castilian words
Some key words used throughout the book I have left untranslated (e.g. *indiana* or printed calico). In the case of these I have used what seemed the most appropriate language – for example *fabricant* (Catalan) rather than *fabricante* (Castilian) but *fábrica(s)* (Castilian) rather than *fàbrica (-ques)* (Catalan).

Measures
The *cana*, which was divided into 8 *pams*, was a length of 1.55 metres.

Exchanges
The Catalan *libra*, which was divided into 20 *sols* or 240 *denarios*, was worth approximately 2 shillings and 2 pence in contemporary sterling terms.
The *real* of *vellón* (copper) was worth approximately 2.4 pence in contemporary sterling.

CHAPTER I

Introduction

Barcelona is a capital of the north with respect to Spain: rich, industrial, hard-working, a bit cold, pragmatic. In contrast it is the most southerly of the capitals of Europe ... the Mediterranean relativizes the harshness of scrupulously capitalist relations of production.

(M. Vázquez Montalbán, *Barcelones* (Barcelona, 1990), p. 37)

This book is a study of the early history of the Spanish cotton industry, in Barcelona. It covers two principal phases in the industry's development: a first, from approximately 1736 to 1783, which was characterized by a concentration above all on calico-printing and a second, from 1783 to 1832, during which there was a gradual expansion in spinning and weaving and a start was made to introducing the cotton machinery which had been invented in England. It is limited, thus, principally to the period generally defined as 'pre-' or 'proto-' industrial; indeed it ends in the year of the foundation of the city's first steam-powered factory, that of Bonaplata, Rull and Vilaregut.[1]

The concentration on Barcelona is justified by the fact that the development of the national industry was largely confined to the city during these two first phases. It was only during the second phase, with the expansion firstly of manual spinning and then the progression to dependence on hydraulic and steam-power, that the extent of this predominance began to be reduced with significant diffusion of the industry to other parts of Catalonia. Even then the lack of local mineral resources, and the consequent need to import

---

[1] First *successful* steam-powered manufacture: there were earlier attempts at use of steam-power which were not persisted with. On these, see below, pp. 264–6. On the Bonaplata mill, see J. Nadal, 'Los Bonaplata: tres generaciones de industriales catalanes en la España del siglo XIX', *Revista de Historia Económica*, 1 (1983), pp. 79–95, and his *El fracaso de la Revolución Industrial en España, 1814–1913* (Barcelona, 1975), p. 198, or the condensed English version of this: 'The Failure of the Industrial Revolution in Spain, 1830–1914', in *The Fontana Economic History of Europe* (London, 1973), IV, pt 2, pp. 609–10.

coal as well as steam engines, led to the continuance of the city's importance as a manufacturing centre. Surveys of the location of cotton spindles in Catalonia carried out in 1850 and 1861 show Barcelona's share to have stood at over a third for both dates and the predominance with respect to steam-power was emphatic: a further survey of 1848 reveals that sixty-six of the eighty-nine Watt engines in use were in mills in Barcelona and its immediately surrounding areas.[2] The 1860s represented a more definite turning-point with diffusion facilitated by the adoption of the water turbine, which increased the advantage of hydraulic power over steam, and the building of railways, which eased the delivery of coal and other cost-influencing products, including grain, to interior areas of Catalonia.[3]

AN INDUSTRIAL HISTORY

The study is intended firstly to serve as a general history of the industry. There is a need for such for although considerable research has been carried out on aspects of, and phases in, its development by Catalan historians in recent years, this work has not been collated into a history of the industry as a whole. The gap in the literature in English is even greater.[4] As a 'general industrial history', it is hoped

[2] Nadal, *El fracaso*, pp. 198–201. See also R. Grau and M. López, 'Revolució industrial i urbanització. Barcelona en la construcció de la Catalunya moderna (1714–1860)', *L'Avenç*, 88 (1985), pp. 14–31.

[3] On this, see E. Camps, 'Migraciones internas y formación del mercado de trabajo en la Cataluña industrial en el siglo XIX' (DPhil thesis, University Institute of Florence, 1990), p. 50, and P. Pascual, *Agricultura i industrialització a la Catalunya del segle XIX* (Barcelona, 1990), pp. 82–130. Coal was needed in interior areas to fuel steam engines which were used to complement hydraulic power whose availability was threatened by drought during the summer months.

[4] The principal published works in Spanish on the industry for the period covered by this book (in addition to those cited in nn. 1–3 above) are as follows: J. Carrera Pujal, *Historia política y económica de Cataluña* (4 vols., Barcelona, 1946–7), IV, pp. 133–65, and *La economía de Cataluña en el siglo XIX* (4 vols., Barcelona, 1961), II, pp. 197–332; F. Torrella Niubó, *El moderno resurgir textil de Barcelona* (*siglos XVIII y XIX*) (Barcelona, 1961); V. Vázquez de Prada, 'Las fábricas de indianas y estampados de Barcelona en el siglo XVIII', *Third International Conference of Economic History* (Paris, 1965), V, pp. 277–91, and 'Un modelo de empresa catalana de estampados en el siglo XVIII; la firma Francisco Ribas', *Primer Congrès d'Història Moderna de Catalunya* (Barcelona, 1984) I, pp. 635–42; P. Molas Ribalta, *Los gremios barceloneses del siglo XVIII* (Madrid, 1970), pp. 519–38; A. Duran Sanpere, *Barcelona i la seva història* (3 vols., Barcelona, 1972–5), II, pp. 291–309; R. Grau and M. López, 'Empresari i capitalista a la manufactura catalana del segle XVIII. Introducció a l'estudi de les fàbriques d'indianes', *Recerques*, 4 (1974), pp. 19–57; C. Martínez Shaw, 'Los orígenes de la industria algodonera catalana y el comercio colonial', in J. Nadal and G. Tortella (eds.), *Agricultura, comercio colonial y crecimiento económico en la España contemporánea* (Barcelona, 1974), pp. 243–94; R. Alier, 'La fàbrica d'indianes de la família Canals', *Recerques*, 4 (1974), pp. 59–91; R. Fernández, 'La burguesía barcelonesa en el siglo XVIII: la familia Glòria', in

that the book will be of service to students of economic history interested in issues such as entrepreneurship, the organization of production, technological change and diffusion, investment practices, capital accumulation, the relationship of industrial change to state policy, the character of markets and the relationship of industrial growth to expansion in trade. The book should also make it possible to incorporate the Catalan example into those few attempts which have been made to adopt a comparative approach to European industrialization. In particular it will contribute to completing the type of comparison in terms of factors of production carried out by Stanley Chapman and Serge Chassagne,[5] and it is hoped, too, that it will make it possible to situate the Catalan example with respect to the contrasting, textile industrialization paradigms posited by Maurice Lévy Leboyer – the 'downstream' pattern, dominated by the basic manufacturing processes, the British case, and the 'upstream', led by the finishing (printing) ones, that of the French.[6]

P. Tedde (ed.), *La economía española al final del Antiguo Régimen*, II, *Manufacturas* (Barcelona, 1982), pp. 3–131; A. Sánchez, 'Los orígenes sociales de los fabricantes de indianas. La familia Rull', *Primer Congrès d'Història Moderna de Catalunya* (Barcelona, 1984), I, pp. 779–88, and 'L'estructura comercial d'una fàbrica d'indianes barcelonina: Joan Rull i Cia (1790–1821)', *Recerques*, 22 (1989), pp. 9–24; J. M. Delgado, 'La industria algodonera catalana (1776–96) y el mercado americano. Una reconsideración', *Manuscrits, Revista d'Història Moderna*, 7 (1988), pp. 103–16; J. Fontana, *Aribau i la indústria cotonera a Catalunya* (Barcelona, 1963); M. Izard, *Industrialización y obrerismo* (Barcelona, 1973); J. Vicens Vives, *Industrials i polítics del segle XIX* (Barcelona, 1958), pp. 45–79; M. Izard, *La revolución industrial en España. Expansión de la industria algodonera catalana, 1832–1861* (photocopied edition, Mérida, 1969). There exists, too, important unpublished work: above all that of A. Sánchez, 'Los fabricantes de indianas de Barcelona a finales del siglo XVIII y principios del XIX: la familia Rull' (Tesis de licenciatura, Barcelona, 1981), 'Los fabricantes de algodón de Barcelona, 1772–1839' (3 vols., DPhil thesis, Barcelona 1987), and 'La era de la manufactura algodonera en Barcelona, 1736–1839' (photocopied text now to be published in *Estudios de Historia Social*). The literature in English is limited to J. C. La Force, *The Development of the Spanish Textile Industry* (Berkeley, CA, 1965), pp. 14–19, 133–44; R. Herr, *The Eighteenth Century Revolution in Spain* (Princeton, NJ, 1973), pp. 137–42, and short sections of general studies on Spanish and European industrialization.
[5] S. D. Chapman and S. Chassagne, *European Textile Printers in the Eighteenth Century* (London, 1981).
[6] M. Lévy Leboyer, *Les Banques européennes et l'industrialisation internationale dans la première moitié du XIXe siècle* (Paris, 1964). See also his 'Le processus d'industrialisation: le cas de l'Angleterre et de la France', *Revue Historique*, 239 (1968), pp. 281–98.

A distinctive industrialization

FROM 'COMMERCIAL' TO 'INDUSTRIAL' CAPITALISM

Dobb and Vilar

The book also relates to some of the major conceptual issues which
have arisen in the course of interpreting the process of Europe's
economic and social development. Firstly, it should serve to throw
light on the debate concerning the movement from a stage of
'commercial' to one of 'industrial capitalism' which apparently
coincides in the Catalan case with the period covered by the book.
The question has its source, of course, in *Capital* in which Marx
distinguishes two possible routes for the change – 'a really revolutionary way' in which 'The producer becomes a merchant and
capitalist in contradiction to the agricultural natural economy and
the guild encircled handicrafts of the medieval town industry' or one
in which 'the merchant takes possession in a direct way of production'
and which though it 'serves historically as a mode of transition
nevertheless ... cannot by itself do much for the overthrow of the old
mode of production, but rather preserves it or uses it as its premise'.[7]
The more general reference point, however, is Maurice Dobb's *Studies
in the Development of Capitalism* which represents the principal
interpretation of the Marxist viewpoint. Dobb's approach is im-
aginative, eclectic and based on wide historical knowledge – later
criticisms of either narrowness, or of having given too much weight to
one rather than another of the principal mechanisms whereby the
transition was achieved, seem misplaced.[8]

Aware that Marx's second 'way', as Marx himself suspected, had
more often represented a cul-de-sac than securing a successful passage
to industrial capitalism, a first of Dobb's emphases was on the
particular circumstances in the English case which caused a
broadening of the involvement in investment in industry so that
middling social groups as well as members of the commercial and
landed elite became involved. He attributed this largely to the
seventeenth-century political changes which led to a decline in the
monopolies and restrictive practices which had previously restricted
commercial opportunities. A second, and the principal, emphasis was

[7] Cited by M. Dobb, *Studies in the Development of Capitalism* (revised edn, London, 1963),
p. 123.
[8] E.g. R. Brenner, 'Dobb on the Transition from Feudalism to Capitalism', *Cambridge Journal
of Economics*, 2 (1978), pp. 121–40, argues that Dobb overemphasizes external causes
(commerce, towns, political changes) in his explanation.

on the process of 'capital accumulation'. By this Dobb meant a 'primitive' accumulation of capital in the Marxist sense – in other words one which preceded, and made possible, the structural shift to a type of economy in which capital accumulation was regular and automatic. Although, again, he was wide-ranging in his identification of causes of the development – he considered the effects of trade and inflation, with its possibly discriminatory effects on groups with different extents and types of property and indebtedness, amongst others – he attached particular importance to those types of accumulation which involved deprivation of one individual by another (such as that of land) and which, thus, had the additional effect of contributing to that other necessary factor of production for a capitalist system, a 'free' (in terms of possessing nothing and thus being dependent on the labour market: the 'freedom' was that of the employer) labour force: 'It had to be enrichment in ways which involved dispossession of persons several times more numerous than those enriched', he wrote.[9]

The framework for discussing the issue in the Catalan case is Pierre Vilar's brilliant study *La Catalogne dans l'Espagne moderne*. The source of the early emergence of industrial capitalism in the Catalan region, and the problems to which this precocity gave rise in a national context in which traditional modes of production dominated both quantitatively and with respect to the holding of political power, represent the unifying themes of the work.[10] For Vilar, Dobb's interpretation is too oriented towards the English example. Influenced himself by the work of the Annales school, and particularly by that of Ernest Labrousse with its emphasis on economic, demographic and social change over the long term[11] – to which Dobb, of course, could barely have had access – he states at the opening of the second volume of the three-volume work that 'It appears clearer and clearer today that the creative power of the eighteenth century – which assured the definitive triumph of capitalist over feudal society – did not only manifest itself in the England

---

[9] Dobb *Studies in Capitalism*, pp. 123–254.
[10] P. Vilar, *La Catalogne dans l'Espagne moderne. Recherches sur les fondements économiques des structures nationales* (3 vols., Paris, 1962). See, for instance, I, p. 154: 'The development of capitalism reserves these sorts of surprises. It is, by essence, an unequal development. It has installed in Spain, between the country as a whole and its industrialized regions, a sort of relationship of backward country to economically advanced country, of colony to metropolis, with the rancour which that supposes. But here the colonized are the majority. And they have the state! It is the origin of the split.' [11] *Ibid.*, I, pp. 16–20, on this influence.

of the Industrial Revolution and in the France of the political revolution, but in the whole of Europe and its American annexes.'[12] He sets the question of the source of this 'creative power' in the Catalan region within a Malthusian framework: the limiting factor on the development of commercial capitalism, he argues, was low agricultural productivity; this occasioned diminishing marginal returns in any period of economic expansion as rising food and raw material prices penalized commercial and industrial investment whilst privileging incomes drawn from the sector of the economy most committed to the old structures – agriculture. This low agricultural productivity, though, as we shall see, he attributes primarily to the manner in which the pre-industrial economy was organized. The eighteenth-century Catalan expansion, he demonstrates, was particularly powerful, largely because it began from such a low starting-point, but it, too, soon showed signs of being vulnerable to the action of this iron, Malthusian law: by the mid-1750s rates of population growth began to decline as densities returned to high levels and consequent restrictions in labour supply some twenty years later threatened advance in the most 'progressive' sectors of the economy. On this occasion, however, the difficulties, rather than representing the prelude for economic regression, evoked an innovatory response: the declining profit margins in the commercial and agricultural sectors gave rise to a large-scale transfer of capital to industry, removing, thus, the principal restrictions to continuous economic progress.

Vilar's explanation of how this had come about is consistent with Dobb's interpretation. There had been a change in 'modes of production', and in particular a great growth in the size of markets, a concentration of wealth and an increase in the 'freedom' of labour, permitting its rapid deployment from the agricultural to the industrial sector. A large-scale switch to industrial investment had thus become for the first time a possibility. The causes of these changes, according to Vilar, were on the one hand certain structural characteristics of the Catalan economy and society – in particular the practice of primogeniture, and the resultant satisfactory size of Catalan land-holdings and disincentive to holding labour on the land, and the area's varied climatic and soil resources, which encouraged specialization and the growth of market production – and on the other the unprecedented extent of the eighteenth-century

---

[12] *Ibid.*, ii, p. 9.

demographic and commercial expansion which led to a maximization of the possibilities of change which these structural characteristics permitted.[13]

Common ground in Dobb's and Vilar's interpretations is the argument that it was only when the high profits which characterized 'commercial capitalism' were eroded by competition that investment on another basis was resorted to. 'Compared with the glories of spoiling the Levant or the Indies or lending to princes', Dobb writes, 'industrial capital was doomed to occupy the place of a dowerless and unlovely younger sister',[14] and Vilar emphasizes the decline in profit margins in the second half of the eighteenth century in Catalonia and the resultant 'patient or passionate search by businessmen for new types of investment outlet: colonial expeditions, industrial investments... the exploitation of a massive labour force'.[15]

This book's contribution

It is not the intention to challenge Vilar's interpretation. On the contrary, a principal of the book's purposes is simply to play a part in what is effectively developing into a collective activity, that of filling the gap occasioned by Vilar's failure to complete a fourth, industrial volume for his study.[16] This purpose assumes a respect for Vilar's characterization of the Catalan growth process, but, in its fulfilment, in addition to presenting material which will effectively do no more than document developments which are anticipated by Vilar, I shall also be concentrating on two phases in Catalan industrial development to which he gave less attention and whose characteristics, it is hoped, will contribute to refining his case.

The first of these is an industrial expansion in Barcelona in the 1740s. Vilar, as we have just noted, focusses principally on the period of industrial expansion between 1770 and 1790 when, it is true, it was at its most rapid, but this earlier growth was substantial – a near quadrupling in the size of the cotton industry was achieved – and is significant insofar as a principal cause for it was the first major participation of merchant capital in industrial investment. In my

---

[13] *Ibid.*, II–III, *passim*. The argument is summarized at the following points: II, pp. 555–81; III, pp. 9–12 and 559–66. [14] Dobb, *Studies in Capitalism*, p. 160.
[15] Vilar, *La Catalogne*, III, p. 562.
[16] That one was originally intended is clear. At the end of III (p. 569), though, Vilar is vague about his future intentions. He refers to 'The phenomenon of Catalan industrialization' as 'too important to be treated as just an appendix of volume III, and too slight, despite everything, in the limits of the eighteenth century, to justify a whole volume to itself'.

fourth chapter I will focus on this episode and test Marxist explanations for the development – in terms of rising demand and crisis in
other trades inducing a transfer of resources to industry – against
others in terms of state policy and supply considerations (the
availability of calico-printing skills). The second of the phases is that
situated between the interruption of the expansion of the eighteenth
century as a consequence of the War of Independence of 1808–14 and
the renewed acceleration in industrial production of the mid-1830s.
It represents the more serious gap in Vilar's work insofar as its
existence makes it impossible to assess the extent of permanence of
those changes in modes of production which he identified. Was the
changed attitude to industrial investment a permanent one? In this
case he has identified the turning-point in the area's economic and
social history. Or did the crises of the end of the century force a return
to the traditional diffidence of commercial capital to industrial
outlets? In this case the change observed is not of such great
significance: the turning-point was a potential one only. Vilar does
consider this period in his short article 'La Catalunya industrial:
reflexions sobre una arrencada i sobre un destí' but, in the absence of
the necessary data, he is forced to adopt guesswork in answering these
questions – he notes scattered evidence for continued industrial
production, hypothesizes that the severity of the crisis in commerce
may have been greater than in industry and thus actually have
favoured industrial growth, and reiterates his previous emphasis on
the importance of the changes in modes of production as another
cause for industrial continuity: 'Catalonia had become used to
producing not for subsistence but to sell.'[17] In chapter 8 an attempt
will be made at providing a stronger empirical basis for interpreting
these years.

'PROTO-INDUSTRIALIZATION'

Catalonia and the debate

The same types of issue which preoccupied both Dobb and Vilar are
of concern to historians today but the vocabulary which they use in
their analysis has altered slightly and there have been some
substantive changes in interpretations. In particular, studies of the

---

[17] P. Vilar, 'La Catalunya industrial: reflexions sobre una arrencada i sobre un destí',
Recerques, 3 (1974), pp. 7–22. Exists also in a French version in F. Crouzet, R. Gascon and
P. Léon (eds.), *L'Industrialisation en Europe au XIXe siècle. Cartographie et typologie* (Paris, 1972).

type of which this book is an example would tend, now, to be grouped within the category of what is called 'proto-industrialization'. Proto-industrialization consists, as the title of one of the principal books on it reveals, in industrialization before 'industrialization'.[18] Its study has been given priority by the belief that it represented a particularly important stimulus to those changes in modes of production on which, we have noted, both Dobb and Vilar concentrate. It is not the only new line of research relating to the rise of capitalism. A parallel debate has been going on which was initiated by an article of Robert Brenner in which a comparative approach was used to identify the variables which permitted or restrained the emergence of a capitalist system in agriculture in different countries.[19] The two approaches are not mutually incompatible but do involve differences of emphasis. Whereas Brenner sees development as being an endogenous process which took place within the European agricultural system, students of 'proto-industrialization' would appear to be giving greater priority to changes coming from outside – trade-induced industrial development, which took the form in particular of the spread of industry in the countryside, which represented a catalyst for agricultural and other changes. The giving of particular emphasis to industrial development in the emergence of industrialization is justified by a belief that 'proto-industry' had certain characteristics – the contribution which it made to breaking traditional demographic restraints, the accumulation of capital to which it gave rise, the growth in merchant and technical skills which it encouraged and the growing need to centralize production to which it gave rise – which if they did not make industrialization proper inevitable at least made it more likely.

The source of the proto-industrialization debate was an article written in 1972 by Franklin Mendels in which he generalized from the findings of his research on demographic and industrial developments in Flanders.[20] There have been various contributors to the debate in the Catalan context. Josep Maria Muñoz has shown in his work on Sabadell and Terrassa that the successful nineteenth-century industrializations of these two wool centres was anticipated

---

[18] P. Kriedte, H. Medick and J. Schlumbohm, *Industrialization before Industrialization* (Cambridge, 1981).

[19] R. Brenner, 'Agrarian Class Structure and Economic Development in Pre-Industrial Europe', *Past and Present*, 70 (1976), pp. 30–75.

[20] F. F. Mendels, 'Proto-Industrialization: First Stage of the Industrialization Process', *Journal of Economic History*, 32 (1972), pp. 241–61.

by eighteenth-century 'pre-industrial' growth characterized by the emergence of a dynamic entrepreneurial class, the erosion of guild restrictions, a growth in scale of production, accumulation of capital, a diffusion of skills and demographic growth connected to the expansion in textile employment – all *a priori* support for the proto-industrial argument.[21] By contrast Assumpta Muset has described a contrary experience in the case of the cloth industries of Esparreguera and Olesa de Montserrat. On the one hand, the character of the eighteenth-century development of the industry in these towns conformed to the principal elements in Mendels's model. It was predominantly a rural industry in which industrial work represented by-employment (though there were some full-time participants), production was for distant markets, there were developments in the organization of production and an accumulation of capital, the commercial (though not the production) side of the trade was dominated by merchant capital and the existence of industrial employment stimulated population growth. On the other hand, the growth was not followed by industrialization proper, the two industries experiencing structural problems and decline during the nineteenth century, their contribution to later industrialization being limited to the provision of labour forces for the new textile factories.[22]

Mendels's original article did not, of course, predicate an auto-matic move towards industrialization but it left the question of the circumstances determining the success of the transition vague. Enriqueta Camps's recent thesis on labour migration in Catalonia during the industrialization period contributes to clarifying the issue and makes it possible to locate the apparently contradictory experiences described by Muñoz and Muset within the general process of textile industrialization in Catalonia. Her study dem-onstrates that during the industrialization period textiles were characterized by high rates of labour mobility as a consequence of technological change and those resultant geographical shifts in industrial location to which reference was made in the first paragraphs of this introduction. The labour force which was drawn to the developing sectors of the industry had its source, pre-dominantly, in areas of proto-industrial activity. Industrialization

[21] J. M. Muñoz, 'La contribució de la indústria rural a la industrialització: el cas de Sabadell i Terrassa al segle XVIII', *Primer Congrès d'Història Moderna de Catalunya* (Barcelona, 1984), I, pp. 399–410.
[22] A. Muset, 'Protoindústria e indústria dispersa en la Cataluña del siglo XVIII: La pañera de Esparreguera y Olesa de Montserrat', *Revista de Historia Económica*, 7 (1989), pp. 45–68.

involved a redistribution and concentration of industry and Camps's study illustrates this. Within such a process the contrary types of experience documented by Muñoz and Muset were to have been expected: some areas, such as the two towns studied by the former, benefited from the geographical shifts in the location of the industry, in which case there was a direct movement from local proto-industry to local industrialization, and other areas were the victims of the changes, in which case there was a movement of unemployed textile workers away from the local proto-industry to the new centres of activity.[23] Both studies therefore demonstrate a proto-industrial/ industrialization link.

In contrast to the studies of Muñoz and Muset, which focus on the experiences of individual towns, Jaume Torras, in two important articles, has provided a general interpretation for industrial development in eighteenth-century Spain which he relates to Mendels's model.[24] The eighteenth century provided an opportunity for industrial growth, he shows, because of rising population (and hence demand) and the policy of encouragement to industry followed by the Bourbon monarchy (though he emphasizes the limitations imposed to the independence of Spanish tariff policy by the Treaty of Utrecht). The opportunity was not taken advantage of to an equal extent by the different Spanish regions: developments in linen production were concentrated principally in Galicia, and those in wool, cotton and silk in Valencia and, above all, Catalonia. Success in linen production did not require any special circumstances – it was combined with agricultural activities and the flax was grown by the producer himself. Success in silk and woollen production did, and Torras attributes Catalonia's and Valencia's achievement in the development of these industries to their industrial traditions – they possessed the necessary skills – and to their prior development of market economies, characterized by specialization between agriculture and industry, and resultant accumulation of capital and developments in organization of production.[25] The existence of this 'proto-industry', Torras argues, contributed to industrialization proper insofar as it led to both higher levels of employment, and thus

---

[23] Camps, 'Migraciones internas', pp. 82–183.
[24] J. Torras, 'Early Manufacturing and Proto-Industry in Spain' (unpublished paper given at workshop held at Warwick University on 'Manufacture and Trade in the Mediterranean in the 18th and 19th Centuries', April 1989), and 'Especialización agrícola e industria rural en Cataluña en el siglo XVIII', *Revista de Historia Económica*, 2 (1984), pp. 113–27.
[25] Torras, 'Early Manufacturing', *passim*.

higher incomes and a deepening of the Catalan market for consumer goods, and also to high levels of rural population, consequent upon peasants undertaking part-time textile employment, and thus later to a source for a factory labour force. It was a means, too, he emphasizes, for the accumulation of capital, the gaining of entrepreneurial experience and for the achievement of technical progress, but he does not judge its role to have been essential in the achievement of changes in these areas nor, for that matter, that such changes, whether they were due to proto-industry or not, were so important in the early stages of industrialization: 'it is not clear', he writes, 'that the necessity of such factors was very great with the beginnings of modern industry nor, above all, that their provision was specific to proto-industry'.[26]

In addition to qualifying Mendels's arguments about the links between proto-industrialization and industrialization in this manner, Torras points out other ways in which the Catalan experience differed from that posited in the model: the initial stimulus to the growth in a market economy and to regional specialization, he emphasizes, came not from an industrial but from an agricultural development – a specialization in viticulture in south-western Catalonia made possible by export demand for wine and eau-de-vie – and the industrial production was directed not to export but to domestic markets.

Urban industry and proto-industrialization

According to a strict definition of 'proto-industrialization' – a process of rural, industrial development and resultant regional specialization – the nature of this study – on an urban industry – would exclude it from consideration in the debate. Torras, indeed, with this definition in mind, cites the examples of Barcelona's and Reus's (another urban cotton centre) prominence in the early stages of Catalan industrialization as further arguments against the 'proto-industrialization' thesis. So exclusive a definition, however, as critics have noted, contributes to the exclusion from the discussion of much pre-industrial activity of undoubtable relevance for later industrialization.[27] For this reason, in this study the term 'proto-industry' will

---

[26] Torras, 'Especialización agrícola e industria rural'.
[27] But see P. Kriedte, 'La ciudad en el proceso de protoindustrialización europea', *Manuscrits, Revista d' Historia Moderna*, 4–5 (1987), pp. 171–208. (originally published in *Die alte Stadt*, 1

be used in the sense of any industrial activity carried out on the basis of technologies which did not make centralization of production essential and the book's utility, it is believed, will consist principally in its documenting such activities in an urban rather than a rural setting.

Urban 'proto-industry's' impact was similar to that of rural industry. It provided a like stimulus to the development of commercial agriculture (the existence of proto-industry boosted urban demand for food), it made possible the creation of new family units which was a permissive element for population growth, it gave rise to capital accumulation, the acquirement of technical skills was facilitated and a commitment to industrial employment which was not easily reversible was created. Some characteristics of such proto-industry in Barcelona, however – and the city was representative in this – were different. Production took place not in family units but in large manufactures – 'proto-factories' these have sometimes been termed in view of their similarity to factories proper. In addition, there was extensive merchant involvement in managerial and entrepreneurial tasks as well as in financing the industry. Consequently, it will be demonstrated that proto-industrialization in an urban context could lead to additional preparatory contributions for industrialization to those considered by Mendels in his original study: they provided experience of centralized production and all that went with this in terms of the development of entrepreneurial and managerial skills and the adaptation of labour to factory production. As a lack of these skills has been argued to have been a principal difficulty confronting English manufacturers during the early stages of industrialization the importance of the contribution is clearly not to be underestimated.[28]

It is probable, though, that more is intended by the criticism of the neglect of urban examples in the proto-industrial literature than the consequent omission of discussion of early examples of concentrated production and their possible contributions to the adaptation to the factory system. The basic assumption behind the model is of an ideal movement towards industrialization in which proto-industry is important insofar as it eroded traditional structures and anticipated

(1982), pp. 19–51), for a thorough survey of the literature relating to urban, pre-industrial industry.
[28] On 'proto-factories', see S. D. Chapman, 'The Textile Factory before Arkwright: A typology of Factory Development', *Business History Review*, 48 (1974), pp. 451–78, and on shortages of managers, see S. Pollard, *The Genesis of Modern Management* (London, 1968).

those of the new type of society that was developing. But while such a process may have characterized the most advanced areas of the European economy, it can hardly be held to have been universal. The more general experience in Europe was one in which a spontaneous movement towards industrialization was complemented, or even overshadowed, by one of importing industrialization from outside. In this second type of process traditional social groups who attempted to adapt the new technology and institutions of industrial society to conform to their priorities and needs were involved. Industrialization became a process in which the old mixed with, and influenced, the new. The 'proto-industrialization' literature up to this date has provided few insights into this second type of process.[29] An urban study such as this, however, can do so for it was cities – ports, capitals and established industrial centres – which predominated in this stage of European industrialization.[30] An intention of this study, thus, will be to demonstrate a duality in the part played by 'proto-industry' in Barcelona's development: as well as contributing to the creation of new structures, its growth in an environment pervaded by economic and social practices of a corporative society caused it to be a central agency for the transmission of 'pre-industrial' patterns into the period of the 'Industrial Revolution'.

'INDUSTRIAL REVOLUTION'

It is the aptness of the use of this last expression in the context of Catalan industrialization which is a third major issue on which it is intended that this study should throw light. Disagreement on this conceptual issue has shown up in discussions among historians of the Catalan experience as it has done in the case of virtually every other European industrialization.

[29] See my chapter 'Variations in Industrial Structure in Pre-Industrial Languedoc', in M. Berg, P. Hudson and M. Sonenscher (eds.), *Manufacture in Town and Country before the Factory* (Cambridge, 1983), pp. 61–92, for an argument of this sort based on the Languedocian experience.

[30] For an argument that Catalan industrialization had this characteristic of being imported, via Barcelona, see R. Grau, 'Cambio y continuidad en los orígenes de la Barcelona moderna (1814–1860)', *Revista de la Universidad Complutense*, 28 (1979), pp. 569–87. On the centrality of Paris to the technology-introducing stage of French industrialization, see L. Bergeron, *Banquiers, négociants et manufacturiers parisiens. Du directoire à l'Empire* (2 vols., Paris, 1975), II, p. 854: 'the remodelling of the French economic space in the nineteenth century was to be ordered, above all other considerations, by the Parisian concentration of capital and entrepreneurs'.

The roots of the difficulty lie in different interpretations of what the central characteristics of the changes which occurred were. From this initial disagreement there follow disputes about the attribution of the events to a particular period. For Pierre Vilar, as has been noted, the turning-point took the form of a change in 'modes of production'. In later discussions on the issue he clarified his position further. Technological change was not essential to the change, he argued: it followed from, rather than being part of, the 'revolution': '"machinism" does not seem to me as essential. *Preoccupation* with "machinism", does', he writes.[31] Such a definition makes it possible for him to argue that a period not characterized by significant technological change represented the roots of modern Catalonia. By contrast the Catalan historian Jordi Nadal sees the changes principally in terms of the adoption of new technology. This type of approach causes him to attach importance to the period emphasized by Pierre Vilar but principally on account of the characteristic which the latter judged not to be essential to it – its engendering of a first acceleration in the rate of technological change. And it is the same type of judgement which causes him to attach greater importance to the impact of the political disturbances of the revolutionary and Napoleonic period than does Vilar. New modes of production may have survived but the movement towards mechanization was interrupted – 'this [the political disturbance] set back the mechanization which had begun with remarkable speed in the early years of the century', he writes. In Nadal's interpretation, consequently, the renewal of the process of mechanization, which, this time, was not to be interrupted, is given prominence. This was marked by the foundation of the Bonaplata mill in 1832. He is careful not to oversimplify and distances himself from the contemporarily expressed view that the establishment of the mill represented the beginning of a 'real industrial revolution' – 'The more it is studied, the more it is shown that the industrial history of Catalonia has followed an intricate path, full of windings and retreats', he has written recently – but the work in which he includes this qualification, the official catalogue for a major exhibition on Catalan industrialization which was entitled *Catalunya, la fàbrica d'Espanya. Un segle d'industrialització catalana, 1833–1936*, suggests a preference for such an approach as well as demonstrating, and

---

[31] Remark made in discussion of his paper 'La Catalunya industrial' (see n. 17 above). Published in Crouzet, Medick and Schlumbohm, *L'Industrialisation en Europe*, p. 433.

promoting, a widespread public identification with such a view-point.[32]

These two types of approaches to categorizing, and dating, Catalonia's industrialization have each had their supporters. Vilar's position has been vulnerable because, as noted, thorough though it is on demographic, agricultural and commercial change it does not include material on industry. The most important contribution to filling this gap has been an article by Ramon Grau and Marina López in which a large number of eighteenth-century notarial contracts recording the terms of companies founded within the cotton industry were used to support Vilar's emphasis on the 'manufacturing era'. Grau and López showed that the development of the industry gave rise to important shifts in modes of production whose character they summarize as follows: 'the key word for defining the historical relation between manufacture and industry could be "accumulation"': of capital, in terms of the building up of an innovating, entrepreneurial class and of a 'proletariat', and in the creation of an urban space adapted to the needs of industrial capital.[33] It is Nadal's approach, however, which has probably received more general support. Jordi Maluquer, for example, in a 1983 essay on Catalan industrialization writes categorically that 'Between 1833 and 1840, the starting point of Catalonia's modern industrial development, the steam engine was introduced and various textile plants became mechanized in the cotton and wool sub-sectors.'[34] Albert Carreras likewise, in his chapter in the more recent *Pautas regionales de la industrialización española*, despite presenting new evidence showing a significant expansion in the cotton industry between 1816 and the early 1830s, a period previously thought of as one of stagnation, concludes that the quarter century between 1835 and 1861 should be 'baptized' 'the Industrial Revolution in Catalonia'.[35]

As will be apparent, the problems which arise in connection with the semantic issue of whether the term 'Industrial Revolution'

[32] Nadal, 'The Failure of the Industrial Revolution in Spain', p. 607, and 'Bonaplata, pretext i símbol', in Ajuntament de Barcelona, *Catalunya, la fàbrica d'Espanya. Un segle d'industrialització catalana, 1833–1936* (Barcelona, 1985), p. 22.
[33] Grau and López, 'Empresari i capitalista', p. 21.
[34] J. Maluquer, 'The Industrial Revolution in Catalonia', in N. Sánchez-Albornoz (ed.), *The Economic Modernization of Spain, 1830–1930* (New York, 1987), p. 177.
[35] A. Carreras, 'Cataluña, primera región industrial de España', in J. Nadal and A. Carreras (eds.), *Pautas regionales de la industrialización española (siglos XIX y XX)* (Barcelona, 1990), p. 271.

should be used to describe the economic and social changes of this period, and the linked problem of attributing such, or another, term to a particular period, are closely related to those which arise in the discussions concerning the movement from 'commercial' to 'industrial capitalism' and about the links between 'proto-industrialization' and 'industrialization'. The detailed documentation of the experiences of Barcelona's cotton industry during this critical stage in Catalan history will, it is intended, contribute to the clarifying of this third issue as well as that of the other two.

REGION OR NATION?

The extent of the regional inequality which displayed itself during Spanish industrialization, and which continues to characterize the Spanish economy today, has had the consequence that economic historians have to a great extent been shielded from the conceptual error to the dislodging of which Sidney Pollard directed his exciting interpretation of European industrialization, *Peaceful Conquest*, in 1981: it is virtually impossible to make anachronistic use of the concept of a national economy and to adopt any other than a regional approach. This is not to say, though, that the Catalan case provides full support for Pollard's argument. A qualification of this in certain minor respects is an additional intention of this book.

Pollard's thesis is that Europe's industrialization before the Railway Age was the achievement of a number of dynamic regions rather than national economies. Such dynamic regions were categorized by industrial specializations, resultant development of market relations with agricultural-surplus areas, and the growth of external economies as a consequence of their concentration of transport facilities, technology and labour markets. Britain's case, he holds, was distinct within industrializing Europe up to the Railway Age not so much on account of any particular social, economic or technological development but insofar as it contained a larger concentration of such industrializing regions which competed with, and in some cases superseded, each other.

Our region was one of those which Pollard lists as possessing these dynamic characteristics. Spain, he notes, 'had one major region which could stand comparison with the classic regions of Inner Europe: Catalonia'.[36] The Catalan case does, indeed, appear to fit

[36] S. Pollard, *Peaceful Conquest* (Oxford, 1981), p. 206.

his paradigm. As our discussions on both the movement from 'commercial' to 'industrial' capitalism and 'proto-industrialization' have shown there was indeed a strong interaction between agricultural and industrial growth in the area, a consequent 'snowballing' effect, growth of 'external economies' and the resultant development of the area into a 'growth pole'.[37] Pollard's argument that there was a need for a national economy to possess several such dynamic regions for the momentum of industrialization to be sustained would also be borne out by the Catalan case – the solitariness of its modernization within Spain was to permit an exceptional industrial concentration in the region but was to act in the longer term as a break on its development and as a barrier to the spread of growth throughout Spain. On the other hand, detailed study on the area suggests that Pollard's argument of an essential unity in the experience of these industrializing regions throughout Europe is an oversimplification if the Catalan case is representative. If the interplay between agriculture and industry was common to that observed in other areas, the institutional and social framework (corporative and interventionist) within which the growth process took place was distinct and this, it will be argued, affected the forms which industrialization took.

If there were important ways in which the Catalan experience was similar to that of other industrializing regions of Europe, it will be shown that there were differences too whose source is well explained by another of Pollard's concepts, but one whose influence he implies was only of relevance to the post-Railway Age. This concept is 'the differential of contemporaneousness', by which Pollard means the differing impact of technological change resultant from its being introduced in countries at different stages of their development.[38] In addition, it will be argued that Pollard's argument that the state's role in industrialization only became significant from approximately 1870 ignores one major reality at least. While the experience of state intervention in eighteenth-century Spain does indeed provide further evidence of the ineffectiveness of direct state involvement in economic development at this stage in Europe's development – the costly failures of Spanish royal manufactures have often been recounted[39] – it demonstrates, too, that other forms of indirect intervention, and in particular tariff restrictions, could have decisive effects on

[37] See *ibid.*, pp. 111–23, on the dynamics of a regionally based growth process.
[38] *Ibid.*, pp. 184–90.   [39] See La Force, *Spanish Textile Industry*, pp. 28–50.

economic development. While Catalonia's economic progress during these years had its roots in that rare capacity for market development which it shared with a select group of other favoured European regions, the extent of the industrial development achieved clearly owed something too to the protective tariff policy pursued by the Bourbon monarchs.[40]

POLITICAL ISSUES

Although the research project which has resulted in this study was initially intended to be confined principally to 'economic' and 'social' issues, I soon discovered that the compartmentalization of the past in this manner was even less practicable in Spain than elsewhere. The mere entering of an archive was sufficient to reveal this – the scattered nature of the documentation (and this was the sharpest of contrasts with the situation in France where I had previously been working) showed a lack of political consensus concerning the administrative control over the industry which I was studying.

I ought to have anticipated the existence of this political dimension. Pierre Vilar's thesis demonstrated emphatically enough the connection of the 'Catalan question' to the area's unique ability within Spain to achieve industrialization at an early stage. In Vilar's work, however, the eighteenth century, on which I was concentrating principally, was portrayed as relatively innocent of the tensions to which the dissatisfaction of the Catalan bourgeoisie with the limited nature of national markets, and the reciprocal fear and jealousy of other regions which felt themselves exploited by the Catalans, gave rise in the nineteenth.[41] Josep Fontana had expressed a similar point of view, arguing that during the eighteenth century what amounted to an informal pact had existed between the Catalan bourgeoisie and the conservative, agrarian-dominated centre with the former being given free access to imperial markets. It was only as a consequence of

[40] On protection, see Torras, 'Early Manufacturing', p. 5. Torras emphasizes, though, that the treaties following the War of Spanish Succession restricted the freedom of the Spanish government with respect to tariffs in most industrial products apart from cotton. See below, p. 68, on this. S. Pollard in his recent essay 'Regional Markets and National Development', in M. Berg (ed.), *Markets and Manufactures in Early Industrial Europe* (London, 1991), pp. 38–40, reconsiders state policy and economic development in the pre-industrialization period and concludes that 'State action, if indeed it had any positive effect whatever, tended to confirm the regional structure of industry.' While accepting a possible state contribution here, he does not attempt any assessment of its impact on the character of regional growth.

[41] Vilar, *La Catalogne*, I, pp. 158–61.

the loss of the Spanish empire following the Napoleonic wars, he posited, that this basis of agreement was broken, a dependence on the national market enforced and compromise became impossible. Catalonia's industrial bourgeoisie could not be satisfied with the feudal restrictions of all kinds which choked the possibility of growth in the national market: it was in this way that it became a 'revolutionary' class.[42]

Recent work on various areas of the Catalan economy has shown, however, that both Vilar and Fontana underestimated the importance of the domestic market for Catalonia's expansion in the eighteenth century.[43] This underestimation does not mean that they were wrong in attributing a change in the character of the relationship between agrarian centre and industrializing periphery to the crisis of the revolutionary period – there is abundant evidence in support of their argument. It does mean, however, that they neglected an important element in the Catalan growth experience during the eighteenth century, one which effectively represents the roots of that dependence of Catalonia on national markets, and that dependence of national markets on Catalonia, which, as noted, is the kernel of the 'Catalan question'. This study will join those to which reference has just been made in throwing light on these eighteenth-century roots of nineteenth- and twentieth-century problems.

My research did suggest, though, that Vilar's belief that the centre–periphery relationship was relatively harmonious during the eighteenth century was substantially correct. Certainly there were no tensions to compare with those which soured relationships between Catalonia and Castile in the nineteenth and twentieth centuries. This, however, I found, was not a justification for disregarding the period from the point of view of the Catalan question. If the relationship was so trouble-free after so inauspicious a beginning with the Catalan loss of its autonomous institutions, and experience of many years of political repression, following its defeat in the Spanish War of Succession, it could only have been as a consequence of successful negotiation between the emerging commercial and industrial leaders of Barcelona and the ministers at the centre. The

---

[42] J. Fontana, 'La primera etapa de la formació del mercat nacional a Espanya', in *Homenaje a Vicens Vives* (2 vols., Barcelona, 1967), II, pp. 143–62.

[43] Especially the articles of Delgado, 'La industria algodonera catalana', pp. 103–16, and A. Muset, 'La conquesta del mercat peninsular durant la segona meitat del segle XVIII: l'exemple de la casa Francesc Ribas i Cia (1766–1783)' *Segon Congrès d'Història Moderna de Catalunya, Pedralbes, Revista d'Història Moderna*, 8, i (1988), pp. 395–403.

Introduction 21

channels of communication, the connections, the arguments and some of the institutions in this dialogue, which was to become so significant and tense later, had their roots too in the eighteenth century. I was not alone in noticing this – in the course of my research Alejandro Sánchez and Roberto Fernández were reaching and publishing similar conclusions.[44] Nor, as might have been expected, was the relationship totally trouble-free: there were moments of difficulty, and it was only by a constant exercise of pressure that decisions unfavourable to local interests were reversed or prevented; some of the tensions of the nineteenth century were anticipated, too.[45] The principal focus of this study is not on these issues – it is primarily orientated towards resolving those questions of defining Catalan industrialization to which reference has just been made. However, in the process of resolving this, issues which are of relevance to these political questions will be raised.

If the mere entering of archives was sufficient to alert me to the political dimension of the work in which I was involved, a growing awareness of the poverty of what these archives contained – and again the contrast with the riches of the Colbertian legacy from which I had benefited in my previous work could not have been greater – was to provide an insight into another, linked issue. The industry which I was studying, despite its large size and its economic importance, had largely escaped political control. There barely existed any documentation of an administrative kind about it despite the fact that from its origins authority over it had been vested in the Junta General de Moneda y Comercio which had been assisted in its task from 1758 by a local Junta de Comercio. The most thorough census of manufactures which existed had been carried out not by these bodies but at the orders of the Bishop of Barcelona, anxious to ensure the religious education of the children employed within them.[46] The industry, it seemed, had enjoyed 'laissez-faire' but not because it had developed in a society in which this principle had acquired an ideological predominance but rather because neither the

[44] A. Sánchez, 'De la Compañia de Hilados a la Comisión de Fábricas. El asociacionismo empresarial en Cataluña durante la crisis del Antiguo Régimen (1771–1820)', Segon Congrès d'Història Moderna de Catalunya, Pedralbes, Revista d'Història Moderna, 8, i (1988), pp. 385–94, and 'La formación de una política económica prohibitionista en Cataluña, 1760–1840', Quaderns del Departament de Geografía i Història de l'Estudi General de Lleida (1988), pp. 3–60; and R. Fernández, 'La burguesía barcelonesa', pp. 98–106.
[45] For documentation of tensions in the 1760s, see A. Ruiz Pablo, Historia de la Real Junta Particular de Comercio de Barcelona, 1758–1847 (Barcelona, 1919), pp. 57–70.
[46] The survey was undertaken in 1786. See below p. 187.

old (the guilds) nor the new (the juntas) interventionist instruments had possessed sufficient authority to control it. This again is not an issue about which I shall be going into in depth but some of the material which I shall be covering will be of relevance to it.

If Vilar argued that the Catalan question only arose following the loss of imperial markets in the revolutionary period, he did attribute its roots to the area's economic distinctness to the rest of the peninsula, a distinctness which had its modern source in its eighteenth-century growth. At the subjective level of interpersonal relationships, the source of the problem was sensed as lying in the fact of the Catalan being different from the people of other Spanish regions. This was the impression from both sides of the relationship though it was evaluated distinctly: what was potentially objectionable in the Catalan to other groups in Spain was generally seen as the source of strengths and virtues by the Catalans.[47] In the course of my research Jaume Torras, in work on the marketing networks of the clothiers of Igualada, a town some 50 kilometres to the west of Catalonia, made some interesting observations concerning the source of this phenomenon. The strength of the felt contrast was not purely a consequence of economic inequality: a contribution to it was also played, he argued, by the manner in which the links between Catalonia and the rest of Spain were organized. Distribution and sales were handled by groups of Catalans, very often linked by family relationships to each other, who retained close links with Catalonia, rarely integrating into the areas in which they were working. The consequence of this was that they appeared as an alien and dominating social group. Torras compares the system with the trading diasporas of the pre-industrial period and formed by minority religious groups which showed similar tendencies to endogamy and non-integration. The persistence of such trading systems was, of course, a sign of Spain's backwardness and the lack of progress achieved in the transactions sector.[48]

In a second paper Torras has added an additional nuance to explaining these subjective reactions of the two parties in the relationship to each other. Unequal economic development from the eighteenth century, he argues, was constantly reinforcing the extent

[47] On the Catalan ideology of hard work and frugality, see J. Vicens Vives, *Noticia de Catalunya* (Barcelona, 1954).
[48] J. Torras, 'The Old and the New. Marketing Networks and Textile Growth in Eighteenth Century Spain', in M. Berg (ed.), *Markets and Manufactures in Early Industrial Europe* (London, 1991), pp. 93–113.

of the social differences between Catalonia and Spain, providing a basis for the formation of rival, national stereotypes and conflicting ideologies. The smallness of the Catalan enclave in which the modernizing ideologies favourable to industrialization were concentrated, however, made it difficult for them to achieve supremacy nationally. It is Torras's argument, therefore, that it was not so much the lack of an early industrial start that caused Spain's nineteenth-century industrialization to fail but the fact that it was concentrated just in one area. He supports this argument with demonstrations of the relatively favourable performance of the Catalan cotton industry with respect to those of other industrializing countries in the nineteenth century.[49] The argument, with its emphasis on the need for a modernizing ideology to achieve predominance for a successful transition to an industrialized society, bears similarities to Harold Perkin's interpretation of British nineteenth-century society in terms of a struggle between different social ideals – a struggle in which, in this case, the middle class and the laissez-faire ideal, it is Perkin's argument, emerged triumphant.[50]

In an article which has already been published I have produced evidence which would support the material bases for Torras's argument – the overwhelming concentration of Spain's modern industry in Catalonia. In it I compare Catalonia's calico-printing industry with that of other parts of Europe and show that Barcelona contained the largest concentration in Europe of such manufacturing activity in the 1780s. In international terms too the extent of industrial concentration was clearly exceptional. I attribute the concentration, as does Torras, to the uniqueness within Spain of the area's commercial and industrial capacity at this stage.[51] In this book I shall develop this line of argument by providing further evidence of the extent of growth achieved by Barcelona's cotton industry and of its lack of diffusion to other parts of Spain. I shall also be arguing that the lack of competition, either nationally or, until the 1790s, regionally, resulted in a similar traditionalism to that observed by Torras in the area's marketing practices in the industry's organization of production.

[49] Torras, 'Early Manufacturing', *passim*.
[50] H. Perkin, *The Origins of Modern English Society (1780–1880)* (London, 1969).
[51] J. K. J. Thomson, 'The Catalan Calico-Printing Industry Compared Internationally', Societat Catalana d'Economia, *Anuari*, 7 (1989), pp. 72–95.

24   *A distinctive industrialization*

STRUCTURE AND CONTENTS

The organizational form chosen for this book is a narrative, one which, if chapter 2, which describes Catalan industrial development over the long term, is included, takes the history of Catalan textiles from the thirteenth to the nineteenth centuries. The reason for this choice is to provide a sense of *process* in the area's industrial development.

The narration takes the following form. Chapter 2, as just noted, consists in a brief survey of Catalan industrial history, focussing on the cloth industry, from the thirteenth to the seventeenth centuries. In chapter 3 the founding of the calico-printing industry in Barcelona is described – in different sections I describe firstly the import trade in calicoes which existed before the industry was introduced, secondly the policy of the government to this trade and thirdly the early efforts at establishing the new industry. Chapter 4, as noted in the first section of this introduction, consists in a description and explanation of the first rapid expansion of the industry during the 1740s consequent upon a significant investment in it of 'commercial capital'. In chapter 5, the consolidation of this progress is described and a full description of what had become a well-established industry by the 1760s is provided. Chapter 6 covers the decades of the 1770s and 1780s when the industry reached its maximal size, benefiting from a second major investment of commercial capital, and expanding its production for the American market. In chapter 7, 'Spinning', three different phases in the industry's incorporation of the spinning processes are surveyed – a gradual expansion in manual spinning from the 1760s to the 1790s, the introduction of the first spinning machinery between 1790 and 1800 and the completion of the incorporation process with accelerated mechanization after the passing of an edict in 1802 banning the import of spun yarn. Chapter 8, 'The crisis of the *fábrica*', documents the response of the industry to the opportunity provided by mechanization and the difficulties occasioned by the disruptions to both internal and external markets by the wars of the period of the French Revolution. Finally in a concluding chapter, 'The Bonaplata mill and Catalan industrialization', a brief description of the industry's development after the revolutionary crises, and of the introduction of new technology in the 1830s, is provided. It is in these last two chapters that an assessment is made of the extent to which the impulse achieved by the Catalan economy in the 1770s and 1780s in any way survives the years of crisis and other questions which have been raised in this introduction are returned to.

The narrative, however, is interrupted at frequent points for the introduction of analysis and descriptions of the industry at various stages in its history. With respect to the former I have attempted to sustain a relatively continuous analytical thread by assessing separately the influence of four major conditioning forces on the industry's growth – government intervention, the availability of capital, market developments and supply influences (in particular the availability of skills, both technical and managerial) – on the different stages of its development between the 1740s and 1780s covered in chapters 4 to 6. With respect to the latter, the fullest descriptions are provided in chapters 5 and 6, at the point at which the industry had grown sufficiently to have developed distinctive characteristics. In the former, details are provided on the size of manufactures, their distribution in the city, their physical appearance, the use of space within them, their managerial structures, their labour forces, the size of investment made in them and its division between fixed and circulating capital, their production techniques, their relationship with the guilds and the character of guild-type regulations which the industry adopted in 1767. In the latter, micro-studies on the manner in which small and large enterprises in the industry functioned are provided, further details on the industry's diffusion in the city are given and an urbanization debate occasioned by the industry's growth summarized.

The pace of developments from the 1790s was such that less scope exists for static analysis, and my priority in the last two chapters has been no more than to establish as far as is possible – the sources for these years are at their worst, administration as well as industry being disrupted by the wars – what happened to the industry in order to provide a firm basis for establishing the extent of the continuities and discontinuities with eighteenth-century growth.

To facilitate the use of what is a long book chapters have been divided into sub-sections, with headings – these are listed in the table of contents.

CHAPTER 2

Catalan industry in the 'long term'

> If trade, contemporary texts often repeat, has survived in the
> Principality, it is thanks to the cloth business
>
> (Vilar, *La Catalogne*, I, p. 545)

The achievement of one of the central purposes of this book – the
assessment of the extent of the discontinuity caused by the growth of
the cotton industry in Barcelona between the 1730s and 1830s –
presupposes a knowledge of the position of industry in the local
economy before the eighteenth century. It is the aim of this chapter
to contribute to providing this. A brief account of different phases of
the history of Catalonia's principal industry until the eighteenth
century, woollen cloth, will be followed by some general comments
on this industry's particularities.

THE DEVELOPMENT OF THE CATALAN CLOTH INDUSTRY

Origins

As Miguel Gual has pointed out, there were two possible sources for
a Spanish textile tradition – a Muslim and an extra-Pyrenean. The
former is the less well documented but it seems to have been
responsible for the existence of concentrations of dyeing-, silk- and
cotton-working skills in certain parts of the peninsula. The latter is
clearly the principal influence on the development of the industry in
Catalonia.

It was first exercised, predictably, on areas close to the frontier.
There appear to have been two principal routes for the industry's
entry: from Aragon, via Jaca and Huesca (mentions of wool
production in 1219 and 1222) and Lérida (famed for its dyeing skills
in the early thirteenth century) and from Catalonia: evidence of a

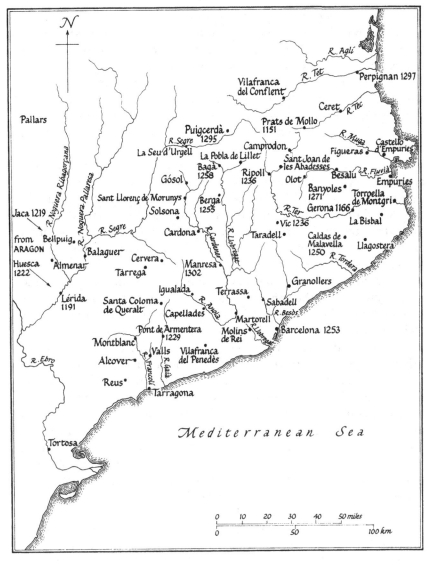

Map 1   Catalonia's cloth industry, twelfth to fifteenth centuries
Centres for which records exist of cloth-making: dates of earliest mentions attest to
the Pyrenean source and southward movement of the industry

cloth industry in Gerona (twelfth century), on the river Ter (1209), at Ripoll and Vic (1236), at Berga and Bagà (1255 and 1258) and at Banyoles (1271). The earliest record of the cloth industry in Barcelona is for 1253. At this stage it was far less important than the city's fustian industry in whose development Moorish influences may have played a role. Other important early cloth-making centres were Prats de Mollo, Puigcerdà, Perpignan, Vilafranca del Conflent, La Bisbal, Olot, Sant Joan de les Abadesses, Moià, Granollers, Sabadell and Terrassa.

The transfer of the industry to Spain was, it is clear, by those mountain Pyrenean routes which were such important channels of communication during the period of reconquest. The gradual southward movement of the industry is detectable both from some of the dates cited in the previous paragraph, and indicated on the map on p. 27, as well as from other evidence: the source of the skills in Perpignan's industry for making cloth with English wools was recorded to be Carcassonne and Narbonne and the origins of the cloth industry in the *comarca* (Catalan territorial division, rather smaller than the county) of the Bagés (capital Manresa, some 50 kilometres inland from Barcelona) is traceable to weavers from Puigcerdà and dyers from Perpignan attracted by municipal privileges granted in 1302 and 1319. If geographical proximity to the necessary technical resources for mounting an industry was one determining factor in this process of proliferation, the existence in both Catalonia and particularly Aragon of abundant wool supplies and good water resources were others. Lérida's early emergence as the first significant industrial centre in the Principality (the name given to Catalonia from the fourteenth century, distinguishing it from the other parts of the Catalo/Aragonese empire – Roussillon, Aragon, Valencia and the Balearic islands) is probably to be explained by its being favourably placed from the point of view of all three of these determinants – it was strategically situated to profit from both routes for the technical introduction of the industry, the river Segre passed through its centre and it was a major centre for the regional wool trade.[1]

[1] M. Gual, 'Para un mapa de la industria textil hispana en la Edad Media', *Anuario de Estudios Medievales*, 4 (1967), pp. 109–68. On the first mention of wool production in Barcelona and on the city's fustians, see Duran Sanpere, *Barcelona*, II, pp. 279 and 288–91, and also C. Batlle, *L'expansió baixmedieval (segles XIII–XV)*, vol. III of P. Vilar (directed), *Història de Catalunya* (8 vols., Barcelona, 1987–90), pp. 127–8. On the wool trade, see C. Carrère, *Barcelone, centre économique à l'époque des difficultés, 1380–1462* (2 vols., Paris, 1967), I, pp. 423–30.

At this early stage, however, the industry's production, with this exception of Lérida, was confined principally to local markets and even with respect to these its impact was minor with comparison to that of imported textiles. Claude Carrère describes the industry as characterized by 'an anarchic production, only satisfying a part of local needs, and, through lack of quality, in no way competitive on the international market'. A sign of this relative inferiority is that if evidence of local cloth production is sparse that of imported cloth is abundant. The sources of the imports to Barcelona included England, Arras, Bruges, Paris, Valenciennes, Châlons, Provins, St Omer, Montolieu (close to Carcassonne), Béziers and Narbonne. Barcelona was both an important market in itself and also a major centre for both the national and international marketing of the imported cloth. Valencia's customs record the names of other foreign sources for imports including Genoa and Avignon.[2]

The fourteenth-century expansion

The turning-point in the industry's development was occasioned, it is now believed, by political events. War and diplomatic tension between the kingdoms of Aragon and France between 1283 and 1313 gave rise to a curious example of anti-mercantilism: Catalan traders, who travelled regularly to Languedoc and Provence to obtain French cloth in return, principally, for bullion, were harassed in various ways, including the obligation to conduct all their transactions through the newly built port of Aigues-Mortes (particularly frustrating for those who had previously confined their trade to western Languedoc) and the subjection to a number of apparently arbitrary taxes. These exactions had the consequence that wartime interruptions in the supply of Languedocian cloth (the Franco-Aragonese war of 1283–95) effectively extended into times of peace.

The resultant shortage of cloth on the Catalan market stimulated a considerable immigration of textile artisans and a sustained attempt to promote the industry in Catalonia. The principal evidence for this is a letter written by the *baile* of Barcelona in 1304 to King Jaume II

---

[2] M. Riu, 'The Woollen Industry in Catalonia in the Later Middle Ages', in N. B. Harte and K. G. Ponting (eds.), *Cloth and Clothing in Medieval Europe: Essays in memory of E. M. Carus-Wilson* (London, 1983), pp. 208–9. Carrère, *Barcelone*, I, p. 431. M. Gual, 'Orígines y expansión de la industria textil lanera en la edad media', in *Produzione, commercio e consumo dei panni di lana. Atti della seconda settimana di studio* (10–16 April 1970) (Florence, 1976), pp. 512–15.

of Aragon informing him that in recent years 'large companies' had been established for the manufacture of 'woollen cloth', that weavers of both sexes had arrived from other countries, that buildings suitable for the industry had been set up, that cloth of a quality and a price to rival that which had previously been imported was being manufactured and that consequently not only would the kingdom of Aragon soon be freed from imports but the local industry would be in a position to supply the national market too.[3]

Peace in 1313 did not bring this development to an end. It would have been reinforced, of course, by the general demographic and agrarian expansion of these years which boosted the local demand for cloth as well by the expanding opportunities in Mediterranean markets consequent upon the Aragonese imperial expansion and the Castilian reconquest which opened Andalusia too to Catalan traders. By the mid-fourteenth century production had expanded considerably: offices for the collection of a tax on it, the Bolla, had been set up in twenty-seven Catalan towns and production was not confined to these. Eight principal centres for the industry can be approximately demarcated (see map on p. 27). These include firstly Barcelona itself, which was by far the largest, with a production capacity of some 30–40,000 pieces a year; secondly Lérida and its surrounding area (including the towns of Tàrrega, Bellpuig, Cervera and Santa Coloma de Queralt); thirdly a Pyrenean concentration: Pallars, Seu d'Urgell, Castelló and Puigcerdà; fourthly a centre coinciding with two Pyrenean river valleys, those of the Ter and the Fluvià (Camprodon, Sant Joan de les Abadesses, Ripoll, Vic, Banyoles and, extending into the plain of the Ampurdan, Gerona, Figueras and Castelló d'Empúries); fifthly that of the Cardener and Llobregat (Bagà, Berga, Pobla de Lillet, Sant Llorenç de Morunys, Cardona and Manresa); and sixthly that of Roussillon (including Perpignan, Vilafranca del Conflent and Prades). The total is completed by a more scattered concentration in south-east Catalonia, including Valls, Montblanc, Vilafranca del Penedés, Tarragona and Tortosa, and finally by the centres beyond Catalonia – Majorca and Valencia. Markets for which the industry produced included Almeria, Genoa, Pisa, Naples, Palermo in the west Mediterranean, Rhodes, Cyprus,

---

[3] J. Reglà, 'El comercio entre Francia y la Corona de Aragón en los siglos XIII y XIV, y sus relaciones con el desenvolvimiento de la industria textil catalana', *Primero Congreso Internacional de Pireneístes* (Saragossa, 1950), pp. 5–16, and reprinted in his *Temas medievales* (Valencia, 1972), pp. 27–47; see also Gual, 'Orígenes y expansión', pp. 515–16.

Beirut, Damascus and Alexandria in the east Mediterranean and Tunis in North Africa.[4]

The expanded industry concentrated above all on the production of cloth of medium and low quality. This is demonstrated by a study of E. Ashtor on cloth prices in the Mediterranean area in the late medieval period which shows that whereas the range of prices charged for Italian cloth was between 25 and 65 *florins* (cloth from Prato at 25–30 *florins*, from Milan and Como at 40–5 and from Florence at 55–65), and for the Flemish centre of Werviq-sur-Lys 26–32 *florins*, that for the many Catalan cloth centres was confined predominantly to between 10 and 22 *florins*, only the production of Perpignan and Majorca exceeding this, the former with prices of up to 31 *florins* and the latter, whose industry experienced a massive expansion in the fifteenth century, selling its *cordellats* at this time at up to 40–5 *florins* (earlier, its production had been amongst the lowest quality of the area).[5] It is not without significance that the price range corresponds with that of the Languedoc industry – that from which it seems likely that the Barcelona industry had predominantly drawn its expertise and that, too, which it supplanted in Mediterranean and peninsular markets. As Carrère comments 'a cloth industry "à la française" had been learnt from them'.[6] Higher quality cloth continued to be imported – the principal sources for this in 1365 were Brussels, Leuven, Ypres, Bruges, Courtrai, Florence, England and a range of French centres.[7] Various attempts to produce higher quality cloth – with imported English wool (in the 1430s and 1440s) and by the introduction of Italian and Flemish workers in 1511 – were to be unsuccessful.[8]

The crisis of the fifteenth century

The medieval expansion of the industry was checked by the demographic crises of the fourteenth and fifteenth centuries which affected Catalonia as they did the rest of Europe. The first of these was a famine in 1333 – later referred to ominously as the 'the first bad

---

[4] Riu, 'Woollen Industry', pp. 211–13; also J. Vicens Vives, *Manual de historia económica de España* (6th edn, Barcelona, 1972), pp. 183–4.
[5] E. Ashtor, 'Catalan Cloth on the Late Medieval Mediterranean Markets', *Journal of European Economic History*, 17 (1988), pp. 227–58.
[6] Carrère, *Barcelone*, I, pp. 433–4.   [7] Riu, 'Woollen Industry', p. 214.
[8] *Ibid.*, p. 219; Carrère, *Barcelone*, II, pp. 818–38.

year' – and this was followed by the Black Death which reached Catalonia between 1348 and 1351 and further plague outbreaks which occurred at approximately two-year intervals well into the fifteenth century. To these demographic crises were added the disruptive effects of the Civil War between 1462 and 1472. Barcelona's population declined from a ceiling of some 50,000 before the first plague outbreak to some 20,000 at the end of the Civil War – a loss of 60 per cent – and that of the Principality which had stood at approximately half a million had fallen to about 268,000 by 1497.[9]

Historians have argued, however, that high levels of industrial production were sustained for some time. This was possible, they emphasize, because of the extent of the concentration on the export trade which was initially relatively isolated from the crises.[10] Vicens Vives thus maintained that it was only in 1416, with the arrival of English competition in the western Mediterranean, and in particular in the Sicilian market, that the industry began to decay and Claude Carrère favours an even later turning-point – the 1430s, when there was a sharp decline in the Levant trade, which provided the principal market: 'stimulus, head and dominating influence of all the commerce' was how the eighteenth-century Catalan historian/philosophe Antoni de Capmany was to describe this trade.[11] Ashtor's study supports Carrère's interpretation with evidence drawn from the Mediterranean markets for which the industry was producing which shows a remarkable Catalan dominance through to the first quarter of the fifteenth century, the industry at Perpignan attaining then its highest levels of production, and then a marked decline, particularly in the Levant and Italian markets, though with the position in the important Sicilian market being better sustained, largely as a result of a transfer of the industry from the troubled mainland to Majorca.[12]

The principal agent for the reversal of Catalonia's fortunes in these markets was the French industry and in particular that section of it whose exclusion from the Catalan market had provided the Catalan industry with its initial opportunity – the industry of Languedoc. And behind the reversal, again, were political events: the policies of the French king Charles VII and his minister Jacques Coeur had led to a recovery in Marseilles' trade with the Levant and to a reassertion

[9] Vilar, *La Catalogne*, I, pp. 461–4; Batlle, *L'expansió baixmedieval*, pp. 85–9, 251–6.
[10] Vilar, *La Catalogne*, I, pp. 472–5.
[11] Vicens Vives, *Manual*, p. 196, Carrère, *Barcelone*, II, pp. 725–70.
[12] Ashtor, 'Catalan Cloth', pp. 233–57.

of control over the spice trade in Occitania. This not only led to a demand for Languedocian cloth in the Levant market – cloth was the principal return product for the imported spices – but also, by making Marseilles into the principal distribution centre for spices in the western Mediterranean, attracted other potential customers for its region's and neighbouring regions' clothiers.[13]

With the loss of its export markets, Catalan producers became sensitive to the issue of the continued large-scale import of high-quality woollens. These appeared unacceptable in view of high levels of industrial unemployment. Pressure was exercised on the Consell de Cent (Barcelona's municipal council, composed of 100 members) for their prohibition. The attempts at fine cloth production during these years which were mentioned above are examples of efforts at import substitution behind such tariff barriers. These steps, though, could only be a palliative: imports of high-quality exports had always existed in Barcelona and it was the loss of position in export markets, caused principally by the switch of the spice trade to Marseilles and the consequent revival of French competition in Mediterranean markets, which was the principal cause of unemployment in the industry.

Although the crisis in cloth exports was delayed till late, it seems probable, though studies on this issue are lacking, that that in industrial production for internal markets – both those of Catalonia and of other parts of Spain – in which the smaller Catalan cloth-making centres were involved showed less hesitation. The agrarian crisis and demographic decline must have affected both the supply and demand situation. How, for example, could a large cloth industry have survived on the plain of Vic where a loss of some 70 per cent in population was recorded?[14] Whatever the precise timing of the crisis in the different sectors of the industry, however, by the second half of the fifteenth century, with the additional disruption of Civil War between 1462 and 1472, it was general: Vicens Vives writes of an 'epoch of *nearly definitive ruin*. Depopulation, flight of workers and emigration of capital, sacking of cities, burning of harvests, confiscations, embezzlement', and Pierre Vilar, similarly, that 'Catalan trade is reduced to only one twentieth of what it had

[13] J. Vicens Vives, *Cataluña a mediados del siglo XV* (Barcelona, 1956), p. 27. G. Feliu in his 'El comercio catalan con Oriente', *Revista de Historia Económica*, 6 (1988), pp. 689–707, confirms the importance of the revival of Marseilles' Levant links but emphasizes, too, the significance of depressed demand conditions in the Levant markets themselves.

[14] Batlle, *L'expansió baixmedieval*, p. 254.

been at the beginning of the century ... Catalonia returns to the local economy'.[15]

A recovery in the sixteenth century

Although the heights of industrial prosperity achieved in the medieval period were not to be returned to, during the sixteenth and seventeenth centuries there was to be some industrial recovery. The initial source of this was the demographic and economic vitality of Castile and the expansion in its imperial trade: 'from the present Principality and from the Counties of Cerdagne', it was reported in 1552, 'a large number of pieces of cloth are generally sent each year to the said kingdom of Castile'. Catalonia's decayed Mediterranean trade had been replaced with a new one in which wheat imports from other parts of the peninsula were effectively financed by the export of cloth to Seville and to the fairs of Medina del Campo, either for local consumption or for reexport for the American trade. As Vilar writes, 'The Catalan effacement in the Mediterranean has not only its compensation, but without doubt also one of its causes in the attraction of the west.'[16] The Castilian cloth industry itself was experiencing a rare period of expansion and prosperity during these years as a consequence of the favourable demand situation in the national market, even achieving some success with its higher quality cloths in the Catalan market.[17]

When this source of stimulus began to flag, with the crises of Habsburg finances of the 1570s and the beginnings of the demo-graphic exhaustion of Castile, the stimulus to Catalan industrial production was sustained by a significant recovery in the local economy, which was experiencing agricultural and demographic growth, and by an expansion in Mediterranean trades, and par-ticularly that with Sicily in which Catalonia enjoyed an effective monopoly – from 1570 until 1620 some sixty Catalan commercial houses are recorded as having regular trading contacts with Palermo. Both favourable trends would appear to have been assisted by a redirection of the Spanish bullion trade with northern Europe

---

[15] Vicens Vives, *Cataluña*, p. 29; Vilar, *La Catalogne*, I, p. 520.

[16] Vilar, *La Catalogne*, I, p. 544. An example of the Castilian and American prosperity – the population of Seville rose from 45,000 to 90,000 between 1530 and 1594 (J. H. Elliot, 'The Decline of Spain', in C. M. Cipolla (ed.), *The Economic Decline of Empires* (London, 1970), p. 177).

[17] Carrera Pujal, *Historia política*, II, p. 163, for details of imports of Castilian cloth into Catalonia.

through Barcelona and Genoa in view of difficulties experienced with the Atlantic route.[18] A considerable colony of Genoese merchants established itself in Barcelona during these years, dominating the wholesale trades.[19]

Direct evidence concerning the response of the Catalan industry to the improved circumstances is again sparse. An indirect sign of activity is the large number of industrial guilds and confraternities founded – 'if there is one domain in which sixteenth-century Catalonia seems creative', Vilar writes, 'it is in that of the artisanal corporations'.[20] In addition, a study on the industry of the small town of Taradell, in the neighbourhood of Vic, shows a steady growth in its labour force from eight *paraires* (cloth-finishers or -dressers and generally in Catalonia the organizers of the entire production cycle and thus the equivalent of the English 'clothier') and weavers in 1553 to fifty-seven, including journeymen and apprentices, in 1599.

There are signs that there was some geographical redistribution of the industry from the larger urban centres to smaller towns and villages during these years: thus the expansion of Taradell has to be set against difficulties experienced by the industry in Vic (complaints in 1597–8 of unavailability of weavers for the city's *paraires*), and the 'manpower' in the Gerona industry in terms of *paraires* and weavers declined from 123 to 41 between 1534 and 1651. The ruralization process, however, is more definitely attributable to the late sixteenth or seventeenth centuries: as late as 1567 a visitor to Gerona reported that large quantities of very fine cloth were being made in the town and sold successfully under the name of 'Perpignan cloth' in a variety of export markets.[21] The reopening of Mediterranean markets seems in fact to have favoured some specialization and concentration of production in urban centres. Reus, and the neighbouring towns of Valls and Alcover, for example, with the help of initial technical assistance from the Majorcan industry, flourished on the basis of

---

[18] Vilar, *La Catalogne*, I, pp. 544–53.
[19] E. Giralt, ('La colonia mercantil francesa de Barcelona a mediados del siglo XVII', *Estudios de Historia Moderna*, 6 (1956–9), p. 223 n. 23) records the presence of forty-nine Genoese merchants in Barcelona during the first quarter of the seventeenth century.
[20] Vilar, *La Catalogne*, I, p. 545.
[21] N. Sales, *Els segles de la decadència (segles XVI–XVIII)*, vol. IV of P. Vilar (directed), *Història de Catalunya* (8 vols., Barcelona, 1987–90), pp. 298–302; J. Clarà, 'Les Fàbriques gironines del segle XVIII', *Primer Congrès d'Història Moderna de Catalunya* (Barcelona, 1984), I, pp. 545–52.

production for the Sicilian market (the population of Reus growing
to over 5,000). Barcelona produced for Italy and Sardinia as well as
for Sicily and Perpignan switched its medieval concentration on the
Sicilian market to a specialization on the production of grey cloth
(*grises*) for Castile.[22]

The crisis of the seventeenth century

From approximately the turn of the century a new period of crisis
opened. The number of textile workers at Taradell peaked – the
existence of fifty-three was recorded for 1622 – and in the 1630s it
was claimed that the Principality's production had fallen by two-
thirds during the previous thirty years with the urban centres being
particularly badly hit (the examples of Gerona, with a decline in the
number of its looms from 500 to 100, and Perpignan, with one from
300 to 30, were given). In Barcelona the crisis gave rise to xenophobia
and demands for protection (as in the 1430s), attempts to improve
the quality of production to prevent *missale*, growing social tension
between *paraires* and weavers as attempts were made to cut wages and
some movement of production processes out of the city to cut costs.[23]

The cause of the crisis was that Catalonia was sharing, to a certain
extent, in the general Spanish crisis and decline of these years. There
was a similar depopulation, particularly in western Catalonia
(around Lérida) and in Roussillon, and, as in the rest of Spain, more
rapid price inflation than in other parts of Europe had pushed up
production costs making industry uncompetitive as well as attracting
imports. Increased competition also contributed and its importance
must be taken into consideration in interpreting the rapidity of the
industrial decline noted in Catalan cities. Marseilles' commerce was
in full expansion, the gabelle of the port rising from an average of
5,224 *livres* between 1600 and 1604 to 26,484 *livres* between 1640 and
1644 and recovery and expansion were occurring in Languedocian
cloth-making centres.[24] Marseilles and France, rather than Genoa,
were becoming the predominant influence on the local economy –
'the large-scale Genoese trade [grand commerce génois] seems from

---

[22] Carrera Pujal, *Historia política*, II, pp. 163, 166–7. Vilar, *La Catalogne*, I, p. 593.
[23] Vilar, *La Catalogne*, I, pp. 592–9.
[24] P. Chaunu and R. Gascon (eds.), *Histoire économique et sociale de la France* (4 vols., Paris,
    1970–80), I, part 1, pp. 333–5, and J. K. J. Thomson, *Clermont-de-Lodève, 1633–1789:
    Fluctuations in the Prosperity of a Languedocian Cloth-Making Town* (Cambridge, 1982), pp.
    91–100.

this point to have less importance than the medium-scale French trade (*le moyen commerce français*). The purchase of drugs and Levantine imports at Marseille is... the heaviest item in the deficit of the commercial balance', Vilar writes.

It was, though, as Vilar himself emphasizes a sharing to a certain extent only. The agricultural economy remained reasonably prosperous with an important exporting sector. There was no decline in the number of Barcelona's merchants. 'Old Catalonia', between the rivers Cardener and Fluviá, suffered no demographic decline. Any gaps that appeared were filled by massive French immigration. Visitors commented regularly on the area's prosperity. If the sixteenth century had seen industry fare better than commerce, the opening of the seventeenth century was apparently witnessing the reverse occurrence.[25]

What was happening? It is clear that not only was the Principality being relatively spared from the economic and demographic disasters which were being experienced in the rest of Spain but also its level of prosperity was being at least sustained by the fact that it was one of the chief entry points for the massive import trade to which the divergence in Spanish price levels from those elsewhere was giving rise. It became a virtual colony of French trade during these years. This was not ideal but it ensured that there was no total collapse in the region.

It is clear that the situation was particularly unsatisfactory for local industrial interests. At least, however, as Josep Fontana emphasizes, the industry was being confronted with an economic reality and so some response was made.[26] This took the form principally of a shift of production out of the cities and a relaxation in corporative restrictions with respect to organization of production: *paraires* were permitted to centralize production processes and to employ workers from outside the guilds.[27]

If the influence of the French on the Catalan economy was strong before 1640, with the outbreak of the Civil War (the *guerra dels segadors*, 1640–52), and the agreement of 1642 whereby Louis XIII became Count of Barcelona assuming sovereignty over the Principality, it became overwhelming. Previous commercial links were

[25] The material for this section is drawn largely from Vilar, *La Catalogne*, I, pp. 588–632.
[26] J. Fontana, 'Sobre el comercio exterior de Barcelona en la segunda mitad del siglo XVII: Notas para una interpretación de la coyuntura catalana', *Estudios de Historia Moderna*, 5 (1955), pp. 216–18.   [27] Vilar, *La Catalogne*, I, pp. 593–9.

broken and French merchants, largely from Marseilles and Languedoc, took the place in the wholesaling trades which had previously
been occupied by the Genoese.[28] With the war, too, Catalonia's
relative insulation from the fate of the rest of Castile came to an end:
Vilar writes of the arrival of 'the worst evils from which the domains
of Castile had been suffering since 1600: excessive public expenditure,
monetary inflation, paralysis of production, depopulation by a
terrible epidemic, and finally, as a conclusion to the international
struggle, loss… of Roussillon'.[29]

Some recovery in the late seventeenth century

From the early 1680s there was a commercial recovery in Catalonia.
The principal evidence for this is an increase in the yield of the
Barcelona *periatge*, a percentage tax on the value of the cargoes of
ships using the port of Barcelona, to levels higher than those recorded
at the beginning of the century. The late 1680s saw a falling back
again in the tax's yield but in the 1690s there was expansion again to
the highest levels recorded for the century. The restriction of the tax
to large ships has the consequence that it is distant trade which it
records: Barcelona was participating in what was a general European
expansion in international trade during these years.[30] Trade with
traditional Mediterranean markets was in expansion but what was
particularly significant was a rapid growth in the Atlantic trade –
Carlos Martínez Shaw writes of the 'extraordinary impulse which
the Catalan commercial presence in the Atlantic ports, and especially
in the Atlantic, receives'.[31] In return for exports of wine, eau-de-vie,
olive oil, nuts and some manufactured goods, colonial products, and
particularly tobacco, sugar and cocoa, were being imported on a
large scale for consumption on the local market and for reexport. A
large tobacco processing plant was established in Barcelona.[32]
Catalonia was participating in what has been termed the 'commercial
revolution': a period of rapid commercial expansion, stimulated

---

[28] Giralt, 'La colonia mercantil', pp. 223–48.   [29] Vilar, *La Catalogne*, I, p. 633.
[30] N. W. Posthumus, *Inquiry into the History of Prices in Holland* (2 vols., Leiden, 1946–65), I, pp.
    39–40, 75, 111–14; J. Meuvret, 'Circulation monétaire et utilisation économique de la
    monnaie dans la France du XVIe et du XVIIe siècle', *Etudes d'Histoire Moderne et
    Contemporaine*, I (1947), pp. 2–3, and Fontana, 'Sobre el comercio', pp. 213–14.
[31] C. Martínez Shaw, 'El comercio marítimo de Barcelona, 1675–1712. Aproximación a partir
    de las escrituras de seguros', *Estudios Históricos y Documentos de los Archivos de Protocolos*, 6
    (1978), pp. 287–310.   [32] Fontana, 'Sobre el comercio', pp. 206, 208.

principally by the introduction of new colonial products whose prices were falling rapidly, and whose impact was largely confined to the commercial sector.[33]

The recovery was not, though, purely limited to Barcelona's overseas trades. The importance of wine exports was one factor which caused it to spread to other parts of the Principality. Substantial population growth is recorded for the towns and villages of the principal wine-producing area, the Penedés (between 1553 and 1717 an increase from 835 inhabitants to 2,805 for Vilanova, of from 605 to 2,050 for Sitges, from 1,930 to 2,530 for Vilafranca, from 215 to 1,250 for San Pere de Ribes, for example).[34] This expansion of the Catalan interior is noted by Josep Fontana in his study on the trade of these years: he emphasizes the leading role played in the recovery by a growing demand for imports occasioned by rising levels of local prosperity.[35] Vilar, too, emphasizes that the prosperity of the tobacco trade was linked to the healthy state of the local market and he provides other indices of prosperity within the Principality: the growth of a string of coastal towns north of Barcelona, and particularly Mataró (this town's growth encouraged it to attempt to attain the status of city in 1702) and the flourishing state of the regional fairs of Verdú and Prades. Citing the 1684 reaction of members of a Barcelona commercial guild to the tendency – small towns, they had noted, 'are growing with the building of numerous houses, and, in certain cases, of whole streets, thanks to trade', and population was being lost to them, now, rather than to foreign countries – he concludes that this widely spread prosperity is to be explained by demographic revival, cheapness of labour and an accumulation of agricultural profits: 'Once again, as in the Middle Ages', he writes, 'it is a whole country, not a simple city, that our analysis should seize.'[36]

In the larger cities disindustrialization continued. There was no recovery in Gerona and the decline in Barcelona's industry was such

[33] R. Davis, 'English Foreign Trade, 1660–1700', in W. E. Minchinton (ed.), *The Growth of English Overseas Trade in the Seventeenth and Eighteenth Centuries* (London, 1969), pp. 78–98. Tobacco prices on the English market fell from 40s. per lb in 1619 to less than 1s. in the 1670s, and the retail price of sugar was halved between 1630 and 1680. Davis compares the impact of these price falls on trade to that occasioned by the fall in prices in cotton goods following mechanization.

[34] E. Giralt, 'La viticultura y el comercio catalan del siglo XVIII', *Estudios de Historia Moderna*, 2 (1952), p. 164.   [35] Fontana, 'Sobre el comercio', p. 207.

[36] The argument of this section is based on Vilar, *La Catalogne*, I, pp. 646–53.

that in 1674 the Consell de Cent recorded that 'The cloth industry
that existed in the present city has almost entirely ceased to exist.'[37]
That qualification which was made with respect to the industrial
decline of the first half of the century, however, has relevance also to
these years: the crisis in the cities was more severe than in the
countryside and in smaller towns. Vilar notes evidence for the
expansion of the production of cutlery in Mataró, of that of hemp
sacking in Vilafranca, Igualada, Cervera, Tàrrega, Agramunt and
Balaguer, of tanning in Gerona, Solsona, Manresa, Igualada,
Vilafranca and Olot and of nail-making in Manresa, Olot and
Ripoll. Fontana, in an analysis of imports during these years, notes a
decline in those of silk, for the luxury industries in Barcelona, but a
rise in those of wool – for the use, it is his argument, of the cloth
industries of the interior. A petition from the *paraires* of Barcelona,
written in 1683, confirms the trend for the wool industry, pointing
out that production was now limited to that of 'different towns and
villages of the present Principality in such a way that those who
previously traded with the *paraires* of the present city today trade with
the *paraires* of the towns and villages'.[38]

The development was not simply a question of the smaller centres
surviving. Jaume Torras has argued that the specialization in
viticulture and rising agricultural incomes of these years contributed
to a growth in textile and other industrial specializations within the
Principality – the 'resulting economies of agglomeration', he argues,
'enhanced the competitiveness of Catalan cheap goods'. This was the
mechanism which was to lie behind the eighteenth-century Catalan
industrial growth: its source, it is clear, is in this period. The contrast
which it represents to the supposed conventional 'proto-industrialization' dynamic, in which industrial, not agricultural, development,
plays the dynamic role, was pointed out in the introduction.[39]

A late seventeenth-century attempt at import-substitution

The extent of the industrial expansion achieved on this new basis
should not be exaggerated, however. The success was limited to some
regaining of terrain in the local market with respect only to lower

---

[37] Carrera Pujal, *Historia política*, II, p. 192.
[38] Vilar, *La Catalogne*, I, pp. 646–50; Fontana, 'Sobre el comercio', p. 210.
[39] Torras, 'Especialización agrícola e industria rural', and for his extension of the argument to
the seventeenth century, see 'Early Manufacturing and Proto-Industry', p. 8.

quality cloths. The position with respect to exports had deteriorated since the 1660s – Fontana's figures show textile exports valued at 104,000 *libras* for 1664–5 against only 44,000 *libras* for 1695–6. And the Catalan balance of trade continued to show a large excess of imports over exports and above all of textile imports for which the 1695–6 figures are again higher than those for 1664–5 (225,000 *libras* against 181,500).[40] The period, however, has a second reason for being regarded as one of recovery: it witnessed the first steps taken to reverse the technological inferiority of Catalan industry, which was the root cause for the heavy import bills, with a number of attempts at imitation of foreign cloths.

Why should these steps have been taken at this stage when such a trading imbalance had been accepted for so long? Four principal causes can be identified. Firstly, if there were some signs of industrial recovery in the countryside, there were none in the city and the extent of the industrial decline was becoming a serious cause of concern as it threatened, as it had in the fifteenth century, social stability. The contemporary preoccupation with the high level of textile imports, and the realization of its link with industrial decline, is revealed by a part of the long title of one of the publications of Narcís Feliu de la Penya, who was to be both the principal Catalan ideologist and agent in the attempted industrial revival: in 1681 he published a *Politico Discurso en defensa de la cierta verdad que contiene un memorial presentado a la Nobilisima Ciudad de Barcelona suplicando mande y procure impedir **el sobrado trato y uso de algunas ropas extranjeras que acaban el comercio y pierden las artes en Cataluña***. The section in bold type reads: 'the excessive dealing in and use of some sorts of foreign cloth which destroy the trade and give rise to the loss of the arts in Catalonia'.[41]

A second permissive element was the growing flexibility which had developed during the century concerning guild regulations. The traditional reaction to crisis had been for guilds to attempt to enforce these more strictly, a policy which reflected on the one hand an interpretation of the crisis in terms of a failure to maintain production standards – stricter application of guild regulations would, it was believed, remedy this – and on the other hand 'Malthusianism': an attempt to ensure that those limited market opportunities which existed were reserved purely to guild masters. Innovation, both with

---

[40] Fontana, 'Sobre el comercio', p. 207. [41] Vilar, *La Catalogne*, I, p. 656.

respect to the development of new types of cloth and organization of production, required, it is clear, a more liberal approach than this and the signs are that the Consell de Cent gradually developed one during the century, showing increasing preparedness to give priority to innovation over the defence of guild traditions. Such flexibility has been noted with respect to the cloth industry earlier in the century and it was exercised towards other guilds too – from 1634 the winding of silk, as well as wool-spinning, was permitted outside the city, and in addition in 1674 silk-weavers were employing larger numbers of journeymen and apprentices than authorized by their guild statutes.[42] This increase in the extent of industrial 'freedom' facilitated the emergence of an entrepreneurial class in the city whose existence is noticed by Fontana: 'Who are those men who give salaries to weavers, have sufficient money to handle considerable amounts of wool and with sufficient weight in the city to be able to avoid protectionist measures of the guilds which could prejudice them, and what do they represent in the city?', he asks.[43]

A third contribution was played by the development of a Catalan strand of mercantilism in which, as elsewhere (this is the period of Colbert), great emphasis was played on the importance of industrial production. Feliu de la Penya, as noted, was the principal author of this and in his important work, *Fénix de Cataluña, compendio de sus antiguas grandezas y medio de renovarlas*, he argued in favour of the creation of a free port in Barcelona to attract trade and the establishment of a large commercial company to finance ship-building, commercial ventures and industrial investment. The title of Feliu's work is again significant – the image of the Phoenix and the mention of Catalonia's past prosperity: Feliu was an historian, as well as an economic commentator, and his concern to further the industrial revival of Catalonia was reinforced by his awareness of the position of commercial and industrial prominence from which the Principality had fallen.[44] There was, of course, a parallel mercantilist programme being enforced in Madrid by reforming ministers of Charles II in which Catalonia had a place – Feliu acted as a local agent for the Madrid-based Junta General de Comercio (the equivalent of the French Bureau de Commerce and encharged with

[42] Carrera Pujal, *Historia política*, II, pp. 176, 192–3.
[43] Fontana, 'Sobre el comercio', p. 211.
[44] On Feliu, see Vilar, *La Catalogne*, I, pp. 655–61; P. Molas Ribalta, 'La represa catalana de 1680–1700. Narcís Feliu de la Penya', in his *Comerç i estructura social a Catalunya i València als segles XVII i XVIII* (Barcelona, 1977), pp. 70–120.

the revival of Spanish industry during the 1680s). In 1692 a local branch of this organization, a Junta Particular de Comercio, was founded in Barcelona.[45] Fourthly and finally, the extent of technical progress which had been achieved during the century, principally in north European textile centres, had had the consequence that there were prospects of high profits to be obtained from the introduction of new technologies. This consideration is clearly of relevance to explaining what was to emerge as one novel feature of these industrial developments – the involvement in them of merchant capital. The principal areas of progress were as follows. Firstly, the traditional broadcloth industry – Catalonia's staple for so many centuries – had been revolutionized by changes in the method of making broadcloth and by the development of the so-called 'new draperies' (lighter woollens for which long staple, combed wools were used); secondly, a variety of mixed fibre cloths (wool and silk, cotton and wool, cotton and silk, linen with all these other fibres, etc.), known as stuffs, involving generally fancy weaves and the use of the draw loom, had been developed; thirdly, there had been significant mechanical progress in what was known as the smallwares industry with the development of the stocking and Dutch ribbon looms; fourthly, there had been a considerable improvement in technique in the linen industry and linen products had emerged as major items in international trade flows; and fifthly, large-scale imports of textiles from India and China, and particularly of printed calicoes, had had a range of spin-offs: they had had a significant impact on design, they had stimulated experimentation with new dyestuffs and they had encouraged the development of a European, import-substituting calico-printing industry.[46] The details of the attempts to introduce these innovations to Barcelona are as follows. In 1665, a grant of monopoly and of freedom from guild regulations was requested in connection with a proposal for the production of *bayetas façon d'Holande*; in 1675

[45] P. Molas Ribalta, 'La Junta de Comerç de Barcelona. Els seus precedents i la seva base social', in *ibid.*, pp. 241–50. On the interventionist policy of Charles II, see N. Florensa, 'Política industrial a Castella sota el regnat de Carles II: 1680–1700' (Tesis de licenciatura, Barcelona 1981), and on the Junta General de Comercio, see W. Callahan, 'A Note on the Real and General Junta de Comercio', *Economic History Review*, 3 (1968), pp. 519–28.
[46] On this textile innovation, see J. de Vries, *The Economy of Europe in an Age of Crisis, 1600–1750* (Cambridge, 1976), pp. 90–4, 100–1; E. Kerridge, *Textile Manufactures in Early Modern England* (Manchester, 1985), *passim*, and A. P. Wadsworth and J. L. Mann, *The Cotton Trade and Industrial Lancashire* (Manchester, 1931), pp. 12–14, 97–110.

production of another Dutch cloth, *herbajes*, was being attempted; in 1677 there is evidence for silk-weavers producing a range of mixed fibred cloths, called *sargas* or *sargiletes* and in 1679 a *paraire*, called Garriga, left Catalonia with 100 workers to promote cloth-making in the 'Dutch-style' in Saragossa.[47] During the 1680s efforts were coordinated by Feliu himself. He arranged for several Catalan artisans to travel abroad to learn new techniques. The details of this industrial espionage, and its fruit, are as shown in table 2.1.

It is clear that the 1680s, the first period of recovery, was a decade of intense activity, for Feliu was not alone in the introduction of new techniques (he mentions, for example, the introduction of French and Italian workers by the ribbon- and lace-weavers to produce plain and flowered ribbons and of gold and silver thread reeling techniques by his collaborator the cloth merchant Martí Piles), and nor was innovation confined to Barcelona: Pere Molas Ribalta has recorded similar initiatives in the Valencia silk industry as well as the introduction of linen manufacturing and new dyeing techniques by a relation of Feliu in Valls and Manresa.[48] For 1688 there is evidence of linen production in Barcelona too and from 1690 Feliu became involved in this activity himself on some scale: he founded the company of Santa Creu to finance it and in 1693 obtained permission to establish a bleaching meadow outside the city walls in this connection. Feliu's ambitions in this area had been clear since the publication of the *Fénix* in 1683 in which he stated his belief that the local climate, well suited for bleaching, would favour it.[49]

Apart from calico-printing (for which there is no evidence), it is clear that a start had been made on introducing the majority of the textile innovations of this period by the 1690s. Four aspects of the process are worth emphasizing. Firstly, the centrality of the role of Feliu himself. In addition to his propagandic role he had arranged and financed the necessary industrial espionage, organized and paid for the introduction of the new techniques in Barcelona and mobilized the support of other merchants for the ventures. Secondly, the extensive institutional participation in the efforts, with the Junta General de Comercio's correspondence with Feliu during the 1680s and establishment of a local branch in Barcelona in 1692, the Consell

[47] Carrera Pujal, *Historia política*, II, pp. 187, 193; Vilar, *La Catalogne*, I, pp. 662–4; Fontana, 'Sobre el comercio', p. 212.
[48] Molas Ribalta, 'La represa catalana', p. 106, and 'La represa econòmica de 1680. Economia i política a finals del segle XVII', in his *Comerç i estructura social*, p. 53.
[49] Vilar, *La Catalogne*, I, pp. 665–6.

Table 2.1. *A late seventeenth-century import-substitution programme:*
introduction of new cloths to Barcelona by Feliu de la Penya in the 1680s

Introducer		Cloth, skill or machine		Organizer of resulting business
Name	Trade	Name	Origin	
Burgada	Linen- and cloth-weaver	*Anascotes Barraganes* and *herbajes*	Flanders and England	Feliu himself who later handed over to a company of ten merchants
		Camelots of worsted and silk	Flanders	
		Cadis	Nîmes	
Gou	*Paraire*	*Droguetos finos* and *comunes*	France	Gou with Feliu, later handed over to *paraires*
		Worsted *sargas* and *mesclas* (*medleys*) of different colours	France	
Cantarell	Dyer	Manufacture and dyeing of scarlet cloth	France	Cantarell with Feliu, later handed over to *paraires*
		Scarlet dyeing of stockings		
Cortines	Silk-weaver	Lustring silk cloth		Three 'individuals' practising in 1683
Julian	Merchant/ stocking-maker	Stocking loom	France	Feliu

Source: H. Kamen, 'Narcís Feliu de la Penya i el "Fénix de Cataluña"',
introductory essay to new edition of *Fénix de Cataluña* (Barcelona, 1983), pp.
14–15.

de Cent's flexibility with respect to guild regulations and direct
participation in some projects – for example, the granting of 275
libras and the use of the Hospicio de la Misericordia to Burgada[50] –
and the participation of the guilds themselves in the commercial
exploitation of the innovations. Thirdly, the fact of merchant
investment in industry: that of Feliu and his colleagues in the
development of linen-bleaching as well as that of the ten merchants
who backed Burgada. It must have been this support which enabled

[50] *Ibid.*, i, p. 664.

the latter to achieve a remarkable rate of expansion in his concern which by 1683 had trained 50 weavers and was employing over 2,000 in preparing and spinning yarn. Fourthly, the concern which was shown on the one hand to spread new techniques – the case just referred to of Burgada; that of Gou, who had trained fourteen workers in the weaving skills for his *droguetes* by 1683, and the three artisans trained in the lustring techniques who, according to Feliu, were sufficient 'to teach the method to the whole of Spain' – but on the other to conserve some of the subtler techniques which had been costly to attain, and from the use of which monopoly profits could be anticipated: Gou had not passed on his dyeing skills, Feliu noted, although he himself had spent a year working with him 'so that he might learn it'.[51]

PARTICULARITIES OF THE CATALAN CLOTH INDUSTRY

Comparing the Catalan cloth industry with that of other parts of Europe, a first point which can be made is that at no stage in its history did it exercise technological leadership. At various points – and in particular during the fourteenth century – the industry was impressive for its size and a reasonable quality of production was attained, but none of its production centres ever attained a status comparable to that enjoyed by Florence from the twelfth to the fifteenth centuries or Leyden during the seventeenth.[52].

The industry bore strong resemblances to that of the neighbouring French province of Languedoc. In both areas cloth-making activities were particularly widely diffused – another contrast with the predominantly urban industries of Florence, Venice and Leyden. The similarities extended, we have noted, to the type of cloth produced, both areas specializing in low to middling quality production. The parallels provide a clue to one, primary cause for the strength of the Catalan industrial tradition: like Languedoc, the Principality was one of the few Mediterranean areas which was well placed both from the point of view of factors of production – raw materials (good wool supplies), water (Pyrenean rivers), labour (densely populated mountainous zones with an urgent need for by-employment), enterprise (primogeniture released younger sons of families for commercial and

[51] Kamen, 'Narcís Feliu', pp. 14–15.
[52] 'Nothing which recalls Florence or the Flemish cloth industry', Vilar writes (*La Catalogne*, I, p. 426).

industrial activity) – and geographical position to supply what until well into the eighteenth century were Europe's principal export markets – the Levant, Italy and Spain itself.[53]

Like Languedoc's, too, the Catalan cloth industry experienced, we have seen, sharp fluctuations in the extent of its prosperity. The explanation for this was on the one hand, as Pierre Vilar has shown, internal – there were periods of lesser and greater demographic and economic prosperity in the Principality which had their impact on both the supply and demand side of its industry – but on the other hand was related to trading conditions in both the international and national economy. This whole question will be reviewed in the conclusion of the book when it will be possible to include in our comparisons consideration of similar fluctuations which occurred in the extent of prosperity of the Principality's industry in the eighteenth and nineteenth centuries.[54]

The character of the relationship of commercial capital with the industry varied. There were a few periods of direct mercantile involvement in industrial activity. These included the fourteenth century – it was commercial capital which was behind the initial expansion of the industry (the mention of large companies, introduction of foreign workers and the building of new manufactures will have been noted) – the mid-fifteenth century when the silk industry, like the wool industry 150 years earlier, was established by wholesale merchants, and the late seventeenth century when, as has just been noted, a range of new types of cloth were introduced with the collaboration of merchants. The direct involvement, however, in no case endured for very long. Claude Carrère notes in the case of the fourteenth-century industry that although the title of 'draper', which had been adopted by merchant participants in the industry, was conserved, the draping roles were in fact soon dropped as merchants came to specialize in the purely commercial roles of importing and exporting cloth: 'for them', she writes, 'the shop counts infinitely more than the workshop...from promoters of the Catalan cloth industry during the first half of the fourteenth

[53] On the history of the Languedocian industry over the long term, see Thomson, *Clermont-de-Lodève*, pp. 89–117; P. Wolff, 'Esquisse d'une histoire de la draperie en Languedoc du XIIe au début du XVIIIe siècle', in *Produzione, commercio e consumo dei panni di lana. Atti Della seconda settimana di studio* (10–16 April 1970) (Florence, 1976). On the importance of the Levant market into the eighteenth century, see R. T. Rapp, 'The Unmaking of the Mediterranean Trade Hegemony: International Trade Rivalry and the Commercial Revolution', *Journal of Economic History*, 35 (1975), *pp.* 502–5.   [54] See pp. 311–17.

century... in less than half a century they became specialized wholesale merchants'.[55] The merchant involvement in silk production was, likewise, not sustained.

Carrère offers two principal explanations for this limitation of direct merchant participation in industry principally to the introduction of new techniques or branches of the trade. Commercial capital, she points out, had plenty of other profitable investment outlets, particularly in the import trades (unlike in some purely industrial areas such as Hondschoote in Flanders) and was not characterized by that 'gigantism' of its equivalents in Augsburg (the Fuggers) or Florence (the Medicis) which permitted investment in very wide ranges of activities; on the contrary, Catalan capitalism was characterized, as Pierre Vilar has emphasized, by its relatively small scale and its dependence on association for major speculations. In addition, she argues that the guild system, which was strengthened in the sixteenth century, placed barriers on direct involvement of commercial capital in industrial activities.[56] Bonnassié, in his study on the organization of production in Barcelona in the late fifteenth century, supports Carrère's argument with respect to this latter point, documenting the strength of the Barcelona guilds, though demonstrating again how the introduction of new industries – he refers to silk and printing – could lead to exceptions as well as contributing to a general taste for greater industrial 'freedom'.[57]

Despite its lack of direct participation in industry, merchant capital could still exercise indirect control over the production process, particularly essential for export trades in which consistent quality of production had to be maintained, by the use of the guild system to enforce regulations – this strategy is documented and explained by Jaume Torras in a general article on industrial organization in the pre-industrial period.[58]

The absence of direct involvement of commercial capital in industry had, on the other hand, important implications for social mobility: the terrain was left open for social advance from within industry. This and the widespread existence of the industry had the consequence that cloth-making was a principal avenue for social

---

[55] Carrère, *Barcelone*, I, pp. 512–22; the quotation from p. 522.

[56] C. Carrère, 'Structures et évolution des entreprises pré-industrielles: le cas de Barcelone au bas Moyen-Age', in *Studi in Memoria di Federigo Melis* (Naples, 1978), III, pp. 37–57.

[57] P. Bonnassié, *La organización del trabajo en Barcelona a fines del siglo XV* (Barcelona, 1975), pp. 148–71.

[58] J. Torras, 'Estructura de la indústria pre-capitalista. La draperia', *Recerques*, 11 (1981), pp. 7–28.

mobility in Catalonia, contributing significantly to the relative dynamism of the area's social structure. The trade of *paraire*, in particular, was the source of many fortunes. Vilar refers to this and cites the eighteenth-century Catalan historian Jaume Caresmar who delighted in pointing out how Catalan noble families with claims to Gothic ancestors in fact owed their origins to fortunes accumulated in the cloth trade.[59]

[59] Vilar, *La Catalogne*, I, pp. 426–7.

CHAPTER 3

The establishment of calico-printing in Barcelona

In the immediate vicinity of the New Gate of this city a
manufacture of printed linens, or printed calicoes, similar to
those which before the prohibition were commercialized from
the Estates General of Holland, has been established.

(AGS, Sección 24, DGR, leg. 438, letter of Julián de
Canaveras, sub-delegate, to Antonio de Sartine, Intendant
in Barcelona, 17 Aug. 1737)

As was noted in the previous chapter, no evidence has yet been found
of attempts to introduce calico-printing among Feliu de la Penya's,
and his collaborators', efforts to modernize the Barcelona textile
industry. This is not altogether surprising because it was a new
industry, which had only recently been introduced in London and
Amsterdam (in 1676), and about whose techniques (in particular the
formulas for mordants) great secrecy was maintained.[1] An aura of
mystery surrounded the trade and the nature of the special
ingredients which imparted the brilliance and permanence of the
colours of printed calicoes. This in itself represented a barrier to the
industry's diffusion: it may not have appeared conceivable. Jean
Rhyiner, introducer of the industry to Bâle in 1716, commented on
this in his 'Traité sur la fabrication et le commerce des toiles peintes',
the first history of the industry. 'As the Dutchman is secretive in his
operations', he wrote (Amsterdam was exercising a near complete
domination of the trade at the time), 'it was believed for a long time
that this art was more difficult and that others than those who were
initiated in these mysteries would not succeed.'[2]

On the other hand, Marseilles was an even earlier centre for the
industry than Amsterdam and London. The industry there has been
traced back to 1648 and was combined originally with the printing of

---

[1] Chapman and Chassagne, *European Textile Printers*, p. 6.
[2] In D. Dollfuss-Ausset, *Matériaux pour la coloration des étoffes* (2 vols., Paris, 1865), II, p. 73.

playing cards and fans with moulds. It expanded considerably from the 1660s, received technical assistance from Armenian workers during the 1670s and experienced some diffusion during the same decade within France and also to Rome to which in 1677 one Vincent Mille committed himself to going to work for a year 'to colour and print linen in the Indian fashion' for a salary of 24 *livres* a month. Given the strength of the links between Marseilles and the Catalan economy during these years, and the extensive French migration into Catalonia, the transfer of calico-printing to Barcelona would appear to have been a practicable proposition. Political circumstances, on the other hand – the war between France and Spain between 1672 and 1678, in which Catalonia was a principal front, and which coincided with the period of expansion and diffusion in the Marseilles industry – may have represented a barrier.[3]

During the 1680s the process of diffusion of the industry was dominated by the internal politics of France. In 1686, a year after the Revocation of the Edict of Nantes, printed calicoes, both imported and produced within France, were banned. The moulds used by calico-printers were to be broken. The measure was designed primarily to protect the woollen and silk industries from the competition of cotton. Its near coincidence with the Revocation, however, was probably not fortuitous. The industry was largely in the hands of Huguenots and this fact must have contributed to removing any doubts about the decision to sacrifice it. The combination of the two measures gave rise to a widespread diffusion of the industry but to Protestant areas, principally Geneva and various towns of north Germany.[4] Despite its geographical proximity to Languedoc, which was the area of maximal diffusion of the industry in France, the religion of Catalonia would have excluded it from sharing in this diffusion.

So the relative novelty of the industry and the secrecy maintained about its techniques, combined with the periods of warfare with France and the fact that the French industry was largely in the hands of Huguenots, might be the explanations for its not being introduced to Catalonia during the period of industrial recovery of the 1680s and

---

[3] H. Chobaut, 'L'Industrie des indiennes à Marseille avant 1680', Institut Historique de Provence, Marseille, *Mémoires et bulletins*, 1 (1939), pp. 81–91.
[4] L. Dermigny, *Cargaisons indiennes, Solier et Cie, 1781–1793* (2 vols., Paris, 1960), 1, pp. 203–6. C. Chassagne, on the other hand, disputes the linking of the two measures (*La Manufacture de toiles imprimées de Tournemine-lès-Angers (1752–1820), étude d'une entreprise et d'une industrie au XVIIIe siècle* (Paris, 1971), p. 45).

1690s which was described in the last chapter. This is assuming, of course, that there was any desire for such an introduction, which is in fact debatable for the industry represented a threat to the staple silk and woollen industries, and the collaboration of the guilds, which we have noted in the case of other industrial innovations of these years, might have been withheld in the case of calico-printing. The arguments in favour of the industry were always weakened by the potential damage it could do to established textile interests and the fact that this was not compensated for by the small amount of employment to which it itself gave rise, particularly when it was printed on imported cloth.[5]

There is indeed direct evidence of the hostility to which imported Indian wares gave rise in Barcelona. In 1667 the silk-weavers resisted an attempt to impose the Bolla on their production of *sargas* and *sargiletes* (cloths made with a range of mixed fibres) by emphasizing the injustice of their having to pay when drapers were selling 'such an abundance of dyed cloths, such as *zangalas*, *blauetes*, *bocaramos* and other cloths of this type...free of the Bolla...making such large profits for foreigners'. The imported Indian wares about which they were complaining were types of cotton cloth dyed in the piece which were only threatening a branch of their trade, that of taffeta for lining dresses, but a list which they included with their petition of the principal purposes for which their *sargas* and *sargiletes* were intended – dresses, bedspreads, curtains, wall hangings, door hangings, carpets, cloaks, handkerchieves, and aprons – shows that the majority of their production was potentially threatened by printed calicoes whose uses were virtually identical.[6]

After the 1690s, the lack of any attempt to introduce the industry requires less explanation – the commercial expansion of these years came to an end in the early eighteenth century, and with the Catalan alliance to the Austrian cause in the Spanish War of Succession, Catalonia became a battleground with disastrous consequences for the local economy. All indicators went into decline. A study by Jordi Nadal and Emili Giralt on the economic structure of Barcelona in 1717–18, based on the new cadastral tax which was imposed after the Bourbon triumph in the war, reveals levels of population which were little higher than those recorded at the worst moments of economic decline in the fifteenth century. They conclude that 'the city

[5] Chassagne, *La Manufacture de toiles imprimées*, pp. 40–6.
[6] Carrera Pujal, *Historia política*, II, pp. 189–90.

appears as if shut in on itself, like in the worst days of the decadence ... a typical pre-industrial society, with no anticipation of the mass features of an industrialization'.[7] The circumstances were clearly not favourable for risky, new industrial ventures. The slowing down in the diffusion of the industry was, besides, an international phenomenon.[8]

For a long period, thus, printed calicoes remained an imported product in Catalonia. The exact date of their first appearance on the regional market is not known but it is likely to have been at some stage after 1650, when the European reexport trade in them began to expand rapidly.[9] By the 1690s a substantial import trade had developed: this is revealed by Fontana's comparison of the city's trade in 1664/5 and 1695/6: at the second date he records imports of 27,000 metres of printed calicoes.[10]

The first section of this chapter will be devoted to a description of this import trade – the substitution for which was to provide the basis for the foundation of the first calico-printing manufactures in Barcelona. A survey of calico stocks carried out in 1732 will be used to establish the extent of diffusion of the cloth in Catalonia, the character of the commercial organization of the trade, the types of calicoes and other cotton goods which were sold in local markets and the uses to which calicoes were put. In a second section, an explanation will be offered for the eventual Spanish decision to follow the precedents of France, England and several other European powers to ban the calico imports, and details will be provided of the resulting legislation and its enforcement. A third section will be devoted to an account of the establishment of the first calico-printing manufactures in Barcelona. In a fourth section some characteristics of the new industry will be described, and in a fifth and final one the role of three 'entrepreneurs' in its introduction will be described.

---

[7] J. Nadal and E. Giralt, 'Barcelona en 1717–1718. Un modelo de sociedad pre-industrial', in *Homenaje a don Ramón Carande* (2 vols., Madrid, 1963), II, pp. 3–31.

[8] On the diffusion of calico-printing, see Chapman and Chassagne, *European Textile Printers*, pp. 6–10.

[9] Davis, 'English Foreign Trade, 1660–1700', p. 82: English calico reexport trade in calicoes rose from nothing to a value of £340,000 between the 1660s and 1699–1701.

[10] Fontana, 'Sobre el comercio', p. 210.

THE IMPORT TRADE IN PRINTED CALICOES

The survey of calico stocks in Catalonia in 1732 on which I am going to base this section was undertaken in connection with the enforcement of the legislative bans of 1717 and 1728 on the import of printed calicoes and other textiles. The first of these measures applied purely to imports from Asia and the second extended the prohibition to European imitations of these. More will be said about these measures in the second section of the chapter. I shall limit myself here to explaining the precise context of the survey.

Its execution was in connection with an attempt to resolve what represented a primary problem in the enforcement of the import prohibitions – the existence of substantial existing stocks of calicoes in merchants' warehouses, drapers' shops and in the hands of tailors which served as a cover for trading in illegally imported calicoes. The carrying out of surveys of stocks was intended to prevent this abuse. Existing stocks were registered by the fixing of seals and, once the survey had been carried out, only this registered cloth was permitted to be sold. The 1732 survey was not in fact the first – a previous one had been carried out in 1729.[11] The need to carry out a second such survey thus reveals the persistent difficulty of enforcing the legislation. In the letter which Julián de Canaveras, sub-delegate of Rentas Generales in the Superintendencia de Hacienda, and encharged with the administering of the prohibitive legislation, sent to Intendant Sartine in Barcelona communicating the orders of José Patiño for the drawing up of the new register, he stressed that so far 'the stage of eliminating them [the imported calicoes] has not been reached, rather their use is so general that there is an abundance of them in all parts', and he confirmed that the principal problem was the selling of illegally imported cloth 'under the pretence of its having been previously registered and sealed'.[12]

The extent of the survey's utility for our purpose is dependent, of course, firstly on the thoroughness with which it was carried out and secondly on the extent of the stocks of calicoes still remaining nearly four years after the extension of the import ban to European imitations of the oriental imports. I shall briefly consider these questions before analysing its content.

---

[11] Carrera Pujal, *Historia política*, IV, pp. 134–5.
[12] The records of the survey are held in AGS, DGR, Segunda Remesa, leg. 4907.

With respect to the former, Canaveras's instructions received a prompt response. Intendant Sartine[13] relayed them to his thirteen *corregidores* on 22 March – they, or, 'in case of an essential duty or other impediment', a substitute, were to carry out the royal orders that in all towns 'in which there was trade and shops in which clothing and cloth of whatever quality were sold all that of cotton and of painted linen which were found were to be registered'. The resulting visits of inspection were carried out between 30 March and 26 April throughout the Principality.[14]

There were, though, considerable variations in the completeness of the surveys. In the *corregimiento* of Gerona, not only was Gerona itself searched thoroughly by the town's mayor accompanied by the local tax officer, but also authority was delegated to two agents to carry out searches in other parts of the district. On the other hand, the *corregidor* of Vic limited himself initially to visiting Vic itself and it was only a full twenty-four days later, by which time word of a forthcoming inspection would surely have gone round, that, having received word that there were 'individuals trading in cloth' in Manlleu and Torelló, he arranged for a constable from the Town Hall to inspect there. In Manresa, too, the orders were not carried out very thoroughly, the *corregidor* merely writing to the leading officials of the small towns and larger villages of his district, requesting reports on sales and stocks of calicoes. In Mataró not even this formality was fulfilled, the *corregidor* absolving himself in his report to the Intendant from extending his searches beyond Mataró itself by referring to the views of 'different experienced people, well informed about the *corregimiento* of this city' that nowhere else 'in this part were there draping shops, nor other types of cloth'.[15]

Clearly there were certain parts of the Principality in which the discovery of illegal calicoes was less likely than in others. For example, the officers to whom enquiries had been directed in the Vall D'Aran reported that there was no 'shop in the valley … in which the said cottons or other types of cloth were sold … there are only some shops which sell some type of fish, eau-de-vie and other foodstuffs'.[16]

---

[13] Antonio Sartine, Intendant of Catalonia 1727–44.
[14] These instructions were recorded in the notarial acts drawn up to describe each visit made. I have quoted here from the notarial act recording the visit made at Valls on 5 April 1732.
[15] This information is extracted from the respective reports for the visits made for these centres – Gerona, 5–12 April, Manresa, 1 April, Mataró, 30 March.
[16] Report of 8 April 1732.

In various cases, however, the likelihood of finding calicoes does not seem to have been the decisive factor influencing the thoroughness of the search. Vic, for example, although predominantly agricultural, contained additional centres to Manlleu and Torrelló in which there would have been a good chance of locating calicoes – Olot, which was a substantial town, with a population of 2,677 (several times those of Torelló and Manlleu), Sant Joan de les Abadesses, Ripoll and Camprodon.[17] So the survey was not complete, but on the other hand, a comparison of the population of the towns visited with that of the total urban population of Catalonia (the 'urban' threshold being set at 1,000) reveals a coverage of over 75 per cent of the Principality. The geographical scope of the survey is thus adequate.[18]

The credentials of the survey from the point of view of geographical coverage have been established. There remains, however, the question of whether the inspections were carried out with sufficient rigour to occasion the recording of all or at least the majority of cotton goods – be they previously registered or smuggled – existing. With respect to the former, it seems likely that they represent a reasonably accurate record. This is because holders of legally imported cloth had a direct interest in ensuring its re-registration and thereby their continued right to trade in it without danger of legal interference. This concern is revealed by the care which drapers can be seen by the survey to have taken to ensure the registration of even very small scraps of calicoes, of 2 *pams* and less. It is highly unlikely, by contrast, despite the thoroughness of the searches that may have been carried out – in the case of Santiago de Arbeca in the *corregimiento* of Tarragona, for example, the inspecting officer reported that he had 'examined and touched one by one the folds of the pieces of cloth' – that they provide a complete record of contraband calicoes. The smallness of the quantity of illegal calicoes found (see table 3.1 below) is one sign of this, for the market, if Canaveras is to be believed, was inundated with the product. It seems likely that there would have been few chances of success in finding such goods, even when the advantage of surprise was enjoyed, as traders in them

---

[17] See Vilar, *La Catalogne*, I, p. 230, II, p. 129, for these demographic details; for the administrative division of Catalonia into *corregimientos*, see F. Mercader Riba, *Felip V y Catalunya* (Barcelona, 1968), pp. 269–80.

[18] The figures for calculating Catalonia's total urban population on this basis are taken from Vilar, *La Catalogne*, II, pp. 118–85. It should be noted that if the 'urban' areas outside Barcelona are isolated the survey emerges as slightly less thorough – a 68 per cent coverage.

Table 3.1. *Cotton goods without seals of 1729 and 1730 seized during the survey of 1732*

Place	Item	Quantity
Balaguer	*Indianas*	21 *canas* 3 *pams*
Tàrrega	Handkerchieves	14½ dozen
Vic	*Indianas*	90 *canas* 4 *pams*
L'Escala	*Bassis d'algodon*	1 *cana* 3 *pams*
Banyoles	*Bassis d'algodon*	7 *canas*
Manresa	*Indianas*	47 *canas* 3 *pams*
Igualada	Small gowns	19
	Indianas	7 *canas* 1 *pam*
Vilafranca	Gowns	8
	Hats	20

would have been used to acting with stealth after the experience of nearly four years of prohibition. And in practice surprise, too, was unlikely. Word must have got round when inspections were being carried out all over Catalonia during a two- to three-week period. In towns with several drapers' shops to be visited, secrecy, it is likely, would only have been maintainable for the first inspection. Significantly, the only substantial haul of illegally imported calicoes achieved was made during such a first visit, in Vic.

So the survey is only of use as a record of the remaining stocks of calicoes and cotton goods imported before June 1728 in some three-quarters of urban Catalonia. As for the second question which was posed – the relationship of these stocks to those which had originally been held in the Principality in 1728 – this cannot be calculated precisely. A clue, however, is provided by the record which exists among the papers of the Junta General de Comercio of a request made in 1729 by Francisco Figueras y Compañia, linen- and silk-draper of Barcelona, to be allowed to import 600 pieces of calicoes which were being detained in Genoa in view of the 1728 import ban. The justification of the request was that the purchase had been made before the edict imposing the restriction was published. It was acceded to.[19] The detail not only serves to give an idea of the scale of the importing activities of one of the city's largest traders in calicoes (Figueras was the fourth largest stockist in 1732 – the 600 pieces

[19] AGS, CSH, reg. 213, fo. 3, consulta of 29 Nov. 1729.

A distinctive industrialization

Table 3.2. *Catalonia's stocks of cotton goods as recorded in the survey of 1732*

Corregimiento/ town	Printed linens and calicoes (canas/pams)	Other cotton cloth	Made-up goods (units)
Barcelona	9,842 – 2½	609 – 5½	591
Gerona	315 – 5	14 – 5	
La Bisbal	21 – 7	0 – 4	
Sant Feliu	51 – 7	162 – 3	
Canet	4 – 5	0 – 2	
Figueras	0 – 3	6 – 0	
L'Escala		1 – 3	
Llança	2 – 4		
Banyoles		7 – 0	
Mataró	47 – 0	8 – 5	
Vilafranca	40 – 4		28
Sitges	16 – 3		
Igualada	7 – 1		19
Tarragona	197 – 0	22 – 2	
Reus	206 – 5	415 – 1½	
Vilanova	21 – 3	30 – 5	
Valls	37 – 4½		
Tortosa	889 – 1		
Vic	103 – 7	5 – 0	
Torelló	three 'bits'		
Manresa	29 – 3½	7 – 3	26
Cervera	248 – 0½	15 – 6½	
Santa Coloma	31 – 5	32 – 0½	
Lérida	459 – 4	35 – 2	
Balaguer	65 – 0		
Tàrrega	39 – 0	14½ dozen handerchieves	47
Puigcerdà		11 – 0	
Urgel	0 – 4½		
Pallars			
Talarn	1 – 0		
Total	12,679 – 7½	1,385 – 0	711

Note: names of *corregimientos* appear in bold type.

would have had a value of some 7,500 *libras* at the retail level – but also can be compared to the quantity – 1,012 *canas* 1½ *pams* – which Figueras is recorded as stocking in 1732. If the 600 pieces in question indeed reached him, and disregarding any holdings which predated this purchase, Figueras's stock in 1732 stood at approximately one sixth of what would have been its level in late 1729 or early 1730. If Figueras's case is representative then it shows that a considerable depletion in the city's calico stocks had occurred by 1732 and the survey thus clearly does not provide a basis for making any quantitative estimates of the size of the trade. The depletion was not, however, it is also clear, total. The survey, for example, records the existence of twenty-six holders of calicoes and other cotton-containing textiles in Barcelona with stocks of 10,450 *canas* or 1,045 pieces as well as a number of made up garments of calicoes. In view of the fact that these stockists not only acted as retailers within the city but also as wholesalers for much of the regional trade – drapers from smaller towns, it is revealed by the survey, were regularly stocking up with calicoes from Barcelona drapers – it would seem probable that supplies, though they may have become scarce by 1732, had not totally dried up and that the survey thus provides a reasonably accurate impression of the diffusion of the trade within most of the Principality.

The instructions of the Intendant to his *corregidores* were to register and describe all the cotton goods found, to note whether legalizing seals had been attached to them and to record their places of manufacture and any customs documentation. As will emerge, not all of these instructions were invariably followed, the data though are sufficiently complete to permit a description of the local trade. This has been organized as follows, firstly, size and whereabouts of calico stocks in 1732, secondly, ports through which these calicoes were introduced and internal distribution networks, thirdly, cloth types (types of cotton textile on which printing had been done, colours and patterns used) and fourthly, uses to which calicoes were being put.

Calico stocks in 1732

Table 3.2 lists the whereabouts and quantity of the stocks of calico and other cotton goods revealed by the survey to have been held in Catalonia in 1732. The table demonstrates comparatively widespread commercialization of calicoes and other types of cotton goods in the region. Stocks were held in twenty-eight different centres and these centres, clearly, would have serviced the requirements of neighbouring villages and smaller towns. Considerable variations, however, in the extent of stocks in different parts of the Principality are detectable. Firstly and pre-eminently, an overwhelming domination

by Barcelona, with its numerous drapers' shops which held some
73 per cent of the region's calico stocks, is revealed; secondly, relatively high densities of stocks in three southern and westerly zones
of the principality are revealed – in Tortosa, the second largest single
stockist, in a group of towns in the *corregimiento* of Tarragona
(Tarragona itself, Reus, Valls and Vilanova) and in a westerly area
including the towns of Lérida, Tàrrega, Balaguer and Cervera;
thirdly, contrasting low densities are shown in the northern *corregimientos* of Gerona, Vic, Manresa, Puigcerdà and the Vall d'Aran.

The survey is of use to us for two reasons. It demonstrates the
existence of a good potential market for calicoes in the region – a
developing industry could expect to benefit from local demand for its
product – and it provides some confirmation concerning the mechanics of the growth process in interior Catalonia which were
mentioned in the last chapter. Jaume Torras, it was emphasized, has
argued that the agrarian prosperity of western Catalonia, largely
brought about by the export of wine and eau-de-vie, lay behind
regional specialization, a growth in a consumer market and the
concentration of textile production in less favoured regions. Vilar,
too, in his interpretation of the recovery of the Catalan region during
the eighteenth century, attributes its origin to an agrarian and
demographic recovery in western Catalonia which began in the first
half of the century and had at its basis the viticultural boom and
repopulation of the Lérida plain. The pattern of the distribution of
calico stocks, suggesting high levels of demand for textiles in south-
west Catalonia and relatively low levels in the north-east, is clearly
consistent with these interpretations.[20]

Points of import and distribution networks

The survey contains little information about the original sources of
the calicoes and the importing trade. Only in one case is the (Dutch)
origins of a draper's stock mentioned. The gap can fortunately be
filled, however, from other sources. Vilar's study of the commercial
affairs of the Alegre family, cloth drapers, shows that Miquel Alegre
in conjunction with Francesc Puget, who administrated his draping
shop, and who was one of the stockists of calicoes recorded in the 1732

[20] See above, p. 40, and Vilar, *La Catalogne*, II, pp. 77–88, 92–9, III, nos. 56 and 57 in appendix
of graphs and maps. For a summary of Vilar's argument, which will also be discussed in the
next chapter, see his 'La Catalunya industrial', especially pp. 11–15.

Map 2 The 1732 survey of cotton stocks in the thirteen *corregimientos* of Catalonia

survey, was involved from 1726 in the import of a range of textiles from Holland, including printed calicoes, in return for exports of eau-de-vie. The trade is thus linked to that agricultural recovery to which Vilar and Torras give prominence. Alegre and Puget not only disposed of their imports in their own Barcelona draping shop but also were suppliers of a wide range of other drapers and tailors in Barcelona, Berga, Manresa, Gerona, Santa Coloma de Queralt and Reus.[21]

Barcelona, as was to be expected, was by far the principal port of entry for the calicoes; it was not, though, the only one. The survey reveals imports through Mataró too – drapers in Reus, Manresa and Vic had obtained calicoes from there and it seems that it was a significant source for illegally imported cloth[22] – as well as an overland route for calicoes from other parts of Spain. Saragossa is revealed as a stocking centre of some importance: Tortosa had received the majority of its calicoes from there and the source of Lérida's stocks is approximately equally divided between it and Barcelona. Saragossa was not, of course, the manufacturer of these calicoes; its merchants would have been distributing imports from the northern coast, probably from Bilbao – the stock of one of the principal drapers in Lérida bore the seals of the customs of Vitoria. Tortosa and Lérida were two of the centres surveyed which were most distant from Barcelona and this would be the principal cause for their dependence on this overland route for their supplies. The strength of this alternative current in the commercialization of calicoes was not, though, inconsiderable. The survey records that part of Barcelona's stock too, described as bearing seals of 'other customs offices of the kingdom', had clearly taken the overland route.

So Barcelona was not alone in playing that role of distribution centre for the local market in calicoes which was mentioned above. The size of its calico stocks, however, reveals its predominance in this role. These in 1732 were in the hands of a total of twenty-six individuals. Of the twenty-six, seventeen were linen- and silk-drapers – this predominance was to have been expected as the marketing of textiles was specialized and divided among different guilds and it was they who had the monopoly of selling silks and non-woollen goods – two were cloth-drapers, six were tailors and in one case no profession is stated. Of the twenty-six only two, Antoni Casanovas and Jaume Guàrdia, were among the city's leading merchants.[23] Registration

---

[21] Vilar, *La Catalogne*, III, pp. 416–17.
[22] The calicoes proceeding from Mataró at Manresa and Vic in neither case possessed the seals certifying legal importation and were duly seized.
[23] On Barcelona's draping guilds, see Molas Ribalta, *Los gremios*, pp. 293–344. Casanovas's and Guàrdia's status as leading merchants is derived from a list of the thirty-nine principal payers of the *cadastro personal* or *ganancial* in Barcelona between 1724 and 1752, which was

details recorded in the survey provided further evidence of the importance of Barcelona's role in supplying the majority of the Principality's markets.

To summarize, the document reveals that the commercialization of calicoes in the majority of Catalonia was dominated by Barcelona though some western zones were under the influence of another, powerful commercial centre, Saragossa. The size of holdings in such centres was on a different scale to that in smaller towns. Only Tortosa and Lérida possessed more than one stockist holding over 100 *canas* of calicoes whereas Barcelona contained sixteen. Drapers in smaller centres, the document shows, rather than holding very large stocks themselves, operated on the basis of regularly replenishing their stocks in their closest, large commercial centre.

There is no evidence about prices at which calicoes from these gradually depleting stocks were selling or of the extent to which the region's requirements of the goods were being fully satisfied. It must be presumed that prices rose and that some scarcity was being experienced. The import figures of printed calicoes to Barcelona for 1695/6, it will be recalled, at an earlier period in the development of the trade (though in one of expansion in the regional economy) stood at some twice the level of the entire recorded stocks for the region in 1732. A hint of the type of commercial transactions which may have been occasioned by the growing scarcity is provided by the record in the survey that the stock of Josep Campllonch, the only significant holder of calicoes in Mataró, had been bought in September 1731 in Barcelona from a merchant from the town of Calaf, Cortadellas.[24] Cortadellas was unlikely himself to have been the original owner of these calicoes and the details of the transaction suggest the existence of some speculative buying and selling.

raised on industrial and trading activities, which is included in Fernández, 'La burguesía barcelonesa', p. 11. Some of the drapers would have been administrating the shops of richer merchants specializing in the wholesale trade – this was the case of Francesc Puget who was administering the shop of Alegre.

[24] A. Cortadellas of Calaf was extensively involved in the American trade some fifty years later (J. Fontana, 'Comercio colonial e industrialización: una reflexión sobre los orígenes de la industria moderna en Cataluña', in J. Nadal and G. Tortella (eds.), *Agricultura, comercio colonial y crecimiento económico en la España contemporánea* (Barcelona, 1974), pp. 362–3). On the Cortadellas family, see also J. I. Gómez 'La burguesía mercantil catalana y su presencia en Aragón (1770–1808)', *Segon Congrès d'Història Moderna de Catalunya, Pedralbes, Revista d'Història Moderna*, 8, i (1988), pp. 405–23.

Types of calicoes

The instructions given to the *corregidores* were vague – to register and to 'describe' the cloth which they found – and consequently there was little uniformity in the character of the registers of the stocks which they drew up. On the other hand, the survey contains enough information to provide a reasonably complete idea of the types of cotton goods which were on sale. I shall differentiate between the different types of printed textiles in terms of the quality of the cloth on which printing had been done and the types of patterns and colours applied.

Four types of cloth, the survey reveals, had been printed on. Two of these were calicoes, in qualities defined as *fina* (fine) or *comuna* (ordinary) (these were invariably listed as *indianas*, the colloquial origin of this term being in several cases acknowledged by the fuller description 'known colloquially as *indianas*'), a third was cotton/linen mixtures and a fourth pure linen. The thoroughness with which the survey was carried out by one Josep Boffarull i Mora in two of the towns of the *corregimiento* of Tarragona with substantial stocks, Tarragona itself and Reus, permits an appropriate calculation as to the relative importance of these different qualities of cloth in the region's markets. The example, as can be seen in table 3.3, did not include pure linens, but this was very much the minority material on which the survey shows printing had been done – there are records of only 166 *canas* 2 *pams* of printed linens stocked. Apart from this omission, there seems no reason to doubt the sample's representativeness. It shows, firstly, that the majority of the printed textiles stocked were *indianas* and, secondly, that the majority of these *indianas* were fine ones.

Descriptions of the colours and patterns with which these textiles had been decorated are yet more erratic and incomplete in the survey. In order to give as accurate an impression as possible of this question, summarized in table 3.4 are all the different descriptions provided and the quantity of cloth attributed to each. What emerges from the summary is the following. Firstly, the types of designs on the *indianas* stocked in the regional market were relatively simple – flower motifs, of various sizes, predominated and in addition there were some pieces with geometrical patterns. Secondly, it is apparent that the colours of the cloth were in majority those obtained by the application of mordants and dyeing in madder – shades of red, lilac,

Table 3.3. *Qualities of textiles on which printing had been carried out in the stocks of Reus and Tarragona*

Indianas finas	243 canas 2 pams
Indianas comunas	64 canas 5 pams
Unpsecified indianas	35 canas 4 pams
Cotton/linen mixture	60 canas 2 pams

Table 3.4. *Colours and patterns (where listed) of printed textiles located in Catalonia according to the 1732 survey*

Description	Quantity
1. Madder-dyed	
Comunas or finas de color	293 canas
Blancas +flores coloradas, encarnadas,	81 canas 1½ pams
decoradas +flores grandes coloradas +flores pequeñas coloradas +flores diferentes coloradas	
Comunas blancas +flores negras	14 canas 7½ pams
Comunas blancas +piques negras	6 canas
Coloradas +flores blancas	9 canas
Pintado de flores	3 canas 6 pams
Coloradas con diferentes colores	7 canas 2 pams
Muscar +flores colaradas y blancas	15 canas 4 pams
Café	6 canas 3 pams
Finas llistadas	7 canas
2. Blues	
Azul +flores blancas +flores blancas grandes	48 canas 2½ pams
Campo azul +picos blancos	6 canas 1½ pams
Azul +flores coloradas	3 canas 2 pams
Azul y blanco	9 canas
Blanco +flores azules	7 canas 2 pams
Hilo y algodon color azul	33 canas

Notes: 1. Omitted from this table is a total of 56 canas 7½ pams of a mixed batch of the following colours and designs: *blancas con flores coloradas, flores pequeñas coloradas, flores grandes; azules con flores blancas grandes, coloradas; vastas azules con picos blancos; obscuras vastas con flores blancas.*
2. Where the terms *coloradas* or *color* are used they refer to the more common madder-based colours. Blues, on the other hand, receive specific mention. This is demonstrated by the list for Tarragona on which all the cloth is described simply as *indianas* (*finas* or *comunas*) *color* except for the blues, described as *color azul.*

brown and black. This was to have been expected. These were the first types of printing methods mastered within the European industry and were to remain the principal ones used throughout the eighteenth century. Thirdly, it is clear from the colours of the stocks of blues that they had been produced predominantly, and possibly entirely, by resist dyeing. This was a totally distinct method of 'printing' from the mordant/madder process which involved waxing a part of the cloth in order to prevent its taking colour when immersed in an indigo solution. It was only practical in the production of white patterns on a blue background for the contrary would have involved waxing the majority of the cloth. The fact that all the blue dyed cloth listed except for 7 *canas* 2 *pams*, short lengths from two pieces, consists in white patterns on a blue background demonstrates the predominance of the resist process in the Principality's stocks.[25] It would be risky on the basis of the evidence of the two short pieces of cloth which were dyed blue on a white background to assert that cloth produced with what was a new method just being introduced – the direct application of indigo dissolved in ferrous sulphate by moulds – was already being marketed in Spain. It is, though, a possibility.[26]

Uses

As will have been noted, the stocks of some drapers and, in the case of Barcelona, tailors, included made-up garments. Descriptions of these, which are summarized in table 3.5, contribute to giving some idea of the uses to which printed calicoes were being put. The details in the table suggest that printed calicoes at this stage were being used principally within the home for house coats, dressing gowns and bedspreads. This is consistent with practices elsewhere. A. W. Douglas has noted the extensive use of calicoes for this purpose in England and he links it to the contemporary fashion for 'undress', characterized by the popularity of 'lightweight clothes cut on fluid

---

[25] On these two dyeing techniques, see P. R. Schwarz, 'La coloration partielle des étoffes', in M. Daumas (ed.), *Histoire générale des techniques* (3 vols., Paris, 1962–8), III, pp. 704–28, and 'Contribution à l'histoire de l'application du bleu d'indigo (bleu anglais) dans l'indiennage européen', *Bulletin de la Société Industrielle de Mulhouse*, 2 (1953), pp. 63–79; P. Floud, 'The Origins of English Calico-Printing', and 'The English Contribution to the Early History of Indigo-Printing', *Journal of the Society of Dyers and Colourists*, 76 (1960), pp. 275–82, 344–9.

[26] This method of direct application of blue, which was not known in India, was being developed in England at approximately the time (the exact date is not known) that the survey took place (Floud, 'The English Contribution to Indigo-Printing', p. 345). Samples of cloth printed according to this method are claimed to exist for approximately the year 1730 (Schwarz, 'Contribution', p. 11).

Table 3.5. *Made-up items of printed calico listed in the 1732 survey*

House coats/dressing gowns for men and women	89
Small house coats/dressing gowns for children	441
Bedspreads	23
Tunics	4
Small tunics for boys/children	23
Hats	107

lines'. A second point which emerges is the predominance of children's clothing among the made-up garments. This too is consistent with England's experience where a large demand for calicoes for children's clothes grew up.

It has already been established that the majority of the printed calicoes stocked in the region were of fine quality and some of the descriptions of these tailor-made garments provide further evidence that at this stage calicoes catered principally for the luxury trade – the fact that the garments were not ones of first necessity is, of course, another pointer to this. The fifteen children's small tunics stocked in Igualada, for example, were 'lined with the same *indiana* with wool stuffing' and the four tunics of *indiana* stocked in Vilafranca del Penedés were with 'cotton and wool stuffing and lined in three cases with *indiana* and the other with painted linen'. This luxury bias is again consistent with the early development of the trade elsewhere.[27]

LEGISLATION AND ITS ENFORCEMENT

The relative lateness of the Spanish government's response to the large-scale import of *indianas* would have been contributed to by the difficulties inherent in devising any form of uniform economic policy in Spain in the late seventeenth century in view of the extensive political freedoms enjoyed by large parts of its territory.[28] It is likely, though, that, as much as such political difficulties, it was the existence of so many other pressing economic problems which prevented an early response. The import of the whole range of European textile production and other manufactured goods, the predominance of foreign merchants in leading commercial centres, and interloping in

[27] A. W. Douglas, 'Cotton Textiles in England: The East India Company's Attempt to Exploit Developments in Fashion, 1660–1721', *Journal of British Studies*, 8 (1969), pp. 28–43.
[28] On political decentralization, see H. Kamen, *Spain in the Later Seventeenth Century, 1665–1700* (London, 1980), pp. 13–20.

the American trades, were threatening to deprive Spain of any semblance of economic independence in the late seventeenth century,[29] and Charles II's death in 1700 without heir seemed likely to make this situation permanent – a primary objective of outside participants on both sides in the ensuing War of Succession was to obtain a share of Spain's domestic and American markets. In such circumstances, an early response to imported textiles was not to have been expected and all the less so in that the vested interests harmed by their introduction, the pressure exercised by whom was crucial to the development of protective legislation elsewhere, were more likely to have been foreign textile industries than domestic producers.

The plausibility of this explanation for the delayed reaction is supported by the circumstances surrounding the publication of the first protective edicts in 1717 and 1718. They formed part of a series of measures taken by Philip V, the Bourbon victor in the Succession War, designed to contribute to the emancipation of the Spanish economy from foreign domination. Additional actions included the founding of royal cloth manufactures, the introduction of foreign (principally Dutch) workers, attempts at fiscal rationalization involving the abolition of internal customs posts (the so-called 'dry ports'), a policy of directing state demands, principally for war materials, to Spanish producers, a drive against contraband and orders to provincial intendants to take stock of, and encourage, local industry.[30] Vilar writes of 'an undeniable improvement in the protection of national interests in front of foreign interests' in this period by means of 'politics directly inspired by Colbertism', in which protective legislation was combined with 'the summons to foreign technicians, the foundation of large privileged royal manufactures'.[31]

The bans on cotton imports were the most radical of these protective measures and Jaume Torras recently has pointed out that a reason for this was that the cotton trade was one of the few in which the Bourbon government had complete freedom of action with respect to tariff policy, maximal levels of tariffs for other industries being prescribed in the international treaties which had been signed at the end of the war. The effects of restrictive government policies

[29] Vicens Vives, *Manual*, pp. 383–5, 394–400, 500–1; G. A. Walker, *Spanish Politics and Imperial Trade, 1700–1789* (London, 1979), pp. 11–15, 19–33.
[30] J. Carrera Pujal, *Historia de la economía española* (5 vols., Barcelona, 1943–7), III, pp. 120–42; A. González Enciso, *Estado e industria en el siglo XVIII. La Fábrica de Guadalajara* (Madrid, 1980), pp. 238–9. [31] Vilar, *La Catalogne*, I, p. 706.

towards cotton on the internal development of the English and French industries have often been discussed but this possible external consequence – Spain's benefiting from the lack of interest shown by its major competitors in the new industry at this stage by the setting up of the necessary protective barriers to establish an import-substituting industry – has not been previously considered.[32]

It was probably symptomatic of the weight of the American trade in the Spanish economy, and the primacy which it held in ministerial concerns, that the actual occasion of the 1717/18 restrictions would seem to have been complaints of merchants from Cádiz and Seville that a permission which had been granted to traders in the Philippines to send Asian textiles on boats to Acapulco had resulted in large imports which were ruining Spanish industry. It would seem likely that these merchants' principal concern was in fact the protection of their trade monopoly for, as the merchants from Manila were quick to point out, they had shown little concern about the impact on the domestic economy of their own export of foreign textiles.[33]

The terms of the prohibition, expressed in the edict of 17 September 1718, were an immediate ban on the import of Oriental textiles, the liquidation of merchants' stocks of these goods within three months and an end to the use of articles composed of the banned materials after 1 July 1719. The penalties for non-compliance were to be confiscation of the offending goods and a fine for a first offence and ten years' banishment and a larger fine (half the offender's possessions) for a second.[34] As has already been noted, it was not an effective piece of legislation. It would seem to have been largely ignored and no evidence has been located of a proper attempt at its enforcement. In 1722 Catalonia's tax administrators were complaining that local markets were still inundated with printed calicoes.[35] Clearly, there were inherent difficulties in enforcing restrictions of this type but in this case the actual terms of the legislation would have contributed to ineffectiveness. The grace which had been allowed for clearing stocks was too limited, the penalties imposed for non-compliance were too Draconian and the failure to include European imitations of Oriental goods in the ban would, in the measure that the imitations were successful, have rendered the measure unenforceable.

[32] Torras, 'Early Manufacturing', p. 5.
[33] Carrera Pujal, *Economía española*, III, p. 124.   [34] AHN, Consejos, libro 1476.
[35] Carrera Pujal, *Historia política*, III, p. 6.

This import of imitations was almost certainly a growing phenomenon during the 1720s. The European industry was increasing in
size, but probably as significant was the fact that the area in which it
could freely sell its wares was gradually decreasing. In 1721 England
had passed new calico legislation, adding to its 1700 ban on the
import of Indian printed calicoes a prohibition on the sale, purchase
or wear of all prints on cotton material.[36] This brought to an end the
use by London printers of calicoes imported in the white from India
with the almost immediate consequence that these were diverted to
Amsterdam to be printed there for distribution in continental
markets. Of these continental markets Spain's must have been the
largest in which sales of European imitations of Indian textiles was
still unrestricted.[37]

It seems likely that the influx of these European imitations of
printed calicoes would have given rise to protests from damaged
parties, as did the imports of Asian textiles in 1717. The royal edict
which was passed on 17 June 1728 to prohibit the import of European
imitations of Asian textiles would in this case have been a response to
such complaints. The measure, however, had an additional purpose,
which complicates the question of the grounds for its adoption. This
was to encourage the development of an import-substituting,
domestic cotton industry. It is revealed by the terms of the edict itself
which excluded from the import restrictions 'unworked cotton,
cultivated on the isle of Malta'[38] – 'unworked' being effectively
interpreted as unwoven, for it was spun cotton which came to be
imported – and was demonstrated further by the second of the two
decrees, that of 1730, passed to establish a system for monitoring the
running down of calico stocks, in which it was stated that 'the real
intention of His Majesty in the rigorous prohibition of the trade in the
said painted linens and cotton cloth... and in the quickest possible
consumption of those which have been introduced in these dominions, [is] to ensure by all the means possible that new manufactures
should be founded in them', and that, in view of this, all printed

---

[36] On the English legislation see Wadsworth and Mann, *The Cotton Trade*, pp. 131–44.
[37] On the diversion from England of calicoes formerly consumed in the domestic market to the
continent via Amsterdam, see D. Ormrod, 'English Re-Exports and the Dutch Staple
Market in the Eighteenth Century', in D. C. Coleman and P. Mathias (eds.), *Enterprise and
History: Essays in Honour of Charles Wilson* (Cambridge, 1984), pp. 104, 107.
[38] This edict is reproduced in J. M. Jover Zamora (ed.), *Historia de España*, xxix, *La época de los
primeros borbones* (Barcelona, 1985), I, p. 253.

calicoes and other cotton textiles produced within Spain were to be exempted from its terms.[39]

The loss of the bulk of the archives of the Junta General de Comercio, in which the measure would have been discussed, prevents establishing the motives for this second purpose of the 1728 decree. Two possible considerations influencing it were (1) the existence of a cotton-working tradition in Spain and the extent to which the use of cotton was already established: to have banned the industry totally in such circumstances would have been extreme;[40] (2) the point raised by Jaume Torras, and just referred to, that cotton goods were the only ones which the Spanish government was free to ban, may have been influential: it meant that cotton was probably the only industry which could be introduced without extensive state intervention in the form of large royal manufactures; the cost of permitting an import-substituting cotton industry to develop was low.[41]

It should be noted that this direct encouragement, which appears to have been intended to ensure the establishment of all the productive processes connected both with cotton manufacturing and printing within Spain and Malta, was unusual within the context of government reactions to the cotton industry and probably made the nascent Spanish industry the most politically favoured of its time. The French industry had been banned, the English industry in the long term was to benefit from its calico legislation – the ban on cotton textiles stimulated domestic linen and linen/cotton production, excluded from the prohibition, which prepared the ground for later progress in cotton – but this was not the intention of the legislation; policy in the Dutch Republic and Switzerland was neutral – no restrictions were applied, which, in view of restrictions elsewhere, caused these areas to be poles of attraction to the industry, but there were no direct encouragements.[42]

The undertaking of the 1732 register of calico stocks, analysed in

[39] Carrera Pujal, *Historia política*, IV, pp. 134–5.
[40] On Barcelona's cotton-producing tradition, see Duran Sanpere, *Barcelona*, II, pp. 288–91. Fontana's study on trade in the 1690s shows substantial cotton imports ('Sobre el comercio', p. 210). That the use of cotton in garments in the Balearic islands was established practice, and that the government was aware of this, is revealed by the granting of an extra year's grace to the inhabitants of Majorca in 1734 to use up calico stocks 'as the people from there use them [*indianas*] for their apparel' (ACA, RA, Cartas acordadas, reg 16, fos. 130–2).
[41] See above p. 68.
[42] See J. K. J. Thomson, 'State Intervention in Catalan Calico-Printing', in M. Berg (ed.), *Markets and Manufactures in Early Industrial Europe* (London, 1991), pp. 60–4.

the previous section, would not appear to have eradicated the problem of contraband. This is suggested by the publication of yet another decree, on 14 April 1734, in which the continued existence of a range of products including printed calicoes, 'despite these strict prohibitions', was announced. Orders were given that these, this time, were to be deposited with local courts of justice within two days: there, lists were to be made for submission to the Consejo de Hacienda where the cloth's fate would be decided upon. An amnesty for previous disregard of the import ban was granted to encourage the surrender of illegal cloth.[43] The decision was not long delayed: a decree of 30 August of the same year ordered that all the deposited calicoes were to be used up within one year.

By August 1736, then, stocks of legally imported calicoes should, finally, have been eliminated. Again, though, the administrative precautions do not appear to have achieved the purpose intended. This emerges from a further letter from Canaveras to Intendant Sartine written in 1737 and requesting explanations for the negligence in customs services which was resulting in the 'inundation' of the Principality with cotton goods. In the same letter, however, he informed Sartine of a development which was to provide a basis for eliminating the imports. In the words which have been used for the epigraph to this chapter he announced that he had received information concerning, and production samples from, a calico-printing concern which had been established in Barcelona.[44]

THE ESTABLISHMENT OF THE FIRST MANUFACTURES

The manufacture about whose foundation Canaveras had been informed was most probably not the first founded. It would seem that the extension of the import ban to European imitations of Asian textiles evoked a fairly prompt response in Barcelona. Bernat Glòria, son of a velvet-weaver, who had risen to become one of the city's leading wholesale merchants, claimed that from the year of the prohibition itself he had devoted 'abundant assets in money to imitating the cloth and composition [referring to the colouring techniques] of the foreign imports'.[45] By 1734, according to Carrera

---

[43] AHN, Consejos, libro 1477.
[44] AGS, DGR, Segunda Remesa, leg. 438, letter of 17 Aug. 1737.
[45] See Fernández, 'La burguesía barcelonesa', p. 62 for the citation and pp. 12–15 for his professional background. The claim to have initiated his printing in 1728 is repeated in a letter to J. B. de Iturralde, Minister of Hacienda, of 22 Aug. 1739 (AGS, SH, leg. 1103).

Pujal, there were several manufacturers in the city who had acquired the necessary technical skills from Swiss members of the city's garrison.[46] Vicens Vives gave a different version, attributing this early manufacturing to French workers.[47] No documentary evidence, however, was cited by either historian and so there remains some doubt about their statements and the extent of printing which took place before 1736 – this is the first year for which there is definite evidence.[48] Glòria in 1738 reported that his early efforts had 'suffered some suspensions' as a consequence of 'the lack of skill of the workmen not experienced in this practice'.[49] It seems likely that any other pre-1736 manufacturing shared this fate.

The 1736 evidence consists in two notarial contracts registered on 4 September 1736. One was by Jacint Esteve, a weaver of esparto, described in the contract as a 'fabricant d'indianas', and two glass-makers, Josep Sala and Geronim Aranyó, recording the terms for the functioning of a calico-printing company for a period of three years. The other was by Esteve alone, on behalf of this company, contracting a Marseillais printer, Joan Benet Huvet, to work for the company. The concern had been running since 24 August. On 25 August the associates had rented for it some huts and adjoining land immediately outside the city's 'Portal Nou', bordering the road to the village of Clot. This was an area of intensive horticulture which possessed good irrigation facilities – the land brought with it irrigation rights for two days in the week from 'the irrigation channel which extends from the reservoir till meeting the barrier of the royal road of Horta and Clot' and possessed its own reservoir and water wheel: it was thus well equipped to serve as a bleaching meadow.[50]

The contracts provide additional evidence for the existence of earlier printing activity within the city. Not only is Esteve already described as a 'fabricant d'indianas' in the contract recording the terms of the company, and as a 'pictori de indianas' in that by which land for the bleaching meadow was rented, but he is also recorded as possessing a stock of printing moulds for the company's use and may also already have possessed the ability to engrave moulds.[51] But it

---

[46] Carrera Pujal, *Historia política*, III, p. 15.   [47] Vicens Vives, *Manual*, p. 487.
[48] On these questions, see my *La indústria d'indianes a la Barcelona del segle XVIII* (Barcelona, 1990), chapter 1: 'Els orígens de la indústria d'indianes a Barcelona'.
[49] ACA, Batllia General, Aa 52, 26 Nov. 1738, fos. 441–52.
[50] AHPB, Severo Pujol, acts of 4 Sept. 1736 and 24 Aug. 1736, fos. 446–7 and 430. Esteve is described as 'esparter' in a contract of 18 Oct. 1734 (Severo Pujol, manual for 1734, fo. 562).
[51] This is the conclusion reached by Duran Sanpere in *Barcelona i la seva història*, II, p. 293.

also supports earlier conclusions about such printing – that it was only carried out at a rudimentary level – for one of the conditions in the contract with the Marseillais printer was that he should teach 'the skill of painting and making *real* indianas to the said Esteve'.

Sala and Aranyó were the principal providers of capital for the new initiative. They, it was stipulated in the company's first clause, 'should see to the provision of the money which will be necessary to buy cotton, weave, purchase paints, rent land ... and other expenses which will be necessary for the said manufacture'. Sala, in addition to advancing capital, was to play a directing role – the expression used, and it was the conventional one in all such companies, was that he was to 'administer' the concern. This meant that he was to exercise financial control. In addition, he was to exercise some managerial functions – the contract recorded his obligation to 'buy the cotton, distribute it to the weavers, collect from them the woven pieces, taking care of their sale after being painted, taking care in the same way to keep a record of the expenses which will be incurred in the purchase of drugs, paying the workers and other items which crop up'. In return for this, Sala was to receive five-twelfths of the profits and a payment of 3 *sols* for each piece of calico which he sold. Aranyó, by contrast, was to be a 'sleeping partner' and his share of the profits only one sixth, as a return on the capital which he had advanced. Esteve's capital contribution was limited to paying one third of the cost of the tools ('expense of the boiling tub, calender, tables, vats and other tools which will be needed for the work'), but he was to receive the same share of the profits as Sala. This was because he was to play the managerial role in the printing, dyeing and bleaching processes, working full time for the company, with the responsibility for accommodating and feeding Huvet and his apprentice and main- taining 'a book for the good control of the entry and exit of *indianas*'. It was this exercising of the managerial role with respect to the central printing processes which was the justification for the company bearing his name even though his authority in the technical sphere was limited by his effective status of apprentice to Huvet: the third clause of the contract expressed 'the obligation which the said Esteve has to paint and make moulds which Joan Benet Huvet will say to be necessary'. The three associates were clearly hoping to obtain a royal privilege in support of their initiative for the last clause in the contract stated that 'whatever privilege which in some time the king should deign to concede ... to the company' was to become its collective property.

The terms of Joan Benet Huvet's employment were generous. In view of his having 'come to this city for the reason inscribed' (the founding of the calico-printing company: he had been recruited for this purpose by Esteve who had signed a contract with him in Marseilles on 10 July), he was promised an annual salary of 175 'pieces of eight', worth 245 *libras*, for three years. In addition, all living expenses were to be paid by Esteve, in whose house he was to live, and his salary was not to be reduced in case of illness. Huvet in return for this, like Esteve, was to work full time for the company – 'the said Joan Benet Huvet has to paint and work in that which corresponds to him not only to make real *indianas*, but also in other things...for the common good of the company'.

The contracts reveal a number of what were to be regular characteristics of the attempts to introduce the new industry to the city. Firstly, it is evident that the three founders of the company believed that their venture was consistent with the royal desire to promote a process of import-substitution – they hoped to receive a royal privilege, it is clear, and the nature of their concern was in conformity with the character of the protective legislation – it included weaving as well as printing. A second point that emerges is that the scale of investment in the concern was relatively large. The commitment purely to paying and feeding Huvet and his apprentice over three years represented a cost of 1,455 *libras*,[52] his recruitment and transport from Marseilles must have involved additional, substantial costs, the rent of the land for bleaching was 90 *libras* a year and in addition cotton, dyes, drugs, tools and other equipment would have had to be purchased. The way this investment was provided, it can be seen, was by what had been since the fourteenth century, when it was introduced from Italy, the general method of financing commercial and industrial enterprises in Catalonia – the founding of a company.[53] The management of the company, following the practice of drapers' shops financed by merchant capital, involved a collaboration between capitalist backers, who exercised financial control (Sala and Aranyó), and an individual from a humbler

[52] In addition to the salary, Esteve was to be advanced 20 *libras* a month over the three-year period for the lodging costs of Huvet and his apprentice.
[53] As Vilar writes, 'the "company" from the great period of the Middle Ages, was the fundamental form, the nearly universal framework of all economic activity' (*La Catalogne*, III p. 383). It was introduced in the mid-fourteenth century (Y. Renouard, 'Les Principaux Aspects économiques et sociaux de l'histoire des pays de la couronne d'Aragon aux XIIe, XIIIe et XIVe siècles', *VII Congreso d'Historia de la Corona de Aragón* (Barcelona, 1962), p. 256.

artisanal background (Esteve), whose commitment to the business was full time and who played the principal role in production as well as providing the trade-name for the concern.

Sala added to the exercising of a financial role – and this too was to be a frequent feature in the new industry – the provision of mercantile services – the buying of raw materials and selling of the finished product. He also fulfilled a managerial task – this was to be less frequent – that of superintending the weaving processes. The calico-printing concerns were unprecedented and initially, in view of the lack of individuals trained in both the production and commercial spheres, a team solution was resorted to for managerial tasks. The resolution of the technical aspects of calico-printing, it can be seen, was being sought by allying skills available already in Barcelona – Esteve's professional training as an 'esparter', esparto being a vegetable fibre with similar qualities to cotton – with skills imported from abroad. By requiring Huvet to train Esteve the company was assuring that at the end of three years one of its members would possess skills in the printing processes and that the dependence on imported skills would thus be eliminated. The terms which had to be offered to foreign skilled workers to perform such a task were, the contract reveals, extremely generous.

In fact the three-year period for which the company was intended to operate was not completed. In February 1737 the concern was functioning. We know this from a request made by Esteve to the Real Audiencia to be allowed to arm guards to prevent overnight theft of his calicoes pegged out in his bleaching meadow outside the city's walls.[54] At some stage of the year, too, Esteve submitted a request to the Junta General de Comercio to be allowed to import calicoes 'in the white' for printing in this manufacture[55] – he was clearly experiencing difficulties either with respect to the quantity or quality of his own cotton manufacturing. On 21 July 1737, however, a notarial contract recorded the company's dissolution and on 10 September Esteve settled outstanding debts with his two backers following the auditing of the company's accounts by the Curia del Corregidor. Huvet had died intestate at some stage between 21 July and September and Esteve was appointed guardian to his orphan son.[56]

---

[54] Carrera Pujal, *Historia política*, IV, p. 135.   [55] AGS, CSH, reg. 248, fo. 176.
[56] AHPB, Severo Pujol, acts of 21 July, 10 Sept., 26 oct. 1737, fos. 284, 360, 406.

The Esteve enterprise was soon replaced by another. In the same month as its dissolution one Antoni Serra, who entitled himself a *negociante*, requested permission from Intendant Sartine to make use of water resources in the neighbouring village of Sant Martí de Provençals for bleaching. In the request he informed the Intendant that he had 'permission from a legitimate superior to found the new manufacture of *indianas*, tapestries, handkerchiefs and other things' and that all that had been lacking to complete his establishment was a 'place in which with all capacity the cotton cloth can be bleached'.[57] As Serra's manufacture was also to be located close to the city's Portal Nou, it is not clear whether it was to his concern or to the recently terminated Esteve manufacture that Canaveras referred in his letter of August 1737.

As had been the case with the Esteve manufacture, Serra hoped to obtain a royal privilege for his concern. In September 1737 he appointed a 'commercial agent' in Madrid to represent him before royal counsels in connection with any request which he should make for 'favour and rewards concerning the new manufacture of *indianas*... undertaken and started in this... city of Barcelona'.[58] Like Esteve, Serra was not to work alone. No contract recording terms of a company has been found, but in an act recorded after his death his widow recorded that her former husband 'had a company established with... Esteve Canals and Bonaventura Canet'.[59] What is not clear is first whether this company was established from the moment of launching the manufacture and secondly whether both Canals and Canet associated with Serra at the same time. The reasons for doubts about these two questions are respectively that a later notarial agreement between the Canals and Canet families records that their association started in 1738 and the fact that the first notarial act located containing significant information about this manufacture mentions only Serra and Canals. In addition, the bleaching meadow which Serra established remained in his full possession, and not in that of a company. This would suggest too that he was initially independent of any company.[60]

---

[57] ACA, Batllia General, Aa 51, 24 July 1737, fos. 285–93.
[58] AHPB, Josep Bosom, act of 12 Sept. 1737, fos. 43–4.
[59] AHPB, Josep Cols, act of 5 May 1741, fos. 92–3.
[60] References respectively: AHPB, Duran Quatrecases, act of 1 Sept. 1759, fo. 147; Josep Bosom, 1st book of wills and inventories, fos 78–80; Josep Cols, act of 16 May 1738, fos. 122–3. In his will Serra expresses his wish that as long as the association with Canals and

The issue is not an important one though, for there is no doubt that the expansion of the manufacture into a substantial concern was with the backing of Canals and Canet. Canals's role, as well as the nature of the manufacture in the early stage of its development, are revealed by the notarial contract just referred to. This consists in an agreement of 16 May 1738 between Serra and Canals and a French printer, Joan Iber, who committed himself to painting 500 pieces of *indianas*, at a fixed rate of 3 *libras* 5 *sols* per unit, 'of all the designs which the said Serra and Canals choose ... at his costs and with his instruments for the space of one year'. Serra and Canals were to provide the cloth for printing 'as it comes out from the house of the weavers' and finished pieces were to be delivered to Canals's house. The manufacture at this stage, it is clear, was not concentrated. It included a building in which weaving was taking place and a bleaching meadow but the actual printing processes, or some of them at least, were being sub-contracted to an independent printer who was using his own tools. Canals was a wealthy cloth-draper, and the delivering of the finished product to his house is a sign that it was he who was encharged with the commercializing of the cloth as well as being already most probably the predominating party in the association. This was certainly to be the case later: the act by which the association between the Canals and Canet family was finally ended on 1 September 1759 recorded that since the establishment of the company its 'administration' had been the responsibility of the Canals family, the *caixa* (cash box) being kept in their house.[61] Bonaventura Canet's utility to the manufacture came from his profession and family links. He was a *corredor de cambios* (commercial broker), and son-in-law of Juame Ferrusola, who represented the interests of Maltese merchants in the city, and he was thus well placed both to handle any financial transactions in which the manufacture might be involved and to secure the crucial supplies of Maltese spun cotton.[62] Finally, Serra: despite his title of *negociante*, his roots were

Canet lasts 'they should not expel my said associates from the bleaching meadow and hut which I have in the place called the Granota as it is my wish that they should continue to use the said things in the way in which since the company was founded it has done'. Not only does the statement show continued ownership of the bleaching meadow but it implies that the association with Canals and Canet dates from after its establishment.

[61] AHPB, Duran Quatrecases, act of 1 Sept. 1759, fo. 147. On Canals and his social progression and economic background, see R. Alier, 'Juan Pablo Canals. Un "ilustrado" catalán del siglo XVIII' (Tesis de licenciatura, Barcelona 1971), and 'La fàbrica de Canals', pp. 59–71.   [62] Molas Ribalta, *Los gremios*, p. 520.

artisanal – he was the son of a stocking-knitter – and he was to play the role of production manager, *fabricant*, in the manufacture, actually living there until his death. Until then, in accordance with the practice of the Esteve manufacture, it was as Antoni Serra & Cia that the company was known.[63]

Up to this point, as has been seen, the undertaking of cotton-weaving and calico-printing in the city had involved a relatively large investment and technological innovation but it had not occasioned any striking changes with respect to organization of production. The Esteve concern had probably been composed of two or three different units – weaving was done on a putting-out basis, it has been seen, printing would have been carried out either in Esteve's house or in the huts which had been rented outside the city walls, bleaching definitely did take place on the land adjoining these huts. That of Canals had bleaching and some processing facilities in Sant Martí de Provençals (a wooden hut had been built on the bleaching meadow), its weaving activities grouped in a 'house of the weavers' and it was sub-contracting at least some, and maybe all, its printing. During 1739, however, not only did the Serra manufacture move towards a form of concentrated production but Bernat Glòria also renewed his efforts in the industry to create another manufacture which was on a quite different scale from that which was normal within the city.

The first sign of the intentions of the Serra manufacture to expand its scale of activities was a request made to the Intendant to be allowed to build a substantial building – approximately 10 by 8 metres and 6 metres high – on its bleaching meadow to contain a fulling mill.[64] The main change, though, was to be the uniting of the weaving and printing activities within one large building and the preliminary to this was the purchase by Serra, on his associates' behalf – the scale of the expansion was clearly beyond his means – of a house, shop and adjoining garden in between the streets of Portal Nou and Cortines, in the heart of the city's artisanal zone. Extensive repairs and changes were then undertaken to these buildings. The costs of these are recorded in table 3.6. The description of the improvements carried out reveals the intention of the building:

---

[63] Serra's family background is revealed in his will – see n. 60 above.
[64] ACA, Batllia General, Aa 52, 17 Dec. 1738, fos. 452–64.

Table 3.6. *Creation of a concentrated manufacture by Canals, Canet and Serra during 1739 (in libras)*

1. Cost of house in Carrer del Portal Nou	1,373– 0– 0
2. Carpenter Henrich's costs at manufacture	204–19– 0
3. Builder's costs for manufacture	400– 1–10
4. Carpenter's costs at bleaching meadow	144– 9–10
5. Builder's costs at bleaching meadow	611–13–11
Total	2,734– 4– 7

mentioned are 'a room (*oficina*) for setting up looms to make *indianas*, another room for printing them, a kitchen to make colours'.[65]

Glòria's renewed involvement in the industry, like Serra's efforts, is first revealed by a request of 26 November 1738 to make use of water for bleaching purposes in Sant Martí de Provençals. The request provides more information on the reasons for the early difficulties in establishing the industry and the manner in which these were resolved. Glòria explained that his early attempts at manufacturing had made him realize that to achieve success it was necessary to have the assistance of an 'individual with perfect knowledge and experience in the practice of achieving colours and the perpetuity and permanence of these' and for this reason he had recruited someone from Hamburg, 'the place in which colours are printed with the greatest perfection and delicacy which exceed those of Holland'. The German printer on arrival in Barcelona had informed him that the water being used by other 'fabricants', outside the Portal Nou, was too dirty for his purpose, in view of its use for agricultural irrigation. He complained that dependence on it would have the result that 'all his application and skill would be fruitless causing the colours to be lost'. It was on his advice, it is clear, that Glòria had decided to set up a new bleaching meadow in Sant Martí de Provençals.[66]

Glòria too had associated with others for the costly business of contracting a foreign worker and establishing a manufacture. The terms of association were recorded on 6 July 1739.[67] The initial investment made had been 8,000 *libras*, though it was stated in the contract that this sum was likely to be exceeded. The capital had

---

[65] AHPB, Josep Cols, Manual for 1739, act of 2 March, fo. 57; and for 1740, acts of 7 Aug. 1740, fos. 102–9.
[66] ACA, Batllia General, Aa 52, fos. 441–52, act of 27 Nov. 1738.
[67] AHPB, Duran Quatrecases, act of 13 Aug. 1743, fos. 323–7.

been divided into sixteenths and subscribed as follows: Glòria 4, Pere Gecseli 3½, Joan Pau Gispert 3, Josep Sala 3½, Geronim Aranyó 1 and Sebastià Vidal 1. Two of the associates, Sala and Aranyó, are already known to us – their presence, as well as some details of the terms, suggest that the new manufacture incorporated elements from the failed Esteve enterprise as well as probably inheriting equipment from the earlier experimentation by Glòria. Gecseli, Gispert and Vidal came from similar backgrounds to Glòria – all three were leading wholesale merchants.[68]

The scale of the enterprise was larger than that of either the Esteve concern or of the Serra manufacture in its original form. The managerial structure was consequently more complex with all but one of the associates playing an active part. The sleeping partner was Sebastià Vidal whose age may have precluded a more active role: his place in the company was soon to be taken by a relation, Joan Vidal. Glòria was to act as the company's administrator, with responsibility for the purchase of raw materials and for the direction of the manufacture; Gecseli's wholesaling company, Pere Gecseli and Cia, was to have responsibility for sales; Sala and Aranyó were jointly to organize weaving; Gispert was encharged with the payment of workers involved in the bleaching processes.

The Hamburg printer's name was Joan Federich Hartung and his terms of employment were as follows: he was to be employed for three years, starting on 1 January 1739, for a huge annual salary of 1,200 *pesos* or approximately 1,680 *libras* (could it have been a payment for the entire period rather than an annual one?) and in return for this he was obliged, in addition to working in the concern, to teach one or two individuals presented to him by the company 'all the secrets and expertise connected with the profession of printing and bleaching *indianas*, composition of colours and other dependent operations in order that at the end of three years those individuals should be capable of directing the work in the due form as master printers of *indianas*'. One of the individuals selected for instruction was Bernat Glòria's brother, Geroni, and the other Josep Sala. For his own, and the company's benefit the former was obliged to note in a book

[68] On Vidal, see Vilar, *La Catalogne*, III, pp. 386, 403; for list of thirty-seven leading tax-payers for commercial activities in the city, which includes Glòria, Vidal, Gecseli and Joan Gispert, father of Joan Pau, see Fernández, 'La burguesía barcelonesa', p. 111; for further information on Gecseli and Gispert, see P. Molas Ribalta, 'La Junta de Comerç de Barcelona. Els seus precedents i la seva base social', in his *Comerç i estructura social a Catalunya i València als segles XVII i XVIII* (Barcelona, 1977), pp. 254, 281.

provided by the company 'all the manner of manipulating the manufacture, the secrets of the composition of colours, the quality and quantity of materials and other things which will be shown to him and which the said printer will have to teach him' and was to work to the Hamburger's orders, 'together with him both in the bleaching and printing as well as in the composition of colours in order that by means of working with the printer ... the two qualities of the practical and the speculative, which are necessary in order that at the end of three years he should be a perfect printer, should be passed on to him'. As with the Esteve concern, the aim was to ensure the training of Catalan workers in the imported skills. An additional characteristic of the new industry revealed in this case is the desire to control the diffusion of the skills whose obtaining had involved such effort and expense. The book in which Geroni Glòria was to record the formulas for mixing the colours was to remain 'always in power of the said company ... so that it should be kept with all secrecy and reserve' and both Glòria and Sala were forbidden either to pass on their knowledge to any other than those named by the company or to use it for their own purposes while the company continued in existence with the penalty of having to pay what it had cost to import the skills should they break this ruling.

During 1739 requests for royal privileges for both these large manufactures were submitted to the Junta General de Comercio. This body considered these on the same day and recommended the acceptance of both but this recommendation was followed by the king only in the case of Serra's concern; Glòria's application was turned down.[69] The injustice would seem to be all the greater insofar as Serra's privilege embraced as many calico-printing manufactures as he wanted to establish in Catalonia – 'No one is to obstruct them in the establishment of this manufacture or in that of others which they placed in the spots which they found convenient in this principality', the first article of the privilege read.[70]

The grounds for the discrimination between the two requests are not known. The historian of the Glòria family has noted that the opposite decision might have been expected, for Canals and Canet were neither as well known to the administration nor as socially distinguished as Glòria (who was a minister in a Junta de Comercio

[69] AGS, CSH, reg. 213, fos. 55, 59. The day was 12 Dec. 1739.
[70] Copies of privilege in AHPB, Josep Cols, Registro de la fábrica de indianas, fos. 1–5.

Marítimo y Terrestre established in Barcelona in 1735).[71] A perusal
of some of the decisions of the Junta during these years provides,
however, some clues as to possible influencing factors. Other requests
for privileges for far less promising manufacturing proposals were
accepted during 1740 and 1741 and noted against the decisions was
a preference for the establishment of manufactures in inland areas –
'I will concede these privileges if these manufactures are established
in the interior of the kingdom, while I do not consider it to be for my
service setting them up on the coasts', it was recorded in one case, 'I
agree provided that the manufacture is established in the interior of
the kingdom', it was recorded in the case of another. It is clear that
a certain reticence existed concerning encouraging industrial developments in areas such as Barcelona, on Spain's periphery, and it may
have been this that had caused the king to limit concessions to a single
privilege. The decision that this individual should have been Serra
rather than Glòria may have been explained by the earlier
establishment of the former's manufacture, or by the fact that it
received a more favourable report from the local sub-delegate of the
Junta General de Comercio encharged with its inspection – the terms
of Glòria's company give the impression of his manufacture having
been put together with some haste and the extent of its progress
by the time of its inspection may not have been very great – or it
may have been the case that Glòria's being better known to the
administration proved a disadvantage rather than being favourable
to his application. A request from another Minister in the Junta
Particular for a privilege for cloth-making was also turned down
during these years and a request of the body as a whole for fiscal
exemptions for its Ministers received exactly the same response as
Glòria's for his manufacturing privilege: its acceptance was recommended by the Junta General but this recommendation was not then
acted upon by the Crown. A third party or body would seem to have
been enjoying the ear of the king.[72]

The royal edict granting Serra's privilege was not published until
1741. Its preamble incorporated the description made by the Junta
General's sub-delegate, Francisco de Montero, of what was to be
Catalonia's first royal cotton manufacture. The description would, it

[71] Fernández, 'La burguesía barcelonesa', p. 63.
[72] For these various decisions, see AGS, CSH, reg. 213, fos. 54–5, 58. On the apparently hostile
climate to the Junta, see Molas Ribalta, 'La Junta de Commerç de Barcelona', pp. 250–4.

seems likely, have been made in 1739, in time for the December meeting at which the Junta discussed the application.

The manufacture consists in two warping machines, which serve to warp the cottons, with the corresponding workers, twelve looms functioning to weave the cotton cloth, in the use of which twenty-five people are employed, both men and women, seven hundred moulds, or designs of all sorts of models for printing cloth, with six tables for this process, a calender, a press, a cloth-burnisher, four vats, and other instruments necessary for the manufacture, in which processes six people are employed. It has a piece of land, or meadow, outside the city walls, surrounded by crystalline water, in which there exists a big vat below its cover, which together serve to bleach, and boil cloth, both before, and after being printed, and to make the colours stand out on the cloth, in which operations five men are employed. In the manufacture there is to be found Pedro Genus of Swiss nationality, an individual skilled in painting any colours on the cloth, and engraving all sorts of designs and drawings for printing, and giving the greatest perfection to the colours which he uses for painting, with a secret, which he has shown already to the associates in the manufacture to ensure in it, in all circumstances, so special a circumstance for the quality and greater perfection of its products.[73]

Like the Esteve and Glòria concerns, that of Serra, it is clear, had obtained its foreign technician and ensured the passing on of his secrets.

CHARACTERISTICS OF THE NEW INDUSTRY

By the time the privilege applications of Serra and Glòria were considered by the Junta General de Comercio in 1739, the first stage in the process of import-substitution intended by the 1728 prohibition had been completed. Colouring techniques had been mastered and an adequate alternative to the foreign product was now available: 'as far as colours are concerned we equal them', Glòria wrote to Juan Bautista Iturralde, Minister of Hacienda, on 22 August 1739, 'and as for prices we will make them as cheaply as they'.[74] The second claim is confirmed by the Serra privilege in which his manufacture's prices were set at a lower level than that previously charged for the imported product.

The type of printing techniques which had been introduced was the more common mordant- and madder-dyeing process. This is clear both from some of the technical descriptions which have been quoted above (for instance, in the description of Serra's manufacture

---

[73] See n. 70.   [74] AGS, SH, leg. 1103, letter of 22 Aug. 1739.

the boiling of the *indianas* after printing 'to make the colours stand out', a clear reference to the process whereby the calicoes to which mordants had previously been applied were boiled in madder to bring out the colours is mentioned), as well as from a later claim made by a printer in 1746 to be the introducer of indigo-dyeing (the principal alternative process).[75] Though an adequate alternative, it is unlikely, however, that the domestic product was quite the equal yet of the previously imported calicoes. This is suggested by further information contained in Glòria's letter: 'experience has shown that very fine cottons are necessary to manufacture cloth of the greatest perfection and fineness equal to the foreign ones which are imported', he wrote, 'and these will not be rid of unless we achieve the manufacture of the said cloth with equal perfection.' Probable difficulties in this area have already been signalled in connection with Esteve's 1737 request to be allowed to import cotton cloth in the white for printing, and Glòria's letter contained a similar request to import fine cotton cloth from Genoa. The quality of the calico on which printing was done was not only important for the obvious reason that on this depended the fineness of the final product – finishing processes could improve but not transform – but also because the quality of the colours obtained from the printing processes depended on it. This was pointed out by Jean Rhyiner in his early treatise on calico-printing – the more the cloth is fine and closely woven', he wrote, 'the more striking the colours'.[76] Glòria, it is clear, had discovered the same for he mentioned that the permission which he was requesting to import fine cotton cloth would ensure that his German printer would be able to 'make use of the ability to give the delicacy and vividness which the colours need in the fine designs'.

The account of the industry's early development given in the last section has shown the character of the process whereby it had reached this state. A few of the salient features of the process will be emphasized here.

[75] ACA, Intendencia, Registros de la Superintendencia, 1/26, fo. 151, 16 Dec. 1747, Campins privilege boasts the achievement of 'up to now not discovered permanence [of colour] of what are known as blauets'.

[76] Rhyiner, 'Traité sur la fabrication', p. 51: Rhyiner continues: 'the reason for that is that the more the threads are compressed and the less space that there is from one to the other, the more the colour with which these threads are dyed should show up... It even happens, if one does fine work on thin cloth, that a part of the engraving and above all the points (*picots*) get lost in the empty spaces of the cloth and interrupt the design, which loses this way a part of its beauty.'

An initial and controversial issue is the role of the state.[77] Although there had been no direct involvement, there is direct or indirect evidence in all the cases which have been discussed of an awareness of the propitiousness of the political climate for the establishment of cotton manufactures and of hopes of obtaining royal privileges. The existence of the 1728 protective legislation and the royal interest expressed in the industry had been, it is clear, essential enabling conditions for the establishment of the industry ensuring as they did respectively the economic (an assured market) and legal (some sort of assurance that departures from guild restrictions would be tolerated) prerequisites for production.

The technical problems involved in introducing the new industry were resolved, it has emerged, by stages. Initially, they were underestimated and it would seem that attempts were made to print calicoes without adequate know-how. A first stage in their resolution had consisted in the introduction of foreign workers with prior training in printing skills, who both carried out printing and instructed Catalan workers in the techniques. The arrival of such workers gave rise, it has been seen from Glòria's experience, to a critical assessment of other aspects of the industry and in particular the inadequacy of its bleaching techniques was exposed. Consequently, from 1737 onwards, the initial facilities used for these – land and irrigation facilities previously used for intensive horticulture, it was noted – were replaced by purpose-built bleaching fields, some distance from the city, on unused land (Glòria's, for example, were set up on 'an abandoned and sandy piece of land which had never been cultivated and which could not be adapted for cultivation')[78] which possessed unexploited, and thus purer ('crystalline water', it was noted in the Serra privilege) water resources. The as yet unresolved problem of ensuring a steady supply of good-quality calicoes on which to print was being confronted in the case of the Serra concern by the association with Bonaventura Canet, which must have assured access to the best Maltese cotton supplies, and in that of Glòria by the dispatch of the director of a woollen cloth manufacture which he had founded a few years previously to Malta

---

[77] On this, see Carrera Pujal, Historia política, IV, p. 142, who states that the extent of protection offered to the Catalan industry was 'derisory', and Vilar, who refers to the historiographical tradition of protectionist writers who exaggerate the importance of protection but who doubts himself the probability of links between 'some general measures of 1717–18' and 'the particular development of the Catalan indianas after 1740' (La Catalogne, I, pp. 706–7).

[78] ACA, Batllia General, Aa 52, 26 Nov. 1738, fos. 441–52.

in order to 'choose the cotton and establish the quality and fineness which they have to have'.[79] The Catalan industry was not, of course, alone in experiencing these difficulties, which were not to be fully resolved until the mechanization of spinning.[80] Its failure, however, to incorporate cotton-spinning until a late stage had the consequence that less effort was put into their solution than elsewhere. Throughout the century it was to concentrate predominantly on the production of lower quality cloth. In this respect the industry did not succeed in equalling the imported product which, as was noted in the second section, had consisted predominantly of fine printed calicoes.

The two significant manufactures which had been established in the industry showed already characteristics which were to be particularly marked in the Catalan industry. Scale of production was becoming large: Serra's manufacture had a labour force of thirty-seven in 1739 without including those preparing warps for weaving, and Glòria's manufacture was planning to use twenty-four looms in the same year and this, if the ratio between looms and weavers was the same as in the Serra manufacture, would have meant a labour force of fifty in the weaving department alone.[81] A movement towards a concentration of production, 'vertical integration', within manufactures is also identifiable. These trends are principally to be explained by economic and technical considerations. Calico-printing was liable to considerable economies of scale and it was an industry which throughout Europe employed large labour forces. It was also an industry in which control over quality was essential for the achievement of good results – concentrated production was thus normal.[82] This second concern in the Catalan case was revealed by the grounds given for the concentrating of looms in one or two places in the Glòria concern: that 'the said Josep Sala and Geronim Aranyó should be able to see them clearly'.[83]

It should be noted, though, that contact with the state was also an important influence. It was the fact that the 1728 import ban restricted the import of both printed and unprinted calicoes which, in view of the lack of a domestic cotton industry, enforced, in contrast to calico-printing elsewhere in Europe, the incorporation of the weaving processes into the Catalan manufactures. It also seems likely that the

[79] As n. 74.
[80] On this, an excellent source is Dermigny, *Cargaisons Indiennes*, II, pp. 214–16.
[81] AHPB, Duran Quatrecases, 13 Aug. 1744, fo. 324.
[82] On some of the factors determining size in calico-printing manufactures, see Chapman, 'The Textile Factory before Arkwright', pp. 451–73.   [83] As n. 81.

possibility of obtaining privileges from the Crown encouraged both scale of production and vertical integration. Is it possible that it is more than a coincidence that the early movement towards vertical integration in the two principal concerns in the industry coincided with their applications for privileges? Certainly the introductory preambles to privileges give the impression that the grounds for requests for them being acceded to included both the size of the investment in, and the actual physical characteristics of, the manufactures for which they had been solicited. Thus in the case of the Serra privilege both the 'big expenses' incurred in the manufacture's establishment and the fact that 'these associates have the manufacture stocked with all that is necessary' are mentioned as justifications for the award. Once privileges had been granted their terms contributed to ensuring that scale of production was maintained or increased – the keeping of its present twelve looms in action and the increasing of this number by 'those that they could in future' was one of the conditions imposed on Serra and his associates.[84]

The existence of a virtually complete guild system in Barcelona was another influence on size and vertical integration. There was no free labour market, nor did existing corporative rules permit general working with cotton. These rigidities would have made the organization of the industry on a putting-out basis virtually impossible and encouraged centralization.

There were clearly strong parallels between the industrial revival of these years and that of the 1680s and 1690s which was discussed in the previous chapter. There were no figures of the status of Feliu involved and no contributions made to mercantilist literature, but there was the similar establishment of a local branch of the Junta General – though coordination between this and the Junta General was not yet perfect – the same involvement of commercial capital in the efforts which were similarly broad (progress was made too in the 1730s and 1740s in the silk, woollen cloth and stocking-knitting industries) and there was the same concern to ensure that imported techniques were passed to Catalan hands.

[84] AHPB, Josep Cols, *Registro de la fábrica de indianas.* On this question of size of manufactures, see also my paper cited in n. 42.

THREE ENTREPRENEURS: JOSEP SALA, BERNAT GLÒRIA AND ESTEVE CANALS

The new industry, as has been seen, was financed and organized by the traditional system of founding companies. Such a system was designed to minimize risk by sharing capital costs. This, and the collective solution to managerial tasks which these companies' charters provided, might cause it to be thought that the consideration of the role of specific individuals in the introduction of the industry would be out of place. In a new industry such as calico-printing, however, as has been seen, the risk element, despite the formation of companies, remained high. In addition, the companies, though collective, had easily identifiable leading members. More than at later stages, when the industry had become established and routinized, an 'entrepreneurial' element was involved at this stage in the industry's development.

Subject to the discovery of further documentation, three key contributors to the introduction of calico-printing to the city are identifiable: Josep Sala, the administrator and a principal financier of the first documented company, and a key participant in the third; Bernat Glòria, probably the first to experiment with calico-printing and clearly the main force behind the establishment of the manufacture which ran in his name from late 1738 or early 1739; and Esteve Canals, who was the dominant influence in the Serra manufacture (which after Serra's death ran in his name and in that of Canet) if not from its moment of launching at least from very soon after it. An additional argument for their having been a significant 'entrepreneurial' element in the establishment of the industry is provided by the fact that these three individuals came from quite distinct social and economic backgrounds.

As noted, Josep Sala was by profession and guild affiliation a glass-maker. His exact professional title was *vidrier de llum*. Members of this profession made decorative, multi-coloured glass for a range of domestic purposes and their guild was one of the most prestigious in the city, rivalling in status that of the silver-smiths.[85] By his original profession, which he does not seem at any stage to have completely abandoned – in 1754, for example, a notarial act records a sale which his son had made on his behalf at the fair of San Fermin, Pamplona,

---

[85] Duran Sanpere, *Barcelona*, II, pp. 401–9.

of seventy-one 'blocks of glass garnet of all colours'[86] – he would have received some experiences relevant to a later involvement in calico-printing: probably some knowledge of dyeing techniques as well as experience in catering for household demand. He was clearly one of the wealthiest members of his guild and his involvement in calico-printing was not the only occasion on which he invested in trades outside his own. Other ventures of which there are records include sheep-rearing, trading in skins, ship-building, trading to Cádiz and, in the 1760s, in old age, prospecting for copper in various parts of Catalonia.[87]

This investment in trades outside his own was not unusual. Molas Ribalta and others have demonstrated how widespread a practice it was for richer guildsmen, with large resources, to do this.[88] From the point of view of both extent of resources and investments there was really very little difference in economic terms between the rich guild-member and the unattached wholesale merchant in eighteenth-century Barcelona. The mere fact of outside investment, therefore, does not mark Sala out, but the eclecticism of his spheres of activity probably does – he would seem to have had an eye for new types of investment and to have been unusually flexible and innovative in his investment strategies. A further sign of this flexibility, and pre-paredness to undertake new activities, was his involvement both in the weaving and printing sections of the new industry. It was he, it will be recalled, who was to be the second of the two individuals who were to benefit from Hartung's instruction in Glòria's manufacture. He was the only one of the three individuals discussed here who actually acquired skills in, and later carried out, the physical processes of calico-printing. That his eclecticism and readiness to undertake things new was conceivably carried to excess is suggested by the fact that he was involved in no less than four different calico-printing manufactures in the 1730s and 1740s, the involvements in each case except the last, when he was producing on his own, ending in legal wranglings.

Bernat Glòria, as was noted above, has been the subject of an extensive study.[89] In this, Roberto Fernández has identified the

[86] AHPB, Duran Quatrecases, act of 13 July 1754, fos. 122–3.
[87] AHPB, Severo Pujol, 12 Jan. 1745, fo. 33, 19 Jan. 1745, fos. 49–50; C. Martínez Shaw, *Cataluña en la carrera de las Indias* (Barcelona, 1981), p. 131; ACA, Intendencia, Registros de la Superintendencia, 1/47, fo. 97, 1769.
[88] Molas Ribalta, *Los gremios*, pp. 198–216.
[89] And except where noted, this paragraph depends on this (Fernández, 'La burguesía barcelonesa', pp. 3–131).

principal stages in his career and pointed out their relevance to his manufacturing role. His origins were within the city's industrial guilds. He was the son of a velvet-maker and although he himself was to become a merchant his connections with the industrial guilds were to be of assistance in his later involvement in manufacturing activities. It was his brother Geroni, a silk-weaver, who was to be Hartung's principal apprentice, it was noted, and who was later to act as *fabricant* for his manufacture and it was he himself who initially took responsibility for contracting the labour force for his concern. His commercial career was most successful and during the 1730s and 1740s he emerged as one of the leading wholesale merchants of his generation. He was the eleventh highest payer of commercial taxation in the city during the years 1724–52, his commercial network extended from the Mediterranean to the Atlantic, and he was one of the first to take advantage of new opportunities in maritime insurance and in the American trade in the 1740s. His commercial training, the extent of his financial resources, his close links with other rich wholesalers and the extensive commercial network which he had built up were clearly other contributing factors in his successful involvement in the industry.

A third significant strand in his career was his links with government. In 1735, as already noted, he was made Minister in the new Junta del Comercio Marítimo y Terrestre, in the 1740s he was extensively involved in catering for state cloth contracts[90] and in the 1750s he and his brother-in-law, Ramon Picó, were commissioned by the leading merchants of the city to act as their joint representatives in Madrid in the negotiation of terms for the establishment of the Real Compañía de Comercio de Barcelona a Indias. The connections between these types of government links and his manufacturing activities were pointed out by Glòria himself in his letter to the Minister of Hacienda of 1739: since obtaining his office in the Junta Particular de Comercio, which had been established in Barcelona in 1735, he noted, 'as so much suits the exercise of my employment, to give an example to the others, my efforts to amplify my ideas, which have always been related to the increase and establishment of manufactures in our Spain, and which the other nations succeed with so well in their countries, have grown'.[91] In fact, though, as has been noted, his interest in manufacturing had preceded his official

---

[90] M. Arranz, 'Demanda estatal i activitat econòmica a Catalunya sota els primers borbons (1714–1808)', *Primer Congrès d'Història Moderna de Catalunya* (Barcelona, 1984), II, pp. 261–3.

[91] AGS, SH, leg. 1103, letter of Glòria to Iturralde, 22 Aug. 1739.

appointment – his involvement in calico-printing dated from 1728 and that in fine cloth production from 1732. The likely causal chain was as follows: his interest in, and links with, manufacturing were probably the principal grounds for his selection as the representative of wholesalers' interest in the Junta (a principal purpose in the foundation of which was the propagation of manufacturing in the Principality) and his holding of this post, as his letter implies, contributed both to the forming of a moral commitment to industrial development as well as to developing a knowledge of the character of state priorities in this area, of how the royal administration functioned and of how assistance could be obtained for his own manufacturing interests. Neither his commitment nor these skills seem to have helped him, it has been noted, in connection with his 1739 application for a privilege but that they did in the longer term is apparent from the fact that Glòria eventually became involved in a wider range of manufacturing activities and obtained more privileges than any other Catalan manufacturer. The details are as below:[92]

1746 for calico printing
1749 for fine woollen cloth manufacture
1752 for importing cotton from America in recognition of promotion of this trade.

Glòria stands out as the individual who played the pioneering role in broadening the range of investments of Barcelona's wholesale merchants to include direct industrial investment. In the pursuance of this interest, and in consequence of his official appointment, and maybe too his cloth contracting with the state, he became the member of this social group with most experience in negotiating with the Crown and one of the architects of the institutions which were to formalize the relationship between the emerging Catalan bourgeoisie, of which he was part, and the Crown.

The Canals family also has its historian, Roger Alier, and it is on his research that this summary will largely depend.[93] Esteve Canals was a first generation immigrant to Barcelona with rural origins – he came from the village of Sant Vicenç de Riells and his father, Jaume, was a peasant – the move to Barcelona taking place at the turn of the

[92] ACA, RA, Diversorum, regs. 491, fos. 1–7, 20 Oct. 1747 (calicoes), 493, fos. 57–74, 22 Dec. 1749 (wool), 499, fos. 129–38, 24 Jan. 1756 (cotton imports).
[93] Alier, 'Juan Pablo Canals', *passim*, pp. 59–91. Again, unless stated, the paragraphs on Canals are drawn from these sources.

century. It was the draping profession which he entered: a document for the year 1705 reveals him acting as an administrator for a draper's shop owned by the commercial company Casanovas-Darrer and shortly afterwards he associated himself with a draper's widow, Mariangela Regàs, to run her former husband's (killed during the siege of Barcelona in 1705) draping shop in the Carrer de Cambis. The relationship soon became a family as well as a commercial one for shortly after it had begun Canals married his associate's daughter, Mariangela Martí. This was as important an event as any in his career, for not only did his wife bring with her a dowry of half of her mother's investment in the draping shop but she also had good inheritance prospects in view of her mother's widowhood and the fact that the only male heir, Geroni, had entered the priesthood. In 1730 this son was left the family property in Mariangela Regàs's will but he in turn named Canals's wife as his heiress. Although there was to be a long delay before they inherited, in practice the fact that Canals and his wife were in line for the succession had the consequence that they enjoyed most of the advantages of ownership from soon after their marriage. They lived in the substantial family properties in the Carrers de Cambis and Agullers – 'three opening doorways... two big, and one small' – and it was Canals, the son-in-law, who came to administer the Martí family affairs: he refers in his will to money which 'I paid and spent ruling and governing the Martí house and family'. By his marriage, thus, Canals effectively stepped into the shoes of the deceased Joan Pau Martí, and acquired a solid base for himself thereby in Barcelona in terms of possession of an established draping outlet, property and family backing. From this base he did not move: his cloth-draping as well as his later calico-printing were run from the Carrer de Cambis.

The appearances are that Canals concentrated all his energies on cloth-draping. The only additional investments of which there are records are some small scale lending of money for interest, the purchase of an office of commercial broker in 1737, which he then rented out for 40 *libras* a year, and some buying of property in the vicinity of the Carrer de Cambis – the inventory undertaken on his death reveals that the 'three opening doorways' had become five by the acquisition of two houses in the neighbouring Carrer de la Caputxeria.[94] His commercial strategy would seem to have been to

---

[94] AHPB, Josep Cols, act of 5 Feb. 1739, fo. 29 (purchase and rent of office of commercial broker).

achieve a gradual but certain accumulation of capital by specializing in the activity in which he had expertise. That this policy bore fruit is apparent from the steady increase which he achieved in the scale of his trade: a slow growth in the turnover of his own shop was followed by investment in other draping outlets. The progress was not checked by his involvement in calico-printing: in 1739, the very year in which the manufacture was undergoing a costly expansion, he associated himself with the brother of Bonaventura Canet, Pere, to open another draping outlet and during the 1740s he was still at the forefront of those city drapers who despite the difficult political situation were importing English and Dutch cloth.[95] His will reveals that at his death he was involved in three different draping shops – that contained in his own house, which he had continued to run, a second one in which he had placed an administrator and that of Pere Canet.

Of the three individuals whom we have been discussing it is clear that it was Canals whose professional interests were closest to calico-printing. He had not himself sold calicoes as he was a *botiguer de tall* (cloth-draper) and it was the *botiguers de teles* (linen- and silk-drapers) who, as we have noted above, enjoyed at this stage the monopoly in the commercializing of cotton goods. He could not, though, have failed to have had knowledge of the trade and an awareness of the excellent prospects for investing in it – he was surrounded by shops stocking the new product, no less than seven of the twenty-six stockists in the city in 1732 being in the Carrer de Cambis.

The character of his commercial career provides some sharp contrasts with those of Sala and Glòria. His relentless concentration on a single type of investment and the narrowness of the circles in which he associated himself professionally is clearly quite distinct from the eclecticism apparent in both the latters' careers from these points of view. Essentially he had just two partners: the Martí family and the Canets, and it is clear that the partnerships were entered into in connection with the two crucial stages in his business career – the first setting him up as a cloth-draper and the second enabling him to progress beyond this profession to make his one, big investment outside his draping activities. The second partnership as well as the first became a familial one for in 1742 Canals's daughter, Gertrudis, married Pere Canet.[96]

[95] AHPB, Miquel Cabrer, 2 March 1739, fos. 132–4 (renting draper's shop); Vilar, *La Catalogne*, III, p. 431 (cloth importing), but note that Vilar (III, pp. 386–7) confuses a Pere Pau Canals with Esteve.   [96] AHPB, Josep Cols, act of 30 Jan. 1742, fo. 32.

Canals's approach, insofar as it can be explained, was that of the newly arrived immigrant to a large city. His lack of resources and background enforced a prudence which came to mark his approach to business activities. If there are special entrepreneurial attributes to be noted which account for his success then they are on the one hand this prudence and simple artisanal qualities of hard work and economy of life style, and on the other his evident ability to collaborate with others. This is revealed both by his successful and harmonious participation in the affairs of the Martí family and by the long collaboration with the Canets. The cordiality of the relationship with Geroni Martí (though it would have been he who in other circumstances would have managed the family affairs) is revealed by his lending of money for the Canals/Canet participation in calico-printing and by his bequeathing of money to one of his nieces by the Canals/Martí marriage. The spirit in which the twenty-one-year Canals/Canet association ran is suggested by the statement in the division which eventually ended it that it had always operated 'with equality in losses and profits despite the fact of the initial capital placed by each of the two being unequal'.

CHAPTER 4

Why did merchant capital move into the industry in the 1740s?

With the addition of the fervorous zeal which the esteem and veneration of the dignities of their sovereign fires in them to their natural inclination to apply themselves to their tasks, the inhabitants of this region naturally involved themselves ardently in constructing opulent manufactures with all the necessary departments.

(AGS, SH, leg. 1103, petition of calico-printers of 1760)

The pioneering efforts which were described in the last chapter were consolidated during the 1740s with the extension of calico-printing to the town of Mataró and with the growth in the industry in Barcelona. Table 4.1 lists the new manufactures and their dates of foundation. By the end of the decade the industry was composed of some eleven concerns[1] with approximately 470 looms and a total labour force in the region of 1,300.[2] Geometrical ratios do not have much significance when the starting-point to which they are related is as low as it is in

---

[1] The company running Campins's manufacture at Mataró went out of business during 1749 – hence eleven and not twelve. It seems probable that Peramás took over the running of the manufacture itself. M. Monjonell Pardás suggests that the manufacture continued functioning even though the company running it was dissolved ('La real fábrica de indianas de Mataró de Jaime Campins y Compañia', (Tesis de licenciature, Barcelona, 1956), p. 61), and that it may have been Rafel Peramás who took it over is suggested both by his initial close links with the manufacture (see p. 197) and by the large size which the Peramás concern rapidly attained: it possessed sixty looms in 1754 (AHPB, Creus Llobateras, act of 7 March 1754, fo. 35: this act was registered by Esteve Peramás i Matas, Rafel's son).

[2] In four cases there is information on looms and labour forces: Canals, 1746, 100 looms, 300 workers; Guàrdia, 1748, 71 looms, 181 workers; Clota, 1749, 48 looms, 117 workers; Pongem, 1749, 40 looms, 120 workers: 259 looms, labour force of 718. This permits the calculation of a loom/workers ratio of approximately 2·75. The labour force of the four other printers on the number of whose looms there is information (Glòria, 34 looms, 1747; French, 28 looms, 1754; Sala, 40 looms, 1754; Peramás, 60 looms, 1754) can be estimated with the help of this ratio: 162 looms, labour force of c. 446. And it seems safe to attribute some 50 looms, and thus a labour force of c. 137, to the three manufactures (those of Capelino, Canals and Planxart) on which there is no information (Canals: AHPB, Josep Cols, Registro de la fábrica de indianas, copy of privilege of 28 June 1747, records 100 looms, and see Duran Sanpere, Barcelona, II, p. 296, for labour force; Guàrdia: ACA, Intendencia,

Table 4.1. *Growth in cotton-weaving and calico-printing in Barcelona and Mataró, 1740–9: founders and (where known) associates*

Existing in	1. **Serra**/Canals/Canet
1740	2. **Glòria** + assocs.
1744/5	**French**, Sala, Brunés, Formentí
1746	**Domingo**, Campderrós, Capelino
	Campins, Villalonga, Llauder, Feliu, Janer, Corominas (in Mataró)
	Guàrdia
	Peramás (Mataró)
1747	**Clota**
	Sebastià Canals
	Pongem, Formentí, Sabater, Just
1749	**Sala**
	Planxart

Notes: 1. Names of founders appear in bold type.
2. There is a solitary reference to another manufacture in 1747, that of Josep Fermantín (AHPB, Josep Cols, act of 10 Nov. 1747, fo. 231).
Sources: Martínez Shaw, 'Los orígenes', pp. 249–50, has references to all these foundations with the following exceptions. **French** (1744/5): AHPB, Rojas Albaret, act of 31 May 1745 (fos. 96–7), forming this company, at this stage composed purely of Brunés and Formentí, and Severo Pujol, act of 19 Jan. 1745 (fos. 49–50), cancelling first act and forming second company, as above. **Domingo**: Grau and López, 'Empresari i capitalista', p. 49. **Peramás**: Llovet, *La ciutat de Mataró*, II, p. 68, for a 1747 foundation but the earlier date of 1746 is suggested by the accounts of the royal manufacture of Mataró with Joan Corominas, *comerciante* of Barcelona, which lists legal expenses incurred on 10 Oct. 1746 in connection with an attempt to get a worker from Campins's manufacture to cease working with Peramás (AHPB, Josep Fontana, Libro de concordias, no. 91, 27 Nov. 1749). **Clota**: 1747 or earlier foundation date revealed by mention in AHPB, Josep Cols, 10 Nov. 1747, of sale of 15 bales of spun cotton to his manufacture. **Sala**: AHPB, Creus Llobateras, act of 8 Aug. 1749 (fos. 54–6), by which Sala's capital in the French concern is paid off in the form of calicoes, and calico-weaving and printing equipment which were used to found his own concern. **Sebastià Canals**: here Martínez Shaw confuses Sebastià Canals with his nephew Sebastià Salamó, who is involved in a later manufacture (see p. 152) and who may have been associated in this: for evidence of families' ties, and earlier collaboration between the two, see AHPB, Miquel Cabrer, 13 July 1742, fo. 257.

Registros de la Superintendencia, 1/26, fos. 214–21, a copy of privilege of 24 Feb. 1748; Clota: Carrera Pujal, *Historia política*, IV, p. 139; Glòria, Pongem: ACA, RA, Diversorum, regs. 491, fos. 1–7, 494, fos. 273–82, copy of respective privileges; Sala and French: Duran Sanpere, *Barcelona*, II, p. 209; Peramás: see n. 1).

Table 4.2. *Manufactures of Canals and Glòria in 1746*

	Canals	Glòria
Looms	100	34
Printing tables	*c.* 16	5
Labour	*c.* 300	*c.* 112
Production	*c.* 7,200	2,448

Note: the report on the Canals concern only details the number of looms. Duran Sanpere, *Barcelona*, II, p. 296, and Alier, 'La fàbrica de Canals', p. 71, who give details on the labour force in 1762 and the number of printing tables in 1756, have been used as a source here with the justification that the manufacture reached a size in 1746 which was then maintained. The production figures have been calculated on the basis of the ratio of six pieces per loom per month which is given in the Glòria privilege. In the Glòria privilege the following partial details of his labour force, are given: seventy-eight weavers (probably included in this figure are the workers devoted to warping), four employed in pressing, eleven in painting – a total of ninety-three without including those involved in the bleaching processes: this would suggest that the loom/labour force ratio of 2.75, as discussed in n. 2, is too low in this case. The ratio between workers employed in the manufacture and in the bleaching field in Canals's manufacture in 1739 was approximately 5 to 1 and on the basis of this ratio I have estimated that Glòria's bleaching fields were employing nineteen. This has been my basis for the estimate of 112 for the total labour force here.

this case but, for what they are worth, growth in looms had been by a multiple of about thirteen and growth in number of manufactures by one of five. The expansion had thus been considerable.

The accepted view of the pattern of this growth is that it took the form of a virtual stagnation until 1746 and then a rapid expansion from this date.[3] The view was developed when the fact of the foundation of the French manufacture in 1744/5 was not known about but, even with the inclusion of this, the table would seem to justify only a slight moderation in it. There exists, however, the possibility that the two existing manufactures in 1740, those of Canals (Canals became the dominant influence in the Serra–Canals–Canet concern after Serra's death in 1740) and Glòria, expanded during the years 1740–6. If this were the case, and the growth was substantial, then it might be necessary to characterize the pattern differently.

The size of the Canals and Guàrdia manufactures in 1746, at the supposed turning-point in the early history of the industry, is revealed

[3] See, for example, Martínez Shaw, 'Los orígenes de la industria algodonera catalana', pp. 248–50.

Table 4.3. *The expansion in the Canals/Canet manufacture, 1740–54*
(prices in libras)

Expenditure up to 1740		2,734– 4–7
March 1741	House in Cortines	330– 0–0
Aug. 1744	House in Cortines	300– 0–0
Nov. 1744	House in Cortines	240– 0–0
Nov. 1744	House in Cortines	260– 0–0
Nov. 1745	House in Cortines	800– 0–0
Jan. 1746	House in Portal Nou	800– 0–0
Dec. 1747	House Cortines/Portal Nou	150– 0–0
1742–7	Repairs/conversion of houses and bleaching fields	4,051–14–2
Feb. 1753	House in Cortines/Portal Nou	2,100– 0–0
March 1754	Purchase of de Clota's bleaching field	4,061– 0–0
Total		15,826–18–9

Sources: Alier,'La fàbrica de Canals', p. 63, and 'Juan Pablo Canals', pp. 93–4; AHPB, Josep Cols, four acts of 3 Jan. 1746, fos. 13–15, and 7 March 1754, fos. 264–8. The value of the de Clota bleaching field I have taken from AHPB, Duran Quatrecases, act of 1 Sept. 1759, fo. 160.

by the privileges which they were granted during this year.[4] The information is summarized in table 4.2. It is clear from this that both manufactures had grown but that the Canals manufacture, benefiting no doubt from the royal privilege which it alone had been granted, had grown most – a multiplication by more than eight in its productive capacity and labour force and an increase in the number of its printing tables from six to *c.* sixteen had been achieved against an increase of not much more than 50 per cent.

The growth is clearly considerable enough to represent grounds for possibly modifying the accepted view of the industry's growth pattern, and the identification of the precise moment in these manufactures' expansion becomes, in view of this, central. This,

---

[4] AHPB, Josep Cols, Registro de la fábrica de indianas, copy of Canals/Canet privilege of 10 June 1747; ACA, RA, Diversorum, reg. 491, fos. 1–7: copy of Glòria privilege of 20 Oct. 1747. The privilege requests were made during 1745, were considered and recommended for acceptance before the Junta General on 16 June 1746, and agreed to by the king on 28 June 1746. Their publication was delayed until 1747, presumably because of the death of Philip V (AGS, CSH, reg. 248, fol. 178, records three 'expedientes conexos' of Canals and Glòria for 'franquicias'; AGS, CSH, reg. 213, fos. 79–80, records the decisions): the visits to the manufactures, on the basis of which the reports were made, probably, therefore, took place during early 1746.

Table 4.4. Capital invested in the Glòria company, 1739–56 (in libras)

1739	8,000
1742	12,000
Dec. 1743	14,400
Aug. 1745	22,000 or 25,064
1756	48,000

Sources: these are the act of 13 Aug. 1744 (AHPB, Duran Quatrecases, fo. 323–6) by which Sala attempted to sell his share in the Glòria concern to Joan Corominas, another of 11 August 1745 (Rojas Albaret, fo. 110) by which Sala was bought out by his associates and Fernández, 'La burguesía barcelonesa', p. 74, for the 1756 figure. Unfortunately, the figures in the two notarial acts for the company's capital in 1743 are difficult to reconcile. The former provides the figure which has been recorded for this year. The latter contains a breakdown of the sum of 3,092 libras, 18 sols, 1 denario by which Sala was bought out as follows: (1) 2,750 libras for two-sixteenth share + profits up to Dec. 1743 + 'the extra estimated for the appreciation of the said two-sixteenth share' (2) 382 libras, 16 sols, 1 denario for 1744 profits. The 2,750 figure would suggest a higher capital value for the firm in December 1743 but it is unclear how much higher for the 'the extra estimated' included in it would seem to apply to growth after this date as well as before, and possibly includes, too, profits for the first half of 1745. It is clear, certainly, that the 1743 figure included in the table does not include the profits earned for that and possibly previous years. In contrast, no problems result for calculating the 1745 capital value of the firm – the figures recorded in the table are for what the capital would have been before and after the 1744 profits had been distributed (there is no evidence as to whether the remaining associates in fact made such a distribution).

fortunately, it is possible to do with some degree of precision as there exists in the notarial archives information relating to the growth of both manufactures during these years – in the case of the Canals concern, records of all its building activities and in the case of that of Glòria, details of the growth in its capital stock. The evidence is summarized in tables 4.3 and 4.4.

The conclusion to be drawn from these two tables is relatively clear. Table 4.3 shows that the size of the Canals concern remained relatively static until mid-1744 when a considerable expansion was undertaken with the purchase of five different adjoining properties, which were then integrated with the manufacture, in the space of eighteen months. Table 4.4 suggests that in the case of the Glòria manufacture too there was some expansion in the pace of its more gradual growth after 1743. There is evidence that the profits earned by it were high during 1744, Josep Sala obtaining a return of at least

13.9 per cent on his share in it during this year.[5] The evidence, and in addition the new information concerning the foundation of the French manufacture (a substantial concern, in which an initial investment of 14,000 *libras* was made), while it would suggest that the return to expansion in the industry was a year or so earlier than previously thought, from other points of view reinforces the established interpretation concerning the timing in the industry's growth insofar as it demonstrates that the existing concerns, as well as new manufactures, participated in it.

The aim of this chapter is to compare and evaluate different explanations which have been given for this pattern of growth whose precise contours have just been checked. In its first half I shall summarize the different views which have been expressed and in its second I shall identify four principal issues which require clarification in order to arbitrate between these views and carry out this clarification by reference to what factual evidence exists. My conclusions will be summarized in a short third section.

DIFFERENT INTERPRETATIONS

Three historians have contributed to the debate on the expansion of the industry during these years. Pierre Vilar's thesis, although it contains little direct evidence on the industry itself, has firstly provided a framework relating to the stages of Catalonia's economic recovery which has important implications for its development, and secondly presents an argument, that political disruptions in the 1740s occasioned a crisis in local capital markets and a consequent reorientation in investment patterns, which clearly has relevance to the increase in industrial investment represented by the expansion of calico-printing. Carlos Martínez Shaw has linked the industry's growth to the prosperity of the American trade.[6] Finally, more recently, Alejandro Sánchez has suggested that greater consideration should be given to supply side causes of the industry's growth.[7] I shall examine these viewpoints in turn. Vilar's I shall survey in detail as it represents so important a contribution to the analysis of the Catalan growth process.

[5] See the notes under table 4.4. The profits for 1744 are recorded and can be related to Sala's investment of 2,750 *libras*. As this figure possibly includes profits for the first half of 1745, the return on his capital during 1744 may have been even higher.
[6] Martínez Shaw, 'Los orígenes', pp. 243–68.
[7] Sánchez 'La era de la manufactura'.

Pierre Vilar's explanation of the Catalan expansion

Catalonia's 'eighteenth-century' growth had its starting-point, Vilar establishes, in the early 1720s.[8] Its roots were in the agricultural economy which benefited from two particularly favourable circumstances. The first was the very extent of the economic collapse caused by the disruptions of the war and the subsequent military occupation – this had resulted in the existence of underutilized land resources, in the existence of slack to be taken up, as well as providing an opportunity for the emergence of new social groups. The second was the high demand which existed in the international economy for wine and eau-de-vie. The importance of this for the late seventeenth-century expansion in the Catalan economy has been pointed out in chapter 2. The combination of these two factors led to a steady agricultural expansion, particularly in western Catalonia, where both the damage occasioned by the war had been greatest and the conditions for intensive viticulture were most favourable. It was a recovery to previous levels of economic activity predominantly, rather than the attainment of new production ceilings, Vilar emphasizes, but he adds that the process of reconstruction gave a particular momentum to the expansion, conferring on it a creative potential which would not normally have been present. 'These reconstructions', he writes, 'which follow a momentary catastrophe impress, from taking place on cleared ground..., a particular vigour to the global growth, allowing the country... to catch up more quickly, to overtake sometimes their neutral or victorious neighbour. That is one of the aspects of the historical dialectic'.[9]

The particularly favourable agricultural conditions, Vilar demonstrates, permitted rapid population growth. On the basis of two local studies, he concludes that the demographic gains between 1708 and 1714 and 1741 and 1744 were massive.[10] This buoyant demographic situation, and the persistence of low food prices (apart from those for

[8] Vilar, *La Catalogne*, I, p. 704.
[9] *Ibid.*, II, pp. 377–9, 540, 555–6; see also III, p. 403, on the special possibilities provided by the extent of the collapse: 'Every war and every defeat implies, in the life of a country, this overthrow of chances and of fortunes, this changing of personnel and sometimes of structure.' See also above, p. 60. Jaume Torras has pointed out that a principal reason for this trade in eau-de-vie achieving such success in Catalonia, despite the area possessing no 'natural' advantages in viticulture over other Spanish regions, is its having possessed with Valencia a less restrictive fiscal system than other parts of Spain in which the production and sale of eau-de-vie were subjected to a royal monopoly ('Early Manufacturing', p. 8).   [10] Vilar, *La Catalogne*, II, pp. 99–101.

wine) until the late 1740s, contributed to wages remaining at low levels – 'there is after 1720 – and that will last until 1760 – *a grinding down of the payment for non-qualified work*', he writes.[11] He thereby establishes that circumstances were particularly favourable for a growth in profits. This growth he demonstrates by reference to the returns on the farming of the royal patrimony in the Principality (which included land and seigneurial dues): during a period in which the stability of agricultural prices might have caused one to anticipate relatively stationary yields, there were in fact increases of up to 200 and 300 per cent between 1726 and 1741 and 1755 and 1760. Having demonstrated the representativeness of these increases, he concludes as follows: 'the rise in the returns on the royal farms, surprising by its amplitude, by its continuity, by its superiority to the corresponding rise in prices, is then at the same time both a sign of the economic dynamism of the century, and one of the motors of this dynamism'.[12]

Catalonia's commerce had been as hard hit as its agriculture – 'it is probable', Vilar writes, 'that the years 1714–30 mark a very accentuated hollow, a minimum comparable to that of the end of the fifteenth century'.[13] Commercial reconstruction initially paralleled, and to a great extent was dependent upon, the agrarian recovery. The farming of the royal patrimony again illustrates this. The auctions for fulfilling the numerous contracts for this were held in Barcelona and some 41 per cent of the successful bidders were Barcelona residents. Here, thus, was a direct agricultural source for a commercial and industrial accumulation of capital. As Vilar writes 'the profit from the farming of seigneurial rights was integrated into Catalan commercial and industrial capital, and its growth in the course of the century forms thus one of the favourable factors in their development'.[14] Similarly linked to the general economic recovery were the profits which merchants obtained as intermediaries between the state and its agencies and the population as a whole in the process of tax-collecting and the provision of bread, meat and other products. 'There exists', Vilar emphasizes, 'between the sums paid by the mass of the population and the public revenues a margin which one can consider as one of the forms, a generally neglected one, of "primitive accumulation" of capital'.[15] By means of a micro-study on the affairs of the *botiguer de tall* (cloth-draper) Miquel Alegre, a representative figure in the commercial recovery, Vilar documents the importance of these types of investments for the emerging mercantile groups: 'all

[11] *Ibid.*, II, pp. 103, 383.   [12] *Ibid.*, II, pp. 478, 491.   [13] *Ibid.*, III, p. 413.
[14] *Ibid.*, II, pp. 489–90.   [15] *Ibid.*, III, p. 389.

those who matter among Barcelona's merchants in the second half of the eighteenth century', he concludes, 'built a part, modest but not negligible, of their original fortunes in the farming of seigneurial dues and taxes'. He accounts for the prominence of this type of mercantile investment in the early stages of the recovery in terms of the extent of the disruptions which had been experienced:

> Catolonia not only became a 'province' in the political sense. It experienced a sort of lowering of potential at all levels. It is normal that the large merchant houses of the previous period seem relegated to the background, while the future directors of the economy of the century, scarcely having emerged from their workshops, seek their safest investments in tax farming, and give the impression in their initiatives of hesitating and fumbling.[16]

This dependence on agricultural incomes was not total. There was a short period of near complete isolation of the regional economy[17] but soon maritime links were resumed. Vilar regards the involvement of the *botiguers*, who were the principal forces behind the commercial recovery of the region, in this external trade as effectively marking their graduation from the status of shopkeepers to that of wholesale merchants: 'As soon as they grow beyond the condition of shop-keepers, they abandon specialization to trade in no matter what product', he notes, '*overseas* commerce is the sign of their pro-motion'.[18] His attachment of particular importance to the par-ticipation in *overseas*, and especially *colonial* trade, is explained in the introduction to his third volume. It is a different type of trading activity ('of another *nature*'), he argues, insofar as it permits speculative profits which are not limited by the resources of the local economy, and thus represents a particularly important source of accumulation for the emergence of a capitalist society. 'Let us say', he writes, 'that... there exists, during the whole of the period studied, a "commercial capital", in certain Catalan centres dedicated to maritime and colonial wholesale trading, in the almost medieval sense of that expression, whose profits, based on situations of distant disequilibrium and monopoly, as well as on the risks of sea-trading, are not essentially raised from the regional production system.'[19]

It is again by means of his micro-study on the Alegres that Vilar plots these developments in overseas commerce. The first trade which was resumed was the most traditional in Barcelona's commercial history, the exchange of foodstuffs – and above all of eau-de-vie and

---

[16] *Ibid.*, III, pp. 385–98. The quotations are both on p. 398.   [17] *Ibid.*, III, p. 398.
[18] *Ibid.*, III, p. 398.   [19] *Ibid.*, III, p. 11.

wine in return for salted cod.[20] The trade, which was handled initially on a truck basis (a sign of the commercial backwardness of the region at this stage), was centred in Reus and the principal trading partners were English shippers. Reus owed its prominence to its combining the role of natural market centre for the expansive agricultural zones, and that of convenient point of contact, in view of its closeness to the port of Salou, with the foreign importers.[21] It became a central growth pole for the principality. Vilar generalizes from the experience – 'the conditions for a new departure were... realized at points which were privileged as usual'.[22] This was not, though the only contact which was achieved with the Atlantic economy during these years. Wines and eau-de-vie were also sent to Seville and Cádiz for reexport – these, Vilar notes, were the 'classical ports for redistribution towards the Atlantic'. This trade involved the *botiguers* in the traditional mercantile activities of insurance, lending money for interest to ships' captains and the taking of shares (*parts de diners*) in shipping ventures.[23]

The next stage in the commercial recovery of the region was the revival of the cloth-importing and redistributing trade. If Miquel Alegre's case is representative, it was franchised during the years 1726 to 1730. The source of the foreign cloth was in part Genoa, but above all Amsterdam, and the commodity exchanged for the imports was, again, principally eau-de-vie. In addition to this extension in the geographical range and commodity make up of Catalan trade during these years, there was also an increase in its autonomy. Rather than relying on the services of foreign merchants, Catalan agents were appointed in Amsterdam, Genoa, Cádiz and Madrid to handle sales and the purchase of return products. In Madrid, Miquel Alegre's son-in-law, Gibert i Xurrich, opened a shop in 1735 which was devoted purely to the sale of imported textiles. A further significant change was the involvement in some industrial exports – ironware principally at this stage – and in the import, via Cádiz, of colonial products for sale in the Catalan region: cocoa became a regular item in the Alegre accounts. By the mid-1730s, with links established between Barcelona, Amsterdam, Genoa, Cádiz and Madrid, the

---

[20] A deficiency in basic foodstuffs but the possession of exportable, Mediterranean agricultural products were two of the conditioning features of the Catalan economy influencing its trading structure, throughout its history, though at this stage, in view of the demographic decline, little grain was being imported. See *ibid.*, I, pp. 336–9.

[21] *Ibid.*, II, p. 322, III, pp. 398–415.   [22] *Ibid.*, III, p. 415.

[23] *Ibid.*, III, p. 409.

preparatory stages for commercial expansion had been completed:
Vilar writes of 'the essential points of the future network of national,
international and colonial relations' having been established.[24]

It is a progressive growth process, it is clear, which Vilar describes.
The agricultural recovery provided a basis for demographic recovery
and contributed to a revival in commercial profits but above all its
being based on an eminently exportable commodity, wine, and its
coincidence with a high level of international demand for this item,
permitted the initiation of a relatively autonomous cycle of commercial expansion. This commercial expansion had its own dialectic,
with a gradual widening and intensification of trading links and a
steady growth in the sophistication of commercial techniques.[25] The
changes of the 1740s, of which the investment in calico-printing is one
but of which the introduction of direct trading with the American
market is the better known example (and that which Vilar analyses
most thoroughly), can be seen as in part a continuation of this growth
process – it represented a further broadening of commercial horizons
by Barcelona's merchants and an increase in the extent of their
control over the international commercial circuit in which Barcelona's commerce had been involved since the 1720s. Vilar shows,
however, that another causative agency played a catalytic role in
these important advances. This was the crisis experienced by the
regional economy during these years as a consequence firstly of the
near total interruption in international trade occasioned by the wars
of Asiento and of Austrian Succession, and secondly of the internal
economic recovery beginning to falter, high grain prices signalling
the possibility of a return to Malthusian conditions between 1749 and
1753.[26] The effect of the crisis was to disrupt the principal trades in
which the region's merchants had previously been involved and to
enforce the modernizing of commercial techniques and the undertaking of new commercial ventures.

Again Vilar uses the example of Miquel Alegre, and of the
company which succeeded it, Alegre & Gibert, to illustrate the

---

[24] *Ibid.*, III, pp. 415–19.

[25] The more general issue which Vilar is exploring on the basis of the Catalan example is the
link between 'commercial' and 'industrial' capitalism, thus in his introduction to his
volume III (p. 12) he writes: 'A concrete study of commercial capital in the origins of modern
capitalist society would consist, then, in seeing how a progressive encouragement to seek new
means – less spectacular, but more continuous – of enrichment corresponds to the erosion of
monopolistic profits, to the diminution of maritime risks, by the establishment of a world
market and the growth of the global volume of exchanges'. See the introduction (pp. 6–7)
on this.   [26] *Ibid.*, II, pp. 556–7, III, pp. 422–3.

creative effects of the crisis. The economic difficulties, he demonstrates on the basis of their archives, affected the majority of trades which Barcelona's merchants had established in the previous twenty years. The import of salted cod was brought to a standstill in 1739; the export of eau-de-vie to, and import of cloth from, Amsterdam first became difficult and irregular and then virtually ceased between 1744 and 1749. Investment outlets in shipping, predictably, suffered a parallel decline – the Alegres experienced low returns on their *parts de diners* in shipping ventures from 1739 and undertook no such investments between 1740 and 1743. 'Around 1744 effectively', Vilar concludes, 'one can say that all the headings of the account book attest to a near total collapse in transactions.'[27]

The search for new investment outlets became essential – it was a question both of employing capital and of being prepared to take advantage of the prospects for speculative profits which would come with the return to peace: 'the reaction of the most enterprising merchants, in face of the collapse in transactions and the circumstances of war, is to chance fate and try something new'. Some of the searching resulted in solutions which were to be of only a provisional nature – for example, locally produced cloth was exported to Cádiz, Genoa and Palermo in 1740 and between 1746 and 1748 grain was exported to Marseilles in return for dyestuffs and colonial products, as well as for the cotton required for the developing calico-printing industry. The interest of these efforts, Vilar comments, 'is not … always to reveal to us future possibilities, but rather it is their demonstration to us of the variety of experiments, the multiplicity of the attempts of a man like Gibert i Xurrich, confronted by the difficulties of the moment'.

Other ventures, by contrast, resulted in the establishment of trades and commercial practices which were to form the foundations for the region's growth over the next fifty years. The principal of these related to the Cádiz and American markets. Firstly, trade to these areas increased. Thus the transactions between the Alegres and their Cádiz correspondent, Tomàs Prats, rose from a level of between 2,000 and 6,000 *libras* a year between 1737 and 1744 to one of between 10,000 and 50,000 between 1747 and 1754. The change, as Vilar notes, is of an order to mark 'a decisive stage'. Secondly, the mechanics of the trade altered. There was an increase in the range of

---

[27] *Ibid.*, III, pp. 422–32, 437–41. The quotation is on p. 432.

manufactured goods exported and raw materials began to be imported in return for these (the exchange is described by Vilar as 'the *double operation*', and he sees it as the paramount stimulus to the trade's expansion); there was an increase in the use of the letter of exchange for the transfer of credit between the two centres; and finally, from 1745, direct shipping ventures to America were undertaken from Catalonia (large undertakings, requiring, Vilar shows, considerable investment which was provided by the founding of substantial commercial companies).

Apart from these changes in the Andalusian and American trade, other import developments encouraged by the crisis included the more regular involvement of commercial houses in insurance and the direct merchant chartering of shipping rather than, as had been the practice, the using of sea captains as intermediaries. The former of these changes is a good example of the modernizing impact of warfare which had made insurance good business and also prevented the resort to the traditional centre of insurance, Amsterdam, impossible: 'The imitation by the Catalan commercial company installed in the major Dutch trading centre [formerly encharged with this insurance] is striking in this case', Vilar notes.[28]

As an example of the extent of the rupture which these changes represented at the personal level, Vilar cites the case of Josep Puiguriguer whose naval rope-contracting company organized and financed the first direct Catalan transatlantic shipping venture: 'It is interesting', Vilar comments, 'to see contracting work for government, an apparently rather routine type of business... give rise to commercial ventures, in their most audacious form.'[29]

So, to his portrayal of a progressive dialectic in commercial development, in his explanation of the region's growth process Vilar adds a strong emphasis on the innovatory force of two disruptions, a first, the devastation occasioned by the War of Spanish Succession and its aftermath, which provided the terrain both for an exceptionally rapid recovery and for the emergence of new, creative social groups, and a second, the rupture of established market links occasioned by the Wars of Asiento and Austrian Succession, which enforced more ambitious commercial undertakings and greater autonomy on the region's capitalism.

---

[28] *Ibid.*, III, pp. 432, 444–63. The quotations are on pp. 432, 434 and 441.
[29] *Ibid.*, III, p. 446.

Both the progressive dialectic and the second of the two disruptions, as noted, are clearly of potential relevance to interpreting the rapid expansion in the calico-printing industry. In addition, the importance of the changes of these years for the industry's future prospects is emphasized by Vilar. Commenting on the cargo list of one of the first Catalan ventures to America he writes: 'Note the absence of any cotton product, and particularly of that of printed calicoes', but he adds that the new market will become 'less than thirty years later, a characteristic destiny of exports. We are here *at the source* of the summons from a market'.[30]

The views of Martínez Shaw and Sánchez

While the relevance of Pierre Vilar's interpretation of the growth in the industry during these years is limited to his emphasis on the likely future impact on it of the growth of the colonial market, and to any implications which can be drawn from his demonstration of the creative consequences of the economic crises of the 1740s, Martínez Shaw, in contrast, in a more recent study has argued for direct links between the commercial trends of these years and the pace of the industry's advance. The influence, he argues, was exercised through the market: it was the war's cutting off of the American market which forced the industry to 'reduce its activities to restrain its initiatives during a period of five years', while the renewal of links with America, with five Catalan-organized and -financed ships sailing from Cádiz to America between 1745 and 1751, led to a 'spectacular return to the ventures of a decade back', with established companies renewing their privileges and new manufactures being founded. He documents his argument with a study of the commercial links of the founders of the manufactures, the majority of whom he shows to have had direct or indirect links with some aspect of the American trade, and with examples of sales by the new manufactures in the American market.[31]

Against this interpretation, more recently, Alejandro Sánchez has argued for supply side considerations being the major influence on the expansion. He notes, like Martínez Shaw, the long gap between the foundation of the Glòria and Canals manufactures and the post-1746 expansion, but argues that this rather than being attributable to

---

[30] *Ibid.*, III, pp. 460–1.
[31] Martínez Shaw, 'Los orígenes', pp. 243–68, the quotations are from p. 251.

'the problems which commercial trade suffered as a consequence of the War of Asiento' was linked more to 'a logical prudence of mercantile groups of the city in face of the progress and the results of these early manufactures' and he speculates that there might be a link between the five-year duration of Canals's 1741 privilege and the gap of similar dimension during which no new manufactures were founded (he was unaware of the involvement of Gregori French in the industry from 1744/5).[32]

TESTING THE INTERPRETATIONS

This will be done as follows. Firstly, the relevance to the industry of Vilar's exposition of the growth process in the Catalan economy, and of his argument about the creative role of the economic crisis of the 1740s, will be assessed by identifying, as far as it is possible to do so, the origins of the fortunes of the individuals who took up calico-printing during these years and the circumstances in which they did so. Secondly, Martínez Shaw's explanation of the expansion in terms of fluctuations in demand in the American market will be checked by establishing, again within the restraints of the limited documentation which exists for the industry during these years, the destiny of the calicoes printed by the industry at this stage in its growth. Thirdly, the possibility of state policy having influenced the timing of the expansion will be examined by reviewing the evidence relating to the links between the industry and the Junta General de Comercio for these years. Fourthly, the possibility that supply restraints, in the form particularly of the extent of availability of the new printing skills, may have been a further determining influence on the pace of the advance, will be examined.

The origins of the new manufactures

The evidence
Of the ten founders of manufactures during these years it is possible to identify the social origins of nine and in four cases there is additional information concerning the identity of a total of thirteen associates. The sources permit, therefore, a relatively thorough reconstruction of the entrepreneurial and financial sources of the expansion in the industry.

---

[32] Sánchez, 'La era de la manufactura', p. 8.

Table 4.5. *Social and commercial background of the founders of calico-printing manufactures in the 1740s*

Founders	Origins	Professional and social career before taking up calico-printing	Career after starting printing
Gregori French, Barcelona	Ireland, merchant	1730–5, correspondent of Miquel Carnisser of Reus; 1739, contractor bread supply Barcelona; 1740, exports eau-de-vie from Vilanova and Salou to Holland; 1742, importing salted cod	From 1746, links with Cádiz; dies in 1750; son runs manufacture till c. 1763
Jaume Campins, Mataró	Mataró, merchant?	1740, contractor to Royal Naval Hospital Cádiz; 1744, + Clota involved privateering venture; 1745, + Clota involved privateering venture; 1746, + Clota organize sailing of *San Francisco de Paula* to Vera Cruz	1747–50, ship-building; 1748–9, represents Catalans in Cádiz; 1749, abandons printing; 1750s, trading in wool, lending money, trading to America from Cádiz; 1764, registered on the *matrícula de comerciantes* of Cádiz
Jaume Guàrdia, Barcelona	*Paraires* of Castelltersol; father Melchior (d. 1730) and son Jaume (d. 1755) are *botiguers de tall*	1714, Melchior tax-farming; 1726, importing cloth from Genoa; 1730s, appoints administrator to *botiga*; from 1730, Jaume involved in contracting for bread and ice supplies; 1734, buys office in Audiencia; 1738, buys seigneurie of Marmellar; 1745, sends goods to Cádiz; 1746, insures cargo of *San Francisco de Paula*	1748, involved negotiations re Royal Company of Barcelona; 1753, *ciutadà honrat*; 1764, grandson Melchior sells manufacture; 1773, grandson Melchior buys seigneurie of Almacelles
Rafel Peramás, Mataró	Son of Francesc, merchant	1710, associated in company trading with Andalusia; 1721, exporting wine to Andalusia; 1731, links with Lisbon; 1744, in society with Campllonch trading to Cádiz	1754, son Esteve running manufacture; 1756, son Rafel matriculated Cádiz

Table 4.5. (cont.)

Founders	Origins	Professional and social career before taking up calico-printing	Career after starting printing
Francesc de Clota, Barcelona, b. 1702	Peasants from San Feliu de Pallerols; father, Jaume, a merchant	1709–23, Jaume a customer of Cia de Gibraltar; 1707–9, Jaume involved insurance company; from 1723, contractor for supplying bread to army with Anton Seguí; 1720s Francesc = young *botiguer de teles*; 1727, Francesc becomes *corredor de cambios*; 1730, Francesc entitles himself *negociant*; 1742, still contracting for bread to army; 1742, trading links with Amsterdam via Bordeaux; 1744, attorney for various noble families, including Duchesses of Alba and Olivares; 1744, enters nobility; 1744/5, + Campins involved privateering from Cádiz; 1746, + Campins organize sailing of *San Francisco de Paula* to Vera Cruz	1747, contracting with Consejo de Hacienda for provision of gunpowder; 1747, trades with Cartagena; 1747, Campins = agent for in Cádiz; 1747, trades with Antwerp; 1748, wine to Amsterdam in association with Campllonch; 1748, links with Paris; 1749, still contractor for bread to army; 1749, still acting for nobility; 1754, abandons manufacture; 1756, deputy to Madrid for creation of Cia de Comercio; 1759–62, director of Cia de Comercio; 1767, appointment as member of Junta de Comercio; 1769, appointment becomes a life one
Sebastià Canals, Barcelona	Silk-weaver	1736, one of the first silk-weavers to establish a commercial company involved in business outside his own guild; 1739, involved in farming Barcelona's bread supply	

| Joan Pongem, Barcelona | Family has fishing/nautical origins in Mataró, he himself is a young *comerciant*, a minor, when he founds his first manufacture, but married already into an old and distinguished commercial family, that of Alabau | 1745, involved shipping venture; 1745, sub-farming royal mills; 1746, visit to Madrid in connection with sub-farming mills; 1746, one of insurers *San Francisco de Paula* | 1748, agent for Valencian merchant; 1749, investor in Perla de Catalunya; 1759, founds a second manufacture; 1773, son Antoni becomes *ciutadà honrat*; 1774, investment in insurance company of La Sagrada Familia; 1781, member of Junta de Comercio; 1792, bankrupt |

Sources: **French**: Martínez Shaw, *Cataluña*, p. 97 (re Irish and Cádiz links); Vilar, *La Catalogne*, III, p. 414 n. 1; AHPB, Duran Quatrecases, act of 3 Aug. 1739, fo. 69, Miquel Cabrer, acts of 27 Aug. 1740, fo. 472, and 13 Feb. 1742, fos. 60–1, Sebastià Prats, 3rd book of contracts and agreements, fo. 50, date of death mentioned; that manufacture was not producing in 1763 is apparent from its non-inclusion in a list of concerns with privileges which was drawn up in this year (BC, JC, leg. 53, no. 1). **Campins**: Martínez Shaw, *Cataluña*, pp. 129–32, contains all this information apart from that concerning the collapse of the Mataró manufacture for which, see his 'Los orígenes', pp. 264–5; Molas Ribalta, *Los gremios*, p. 330, and *Comerç i estructura social*, pp. 230, 290; for Andalusian links, see Martínez Shaw, 'Los orígenes', p. 256. **Perramàs**: Martínez Shaw, *Cataluña*, pp. 34, 54, 87, 108, 134; Molas Ribalta, *Los gremios*, p. 213; AHPB, Creus Llobateras, act of 7 March 1754, fo. 35. **Clota**: Molas Ribalta, *Comerç i estructura social*, pp. 229–30, 270, 275, 280; AHPB, Miquel Cabrer, 28 Dec. 1742, fos. 8–10, 25 May 1742, fos. 195–6, Francesc Albia, 22 Oct. 1744, fo. 116, 17 June 1747, fo. 34, 27 Aug. 1749, fo. 59, 21 March 1750, fos. 10–11, Seabastià Prats, 16 Dec. 1747, fos. 369–70; 15 June, 26 June, 6 Nov. 1748, fos. 263–4, 290, 450, Josep Cols, 7 March 1754, fos. 264–8; Martínez Shaw, *Cataluña*, 1739. fo. 69. **Pongem**: Molas Ribalta, *Comerç i estructura social*, pp. 148–9, 179, 220, 270, 279, 284, 290, and *Societat i poder política a Mataró, 1718–1808* (Mataró, 1973), pp. 41–2; Molas Ribalta, *Los Gremios*, p. 471; AHPB, Duran Quatrecases, act of 3 Aug. 1739. fo. 69; AHPB, Olzina Cabanes, manual, 18 Sept. Vilar, *La Catalogne*, II, p. 434 and III, p. 204; Martínez Shaw, *Cataluña*, pp. 168, 180; AHPB, Olzina Cabanes, manual, 18 Sept. 1748, fo. 13, 3rd book of marriage contracts, 17 Sept. 1748, fo. 335; Josep Francesc Fontana, 21 July 1746, fos. 105–11.

With one exception, that of Domingo, who was a *cotoner*, all these
founders were either *comerciantes*, with no guild attachments, or guild-
members involved in wholesaling-type activities outside their own
guilds. French, Campins, Peramás, Clota and Pongem were in the
first category, Guàrdia, like Canals and Alegre a *botiguer de tall*,
Sebastià Canals, a silk-weaver, and Sala, the 'glass-maker' whose
participation in two other calico companies was noted in the last
chapter, in the latter. Domingo's is the only case of a link with the
small-scale cotton industry which already existed in Barcelona. His
example can be dealt with rapidly as it was an initiative of a different
size and scale from the others: the company which he founded with
two silk-weavers, Josep Capelino and Pau Campderrós, only involved
an initial investment of 900 *libras* and was purely for the production
of cotton cloths, not for printing.[33] There are records of the purchase
of its product by one of the large calico-printing concerns.[34]

In most cases it is possible to gain an approximate idea of the trades
in which these eight wholesaler participants in the new industry had
been involved and also of their status within the city's commercial
community. The available details are summarized in table 4.5 (Sala
has been omitted from the table as his case was discussed in the
previous chapter). In table 4.6, briefer details are provided concerning the backgrounds of the individuals with whom these founders
of calico-printing concerns associated themselves.

A few extra details on some of these partners will contribute to
enlightening the grounds for their involvement in calico-printing.
Brunés was a minority investor in the French concern (2,000 *libras*
against the 6,000 each invested by French and Sala) and his
managerial contribution to the manufacture was limited to the
supervision of its, and its bleaching meadow's, construction in the
'*horta* [irrigated land/vegetable garden] of St Pau'.[35] It was the first
concern in the industry to be situated in what was eventually to be
the city's principal industrial zone – beyond the Ramblas, on the
city's west side, between the inner and outer city walls, an area
known as the Raval or Arraval, occupied largely by religious

---

[33] AHPB, Josep Cols, act of 2 Feb. 1746, fo. 19: 'una fàbrica de blauets'. On Barcelona's small,
existing cotton industry see Duran Sanpere, *Barcelona*, II, pp. 284–91, and Molas Ribalta, *Los
gremios*, p. 255: two 'cotoners' in 1729.
[34] In the accounts of Campins's manufacture with Joan Corominas in Barcelona, one of the
first transactions concerns cottons taken to 'Casa Capelino' (AHPB, J. B. Fontana, Libro de
concordias, 91).   [35] AHPB, Severo Pujol, 18 Jan. 1745, fos. 45–6.

Table 4.6. *Social origins of partners in manufactures founded in the calico-printing industry during the 1740s (geographical origin being Barcelona except where stated)*

---

1. Josep Sala: origins discussed in previous chapter
2. Jaume Brunés: an apothecary
3. Miquel Formentí: silk-weaver, ex-apprentice of Geroni Glòria and thus probably ex-employee of Glòria's manufacture
4. Antoni Llauder (Mataró): *ciutadà honrat* of Barcelona, landowner in Mataró
5. Galceran de Villalonga (Mataró): *ciutadà honrat* of Barcelona, landowner in Mataró
6. Francesc Feliu (Mataró): *ciutadà honrat* of Barcelona, landowner in Mataró
7. Salvador Janer (Mataró): merchant
8. Joan Corominas: merchant
9. Josep Sabater: a stocking-knitter
10. Francesc Just: a *paraire*

Note: excluded from the table are Capelino and Campderrós, whose origins have been mentioned above. Formentí was associated in two different concerns which is why there are only ten names here.

establishments and market gardens (see map on p. 168).[36] Brunés's connection with the industry may have arisen from his involvement as an apothecary in the import and mixing of drugs.[37] Formentí's contribution to the French manufacture was restricted initially to the technical side – he was to be its *fabricant*. Indeed, he was initially purely an employee, though he was to be given a 10 per cent share of the profits and once he had accumulated 500 *libras* on this basis he was to be allowed to invest in the company and to become a subordinate associate ('with neither active nor passive voice' in its direction).[38] His qualification for his position came from his possession of both weaving, as a consequence of his professional formation as a silk-weaver, and printing skills, apparently obtained by working in the Glòria manufacture.[39] The share in the profits which he was

---

[36] On Barcelona's urban development, see R. Grau, 'La metamorfosi de la ciutat emmurallada: Barcelona, de Felip V a Ildefons Cerdá', in M. Tarradell, *Evolució urbana de Catalunya* (Barcelona, 1983), pp. 65–81.
[37] On the importance of this sort of background to later participation in the industry, see Molas Ribalta, *Los gremios*, pp. 275, 524.
[38] AHPB, Severo Pujol, 19 Jan. 1745, fos. 52–3.
[39] Molas Ribalta, *Los Gremios*, pp. 470, 481 n. 108.

granted, and the high salary of 300 *libras* which he was accorded as *fabricant*, made it possible for him to join the Pongem manufacture on a stronger footing in 1747 – his investment was 4,000 *libras*.[40] Llauder's, Villalonga's and Feliu's cases illustrate a point on which Vilar and others have placed much emphasis – the range of the social groups who participated in commercial companies and the inclusion within this range of members of the nobility.[41] In this case it was an ex-commercial nobility, predominantly, but one already with some tradition – the Llauder's title dated from at least the 1680s[42] and Francesc Feliu de Sayol was a great grandson of the Narcís Feliu de la Penya who had been made *ciutadà honrat* (noble status conferred on leading urban citizens, similar to French *bourgeois*) in 1670 and had played so central a role, we saw in the penultimate chapter, in the Catalan commercial and industrial expansion in the period leading up to the Spanish War of Succession.[43]

As well as capital it was space which these landowners could offer for the Campins manufacture in Mataró – the *horta* on which it, and its bleaching meadow, were situated was rented from Feliu and a house 'which serves as a warehouse' was rented from Llauder. Llauder also served as cashier to the manufacture.[44] Janer and Corominas had had previous commercial connections before their participation in the Mataró concern. Since 1740 they had been associated with a third merchant in the export of textiles to Cádiz.[45] Their contributions to the production side of the Mataró manufacture were crucial as Janer acted as director and it is clear from Corominas's accounts with the concern that he was the main link with Barcelona whose near ten-years' experience of the industry by 1746 made it an essential source for equipment, labour and legal and administrative services.[46] Josep Sabater was one of the wealthiest members of the silk stocking-knitters' guild.[47] He did not abandon his stocking-knitting on associating himself with Pongem.[48] He was

---

[40] AHPB, Olzina Cabanes, 3rd book of marriage contracts, 31 oct. 1747, fo. 335.
[41] See, for example, Vilar, *La Catalogne*, III, pp. 189, 446, 453.
[42] J. Llovet, *La ciutat de Mataró* (2 vols., Barcelona, 1959–61), II, p. 125.
[43] Molas Ribalta, 'La companyia Feu-Feliu de la Penya (1676–1708). Comerç de teixits vers 1700', in his *Comerç i estructura social a Catalunya als segles XVII i XVIII* (Barcelona, 1977), p. 159, and Vilar, *La Catalogne*, I, pp. 655–61.
[44] For accounts of the manufacture, see AHPB, J. B. Fontana, Libro de concordias, 91.
[45] Martínez Shaw, *Cataluña*, p. 127.   [46] As n. 44.
[47] Molas Ribalta, *Los gremios*, pp. 512, 523; in 1753 he was the fourth largest silk importer in the guild.
[48] In 1756 he was trying to obtain a privilege for this manufacture (AHPB, Creus Llobateras, act of 12 June 1756, fo. 45).

encharged with sales in the new company.[49] It was partly in connection with this role that he participated in the foundation in 1750 of a small company in conjunction with Jaume Pujades, Joan Batista Pau and Josep Llauger, respectively two merchants and a sea captain from the coastal port of Canet, for the purchase and export of Catalan products to Cádiz where 'a shop or house' was to be established for their sale.[50] Sabater was intended to be the Barcelona agent of this company, purchasing products for export, but from 1753 he himself resided in Cádiz, acting there not only for the Pongem manufacture but also for that of Canals and Canet.[51] Francesc Just was a *paraire* and brother-in-law of Sabater. Like the latter he continued with his original profession – in 1758 he was the third largest cloth-producer in his guild. In the Pongem manufacture he was encharged with the purchase of cotton and other raw materials.[52]

Interpretation

Firstly, it is clear that the predominating group which took up calico-printing during these years was that with which Vilar was concerned in his analysis of the growth of commercial capitalism in the region. It was the movement of wholesalers into the industry, be they independent *comerciantes, botiguers* like the Alegres, or members of other elite guilds, which was the principal cause for its expansion.[53] The scale of this movement was not insignificant given the approximate size of the city's commercial elite. Members of at least seven of the thirty-seven families paying the highest rates of commercial taxation in the city between 1724 and 1752 had invested in the industry by 1750.[54] What is more, it was some of the most dynamic members of this commercial elite which had become

---

[49] As n. 40.

[50] AHPB, Duran Quatrecases, 2nd book of agreements, 13 Nov. 1750, fos. 70–1, and Martínez Shaw, *Cataluña*, pp. 122–3.

[51] Martínez Shaw, *Cataluña*, p. 128, and AHPB, Duran Quatrecases, Inventaris i Encants, act of 1 Sept. 1759, fo. 161: which shows that Sabater is acting as an agent of Canals and Canet and residing in Cádiz but on behalf of the company of Anglí & Sabater.

[52] Molas Ribalta, *Los gremios*, pp. 390, 402.

[53] The relationship with the Alegres was close in the case of at least two of the investors in calico-printing. Sebastià Vidal, a member of the Glòria company, was, like Alegre, a 'shopkeeper with merchant ambitions', and he had been Alegre's principal associate during the early stage of his career, and the Guàrdias were involved in several of the same companies as the Alegres (Vilar, *La Catalogne*, III, pp. 386–7, 416).

[54] The list of these payers of the cadastre for commercial earnings (*ganancial*) was drawn up by Fernández, 'La burguesía barcelonesa', p. 111. The seven families are those of Guàrdia, Glòria, French, Clota, Gesceli, Gispert and Vidal.

involved. Glòria's case was discussed in the last chapter. Guàrdia and Clota were comparable to Glòria in the range of their investments and the social mobility which they had experienced during these years of reconstruction and economic expansion. In 1736, a report made on the former in connection with his application for the position of consul in the guild of commercial brokers described him as 'according to common opinion ... one of the merchants with greatest fortune, credit and intelligence who there is in this capital, having circulated in various provinces to instruct himself in the rules of trade'. This commercial travelling had extended to Flanders, Holland and France: 'he is the most able of them all', the report continued.[55] Clota's starting-point may have been slightly more favourable than that of either Guàrdia or Glòria. It was his father who had initiated the involvement in military bread contracting, and that the family already possessed considerable resources at the beginning of the century is revealed by the fact that it lost fourteen houses as a consequence of the destruction of a part of the area known as the Ribera (the half of the city to the east of the Ramblas) for the purpose of the construction of the fortress of the Ciutadella following the end of the War of Succession. His progress, however, was similarly impressive. Martínez Shaw describes him as 'one of the most representative members of this first bourgeois generation and also one of those who was able to spy out best the paths of the future'.[56]

Campins is described by Martínez Shaw in a similar manner as 'one of the most enterprising businessmen of the middle years of the century'. The range of his investments during the 1740s and 1750s, as revealed in table 4.5, clearly justifies the description. He remains, however, a slightly enigmatic figure. The information on his Catalan background is sparse. No evidence has been located of any commercial activities in which either he or his father were involved in Catalonia before he established himself in Cádiz, though it is probable that he was related via his mother to a Josep Barnola (his full name was Campins Barnola), a silk manufacture, who played a prominent role in shipping and silk-manufacturing developments during these years and who was a major backer, investing more than the Alegre company, of the third Catalan-organized trading venture

---

[55] ACA, RA, Papeles de su excelencia, leg. 249, 16 May 1736.
[56] *Ibid.*, and Martínez Shaw, *Cataluña*, p. 70.

to America.[57] He was one of the first Catalan merchants to establish himself in Cádiz. His career there prior to his involvement in calico-printing had three particular characteristics: firstly, the closeness of his links with leading merchants both in Catalonia and Andalusia, secondly, his involvement in all aspects of the Catalan/American exchange – ship-building, importing of Catalan products, in particular eau-de-vie, to Cádiz for reexport and shipping ventures to America – and thirdly, his connection with government (his office in the Royal Naval Hospital and the royal authorization which he would have required for his 1745 privateering venture).

The prominence within Barcelona's commercial community of these wholesalers is also demonstrated by the fact that some of their number were among the first of its members ennobled – Glòria and Guàrdia with the titles of *ciutadans honrats* in 1748 and 1753 respectively (the second and fourth awards of this honour) and Clota with that of *cavaller* (knight) in 1744.[58] It is clear that participation in calico-printing at this stage was an avant-garde investment undertaken by the leading participants in the Catalan expansion.

It is also clear from table 4.5 that the stages by which the merchants who involved themselves in calico-printing had accumulated capital corresponded approximately to those represented by Vilar as typical in the process of recovery which followed the defeat in the War of Succession. In most cases, it can be seen, there had been some sort of involvement in trades linked directly or indirectly to the state – French, Guàrdia, Clota and Canals had been involved in contracting for urban and military bread requirements, Campins, as just noted, had been contractor to the Royal Naval Hospital in Cádiz since 1740 and Pongem was the sub-farmer of the royal mills in Catalonia. There is also evidence of involvement in the exchange of foodstuffs (French was a salted cod importer and he, Clota, Campins and Peramás had all participated in the export of wine and eau-de-vie) as well as in the international cloth trade (Guàrdia and Clota principally).

If the evidence suggests the predominance of a rising social group, and newly accumulated capital, in the industry's expansion, there are also a few signs of links with the Principality's previous period of prosperity. This was to have been expected: 'That the crisis,

[57] Martínez Shaw, *Cataluña*, pp. 67, 129–32, and 'Los orígines', pp. 256–8; Vilar, *La Catalogne*, III, pp. 452–3.   [58] Molas Ribalta, *Comerç i estructura social*, pp. 283–4.

prolonged and concluded by the resistance and the fall of Barcelona, should have carried away the majority, the near totality, of the old merchant fortune, that cannot surprise us', Vilar writes, 'But is it likely that all the enriched of the period of growth, of the war contracts and of the presence of the court in the Catalan capital, should have been carried away in the catastrophe?'[59] The Clota family, whose relatively advantageous financial position at the beginning of the century has been mentioned, and which was an important customer of the Gibraltar Company in 1711, was probably one such survivor and Joan Pongem by his marriage, was linked to the Alabau family, which came from the commercial elite of the beginning of the century, having been elected onto the 'matrícula de mercaders' (a list of leading wholesale merchants, inclusion on which brought with it political and judicial responsibilities, but which fell into disuse following 1714) in 1705. Similarly, the involvement of the Peramás family in the export of wine to Andalusia since at least 1710 links them, too, to an earlier stage of Catalonia's commercial development – that of the first shift away from the Mediterranean and towards the Atlantic which had its source in the last quarter of the seventeenth century, which was referred to in chapter 2 – and the presence of Llauder, and above all of Feliu, in the Campins company is another sign of elements of continuity. The prominence of Mataró in the expansion (two manufactures founded and the Pongem family originating there) is in itself worthy of note. It reflects the continued commercial prosperity of what for a while was Catalonia's second city and that the individuals who founded manufactures there were those whose links with the earlier phase of Catalonia's growth were strongest is a possible confirmation of a remark of Vilar's, that the town was a centre for members of the local elite who were opposed to the Bourbon succession.[60]

A minor discrepancy from the pattern argued for by Vilar is provided by Campins's case. His example suggests that at least a part of the capital invested in the new industry had an extra-regional origin. It is clear from the list of his activities before he took up calico-printing that he had been involved as much in *Andalusian* as in Catalan trading activities since he had established himself in Cádiz, so capital which he invested in the industry can at the most only be categorized as being partly regional. In addition, there are signs that Andalusian merchants participated in his huge investment of 33,600

[59] Vilar, *La Catalogne*, III, pp. 402–3.   [60] *Ibid.*, I, pp. 668–9, II, pp. 70–1.

libras in the industry. (This was more than half of the 58,800 *libras* which was invested in the Mataró concern and by far the largest investment of which there is record – compare Glòria's, French's and Pongem's initial investments in their concerns of 2,000, 8,000 and 6,000 *libras* respectively.) The signs are in the accounts of the manufacture in which this large investment is recorded as being of 'Dn Jayme Campins de Cádiz *and his associates*'.[61] Campins, as also noted in table 4.5, was involved in a variety of partly Andalusian-financed ship-building ventures during these years in Catalonia and so the associating with Andalusian finance for his calico-printing would have been consistent with his commercial practices. The possible involvement of Andalusian capital in the financing of this concern (though it would seem to be the only case) is a useful reminder that this was still a relatively early phase in the recovery of the Catalan economy, that Barcelona was still a secondary commercial and financial centre compared to those of Andalusia, and that the local resources for investment were relatively small by international standards (a smallness which was compensated for, as Vilar has noted, by the exceptional capacity of the region's merchants for organizing collaborative enterprises).[62]

Finally, table 4.5 provides evidence which is at least consistent with, even if it does not prove, Vilar's explanation of the undertaking of new types of commercial investment during these years in terms of the need to respond to the economic crisis occasioned by the wars of Asiento and Austrian Succession. It has already been noted that the timing of the expansion of the industry conforms exactly with this hypothesis. In addition, the previous investments of some of the founders of the calico-printing concerns, and particularly those of Guàrdia, Clota and French, were in trades which were interrupted by the wars. The very scale of the investments made in the new industry might be a sign of the existence of surplus, temporarily unemployable funds in the regional capital market – those in Guàrdia's and Clota's manufactures must have been as large, or probably larger in the case of the former, than that in the Mataró

---

[61] AHPB, J. B. Fontana, Libro de concordias, 91. The associates are revealed at another point of the account included with this agreement to be Pedro Virgilio and Jaime Sala i Millàs. The latter may have been of Catalan origin but had been working some years at least in Andalusia (Martínez Shaw, *Cataluña*, pp. 118, 130–1).

[62] It is an additional illustration of Martínez Shaw's argument concerning the importance of the Andalusian contribution to the early stages of Catalan growth. See his *Cataluña*, pp. 98–105, 144–54.

concern.[63] Evidence (in table 4.5) of first-time involvement by these merchants in a range of other trades during these years provides further support of the need which they must have been experiencing to find outlets for their capital, and that the wars induced a preparedness to take risks which was not typical of commercial capitalism, and which, too, could be of relevance to the movement into industrial activity, is demonstrated by the involvement of Campins in privateering activity in 1745 before he became with Clota the joint organizer of the second Catalan organized trading venture to America in 1746.

The individual whose case would appear to fit Vilar's explanation best is Gregori French. His commercial activities seem to have been focussed in particular on the trade which was most severely interrupted by the wars – the exchange of eau-de-vie for salted cod. In 1740 his two English-speaking brothers were situated respectively in the ports of Vilanova and Salou to assist in this trade and the extent of his commitment to this zone of Catalonia is demonstrated by the marriage in 1756 of his daughter, Antonia, into the Tarragonese nobility. The timing of his substantial investment in calico-printing conforms perfectly with a theory which would account for it in terms of the blocking off of his previous investment outlets and finally the inventory of his possessions undertaken on his death demonstrates that his manufacturing activities had become by far his principal ones: his investment in calico-printing accounted for at least 66 per cent of his total capital.[64]

[63] Guàrdia had 'created a house capable of having 100 looms established in it' in the quarter of the Raval and at the time of the granting of his privilege had seventy-one looms in action. Clota's concern, also in the Raval, was operating with forty-nine looms in 1749, whereas the 58,800 *libras* in the Campins manufacture had created a concern with only thirty-six looms at the time of its obtaining a royal privilege in December 1747 (ACA, Intendencia, Registros de la Superintendencia, 1/26, fos. 151, 214–21, 16 Dec. 1747, 24 Feb. 1748, Campins's and Guàrdia's privileges detail the number of their looms; for Clota's manufacture, see Carrera Pujal, *Historia política*, IV, p. 139). It is possible that Guàrdia financed this manufacture by himself as in the inventory drawn up on his death there is no mention of any associates – the entire manufacture is detailed as forming part of his patrimony (AHPB, Sebastià Prats, 4th book of agreements, 7 Sept. 1755, fos. 211–25).

[64] AHPB, Miquel Cabrer, 27 Aug. 1740; in this act French's orders to his brothers in Vilanova and Salou are recorded in English. His brother Nicolas was one of the Alegres' correspondents in Reus (Vilar, *La Catalogne*, III, p. 415 – Frenys, the surname recorded, would seem to be a local spelling of French). For the marriage of French's daughter and the inventory on his death, see AHPB, Sebastià Prats, 3rd and 4th books of contracts and agreements, 8 June 1752, fos. 50–7, and 9 July 1756, fos. 183–5. French's career suggests that the links with England occasioned by the alliance during the Spanish War of Succession may have been an important element in the successful trade which developed later in the exchange of eau-de-vie for salted cod. The family's links with the area would seem to have

Markets

The assessing of the validity of Martínez Shaw's explanation of the expansion of the industry in terms of the possibilities of the American market is complicated by the sparsity of documentation existing. The only sources available are firstly the inventories of the business transacted by the Junta General de Comercio (the sole records which exist for this body during these years) in which there are a number of references to difficulties experienced by printers in securing respect for the fiscal exemptions, granted by their privileges, on sales in a variety of markets, and secondly notarial registers which include a comparatively large number of acts by which printers named agents to commercialize their cloth, some others in which actual sales of calicoes are recorded and two inventories of manufactures in which lists of outstanding debts make possible the identification of customers.

The limitations of these sources are evident. The experiencing of difficulties with respect to the fiscal exemptions could only affect manufactures which possessed privileges (the Glòria concern, it was noted in the last chapter did not receive one, and nor did Gregori French's until 1750) and in the case of these it was not a sufficiently regular occurrence for its record to provide full details of commercial networks. The naming of agents before notaries, in contrast, was a regular practice: the difficulty here is firstly that it was one which was generally only resorted to once for each centre (though there are some cases of printers changing their agents), and secondly that the acts recording it are scattered among too wide a range of notaries for full details to be compiled. Both sources tend to record initial contacts with markets principally: it was the first attempts to obtain respect for fiscal privileges which generally ran into trouble and the naming of an agent was clearly the preliminary measure for penetrating a new market. Neither is of assistance with respect to the regional market in which neither difficulties in obtaining fiscal exemptions occurred nor the naming of special agents for cloth sales was necessary, local drapers continuing, as they had in 1732, to purchase

originated during the war. On other commercial consequences of the English alliance, see G. J. Walker, 'Algunes repercussiós sobre el comerç d'Amèrica de l'Aliança Anglo-Catalana durant la Guerra de Successió Espanyola', in Comissió Catalana del Cinqué Centenari del Descobriment d'Amèrica, *Segones Jornades d'Estudis Catalano-Americans* (Barcelona, 1987), pp. 69–81.

Table 4.7. *Markets for the Catalan calico-printing industry, 1741–58*

1. *Interior Spain*

Madrid	CANALS (1741), *Canals* (1741), **Campins** (1747), *Glòria* (1748), *Canals* (1748), *Guàrdia* (1748), CLOTA (1749), GUÀRDIA (1750), CLOTA (1750), CANALS (1753), *Canals* (1753), *Seguí* (1753), CANALETA (1753), FERRA (1755), *Canals* (1756), CANALETA (1756), **Guàrdia** (1756); **Canals** (1759)
Saragossa	**Campins** (1747), **Canals** (1750), **Guàrdia** (1756)
Barbastro	**Canals** (1759)
Toledo	CANALETA (1755)
Valladolid	CANALS (1755), **Canals** (1759)

2. *Local maritime links*

Majorca	CANALS (1741), *Canals* (1741), **Campins** (1748), FRENCH (1749), **Canals** (1759)
Valencia	CANALS (1741), *Canals* (1743), **Campins** (1748), GUÀRDIA (1748), CLOTA (1749), **French** (1752), *Guàrdia* (1752), SEGUÍ (1753), *Pongem* (1753), CANALS (1754), *Guàrdia* (1754), *Guàrdia* (1755), CANALETA (1754), *Glòria* (1755), **Guàrdia** (1756), **Canals** (1759)
San Felipe (Játiva)	**Guàrdia** (1756)

3. *Central Mediterranean Spain*

Alicante	**Guàrdia** (1748), CLOTA (1749), **Guàrdia** (1756)
Cartagena	GUÀRDIA (1750), SEGUÍ (1755), **Guàrdia** (1756)
Murcia	*Guàrdia* (1751), **Guàrdia** (1756), **Canals** (1759)
Orihuela	**Guàrdia** (1756)

4. *Andalusia*

Cádiz	**Campins** (1747), CLOTA (1749), *Canals* (1749), **Guàrdia** (1750), **French** (1750), GUÀRDIA (1751), *Guàrdia* (1753), SALA (1755), **Canals** (1755), **French** (1755), **Guàrdia** (1756), **Sala** (1756), **Canals** (1759)
Jerez	FRENCH (1751)
Seville	**Campins** (1747), GUÀRDIA (1748), CLOTA (1749), **Guàrdia** (1750), *French* (1751), GUÀRDIA (1751), GUÀRDIA (1751), *Seguí* (1756), **Guàrdia** (1756)
Málaga	**Campins** (1748), CLOTA (1749), **Guàrdia** (1756), **Canals** (1759)
Córdoba	CLOTA (1750)
Granada	**Guàrdia** (1756)

Key: capitals = naming of sales agent at centre; italic type = problems experienced with receiving fiscal exemptions; bold type = record of sale of calicoes in the centre in the year named.

Sources: 1. AGS, CSH, reg. 213, fo. 98, reg. 248, fos. 178–87 (difficulties experienced by printers in different markets in securing fiscal exemptions to which their privileges entitled them).
2. Notarial references: **Campins**: AHPB, J. B. Fontana, Libro de concordias, 91 (see also Martínez Shaw, 'Los orígenes', p. 264); **Canaleta**: AHPB, Creus Llobateras, 22 Sept. 1753, fo. 48, 4 June 1754, fo. 71, 2 July 1755, fo. 54, 7 Jan. 1756, fo. 3, 12 Feb. 1756, fo. 15; **Clota**: AHPB, Sebastià Prats, 27 July 1749, fos. 262–4, 30 Jan., 26 May 1750, fos. 48, 182; **Canals**: AHPB, Josep Cols, Registro de la fábrica de indianas, fos. 6–8, Josep Cols, 5 Sept. 1753, fo. 169, Duran Quatrecases, 20 Oct. 1754, fo. 179, 19 Feb. 1755, fos. 311–12 (see also Martínez Shaw, 'Los orígenes', p. 260); **Ferra**: AHPB, Creus Llobateras, 10 June 1755, fo. 49; **French**: AHPB, Sebastià Prats, 21 Dec. 1749, fo. 304, 15 July 1751, fos. 241–2, 3 Oct. 1755, fos. 311–12, and 3rd book of agreements, 8 June 1752, fo. 51 (see also Martínez Shaw, 'Los orígenes', p. 261); **Guàrdia**: AHPB, Sebastià Prats, 22 June, 3 July, 4 Sept., 30 Oct., 8 Nov. 1748, fos. 286, 327, 356, 428–9, 435–6, 8 and 30 May, 9 June 1750, fos. 152–3, 188–9, 205, 18 Aug., 9 Oct., 5 Nov. 1751, fos. 283, 376, 399–400 (see also Martínez Shaw, 'Los orígenes', p. 261); **Sala**: AHPB, Creus Llobateras, 9 July 1755, fo. 59; **Seguí**: AHPB, Creus Llobateras, 3 Dec. 1753, fo. 69, 10 June 1755, fo. 48, Sebastià Prats, 1 July 1756, fo. 145.

Table 4.8. *Sums owing to Canals and Canet by their customers in 1759*
(*in* libras)

1. *Outside Catalonia*	31,706– 9– 0
2. *Within Catalonia*	
Barcelona (tailors)	2,446– 7–10
(drapers)	1,276– 7– 4
(misc.)	536–13– 2
Mataró	6,076– 1– 7
Tortosa	82–19– 0
Olot	461– 4– 0
Castelló d'Empúries	97–18– 9
Calaf	186–19– 0
Calella	2,454–18–11
Sant Feliu de Codines	354– 4– 7
Copons	1,884–12– 2
Total within Catalonia	15,858– 6– 4

Source: AHPB, Duran Quatrecases, 1 Sept. 1759, fos. 147–86.

their stock themselves in Barcelona. This gap is clearly a significant one in view of the widespread demand for calicoes in Catalonia which was documented in the last chapter.

Despite these drawbacks, it has been possible to locate a comparatively large number of mentions of different markets from these two sources. These are listed in table 4.7. The table provides, it would seem, a reasonably clear impression of the industry's principal markets during these years – it is unlikely that many significant outlets (outside Catalonia that is) have been omitted. In addition, the existence of the two inventories which were mentioned, for the Canals and Guàrdia manufactures, and particularly full documentation which exists on both the Clota and Campins concerns, partly compensates for the unsystematic nature of the other two sources providing reasonably complete information on the marketing networks of four important companies (including the regional market in the case of the Canals and Guàrdia concerns) which between them probably accounted for over half the industry in 1750. This information has been summarized in tables 4.8–4.10.

Table 4.7 suggests that the most important market for the industry outside Catalonia was Madrid. The assessment of the relative importance of markets has been done by the simple method of adding

Table 4.9. *Towns and villages in the Catalan region with* botiguers *owing money to Jaume Guàrdia in 1756*

1 *botiguer*: Arbeca, Canet, Cervera, Esparreguera, Igualada, Malgrat, Manresa, Olot, Solsona, Torà, Tortosa, Valls 2 *botiguers*: Vic, Vilanova, Balaguer 3 *botiguers*: Lérida

Source: AHPB, Sebastià Prats, 4th book of agreements, 7 Sept. 1756, fos. 211–25.

Table 4.10. *Marketing networks (outside Catalonia) of Guàrdia, Canals, Clota and Campins*

	Guàrdia 1756	Canals 1759	Clota 1750	Campins 1746–8
Granada	15%			
Seville	15%		*	*
Málaga	14%	13%	*	*
Cádiz	9%	23.7%	*	*
Córdoba			*	
Madrid	14%	7%	*	*
Valladolid		4.3%		
Saragossa	2%			*
Barbastro		3.6%		
Cartagena	5%			
Murcia	15%	34%		
Alicante	4%		*	
Orihuela	1%			
Valencia	4%	11.9%	*	*
Játiva	2%			
Majorca		1.9%		*

Sources: as table 4.7.

the number of references which it has been possible to locate to each – Madrid, with a total of eighteen, is that for which most have been found. The importance of demand in the capital was to have been expected: as was pointed out in the previous chapter printed calicoes at this stage were a luxury item, not one of first necessity, and the combination of the presence of the Court, of the largest urban population in the peninsula (150,000 in 1787) and great concentrations of wealth made Madrid the principal centre for luxury consumption in Spain.[65] Apart from to Madrid, however, there are few signs of Catalan calicoes penetrating extensively to interior parts of Spain at this early stage in the development of the industry. Canals's production for Valladolid and Canaleta's for Toledo in the mid-1750s are the two exceptions which appear in the table and in addition Canaleta gave his Valencia agent powers to sell his calicoes in the 'Kingdoms of Castile' as well as in the Valencia area. It is of some interest that the industry's pioneers in, respectively, the original establishment of the printing techniques and the movement into spinning, were also, possibly, leaders in the exploitation of Spanish interior market. Rather than for the internal market, the table demonstrates quite clearly that most of the production of the new industry was directed by sea to ports along Spain's Mediterranean and southern Atlantic coastlines: Majorca, Valencia, Alicante, Cartagena, Málaga and Cádiz, with some incursions inland from these centres – Játiva from Valencia, Orihuela and Murcia from Cartagena or Alicante, Granada from Malaga, Jerez, Seville and Córdoba from Cádiz. Of the individual centres the most important were Cádiz and Valencia (with thirteen and sixteen entries) and of the different geographical areas serviced by the industry during these years the Andalusian appears to have taken the largest share of output (twenty-nine entries against twenty-two for 'local maritime links').

The timing of the first recorded contacts with different centres provides an approximate idea of the stages in the creation of the industry's market network. (As just emphasized, it is the early connection with markets which are most thoroughly recorded by the two principal sources and so the table is possibly at its most reliable in tracing this process.) The Canals manufacture (responsible for all the pre-1747 evidence) produced initially, it can be seen, for the local trade (there are several records of sales to Barcelona drapers which have not been included in the table), for the closest seaborne markets of Majorca and Valencia and for Madrid. During the second half of the decade the industry's sales were extended southwards, with an initial emphasis on the Andalusian area in particular, and with Campins's manufacture of Mataró playing here a pioneering role – sales in Cádiz and Seville from 1747, and Málaga from 1748 – but receiving support from the manufactures of Clota (Cádiz, Málaga,

[65] Herr, *Eighteenth Century Revolution*, p. 87.

Seville and Alicante from 1749) and Guàrdia (Alicante and Seville
from 1748, Cádiz from 1750, Cartagena from 1750 and Murcia from
1751). The Canals manufacture, in this particular respect, would
seem to have followed others rather than setting a lead, the first
record of production for Andalusia being for 1749. As just noted, the
industry appears to have made its first (Madrid apart) contacts with
interior Spain in the mid-1750s.

Table 4.8 suggests that regional Catalan demand was accounting
for about one third of the production of the Canals concern. There is
some danger, however, in using this table for other purposes than
gaining an impression of this firm's penetration of the local market,
for the inventory on which it is based was drawn up for the purpose
of the manufacture's division between its two associates and to facilitate this process there are signs that its liquidity position had been
maximized, outstanding debts having been called in: it probably
only records fragments of its marketing network. Even were it
complete, it is doubtful whether the relationship between regional
and extra-regional sales for the industry as a whole could be assessed
accurately on its basis – some of the originalities in the nature of its
marketing network were implied in the previous paragraph: the
combination of its having been the first manufacture founded, and of
having had at its head Canals, with his background in local draping
activities (unlike the international merchanting activities of the
majority of founders of concerns after 1745), caused it to concentrate
to a greater extent than later foundations on the local trade. The list
can be used, however, to demonstrate further the size of the market
which must have existed for calicoes in the Principality as it shows
that even quite small towns and villages such as Copons (population
of 186 in 1718 and 468 in 1787) and Calella (768 in 1718 and 2,637
in 1787) contained several customers for calicoes (five in the former
case and three in the latter).[66]

Table 4.9 consists in a list of the towns and villages in which there
were cloth-drapers owing money to Jaume Guàrdia at the time of his
death in 1756. Clearly some of these debts would have been for other
types of cloth than calicoes, for Guàrdia had continued his general
cloth-trading after taking up calico-printing, and excluded from the
list are both retail customers and, of course, any client who had not
resorted to credit. Despite these limitations, however, the table
provides an approximation of the local marketing network of an

[66] Vilar, *La Catalogne*, II, pp. 119, 156.

important wholesale participant in the new industry. It can be seen that Guàrdia had commercial relations with at least twenty-one drapers in a total of sixteen different centres. The scale of the business transacted, on the other hand, was not apparently large, the size of the debts recorded ranging from approximately 10 to 300 *libras*, considerably less than those of some of Guàrdia's Barcelona draper clients and also than the value of the calicoes deposited with his agents in the Mediterranean markets for which he produced (see tables 4.7 and 4.10): one of Barcelona's *botiguers*, Anton Darrer i Duró, owed him over 5,000 *libras* and the value of calicoes held by his agents ranged from some 400 libras in Orihuela to some 5,000 in Granada, Seville and Murcia.[67] It seems probable that Guàrdia gave priority in his calico-printing manufacture to production for more distant markets.

The existence of variations in the character of the market networks established by printers who came from distinct professional backgrounds, and who joined the industry at different stages in its development, which has just been hinted at in the discussion on Canals's and Guàrdia's marketing networks, is demonstrated more systematically in table 4.10. In this are listed the markets for which four printers were working at different points in time and, in the two cases for which the sources permit, the calculation of the relative importance of the different markets. In comparing the slightly distinct marketing networks which the table reveals, a first point which stands out is the extensiveness of that which Guàrdia had built up during his some ten years of involvement in the industry before his death in 1756. It was apparently larger than that of the Canals concern which in 1759 was over twice as old. The table thus provides further evidence of the large scale of Guàrdia's investment in the industry as well as illustrating some of the probable advantages which had accrued to him from his prior possession of a large distribution network as a consequence of his previous involvement in the international cloth trade. All four cases show the importance of sales along the Mediterranean and south Atlantic coastline, and especially in the Andalusian market: the latter accounted for 53 per cent of Guàrdia's calico stocks and 36.7 per cent of the sums owed to Canals. Apparent, though, are definite variations in the extent of

---

[67] Prices calculated on the basis of 25 *sols* the *cana* for the 25 pieces on deposit at Orihuela and 375 pieces at the other centres, though such a price would be on the low side, Campins's manufacture in 1748 recording average selling prices of 1.38 *libras* for *indianas comunas* and 2.77 *libras* for *finas* (AHPB, J. B. Fontana, Libro de concordias, 91).

dependence on the latter market – it was weakest for the Canals concern (two out of eight recorded markets situated there), Guàrdia's situation was an intermediary one (four out of twelve selling points were in Andalusia, though, as just noted, they accounted for over 50 per cent of his total stocks) and the dependence was greatest in the case of Clota and Campins, with respectively four and three of the seven markets, for which there are records of their having produced, situated there.

If it has been established that the growth of the industry from 1746 was connected with an expansion in its market network along the Mediterranean and south Atlantic coastline, and that particularly important to it, and especially so for some manufactures, was the development of sales outlets in Andalusia, links with the American trade have not yet been documented. It might, of course, be argued that the sales in Andalusia were indirectly connected with this because it was what contributed to this area's prosperity and made it (clearly) so good a potential market for the industry. Martínez Shaw's argument, however, does not take this form: he infers that a significant proportion of the calicoes sent to Andalusia, and particularly those directed to Cádiz, were intended for reexport to America.

The survival of the accounts of the Campins's manufacture of Mataró makes it possible to check this argument for they contain relatively complete records of sales in the area in which exports are distinguished from the local trade. Table 4.11 contains the complete details for the first one and a quarter years of the manufacture's trading activities. It shows that even in the case of Cádiz, which it might have been thought was purely a staging post for exports to America, nearly as many calicoes had been sold locally as exported. All the calicoes sent to Seville were, clearly, for local consumption. Calculated in percentage terms exports represented 27 per cent of the total sales achieved and 22 per cent of the total quantities of calicoes which had been sent to the area. Some of the local sales in Cádiz could have been to merchants for later export but that this was very often the case is unlikely in view of the relatively small lots in which the calicoes were sold: the biggest individual local transaction was for thirty pieces of ordinary calicoes. Campins himself had handled the sales in Cádiz and his agent, Jaime Sala Millàs, those in Seville. The fact that the latter had sold considerable quantities of calicoes at the local fairs of Ronda and Villamartín demonstrates that it was the

Table 4.11. *Sales of the Campins manufacture in Andalusia, February 1747–June 1748*

	Calicoes received	Destiny of calicoes	
1. Cádiz	199 fine	Sold locally	554
	1,263 ordinary	Exported	555
		Presents	9
		Stocked	11
		Inferior	27
2. Seville	158 fine	Sold at Seville	675
	890 ordinary	Sold at fairs	
		of Ronda and	
		Villamartín	272½
		Stocked	100½

Source: AHPB, J. B. Fontana, Libro de concordias, 91.

regional as well as the urban Andalusian market which was being exploited. That this was the general practice is revealed by the fact that in many cases printers gave specific authority to their sales agents to extend their activities beyond the principal city in which they were situated. Guàrdia, for example, in 1751, authorized Tomàs Prats in Cádiz and Jaume Graner in Seville in separate notarial acts to sell his production 'whether it be within the said city...or outside it'.[68]

The strength of the evidence provided in table 4.11 about the relative importance of the American vis-à-vis the regional Andalusian market in the expansion of the industry is strengthened by the fact that it is taken from the manufacture which, as noted, was the pioneer in the establishment of links with the area and whose founder was the principal agent in the creation of more intense trading links between Catalonia and America during these years (see table 4.5). It emerges that even in this case production for the American market was of only secondary importance. What is more, further details in this manufacture's accounts reveal that the decision to export calicoes to America was a personal one of Campins himself: he was obliged to take full financial responsibility for the operation because, it is recorded, 'neither as interested party, nor associate of that manu-

[68] AHPB, Sebastià Prats, 18 Aug., 5 Nov. 1751, fos. 283, 399–400.

facture, could he export (*navegar*) them (*indianas*) according to the law
and tradition (*estil*) of trade without express and positive consent of
all the other associates, *which is not registered (no consta)*'.[69] The
prospect of selling in the American market was clearly not raised in
the discussions which would have preceded the founding of the
Mataró manufacture. The example of Campins's export of calicoes to
America was without doubt to be an important one but at this stage
his principal contribution to the development of the industry's
markets lay in his promotion of the sale of calicoes in Andalusia. A
detail in his manufacture's accounts provides an insight into one of
the selling techniques which he used to achieve this end: in Cádiz he
had given away as presents nine pieces of fine calicoes 'to different
individuals it was necessary to reward in order to introduce them by
their use'.[70]

Government and the expansion

In the last chapter it was emphasized that governmental encouragement was essential to the progress of the industry from its very
beginnings. It was the protective legislation of 1717 and 1728 which
provided the initial opportunity for import-substitution and it has
been seen that all the early manufactures were founded with the hope
of obtaining privileges from the Crown.

Some signs of a possible wavering in governmental attitudes
towards the industry at the turn of the first decade in its development
were also noted – the refusal of a privilege for Glòria's manufacture
and the preference recorded in the inventory of the archives of the
Junta General de Comercio for inland rather than coastal manufactures. This apparent lack of enthusiasm for the new industry was
paralleled, it was noted, by the failure to give backing during these
years to the attempts of the Junta de Comercio Marítimo y Terrestre,
which had been founded in Barcelona in 1735 to assert its influence.[71]
The policy of import-substitution, or the Catalan manufactures
which had been the only ones to take advantage of this policy, were
apparently out of favour. A yet more emphatic demonstration of this

[69] 'Sentencia Arbitral' of Francesc Oller and others concerning the Mataró company, 27 Sept.
1749, AHPB, J. B. Fontana, Libro de concordias, 90. My emphasis.
[70] The accounts reveal that a further twenty-nine pieces and seven shorter lengths had been
given away for the same purpose ('the indispensable gratification to different individuals,
with the intention that by these using them, their consumption should be established') in
Mataró, Barcelona, Saragossa and Madrid.
[71] Molas Ribalta, 'La Junta de Commerç de Barcelona', pp. 250–4.

is provided by the royal edict of 19 October 1742 which revoked the 1728 protective legislation, permitting again the import of foreign calicoes. This measure gave rise to a strong reaction from the developing industry in Barcelona, Canals and Canet submitting a petition to the Junta General protesting that the permission to import 'will cause the loss of the manufactures of these products which... there are in Barcelona'.[72] This protest would seem to have convinced, for the Junta on 20 December 1743 renewed the ban on the grounds of the damage which imports were doing to the industry, explaining the apparent inconsistency of its fluctuating policy (mysteriously) by the fact that 'then [the previous year?] they [the manufactures] had not attained the perfection and number which they are in today'.[73]

The precise background to these apparent fluctuations in the extent of the government's commitment to fostering development in the Catalan area is not completely clear. González Enciso writes of them being possibly the consequences of 'the pressure of the new liberal ideas which were already starting to filter through' in the administration of industry during these years.[74] If he is correct then it seems probable that José Campillo, who became the Minister of the Departamento de Hacienda in 1741 until his death in 1743, was the principal medium for this infiltration. He was a believer in fiscal reform whose book the *Nuevo sistema económico* was to be of much influence on some of his successors in the administration and particularly on Bernardo Ward who, as will be discussed in a later chapter, was to back policy which was similarly unfavourable to the interests of the industry in the 1750s.[75] Another fiscal measure of his ministry, the extension of the royal eau-de-vie monopoly to Catalonia, was also widely opposed and is another sign of a temporary lack of effectiveness of Catalan pressure groups in the capital.[76]

If the cause of the wavering is uncertain, its consequences for the progress of the industry are not to be doubted. Canals and Canet

[72] AGS, CSH, reg. 213, 7 March 1743, fo. 65.
[73] Carrera Pujal, *Historia política*, IV, p. 137. For the precise dates of the two pieces of legislation, see AGS, SH, leg. 1103. petition of 1760 of Barcelona calico-printers.
[74] González Enciso, *Estado e industria*, p. 241.
[75] M. Artola, 'Campillo y las reformas de Carlos III', *Revista de Indias*, 12 (1952), pp. 685–714. On Campillo's appointment and death, see Jover Zamora, *Historia de España*, XXIX pp. 127–30, 259–62.
[76] Martínez Shaw, *Cataluña*, pp. 213–17. AGS, SH, 22, leg. 1103, for a petition from leading Catalan merchants, including Glòria, Domènec Gispert, Gibert (Alegre's son-in-law), Josep Puiguriguer and Francesc and Joan Puget against dues being charged on eau-de-vie in Cádiz before export to America.

warned of the danger of the loss of the industry. This was doubtless an exaggeration as 30 per cent import dues were still being charged which should have ensured adequate protection, but clearly the removal of the import ban would have been a temporary discouragement to further major investments in the trade. The conditional nature of the local commitment to the industry is apparent from the promise which Canals and Canet made in their request for the renewal of their privilege in 1746 to maintain the 100 looms which they had in action by this date 'under the supposition that the prohibition of foreign printed calicoes in the dominions of his majesty will be maintained'.[77]

If the government's tariff policy was one possible influence on the rate of expansion of the industry (the timing of the expansions in the Canals and Glòria manufactures, as well as that of the founding of the French concern, is certainly consistent with such an interpretation) another, it seems probable, was its approach to granting privileges. The decision of 1739 to grant a privilege solely to Serra and his associates, and the actual terms of this privilege as it was published in 1741, which extended its applicability to any printing manufactures which they founded in Catalonia, must have served temporarily to discourage further involvement in the industry on the grounds that successful applications for privileges must have seemed unlikely in view of the rejection of Glòria's request and the apparent preference of the government for monopolistic production in the area.

The Serra/Canals privilege had, though, a time limit. Sánchez, it seems likely, is correct in emphasizing the significance of this with respect to the timing of the expansion of the industry. The date at which the Serra/Canals privilege ran out must have appeared as potentially a key one both to existing and prospective participants in the industry – the question of the privilege's renewal would force the Junta General to define its policy to the future of the industry and it was clearly possible, in view of the manufacture's success, that privileges would from that point be granted more readily. If one possible cause for Canals and Canet's rapid expansion in the size of their concern from early 1744 was the reassurance which the restoration of the import ban had provided, another, it seems highly likely, was the desire to ensure that the report which would have to be submitted in connection with the question of the renewal of its privilege would be as favourable as possible. In this they were

[77] AHPB, Josep Cols, Registro de la fábrica de indianas, fo. 14.

Table 4.12. *First evidence of manufacturing intentions during 1746*

February	Domingo/Capelino calico-weaving firm set up
April	Guàrdia purchases house and gardens for prospective manufacture
June	Mataró manufacture initiated
(June	Canals and Glòria privilege requests granted)
October	Clota hires colourist for a manufacture
December	Formentí purchases bleaching meadow for eventual use by Pongem's concern

Sources: (those not already provided): AHPB, Olzina Cabanes, 27 Sept. 1747, fo. 587, and 3rd book of marriage contracts, 31 Oct. 1747, fos. 335–40 (ref. to Guàrdia's and Formentí's property acquisitions), Francesc Albía, 16 oct. 1746, fos. 315–16 (Clota).

certainly successful: Francisco de Montero reported to the Junta General that the associates had

increased...the material building adding to it a portion of land and increasing its offices, and that they had 100 looms functioning with their equipment, and workers necessary for their respective manoeuvres, in such a way that under a single roof all the manoeuvres of the manufacture were carried out...which made it appear very colourful (*vistoza*) for the beauty and disposition of the site (*materialidad*) of the building, and its manoeuvres.

The benefits from its growth to the public and especially to 'the large number of people which it is necessary to employ in its respective processes' could not be doubted.[78] The importance of the pendant decision not only for the Canals concern but also for that of Glòria is revealed too by the pressure which they exercised on the Junta General during 1745: three 'linked expedients' were submitted in connection with the granting of new privileges – the two manufactures were clearly collaborating in their efforts to secure a good future for the industry.[79]

With respect to the new entrants to the industry, there is no evidence of requests for privileges until a favourable decision had been made (on 16 June) concerning the Canals and Glòria applications,[80] but that the discussions which must have been going on about the future of the industry (maybe there was positive feedback from the Court at a fairly early stage in the proceedings)

[78] *Ibid.*, fos. 17–20.   [79] AGS, CSH, reg. 248, fo. 178, reg. 213, fo. 80.
[80] The first request for a privilege was from Guàrdia during 1746 (the date is not specified). This was consented to on 20 Nov. 1747 (AGS, CSH, reg. 248, fo. 178, and reg. 213, fo. 87).

may have precipitated the decision to initiate production is suggested
by the fact that no less than five manufactures were initiated – after
so many years in which few had been established (see table 4.12) –
during the year. One of these first steps towards establishing a
manufacture came to nothing – Clota's contract with the colourist
Ferrer was cancelled in July 1747, though his manufacture was
established by this stage[81] – and Pongem's manufacture was not fully
launched until October 1747: these details, though, do not subtract
from the point which is being made here which is that, if the Glòria
and Canals manufactures are included, decisions relating to the
establishment, or the future development, of seven concerns, the bulk
of the industry until the mid-1750s, when a further expansion took
place, were made within the space of eleven months.

The belief that government policy was becoming more favourable
to industry – if it was indeed an influence on the acceleration in the
rate of expansion of the industry which occurred from 1746 – turned
out to have been correct. The favourable response to the Canals and
Glòria privilege requests was not an isolated event. There was a string
of concessions of commercial and manufacturing privileges made
during these years – the Reales Compañias de Comercio y Fábricas
of Extremadura and Aragón were founded during 1746, of Granada
and Seville during 1747 and of Toledo and La Unión during 1748. In
addition, state manufactures were boosted – in 1746 land was bought
for the Real Sitio de San Fernando, which was to be an important
industrial centre, and in 1750 a succursal of the royal cloth
manufacture of Guadalajara was set up at Brihuega.[82] Participants in
the new calico-printing concerns were not slow to take advantage of
the clearly favourable environment for the obtaining of industrial
concessions. Campins actually attended the Court in person on
behalf of his company for this purpose for a total of six months (21
December 1746 – 27 February 1747 and 10 August – 8 December
1747) and was rewarded for his pains both by a privilege (granted on
19 October 1747, a month earlier than Guàrdia's though the latter's
request was made earlier) and the redemption of import dues on a
large number of pieces of fine calicoes which he had imported in the

---

[81] AHPB, Francesc Albìa, act of 12 July 1747, fo. 43. The existence of Clota's concern during
1747 is demonstrated by records of the purchase for it of 15 bales of cotton (ibid., Josep Cols.,
16 Nov. 1747, fo. 231).
[82] La Force, Spanish Textile Industry, p. 54; González Enciso, Estado e industria, p. 239; M. J.
Matilla Quizá, 'Las compañias privilegiadas en la España del Antiguo Régimen', in M.
Artola (ed.), La economía española al final del Antiguo Régimen (4 vols., Madrid, 1982), IV, p. 323.

white from Marseilles.[83] Canals and Canet intervened too obtaining during 1747 an improvement on the terms of the renewed privilege which they had been granted during the previous year – the price controls which had been imposed on their production were lifted – and privileges for other manufactures were granted as follows: Clota, 12 December 1748, Sebastià Canals, 20 February 1749, French, 13 August 1750 and Pongem, 6 August 1751.[84]

The grounds for the renewed priority which was being given to industrial development were various. A change in monarch and a change in advisers was one. José Carvajal, who became Secretary of State and President of the Junta General de Comercio in December 1746, was a Colbertist, strongly favourable to manufacturing interests. As important as the actions of individuals, however, was a growing realization of the political and economic damage which had been occasioned by the eight years of war: there is evidence of a general desire to revive the flagging policy for economic recovery, which had been initiated after Utrecht, as well as to rethink the international alliances which had contributed to the war – links with England were to replace those with France.[85] Manufacturing interests, including Barcelona's calico-printers, stood to benefit from this trend in public opinion.

From 1746 onwards, thus, it is certainly justifiable to regard the influence of the government on the industry as a positive one, contributing to the acceleration in its growth. The commitment to the 1728 import ban had been confirmed, the Canals privilege renewed and between 1746 and 1751 seven new *franquicias* had been granted. In addition, price restrictions had been removed – probably a not inconsiderable advantage, for the prices which had been imposed on the production of the Serra concern in 1741 were between 1 *libra* 2 *sols* and 1 *libra* 7 *sols* 6 *denarios* depending on (a) quality and (b) whether the sales were wholesale or retail, whereas the average price which was being paid for the production of Campins's manufacture in 1747 was 1 *libra* 7 *sols* 7 *denarios* for *indianas*

[83] AHPB, J. B. Fontana, Libro de concordias, 91, and AGS, CSH, reg. 213, fo. 84. The revised version of the Canals privilege is in AHPB, Josep Cols, Registro de la fábrica de indianas, fos. 17–20. The other grants of privilege as follows: AGS, CSH, reg. 213, fos. 87, 92–3, 95, 111, 126.

[84] AHPB, Josep Cols, Registro de la fábrica de indianas, fos. 17–20; AGS, CSH, reg. 248, fos. 180, 181, 182.

[85] Jover Zamora, *Historia de España*, XXIX, pp. 133–5, 641–76; Carrera Pujal, *Economía española*, III, pp. 334–5.

comunas and 2 libras 15 sols 5 denarios for finas – and concessions were being granted more readily with respect to the import of calicoes in the white for printing. Campins's manufacture took advantage of this massively, importing 915 pieces of fine calicoes from France between 1 August 1746 and 11 August 1747 at a cost of just under 15,000 libras, a quarter of the total sum invested in the concern.[86]

Supply restraints

In the last chapter, certain of the technical difficulties which beset the first manufactures with respect to the essential colouring, printing and bleaching techniques, as well as the manner in which they were resolved by the introduction of skilled foreign printers, were described. Mention was also made of the obligation which was placed on these foreign artisans to pass on their skills to Catalan workers and of the efforts which were made to ensure that the diffusion of the expensively acquired technical expertise was restricted.

An important dimension of the history of the industry in its second decade would be missed if no further consideration was given to this side of its development. There can be little doubt that a shortage in the necessary dyeing and printing skills remained a conditioning factor on the rate of its expansion. The secret techniques, whose mastery was necessary for successful calico-printing, represented the most exotic aspect of the trade and a real as well as psychological barrier to its diffusion. The 1746 contract between Clota and the 'painter' Ferrer, to which reference was made in the last section, provides an insight into the mystery, secrecy and only vague technical understanding which surrounded the central colouring techniques at this time, and which is clearly relevant for a full understanding of the circumstances surrounding the expansion of the industry. Ferrer, it was stated in this agreement:

should...communicate to the said Don Francisco de Clota all the secrets that he has and will acquire in future concerning the permanence of colours, should apply this secret, or materials, in order that the dyed cloth leaves the colour intact there where the secret will have been applied, and [should apply] others which he may know, without any reserve, making it clearly understood, by presenting evidence to Sr de Clota, that there remains nothing for him to communicate.[87]

---

[86] AHPB, Josep Cols, Registro de la fábrica de indianas, fos. 1–5, and J. B. Fontana, Libro de concordias, 91.   [87] AHPB, Francesc Albìa, 16 oct. 1746, fos. 315–16.

Proof of the continued existence of a shortage of these skills is provided firstly by the evidence of continued efforts to ensure secrecy in the existing manufactures – there would have been little point in these precautions if the labour market had been satiated with skilled printers – and secondly by the high salaries and favourable conditions offered to printers trained in the techniques – the scarcity of the skills gave rise to high rewards for those who possessed them.

With respect to the former, it is necessary to consider the procedures adopted in two different types of company – those run by capitalist investors who hired the services of skilled printers and those in which one or more of the associates themselves carried out the printing processes. Glòria's concern, it will have been noted, was of the first type, Esteve's and Serra's of the second and the new manufactures of the 1740s, for which evidence exists, divide as follows: Guàrdia, Campins and Clota (as just noted) employed printers (in Guàrdia's privilege the existence in his manufacture of a 'Skilled painter who has communicated his skill to another in order that this precise and essential circumstance should not be lacking' was recorded),[88] and in French's, Pongem's and Sala's manufactures one or more of the associates carried out the printing.

The type of arrangements adopted in the first type of company has already been described for Glòria's concern. Those taught the skills were sworn to secrecy and were denied the right to use them on their own behalf. The death of Serra was to oblige the Canals/Canet company to draw up similar contractual agreements with a printer to those in force in the Glòria concern. Having initially taken on a brother of Canet, Tomàs, formerly a peasant, to take the place of Serra (a choice which reflected what was to be throughout a central concern with respect to these technical secrets – the desire to ensure that knowledge of them was confined to members of the families which possessed them), the associates signed an agreement in 1743 with Josep Canaleta, a silk-weaver, who had probably been working in the manufacture since 1739. In this, Canaleta, in return for Canals's and Canet's commitment 'to get Tomàs Canet to teach him free of charge... the secret to make colours to paint, or to print *indianas*, as well as the manner to make the boilings, soakings, brightenings, masticiations (*bullisatjes, trempatjes, lluminatjes, masticatjes*) and other necessary skills to get the said *indianas* into the state

[88] ACA, Intendencia, Registros de la Superintendencia, 1/26, 24 Feb. 1748, fos. 214–21.

of perfection in which they should be', committed himself to working full time as *fabricant* for the company and to retaining secrecy about the skills which he was to be taught, only passing them on to individuals named by his employers. A penalty of 1,000 *libras* was imposed for *each* failure by Canaleta to respect this last requirement.[89] The associates of the Mataró manufacture similarly were dependent on the services of a skilled printer. One Jacob Lund, a Swede from Stockholm, had been recruited and reached the manufacture via Cádiz during July 1746. The secrecy which surrounded the colouring processes which he carried out for the manufacture is demonstrated by the fact that the room in which he carried out his mixing of mordants and colours was known as 'the room of the secret'. It was not only competitors but the partners themselves who seem to have had difficulty in finding out what went on in this room. This is revealed by details in the manufacture's accounts. Payment of a bounty to Josep Campins, Jaume's brother, is recorded for 'the troubles gone to... in the toleration of the Swede to assure the secret for the company despite his cautious dissimulations' but this payment was not authorized in the final settlement of the company's affairs 'in consideration that the said Don Josep Campins did not succeed in the ascertainment of the secret'.[90]

An example of the second type of company, Pongem's, suggests that the centrality of the secret formulas for printing for successful participation in the industry gave the associate possessing them a position of exceptional power. Formentí, who it will be recalled had initiated his career in the industry with minimal resources, had been granted exceptionally favourable terms within the French concern and had, on the basis of these and the high salary which he had been paid, accumulated enough capital to be a major investor in this manufacture, was to be this company's most influential member – Pongem was to administrate but he was to have responsibility for the entire production process and the taking on of labour. The arrangements with respect to the colouring processes were as follows. Formentí committed himself to teaching the techniques to two 'youngsters' acceptable to the associates 'except the secret of the colours'. This, as in the case of Glòria's company, was to be recorded in a book to be kept in the 'cash box' of the company which was to be locked with two keys, one to be retained by Formentí and the

---

[89] AHPB, Josep Cols, 8 Nov. 1743, fos. 275–6.
[90] AHPB, J. B. Fontana, Libro de concordias, 90 and 91.

other by the 'cashier', Pongem. In the case of Formentí separating from his associates, the book was to be returned to him 'in the same form that it was handed to the company'. It was explained that the purpose of depositing the book in this way was purely 'in case of what could happen on the death of Formentí, and the manufacture consequently being deprived of this secret'. In the event of death, Formentí's son, who was a minor, was to be taught the colouring secrets by the individual whom the associates chose to take his father's place, should he desire such instruction, 'so that if capable and of a good disposition he could take on the job of "fabricant"'.

It is worth emphasizing the differences between these terms and those accorded to dependent printers, as in Canaleta's case. Formentí's property rights over his secrets had been acknowledged in two ways: they were not to be passed on, either to the 'youngsters' whom he was to train or, it seems, to his partners: it is stated that the only grounds for recording and depositing them in the company's 'cash box' was as an insurance in case of his death ('the intention of the said associates is only to hold the said book for what could happen on the death of the said Formentí'); and the inheritance rights of his son with respect to them were to be respected. In contrast to Canaleta's case, there were no restrictions placed on Formentí should he want to leave the company to work on his own or with other associates (both the possibility of his leaving the company in the event of a disagreement with his associates or simply because he wanted to were catered for in the company's terms). Instead, it was the other associates who were bound: 'it is agreed', the 15th clause in the company's terms reads, 'that no innovation of any sort can be made with respect to the permanence of the said Formentí as *fabricant* of the said manufacture'.[91]

The size of the financial rewards which the scarcity of the printing skills occasioned has already emerged from Formentí's case and from the evidence of the high annual salaries which were paid to Huvet and Hartung within the Esteve and Glòria concerns. Other evidence can be added: Formentí's salary within the Pongem concern was to be 360 *libras* and he was also to enjoy free residence in the manufacture; Canaleta's salary was less, 250 *libras*, but, as noted, he did not take up his position in possession of his skills, but was himself to be trained in them, free of charge, before exercising his role;

[91] AHPB, Olzina Cabanes, 3rd book of marriage contracts, 31 Oct. 1747, fos. 335–40.

Ferrer, by his contract with Clota, was to be given a salary of 300 *libras* and a free gift of a 1,000 *libras* capital stake in the manufacture which was to be created.[92] The fullest and most impressive evidence, however, of the potential gains open to the qualified printer comes from the records of the Mataró company: between 27 July 1746 and 13 August 1747 Lund was paid a total 2,172 *libras* 8 *sols* 6 *denarios* in wages – it is not clear whether he had to pay an assistant or assistants out of this sum – and his creature comforts had been well catered for too: among items purchased for his use were silver cutlery, pewter and crystal candlesticks, a chocolate mill, Dutch-style upright chairs, six armchairs, two mirrors, a walnut table, a bed with a gilded head board, pewter plates and, for his northern dietary needs, large barrels of beer were supplied to him at regular intervals.[93]

Predictably, the various attempts to restrict the diffusion of the printing techniques eventually gave rise to legal disputes. The first of which I have found record was between Sala and his associates in the Glòria company. In August 1744, Sala sold his two-sixteenths share in this concern to Joan Corominas (two years later a partner in the Mataró concern) for 2,750 *libras*. He did not inform his associates of this sale and took precautions, it appears, to prevent them discovering about it in the near future: in the sales act signed it was agreed that Sala should attend the annual December meeting of the company at which profits were distributed and business strategy discussed avoiding, thereby, the possibility of suspicion about his changed status within the concern.[94] The grounds for the secrecy would seem to have been as follows. The decision to sell his shares in the company appears to have been linked to a need to raise capital for involvement in another calico-printing manufacture which had been founded in May 1744 by Jaume Brunés and Miquel Formentí, probably with his collaboration.[95] In January 1745, as noted above, this concern was absorbed by a formal company composed of French, Sala, Brunés and Formentí in which Sala invested 8,000 *libras*.[96] Secrecy was necessary as his actions were technically illegal on two scores: firstly, it was a generally observed convention that members of companies were not allowed to sell shares without first obtaining the consent of their partners, and secondly, his involvement in a rival calico-

---

[92] For references, see above nn. 87, 89, 91.
[93] AHPB, J. B. Fontana, Libro de concordias, 91.
[94] AHPB, Duran Quatrecases, 13 Aug. 1744, fos. 323–7.
[95] AHPB, Rojas Albaret, 31 May 1744, fos. 96–7.
[96] AHPB, Severo Pujol, 18 Jan. 1745, fos. 45–6.

printing manufacture was in opposition to the commitment which he had made in 1739 not to use the technical secrets which he had learnt from Hartung for his own purpose as long as the Glòria company existed. On 22 July 1745, at another reunion of the Glòria company, Sala finally informed his partners of the sale of his shares and requested that Joan Corominas be instated as associate in his place. The response of his partners to this request was, understandably, not enthusiastic. Glòria, on their behalf, two days later registered a complaint at the Curia del Corregidor which was notified to Sala by this body's sworn messenger: the associates in the company, the complaint read, were not obliged to accept the sale of Sala's shares, nor Sala's continued membership of the company 'as [Sala] had abdicated from the right which he possessed by the expressed cession and also because information had been received that he was associated in another newly established manufacture of printed calicoes which could be prejudicial to the said company'. Sala responded to this challenge by accepting the right of his associates not to accept Corominas into the company but insisting that thereby the status quo had been returned to – that he himself had become a full associate again. He challenged the right of the associates to debar him from continued membership, offering to 'meet together for the business affairs of the said company for its greater utility and profit'. Such an invitation was unlikely to have been accepted in view of Sala's abuse of his associates' confidencè and some two weeks later Sala's shares were bought out.[97]

This dispute may appear as of only anecdotal significance but it does in fact throw some light on various aspects of the development of the industry at this stage. It illustrates the atmosphere of secrecy and rivalry which surrounded the establishment of the new manufactures. The operation of the restrictions to the spread of the industry which have been described in this section are apparent – subterfuge was enforced to get round them. The apparently limited effectiveness of these restrictions when they were purely legal in nature, however, is clear: Glòria's riposte to Sala amounted to no more than ensuring that the latter should no longer remain a partner in his concern. Once secrets had been passed on, it would seem, little could be done to prevent them being exploited commercially – though this is not, of course, to say that the precautions taken against their initial passing on were not effective: on the contrary, with experience, and Sala's case was an important part of this experience, they appear to have been enforced more carefully.

CONCLUSION

It is now possible to draw the strings together and attempt some overall assessment of the forces behind the expansion of the industry during these years. Before doing so, however, it seems justifiable for consideration to be given briefly to how important a question this is. It is not only that the rate of the expansion of the industry after the many years of hesitant growth was, as has been noted by historians, and it is the principal reason for the issue having attracted attention, particularly rapid – in the space of a few years the industry nearly quadrupled in size. It is also the fact that such extensive involvement of wholesale capital in manufacturing activities was, as we have seen in chapter 2, a relative rarity in Catalonia's industrial development and was to represent the launching of Barcelona's modern manufacturing tradition (which, as noted in chapter 2, had been on the wane since the first half of the seventeenth century). Even if the perspective is a national one, the events appear as of some note – in terms of the debates about the supposed Spanish ineptitude for manufacturing activities, the moment at which the successful establishment of a large-scale industry was achieved is clearly of some importance. That the participants in the achievement were themselves aware that it represented something of a change is suggested by a phrase which they used in a petition directed to the Minister of Hacienda in 1760: in connection with discussion in this concerning the large size of their manufactures they mention that one of the reasons for their having been constructed in this way was to 'oblige the skilled foreign manufacturers to prefer the *then doubtful prospect of the manufactures of Catalonia* to the already operating and secure ones in which they were employed' (referring to the introduction of foreign skilled printers to the early mills).[98]

The documentation, it has been seen, is not sufficiently complete to provide as full an explanation of this novel development as would be desirable; however, the assessment of that which exists has permitted some refinements in traditional interpretations. I shall briefly summarize here the principal conclusions which have been reached

[98] AGS, SH, leg. 1103. My emphasis.

in the different sections of this chapter and attempt to relate them to each other.

Firstly, it has been seen that Pierre Vilar's theory of a crisis in the region's capitalism, caused by the warfare of this period, occasioning an intensification in some traditional investments and a search for new ones, although it was not related by him to the movement into calico-printing, is apparently of some relevance to it. The timing of the expansion in calico-printing is consistent with Vilar's theory; the details of the prior investments of some of the founders of the concerns show that they had been previously involved in trades interrupted by the war; in at least one case the investment in calico-printing seems to have taken the place of that previously made in an interrupted trade with northern Europe; the very size of the investments in the industry appears to signal the temporary existence of surplus capital because of the blocking off of so many investment outlets.

If, though, investment in calico-printing clearly presented itself as an attractive, alternative investment during these years, some of the reasons for this being the case have to be sought on the supply side.

Firstly, from late 1743 the government's commitment to protection was renewed, and secondly, from 1746 the whole tenor of government economic policy, it has been seen, became openly supportive to industrial development. These types of assurance were, it would seem, absolutely essential pre-conditions for the large investments in calico-printing which took place, and the precise timing of the growth in the industry, it has been observed, seems best explained in terms of the slight fluctuations in government industrial policy.

Secondly, it is clear, too that the existence of expertise and equipment in Barcelona were essential enabling factors for the industry's growth. There were two types of requirements. Firstly, there was a need for the basic tools, machinery and production skills and these, by the mid-1740s, would seem to have been generally available in Barcelona as a consequence of the some ten years' prior experience of the industry. In addition, of course, there would have existed within the city a wide range of other industrial crafts of relevance to calico-weaving and calico-printing (silk and wool dyeing and weaving, the metal and carpentry trades for the building of furnaces and provision of looms, vats, cauldrons, calenders, presses and other equipment). Coromina's role in the Mataró manufacture, it was noted, had consisted essentially in acting as an agent for the obtaining of these types of equipment and a variety of other necessary

services in Barcelona and he does not seem to have experienced any
difficulty in exercising it. Secondly, there was a need for access to the
'secrets' whose diffusion, it was noted in the fourth section of the
chapter, had been controlled with such care. The influence of this
factor on the expansion of the industry is complex. On the one hand,
it must have slowed down the diffusion process – difficulties on this
score during the 1730s were noted in the previous chapter and a skills
scarcity has been documented in this – but on the other hand, it
possibly influenced the form which the expansion took by favouring
the chances in the industry of those wholesale capitalists whose
movement into the industry during these years was the principal
cause for its expansion: they were the only social group in the city
whose international economic links meant that they could, if
necessary, import the skills from abroad and their participation in the
industry must have been encouraged, too, by the near monopolistic
producing conditions which the scarcity of these fundamental skills
initially induced.

The attempt to link the pace of growth of the industry with the
expansion of trading with the American market has emerged as a
slight red herring. The reasons why hitherto such prominence has
tended to be given to this supposed connection seem to be as follows:
the fact that the American trade became later, as Vilar emphasized,
so important to the trade; the coincidence observable between the
achievement of the first direct trading links between Catalonia and
America and the founding of the new calico-printing concerns; and
finally the rapidity of the industry's growth, explicable only, it seems
to have been thought, in terms of the development of a completely
new market. All three grounds would seem to be flawed. The first errs
for its anachronism and is all the more at fault in view of recent
studies which have tended to revise downwards the importance of the
American market to the industry's development even at later dates.
In the case of the second the error arises from a concentration on
what was completely new in local investment fashions to the
detriment of what had been going on for some time: more important
than the contemporaneous involvement in the American trade in
explaining the market developments in the new industry, it is clear
from what has been revealed in the second section of this chapter,
were the gradual increases in the range of Barcelona's commercial
network which had been occurring during the previous thirty years
and particularly that along the route to the Atlantic. Guàrdia's rapid

development of so extensive a sales network for his calico-printing concern can only be explained in terms of these. Finally, although the existence of only a finite demand for textile production within Europe has often been emphasized by economic historians, the position of cotton production and calico-printing within Spain at this stage was distinct: it was an import-substituting industry, a large domestic market for which already existed, and so there is no need to look too far for sources of demand. The industry had taken a second, important step during these years in occupying the place in the domestic market which had previously been held by foreign producers, and, as shall be seen in later chapters, there was going to be space for further steps too.

Before, though, rejecting the American argument out of hand, it should be noted that the *illusion* of exploiting this market was clearly high in the list of priorities of two of the founders of calico-printing concerns during these years, Campins and Clota, who in the year prior to their involvement in printing had jointly organized one of the first Catalan shipping ventures to the New World. An example had been set, it has been noted, and Campins, it should be said, with one foot in Andalusia and another in Catalonia, his extensive and prestigious commercial contacts in both centres, his connections with the northern European calico trade (the introduction of Lund), his pioneering role in the development of the Andalusian market, his illusions for the American trade, his awareness of the importance of the political dimension and his assiduity in maximizing his advantages in this respect and the large scale of his investment emerges as very much the representative figure in this second and crucial stage in the industry's growth. That his manufacture failed, and that his career in the 1750s does not appear to have fulfilled the promise of the 1740s, and that Clota's manufacture only outlived his by a few years, are useful indicators of the speculative element which partly explains the speed of the expansion while it does not remove the significance of the investment which had been made. The equipment, buildings, bleaching meadows and skilled workers which had been assembled, and the markets which had been developed, could be made use of by others.

CHAPTER 5

The development of the industry in the 1750s and 1760s: adaptation to the requirements of 'merchant capital'

> Only those...which have at least twelve looms running, their own meadow or a hired one for bleaching, moulds, tables for painting, vat for boiling, calender, burnisher and other necessary tools will be deemed manufactures.
> (First article of regulations adopted by the industry in 1767, cited by Grau and López, 'Empresari i capitalista', p. 25)

The spurt of the mid-1740s in the growth trajectory of the industry gave way to a steadier pace of expansion in the following two decades. As can be seen in table 5.1, the total number of manufactures in Barcelona (Mataró has been excluded from the table) rose steadily to the figure of twenty-nine by 1768. A total of thirty-seven new manufactures were founded. The growth, it is clear, took place in two principal phases, 1753–6 and 1761–8 (ten and twenty-four new manufactures founded respectively – including those listed for 1760–8). There were also twelve manufactures lost during the second phase, it can be seen, showing it to have been characterized by increased instability.

What were the origins of these thirty-seven new participants in calico-printing? We have seen from the last chapter the importance of answering this question for interpreting the sources of the industry's expansion. In addition, as was the case in the 1740s, it was companies, rather than individuals, who founded the majority of concerns: there is evidence for nineteen manufactures being run by companies and five by family associations. A second question, therefore, which will require resolution is the identity of the participants in these companies. Finally, what were the sums invested in the industry? Where the information exists this too will be recorded.

These questions will be dealt with in the first section of the chapter – which will consist, consequently, principally in the presentation of data. In the second section, this data will be used (on the pattern of the previous chapter) as a basis for an assessment of the relative importance of government intervention, supply factors (skills, enterprise, and availability of capital) and the home or export market in the expansion of the industry. A third section will be devoted to a description of the type of industry which had come into existence by the end of this period in terms of the size of manufactures, their distribution in the city, their physical appearance, the use of space within them, their managerial structures, their labour forces, the size of investment made in them, and its division between fixed and circulating capital, their production techniques, their relationships with the guilds and the character of its own guild-type regulations which it adopted in 1767.

THE EXPANSION

Identity of founders

Of the thirty-seven individuals in whose names these manufactures were founded it has been possible to identify the professional origins of twenty-five. Eleven were of merchant status or its equivalent, eight came from the industrial guilds and six from within existing calico-printing concerns. I shall deal with each category in turn.

Of the eleven of merchant status, four came from the same world of wholesalers that had been so prominent in the expansion of the industry during the 1740s. These were Josep Francesc Seguí, whose father, Anton, had been a close collaborator of Campins,[1] the Magarola brothers, one of whom was described as a 'journeyman merchant' (*mancebo de comercio*) in 1755,[2] Alegre i Gibert, the successor to the company of Miquel Alegre, the growth in whose commercial fortune provides the principal data for Vilar's description of Catalan expansion during the first half of the eighteenth century which was summarized in the previous chapter and finally Jaume Canet, son of Bonaventura, co-founder of the Serra/Canals concern, which split into two during the 1750s.[3] Three others were drawn from the elite

---

[1] AHPB, Sebastià Prats, act of 12 Aug. 1747, fo. 252, together with Glòria and Clota (showing the closeness of his links with other founders of calico-printing concerns), he made Campins his agent in connection with a transatlantic venture.

[2] AHPB, Sebastià Prats, act of 12 Dec. 1755, fo. 349: status of *mancebo* shows that they belong to a younger generation of merchants to that of Glòria, Campins, etc.

[3] BC, JC, leg. 5, no. 8, contains documentation concerning Canet's 1764 acceptance on to the *matrículo de comerciantes*.

Table 5.1. The expansion in calico-printing in Barcelona, 1750–February 1768

Year	New manufactures	Manufactures which cease	Running total	Names of new manufactures	Names of manufactures which cease
1750			8		
1753	3		11	Canaleta, Ferrà, Seguí	
1754	3	2	12	S. Salamó, Ayguasanosa, Roca & Serralt?	Clota, S. Canals?
1755	2		14	Magarola, De Las Casas	
1756	2	1	15	Cantarell, Aldrich	De Las Casas
1758	1	1	15	Canet	Roca & Serralt
1759	1		16	Formentí	
1760	1		17	Llorens (Cathalà/Llorens from 1762)	
1761	2		19	Alegre, Capelino?	
1762	1		20	Aymar (J. Ribas from 1767)	
1763	3	1	22	Carrera, Buch & Armengol, Igual?	French?
1764	1	1	22	Llagostera?	Ayguasanosa
1766	2	2	22	F. Ribas, Alabau?	Aldrich, A. Salamó
1767	6	1	27	Illa, Iglesias, Rigalt?, Pallarès?, Pagès?, Crous?	Llagostera?
1768	3	1	29	Sirés?, G. Soler?, Esteve?	Carrera?

1760–8: Anton Riera, Pau Sanaüja, Onofre Arquimbau, Félix Parera, Josep Monblanch, R. Soler start and cease during these years

Notes: 1. Existing manufactures in 1750 were: Canals, Glòria, French, Guàrdia, Clota, S. Canals, Pongem and Sala.
2. In some cases, indicated by ?, only approximate evidence of foundation or departure from industry exists.
3. The following manufactures about which there is inadequate information have been omitted: Domingo, Planxart (from 1740s), Bernat and Francesc Fontanelles (mentioned 1754), Josep Giral (1760), Josep Font (1763).
Sources: New manufactures: Canaleta – Martínez Shaw, 'Los orígenes', p. 250; Ayguasanosa, Formentí, Alegre, Cathalà, Aymar, Carrera, Buch/Armengol, J. Ribas – Grau and López, 'Empresari i capitalista', pp. 28–9, 49–50; Magarola, Aldrich – Molas Ribalta, *Los gremios*, pp. 522, 528; Roca & Serralt – Duran Sanpere, *Barcelona*, II, p. 299; F. Ribas – Vázquez de Prada, 'Un modelo', p. 635; G. Soler, Sirés, Esteve – 'Relación de fábricas de indianas de Barcelona en 1768', in Fernández, 'La burguesía barcelonesa', p. 67; Illa, Iglesias, Pallarès, Rigalt, Pagès,

Crous – complicated, for although their manufactures are not included on the 1768 lists, each is recorded in a document of December 1770 as a *fabricante de si mismo*, in other words, in their own manufactures, at the time of the publication of regulations for the industry in 1768. Later, in 1774, it was recorded that these (and other) manufacturers were practising at the time of the edict by which these regulations were prescribed – 4 October 1767 and so I have attributed (tentatively) the foundation of four of these manufactures to 1767. The more definite attributions of Illa's and Iglesias's concerns to this year are justified by the fact that up to 1766 at least both were working as *fabricants*, the former for Cathalà and the latter for Guàrdia: BC, JC, leg. 53, no. 40, fo. 4, no. 21, fo. 2; Arxiu de la parròquia de Santa Maria del Mar contains a copy of Isidro Cathalà's five-year agreement of 1762 with Illa; Molas Ribalta, *Los gremios*, p. 329, records Iglesias's working for Alegre in 1766; Seguí, Llorens – ACA, Batllia General, Indice del llevador general de concesiones de agua desde el año 1752 hasta 1768, fos. 59, 269, 23 June 1753, 11 Sept. 1769; Capelino, Llagostera: Arxiu de la parròquia de Santa Maria del Mar, Cathalà papers, copies of/references to agreements concerning bleaching meadows, 12 Jan. 1762 and 9 Sept. 1764; Ferrà – AHPB, Josep Cols, act of 7 May 1753, fos. 90–1; Salamó – AHPB, Creus Llobatera, act of 4 March 1753, fo. 30; De Las Casas – ACA, Batllia General, Concesiones de agua, 11 Dec. 1755, fos. 158–9, and Arxiu de la parròquia de Santa Maria del Mar, Cathalà papers, contains a copy of notarial act of Creus Llobateras, of 6 May 1756, in which reference is made to 'fàbrica de Indianas…novament…establert'; Cantarell – BC, JC, leg. 53, no. 1, details of various privileges including his, granted on 18 June 1756; Canet – BC, JC, leg. 5, no. 8, fos. 8–11, copies of notarial acts by which he converted houses to form his manufacture; Igual and Alabau – mentioned in BC, JC, Acuerdos, reg 1, fos. 77, 372; 1760–8 group – BC, JC, leg. 53, no. 4, fo. 2. Manufactures which cease: Ayguasanosa and Salamó – AHCB, Arxiu comercial, B 298, 300; Aldrich – Molas Ribalta, *Los gremios*, p. 528; Clota – sells his bleaching meadow to the Canals/Canet company on 7 March 1754 (AHPB, Josep Cols, 1754, fos. 264–8); S. Canals – not included in 1754 survey of industry (Duran Sanpere, *Barcelona*, II, p. 299); De Las Casas – his bleaching meadow is sold to Joan Torras, associate in Ayguasanosa's concern, on 11 Dec. 1756 (ACA, Batllia General, BB3, Cabreo del corregimiento de Barcelona, 1748–62, act of 15 Nov. 1761, fos. 285–6); French – he pays off his associate Brunés in 1757, having sought renewal of his privilege in the previous year, but this is the last reference which I have for his manufacturing activities. He was not among those recorded as possessing *franquicias* by the Junta de Comercio in 1763 (AHPB, Creus Llobateras, 29 Jan. 1757, fos. 14–16; AGS, CSH, reg. 248, fo. 186; BC, JC, leg. 53, no. 1); Roca & Serralt – his bankruptcy is documented in AGS, CSH, reg. 248, 20 July 1758; Llagostera – included in list drawn up in June 1768 of eight manufactures which had ceased production (BC, JC, leg. 53, no. 4, fo. 2); Carrera – in this year he is recorded as working as *fabricant* for Pongem (BC, JC, leg. 53, no. 40, fo. 4). Cases for which data are insufficient: Fontanelles – Duran Sanpere, *Barcelona*, II, p. 289; Giral – AGS, CSH, reg. 248, fo. 189; Font – BC, JC, leg. 53, no. 1.

retailing guilds of the *drogueros* and *cereros* (dry-salters and wax-chandlers), which were known as *colegios* rather than *gremios*. These were Gaspar Soler, Joan Batista Sirés and Segimon Aldrich.[4] The rest of the group was made up of a tailor/*comerciante*, Bernat de Las Casas, who had been involved in contracting for military cloth in 1743,[5] a *botiguer de drap*, Agustí Salamó, who worked with his brother Sebastiá,[6] a *comerciante* Joseph Buch, who was associated with the silk-weaver Manuel Armengol[7] and an employee of the royal tax service, Josep Igual.[8]

Members of industrial guilds who moved into the industry included Joan Ayguasanosa (a linen-weaver), Mateu Ferrà, Josep Capelino and Francesc Alabau (silk-weavers), Ramon Soler (a silk-braider) and Lluís Cantarell, Josep Aymar and Eudalt Llorens (wool-dyers and a silk-dyer).[9] The six ex-employees of calico-printing concerns were Josep Canaleta, Miquel Formentí, Antoni Carrera, Francesc Ribas, Pau Illa and Olaguer Iglesias. Canaleta and Formentí were encountered in the previous chapter. The former terminated his agreement with Canals and Canet in 1752 to found his own manufacture and the latter took over Pongem's concern in 1759, leaving the latter to found a separate manufacture. About Carrera little is known except that he was a qualified printer when he launched his manufacture with merchant backing in 1763 but Ribas's case is better documented: he served as Canaleta's technical assistant before working on his own behalf, initially making use of the

[4] Molas Ribalta, *Los gremios*, pp. 272–5, 524–8; J. Doncel, 'Els adroguers i sucrers de Barcelona, 1700–1820. Un exemple d'élite gremial', *Primer Congrès d'Història Moderna de Catalunya* (Barcelona, 1984), I, pp. 689–98.
[5] AHPB, Josep Cols, act of 9 Nov. 1743, fo. 276.
[6] AHPB, Creus Llobateras, acts of 4 and 13 May 1750, fos. 50–1, 53, for details of professions. There is some confusion with respect to the Salamó manufacture. My interpretation is as follows. Sebastià Salamó was son-in-law of Sebastià Canals with whose 1747 manufacture he may have been connected. During 1754 there are several references to the manufacture of Agustí Salamó, Sebastià's brother, and also to Sebastià's establishment of a bleaching meadow but none to his possessing a separate manufacture until the 1760s. It seems likely that the two brothers in fact worked in association, Sebastià acting as *fabricant* (he was a qualified printer). The listing of the company in Sebastià's name after 1760 would be explained by Agustí's death – his name disappears from the cadastre between 1759 and 1764. (For his relationship to Canals, see AHPB, Miquel Cabrer, fo. 257, 13 July 1742; for Sebastià's bleaching meadow, see ACA, Batllia General, Concesiones de agua, fo. 159, 11 Dec. 1755; for his qualifications as printer, see BC, JC, leg. 53, no. 40, fo. 4: he is one of four qualified *fabricantes* who on the day of publication of regulations for the industry was *sin exercicio*; for cadastre for 1759 and 1764, see AHCB; other relevant references follow table 5.1 above.)   [7] Molas Ribalta, *Los gremios*, pp. 537.
[8] E. Herrera Oria, *La real fábrica de tejidos de algodón estampados de Avila y la reorganización nacional de esta industria en el siglo XVIII*, (Valladolid, 1922), p. 56.
[9] Molas Ribalta, *Los gremios*, pp. 417, 481, 525, 537.

industrial plant of his employer. Pau Illa's first contact with the industry was as a painter in the Campins manufacture in 1747. In 1762 he became the *fabricant* for, and a small-scale participator in, the Cathalà Llorens manufacture and in 1767 he established his own manufacture. Iglesias was by origin a gardener and possibly related to Francesc Iglesias who had been instructed in the colouring secrets by the cloth-dyer Francesc Aymar in 1756. In 1766 he was *fabricant* for the Alegre manufacture and a year later he founded his own concern together with his son.[10]

Associates in companies

Of the nineteen companies of which there is evidence I have details of the partners, or some of the partners, in fourteen. Starting with those formed by merchants or those of merchant status, I have information on three. The Buch & Armengol association has already been mentioned. There is little information available concerning Josep Buch but there is concerning Manuel Armengol – he was one of the wealthiest members of the silk-weavers' guild with twelve looms in 1753 and he had obtained a royal privilege for the manufacture of silk stockings in 1751.[11] De Las Casas was associated with another tailor for his brief involvement in the industry. No evidence of the foundation of a company has come to light in the case of Jaume Canet but later evidence shows that he was working in close collaboration with the important wholesale company Anglí & Sabater which had strong links in Cádiz and had been involved in the commercialization of the output of the Canals/Canet manufacture. Aldrich's associate was a commercial broker, Ermengol Burgès, and Igual associated himself with Bernat Busquets, a trained calico-printer.[12]

Information on companies formed by the new calico-printers who

---

[10] References as in sources for table 5.1. In addition, on Illa, see AHPB, Creus Llobateras, act of 3 June 1747, Paulus Illa, *pictor*, witnesses an act registered by Jacob Lund; and on Francesc Iglesias, see AHPB, Josep Cols, 27 April 1747, described as 'mancebo fabricante de indianas' in the Canals/Canet concern, and P. Molas Ribalta, 'Los gremios de Barcelona en el siglo XVIII' (4 vols., DPhil thesis, Barcelona, 1968), IV, p. 238 n. 22.

[11] Molas Ribalta, *Los gremios*, p. 493; AGS, CSH, reg. 248, fo. 118.

[12] On Anglí and Sabater, see BC, JC, reg. 5, 1 Dec. 1774: 'the manufacture of Jaume Canet has always been considered and has generally been taken for belonging not only to him but also to Sebastián Anglí y Pablo Sabater'. On their links with the Canals/Canet concern, see AHPB, Duran Quatrecases, 1 Sept. 1759, fo. 162: among debtors for calicoes are 'Josep Sabater living in Cádiz and on his behalf the Srs Anglí y Sabater of this city'. On Aldrich's association, see AHPB, Creus Llobateras, act of 3 March 1758, fos. 24–5; other references as sources for table 5.1.

came from the industrial guilds is more abundant. I shall provide the
details in the chronological order of the companies' foundations as
this will contribute to informing on the process of the industry's
development. Joan Ayguasanosa founded two different companies
during 1754, one in which he allied with two fellow-linen-weavers, an
engraver/colourist who was a former employee of Canals and a
cutler's widow, and the other with a different linen weaver, the
engraver and a stocking-knitter.[13] Lluís Cantarell, wool-dyer, began
printing in 1756 in association with his brother-in-law Ramon Pujol,
son of a tailor and himself a successful merchant. The concern was
later to be known as Pujol/Canterell.[14] Josep Capelino's first
connection with the industry, we have seen, was the establishment of
a calico-weaving manufacture in 1746 for which he was *fabricant*: it is
possible that his involvement was continuous from that date. The first
evidence for his calico-printing, however, is for the year 1761 when he
was working in association with a rich member of the ribbon-makers'
guild, Francesc Tomàs.[15] The silk-dyer Eudalt Llorens's first involvement in the industry was as a junior partner of the Magarola
brothers in 1757. In 1760 he founded his own concern. Whether he
received support from other investors at this stage is not clear but on
his death his widow associated with Isidro Cathalà, a wealthy silk-
weaver, already owner of a large silk-painting manufacture, and four
others – Anton Gispert, *botiguer de teles*, Nicolau Sivilla, another
wealthy silk-weaver, Joan Aran, a *comerciante* and Pau Illa, a calico-
printer – to form a far larger concern.[16] Finally, Josep Aymar, a
wool-dyer: the first evidence of his manufacturing is for 1761. He was
receiving backing from Josep Ribas, a prosperous builder, involved
in a wide range of different commercial spheres. By 1767 the
manufacture was no longer in Aymar's hands – it was running in
Ribas's name and Aymar was working as *fabricant* for the *droguero*
Sirés who had just taken over, or was about to take over, the large
Alegre manufacture.[17]

Again, respecting the chronology of their foundations, companies

[13] AHPB, Duran Quatrecases, 28 July 1754, fos. 108–9, Josep Bosom, 5 Dec. 1754, fos. 225–6.
[14] Molas Ribalta, *Los gremios*, pp. 417, 424.   [15] *Ibid.*, pp. 481, 501.
[16] AGS, CSH, reg. 248, fo. 188; Arxiu de la parròquia de Santa Maria del Mar, Cathalà
papers, contains a copy of the 1762 terms. The possibility that Llorens had been associated
with Aran and Illa before the establishment of the Cathalà company is suggested by the fact
that his widow and the two others are declared by the terms of the contract to be liable for
'debts brought over with the capital contribution to the present company'.
[17] Grau and López, 'Empresari i capitalista', p. 29, and BC, JC, leg. 53, no. 40, fo. 4, list of
fabricants practising in 1768.

formed by calico-printers were as follows. Josep Canaleta was backed by relations principally – his partners were his brother Francesc, who had followed the parental trade of glass-making, his brother-in-law, Miquel Vidiellas, a silk-weaver like himself, and Antoni Grau an inn-keeper.[18] Miquel Formentí, when he took over Pongem's concern in 1759, continued his association with the partners in the original concern, the stocking-knitter Josep Sabater and the cloth-dresser Francesc Just, whose backgrounds were described in the previous chapter. Both had expanded the roles which they had initially exercised purely for the Pongem manufacture: Sabater represented the interests of other printers in Cádiz and Just had developed a large-scale specialization in cotton-trading (he had been encharged with the purchase of cotton by Pongem): his son Magí was to have responsibility for the supplying of some thirty printers with cotton from the 1770s.[19] Antoni Carrera's initial associates in 1763 were Baltasar Bacardit, by profession a tailor who had been involved like de Las Casas in extensive contractual work for making uniforms, a builder and sword-maker.[20] Finally, Francesc Ribas received backing in 1766 from Joaquim Roca Batlle, son of a *botiguer* from Vilafranca, and himself one of the city's most prosperous and reputed wholesale merchants.[21]

Size of the investments

Information on this exists in the contracts for founding or renewing companies which generally ran for five years initially. Table 5.2 includes information from the 1740s, in order to provide as full a picture as possible of investment in the industry during these years. The third column represents first investments in the industry – which is what we are principally interested in at this point. The fourth column provides details of accumulated capital based on inventories made for running concerns. These figures will be referred to in the third section of the chapter.

---

[18] Molas Ribalta, *Los gremios*, p. 522.

[19] See above p. 117, and *ibid.*, p. 523; on Sabater, see AHPB, Duran Quatrecases, 2nd book of statutes and agreements, act of 28 July 1754, fos. 108–9, and manual for 1759, act of 1 Sept., fo. 162; on Just, see Delgado, 'La industria algodonera catalana', p. 114 n. 21.

[20] Molas Ribalta, *Los gremios*, p. 528.

[21] Vázquez de Prada, 'Un modelo', p. 635. In 1772, Ribas had twenty-four looms set up in Roca's house in the Carrer de Mercaders (BC, JC, leg. 53, no. 7).

A distinctive industrialization

Table 5.2. Capital formation, 1739–72 (in libras)

Company	Year	First investment	Accumulated capital
Glòria	1739	8,000	
	1742		12,000
	1743		14,400
	1744		22,000
	1755		48,000
	1756		96,000
French	1745	14,000	
	1749		21,326
	1752		29,692– 5– 2
Campins (Mataró)	1747	58,800	
Pongem	1747	15,000	
Canaleta	1753	16,000	
	1766		46,915
	1770		33,401–14–10
Ayguasanosa	1754	1,420	
	1754*	4,800	
	1760		7,070–13– 8
Guàrdia	1756		115,655–10– 0†
Canals/Canet	1758		156,449– 5– 2
Alegre	1761	9,000	
Aymar	1762	12,000	
(as J. Ribas)	1772		20,425
Cathalà	1762	26,000	
	1768		53,381
Carrera	1763	12,000	
Buch & Armengol	1763	7,000	
	1767		24,000
Ferrà	1764		12,000†
F. Ribas	1766	4,000	
	1768		10,150

* Second company founded by Ayguasanosa in 1754.
† Neither of these two figures include fixed capital.
Sources: Grau and López, 'Empresari i capitalista', pp. 28–9, 38, 48–57. For Glòria, see p. 100, and Fernández, 'La burguesía barcelonesa', p. 74; for French, see AHPB, Severo Pujol, act of 18 Jan. 1745, fos. 323–7, Creus Llobateras, 8 Aug. 1749, fos. 54–7, and Sebastià Prats, 3rd book of contracts and agreements, 9 June 1752, fo. 51; for Mataró, see AHPB, J. B. Fontana, Libro de concordias, 90 and 91; for Cathalà, see Arxiu de la parròquia de Santa Maria del Mar, balances of Cathalà manufacture; for Ribas and Canaleta's 1766 figure, see Sánchez, 'La era de manufactura algodonera en Barcelona', p. 12; for Guàrdia, see AHPB, Sebastià Prats, 4th book of marriage contracts and agreements, 7 Sept. 1756, fos. 211–25; for Canals/Canet, see AHPB, Duran Quatrecases, 1 Sept. 1759, fos. 147–86. The inventories on which Guàrdia's figures for 1756 and French's for 1749 are calculated purely list quantities of stock and do not state prices. Prices from the Canals/Canet inventories have been used to calculate the value of all Guàrdia's stock and all that of French's apart from his cotton and pieces of calicoes which have been calculated on the basis of the prices in French's 1752 inventory.

WHAT WAS BEHIND THE EXPANSION?

Government

It was established in the last chapter that government measures were important influences on the expansion of the industry. There was no direct state investment – historians have correctly pointed out the contrast beween royal policy towards the wool industry in Castile in this respect and that towards cotton in Catalonia – but the character of tariff policy and the readiness to grant *franquicias* were, it has been seen, important influences on the timing of investment in the industry.

The extent of the expansion achieved in the industry during the years with which we are now concerned attests again to the relatively favourable conditions which government tariff policy had created for the industry. In addition two new measures had specific consequences.

The first of these was a decree of 24 June 1752 making the fiscal privileges which royal manufactures possessed generally available to other existing or newly founded manufactures. Entrepreneurs had still to apply to the Junta General de Comercio in order to benefit from this measure but this was much simpler than obtaining individual privileges. The founding of new manufactures, as well as the continuation of old ones (the legislation represented an alternative, too, to renewing existing privileges), were thus significantly facilitated. The measure also represented further, reassuring evidence of the royal commitment to import-substitution. It thus seems probable that the concentration of calico company foundations noted for the period 1753–6 was contributed to by this measure. It was not, it should be stressed again, a case of government being directly responsible for the foundation of manufactures but of a government measure having possibly represented an influence on the timing of the decision to start production. Canaleta, Salamó, Ferrà, Seguí, Canals, Peramás and Sala all made use of the edict (in the case of Canals to renew his previlege and in those of Peramás and Sala to gain privileges for existing concerns).[22]

The second innovation has received more comment. The accession of Charles III in 1759 brought with it a movement in the direction of

---

[22] González Enciso, *Estado e industria*, p. 243; AGS, CSH, reg. 248, fos. 184–6.

economic liberalism and on 15 May 1760 the prohibition on the import of cotton goods was changed for import duties of 20 per cent for a period of ten years. There is no question that for a while the Catalan industry was out of favour with the government. The large size of its manufactures, and the fact that many of them had received royal privileges, seems to have caused them to have been seen in the same sort of terms as state manufactures, which were also out of favour. Barcelona's newly founded Junta Particular de Comercio (in 1760) recorded the types of criticisms which had been made by Ministers: that the calico-printing manufactures were only of service to their owners, that what success they had achieved was owed purely to their privileges, that their prices had not come down, that they did not contribute to exports and that their owners were moved by gross egoism – 'they want all for themselves and nothing for the needs of the Crown', it had been complained. In place of prohibition it was felt that the admission of cotton goods with payment of duty would boost customs income and also make available a wider choice for the consumer – the king's subjects would have thereby 'cloth of better quality, greater beauty and more beautiful designs and colours'.

In fact the 1760 measure was repealed before the end of the anticipated ten-year trial – printed calicoes were prohibited again from 8 July 1768 and this ban was extended to cotton cloth in the white during 1769 – but for several years the industry was slightly less fully protected than previously.[23] As can be seen from table 5.1, there was no collapse. The change in the tariff situation had selective effects. It hit the cotton manufacturing processes most. The printing sector could in fact benefit from the freedom which the measure conferred to import cloth in the white. The larger companies could thus adjust to the situation by reducing their weaving activities while expanding their printing ones, but the sector of the industry whose principal activity was weaving, and also another which was purely producing varieties of cotton cloth for sale in the white, were seriously affected. Bankruptcies among calico-printing concerns were confined principally to the first of these vulnerable categories and the second was totally eliminated: in 1760 there were said to be 100 looms, employing 100 men and 500 women, working in it but by June 1768

---

[23] Carrera Pujal, *Historia política*, IV, pp. 142–3, 147–8, and a more recent summary of legislation in Izard, *Industrialización*, pp. 16–22; BC, JC, reg. 82, letter of Junta of 21 Nov. 1761, for summary of government criticisms of the industry.

the majority of these had gone out of production.[24] The initial reversion in 1768 to prohibiting the import of printed calicoes only, and not cloth in the white, aggravated the situation further. This was complained about by the principal calico-printers who warned that such a tariff structure would cause the industry to concentrate purely on the printing processes.[25]

The effects of the switches in tariff policy during the 1760s were not, therefore, uniform. Smaller, artisanal weaving firms had been worst hit but at the same time the freedom to import calicoes in the white was probably the cause for an expansion in the number of firms confining their activities to the printing processes – table 5.1 shows the rapidity in the expansion of concerns in 1767 and early 1768 and most of them were of this type. Larger manufactures, though they had survived the difficulties better than small, were threatened by this latter development because of their commitment to manufacturing activities, and the scale of their production. Their structures were in conformity with a total import prohibition of printed calicoes and cloth in the white – this explains their opposition to the continued permission to import cloth in the white after 1768. The vulnerability to alterations in tariff policy, to which the industry's protected status exposed it, had again been demonstrated.

Skills and capital

It is a long and important period in the industry's history that is being summarized. It presents some contrasts with the 1740s. It is not uniform itself – the 1750s were different from the 1760s.

During the 1750s 'wholesale capital', our data show, ceased to be the principal source of new calico-printing concerns. There were further investments from this source, we have seen, but they were not on the same scale as in the previous decade. It might be said that the wholesalers had given an impulse to the industry from which smaller fish could now benefit. The principal sources for new concerns were on the one hand the artisanal guilds with skills which could be used in the new industry – linen- and silk-weavers and dyers (Ayguasanosa, Ferrà, Cantarell, Llorens) and on the other the industry itself (Canaleta, Canet and Formentí). This was one novelty of the

---

[24] BC, JC, leg. 53, no. 4, has information on the crisis. On employment in the production of cotton cloth in the white in 1760, see AGS, SH, leg. 1103, letter of 1760 from calico-printers complaining about measure of 15 May 1760 removing protection.

[25] BC, JC, leg. 53, no. 4, fos. 2–6, petition of *fabricants* of *indianas* of 14 Sept. 1768.

decade: the new industry had itself become a means of capital accumulation and social mobility and the source of new concerns. This latter development was sustained during the 1760s – firms of Ribas and Iglesias. There are, too, further entrants from relevant industrial guilds – Alabau, Aymar. But our data also reveal a widening in the sources of investment in the industry. It was a widening in four principal directions. Firstly, there was a growth in the participation of trades with close commercial relationships to the industry – that of the dry-salters and wax-chandlers, who were the source for the industry's drugs and dyestuffs being the principal example (tailors had invested in the industry in both decades). Secondly, leading members of the silk industry became involved in the industry – Català, Armengol and Tomàs. A distinction has to be made here with respect to this development and the involvement of silk-weavers in the industry in the 1740s – this was a case not of individuals with work skills relevant to printing transferring to the new industry but of a transfer of capital from one industry to the other. Català's example demonstrates this – rather than he himself working in the industry his company employed its two junior associates to act as *fabricant de teixits* and *fabricant de pintar*; Català's role was limited to acting as administrator. Thirdly, there is the appearance in this period of what might be termed 'rentier'-type investments in the industry. By this is meant investment by individuals who simply wanted a certain return on their capital – for whom there were no familial, professional or commercial motives for their participation. The foundations which fall into this category are those of Carrera, with its builder and sword-maker among its associates (Carrera's share in the capital of the concern was minimal), and of the builder Josep Ribas, which took the place of that of Aymar. In addition, Roca's investment in Ribas's concern was a passive one and there is evidence of the existence of a market for the shares in Glòria's concern during these years. The development was a sign of the extent to which the calico-printing industry had become an established one – investment in it was beginning to be as normal as that in ship-building projects and in drapers' shops or the farming of taxes or seigneurial dues. The principal enabling fact for this development clearly was the growth in the availability of trained managers and a labour force. Finally, as has already been mentioned, these years witnessed the emergence of mini-manufactures, run by ex-members of the labour forces of the large concerns.

The information concerning companies reinforces this view of the variety of different types of enterprise moving into the industry during these years. There was a corresponding variety in the types of company founded. There were several family associations, it has been noted, for which no formal company foundation was necessary. In addition, some of the formal companies were formed effectively from members of the extended family – Canaleta's, Formentí's, Cantarell's being the principal examples. There were then companies whose main purpose was to pool manual skills – that of Ayguasanosa is an example of this – and others formed to pool managerial ones – Cathalá's, Formentí's and Canet's are the principal examples of these (and there were other examples, it will be recalled, in the previous chapters). In Català's company, in addition to Català's responsibility for administration and sales, and that of Aran and Illa for the principal production processes, Sivilla shared with Català that for the buying of raw materials and was encharged with collecting cloth from the weavers and paying the labour force. Finally, what I have characterized as the 'rentier company' tended to take the form of a group of passive investors either associated with, or employing, a *fabricant* with responsibility for all the managerial and production roles.

With respect to the size of initial investments as recorded in table 5.2, it is clear that during the 1750s and 1760s there were none to compare with those of Mataró and the other very large concerns founded during the 1740s. Another contribution of the pioneers in the industry would have been to create externalities from which later participants could benefit. What emerges from the table is that there was a relatively standard amount required for an initial investment in a large-scale printing concern of between 8,000 and 16,000 *libras*. This did not represent a particularly large investment. As Ramon Grau and Marina López write in their outstanding study on the industry: 'Compared with investments in other types of contemporary businesses – even in draping shops – the capital of a manufacture is small.'[26]

[26] Grau and López, 'Empresari i capitalista', p. 27.

Markets

The analysis of the market network of the industry which was done in the previous chapter extended into the mid-1750s and much of what was concluded there has relevance for this period too. Calico-printing, it was noted, was an import-substituting industry. There is no need to discover some new source of demand. It was stepping into previously occupied shoes. There are questions which need settling, however. These are firstly, the importance of the American market – this question has no more been resolved for these years, and those leading up to the end of the American War of Independence, than it has been for the 1740s – and secondly, the extent of the penetration of the peninsular market achieved by the industry – up to the early 1750s, it has been noted, contact had apparently been limited principally to the coastal areas, Andalusia and Madrid.

With the foundation of the Real Compañia de Comercio de Barcelona a Indias in 1755, the possibility of exploiting the American market clearly increased. The evidence concerning the extent to which this possibility was taken advantage of is not, however, conclusive. On the one hand, a visitor to the city in 1765 reported that he had been told that an average of 40,000 pieces of printed calicoes, for a value of 400,000 *pesos* or some 560,000 *libras* – this would probably represent over half the city's production – were exported, and that two-thirds of Canaleta's production of 6,000 pieces was being sold to the Caracas company for American export.[27] On the other hand, Josep Maria Oliva's study on the Barcelona company between 1756 and 1785 shows only minimal textile exports – of the company's total exports only some 4.4 per cent consisted in textiles *of any sort* (not purely calicoes) whereas exports of agricultural products (wine, eau-de-vie and flour) were massive (22.5 per cent, 29.78 per cent and 29.26 per cent respectively of the total exports).[28] Another recent study, on the commercial company of Ermengol Gener, which specialized in the American trade, gives a similar picture – it shows an overwhelming predominance of agricultural products among exports, eau-de-vie providing 77.6 per cent of total exports to Cádiz, whereas sales of printed calicoes, printed linens and

---

[27] J. Albareda and S. Sancho, 'Catalunya el 1765: un informe econòmic i polític', *Segon Congrès d'Història Moderna de Catalunya, Pedrables, Revista d'Història Moderna*, 8, i (1988), pp. 293–4.

[28] J. M. Oliva, *Cataluña y el comercio privilegiado con América* (Barcelona, 1987), pp. 267–79.

cotton goods only amounted to 4.26 per cent of the total.[29] If the export of printed calicoes to America had been on a big scale it would have been thought that this would have shown up in the accounts of one or the other of these commercial organizations over so long a period.

Recent research has thrown light on the question of the deepening of the interior market during these years. Jaume Torras, in a study on the sales network of Torelló, a woollen cloth-maker of Igualada, has shown that his markets developed as follows: 1761–5: sales divided between the local market (Aragon/Catalonia) and Madrid (60.3 per cent and 39.7 per cent respectively); 1766–70: reversal of previous balance (local now 22 per cent and Madrid 77.5 per cent); 1776–80, development of a third important sales area in Castile (Catalonia/ Aragon, 27 per cent Madrid, 39.3 per cent, Castile, 32.3 per cent). The pattern is similar, it will be recalled, to that observed some twenty-five years previously in the cotton industry – initial concentration on the local market and that of Madrid and then a shift to remoter sectors of the national market (though the calico-printers concentrated initially on the Mediterranean coastal and Andalusian markets before selling in Castile). Torras argues that his example suggests that 'the Spanish markets had a greater importance earlier than is generally supposed for the growth of the cloth industry'.[30] A second study, this time on the Terrassa clothiers Anton and Joaquim Sagrera, shows a similar predominance of national markets for the years 1792–1807 – two-thirds of its sales were in Catalonia, 30 per cent in Aragon and 5 per cent in Castile.[31]

The only study which exists on the sales networks of the calico industry during these years – one on the company of Francesc Ribas between 1766 and 1768 and 1774 and 1783 – conforms with these two studies on the wool industry. Its results are summarized in table 5.3. The product of this company, it is evident, was directed almost exclusively to the domestic market and above all to Castile.

There are dangers, clearly, in drawing conclusions from such incomplete data. In particular the examples of single companies

[29] M. Andreu, 'Catalunya i els mercats espanyols al segle XVIII. La casa Ermengol Gener', *Primer Congrès d'Història Moderna de Catalunya* (Barcelona, 1984), I, pp. 533–44.
[30] J. Torras, 'Mercados españoles y auge textil en Cataluña en el siglo XVIII. Un ejemplo', in *Haciendo historia: Homenaje al Profesor Carlos Seco* (Madrid, 1989), pp. 213–18.
[31] J. M. Benaul, 'La comercialització dels teixits de llana en la cruïlla del XVIII i XIX. L'exemple de la fàbrica de Terrassa Anton i Joaquim Sagrera, 1792–1807', *Arrahona, Revista d'Història*, 2 (1988), p. 38.

Table 5.3. *Sales of F. Ribas & Cia, 1766–8 and 1774–83*

Castile	53.27%
Andalusia	5.80%
Valencia	5.34%
Murcia	2.38%
Basque country	0.50%
Aragon	0.69%
Galicia	0.69%
Extremadura	0.29%
Majorca	0.15%
Catalonia	24.06%
Export	0.69%
Uncertain	6.22%

Source: Muset, 'La conquesta del mercat peninsular', p. 396.

cannot automatically be taken as representative of the industry as a whole – the individuality of different concerns and their marketing networks was demonstrated in the previous chapter and has been emphasized by other historians.[32] However, the combination of the evidence of the predominance of the domestic market provided by these three case studies with the lack of signs of significant textile sales in America in either the accounts of the Royal Company or those of Ermengol Gener suggest that the progress of the industry in this period continued to be based principally on the domestic market.

It seems probable (though clearly more research needs to be carried out into this question) firstly that the information passed on to the visitor to the city in 1765 concerning the extent of sales achieved in the American market at this stage was exaggerated (possibly 'exports' to Andalusia were being taken for exports to America), and secondly that whatever sales were being achieved in the American market at this stage – the evidence concerning Canaleta seems solid enough – represented a cyclical peak. There is a variety of evidence for this latter argument. There was a shortage of printed textiles and other types of cotton goods on international markets during these years because of the Seven Years War, which gave rise to an expansion in the exports of the English industry, and it is possible that Barcelona's industry benefited from this.[33] In addition, the permission which had existed since 1760 to import

[32] Especially by Torras, 'The Old and the New: Marketing Networks and Textile Growth', pp. 93–113.   [33] Wadsworth and Mann, *The Cotton Trade*, pp. 157–60.

calicoes in the white for printing, damaging though it may have been to the industry's position in the domestic market, would have permitted the growth in the export trade in *pintados* (the name given for prints on imported white linens). Finally, in October 1765 a royal edict was passed liberalizing the American trade by conferring on nine Spanish ports, including Barcelona, the right to trade directly with the West Indies.[34] A short-term increase in American exports could have followed from this. Certainly there are signs of a strong interest in the American trade in Barcelona during these years – it was in 1765 that plans for introducing supplies of American cotton for spinning to Catalonia were first mooted and in 1768 Canaleta requested the use of two ships from the Junta General de Comercio to facilitate the development of this trade (demonstrating, thereby, though, the primitive state of the trade at this stage). The movement into cotton-spinning to which these imports of American cotton gave rise will be described in chapter 7. It was to come to an end in approximately 1775 and it seems likely, too, that the extent of importance of the American market for the industry had declined by then only to revive with the further liberalization of the American trade brought about by the 'Regulation of Free Trade' of 1778.[35]

The expansion of the industry during this period would appear thus to have owed most to the national market. What was occurring, it is clear, was an extension of that process of import-substitution which was detected as being behind the expansion of the industry during the 1740s, in particular an extension beyond the primarily peripheral zones on which the industry had concentrated in the 1740s, into the Spanish interior and, above all, the records of Ribas's concern suggest, into Castile.

In this expansion of its sales in the domestic market there are signs that the leading printers in the industry attempted to gain acceptance of their wares in the Court in view of its importance both as a consumption centre and as an influencer on fashions. An extract from

[34] On the liberalization of the American trade, see J. Fisher, *Commercial Relations between Spain and Spanish America in the Era of Free Trade, 1778–1796* (Liverpool, 1985), pp. 9–19.
[35] The post-1778 American trade was to consist above all in the export of *pintados*. The imported linens were of a higher quality, and gave better results when printed, than the domestically produced calicoes. The possibility of exporting them thus enabled the Catalan printers both to increase their output rapidly (as was necessary in a speculative international trade) and possibly to compete more effectively in the less well-protected American market. On cotton-spinning and the later developments in the American trade, see below pp. 211–12, 236–48. On Canaleta's shipping requests and the importing of American cotton, see Carrera Pujal, *Historia política*, IV, pp. 146–8.

the correspondence of the Barcelona Junta de Comercio provides an insight into some of the commercial methods used in this process: writing to their representative in Madrid in 1766, they recorded their pleasure that 'the exquisite piece from the manufacture of Isidro Cathalà and printed handkerchieves from that of Ribas... should have enjoyed the approval of such senior individuals, even the Prince and Princess of Asturias having seen them and most recently the King Our Lord' and informed him that they were writing to all the printers in the industry advising them to produce 'some special printed cloth' in order to promote their sales.[36]

The technical capacity of the industry was gradually improving – this is something about which we shall go into greater depth in the final section of this chapter – and this enabled it to provide alternatives for higher quality imports. This is revealed by a report of Joan Pau Canals, son of Esteve, on the development of copper-plate printing by Capelino and Tomàs in 1770. He mentions that the cloth produced by the technique, and the design chosen (chinoiseries), represented a successful imitation of 'those from England, which I saw in the Court in 1768 particularly in the room destined for the most excellent Duke of Alba in the Royal Palace of Aranjuez'.[37] The institutional as well as the elite market was being tapped – Igual's manufacture had won the contract for the provision of flags for the Spanish navy and had had the honour of one of its samples being presented to the king.[38]

DESCRIPTION OF THE INDUSTRY IN 1767–8

The manufactures: distribution in the city, exteriors, interiors

The industry was dominated by large manufactures. Calculations for 1754 show average labour forces of 114.[39] These substantial establishments were concentrated above all in the north-west corner of the city, close to where Esteve and Canals founded the first concerns. Of the twenty-seven of the twenty-nine concerns documented in table

---

[36] BC, JC, reg. 83, letter of 6 Dec. 1766.
[37] BC, JC, leg. 53, no. 10, fos. 5–6, report of 15 Dec. 1770.
[38] E. Herrera Oria, 'Ideas de Ramón Igual sobre la organización en España de la industria de tejidos', *Revista Historica: Investigaciones, Bibliografia, Metodologia y Enseñanza* (Valladolid) (1924), p. 51.
[39] These figures are calculations on the basis of numbers of looms (see p. 96n on this). Looms for 1754: Duran Sanpere, *Barcelona*, II, p. 299.

5.1 whose location it has been possible to identify, ten were in a circle of streets surrounding the Portal Nou – the Carrers de Cortines and Rech Condal, the Bassas de San Pere and Plaças de Marquilles and San Pere – none of them more than 150 metres from the Canals concern – and a further six were in streets linked to this circle – San Pere Més Alt, San Pere Més Baix, Carders and Llàstics. Apart from this concentration, the eastern half of the city contained two other concerns – in the Carrer de Jonqueres, neighbouring Carrer San Pere Més Alt, and in the Carrer Merced (an unusual situation in the commercial quarter of the city – this was Glòria's concern). The eastern half of the city thus dominated over the west (the Raval) – eighteen out of twenty-seven concerns. In the latter there were two concentrations, one in its southern corner (four manufactures in the Carrer de Trentaclaus and two others between the Ramblas and the Carrer de Santa Monica) and a more scattered one in its northern half – in the Carrers de Tallers (the Magarola concern), Cera and Botella (see map on p. 168).[40]

The reasons for the concentration of the industry in this way are clear. The area around the Portal Nou had been the heart of the city's great medieval cloth industry: where the Carrer del Portal Nou crossed with the stream the Rech Condal was situated the 'consolat del pont de Campderà' from which the wool industry was administered, and adjacent to this was the Carrer de Tiradors which gave on to a 'hort de Tiradors' – which had served for stretching the completed pieces of woollen cloth to the correct sizes; the Plaça de San Pere had been the centre for the dyeing processes.[41] The industry still existed but as a shadow of its former self. Labour with textile skills was thus available in the area; property prices in it were low; there were buildings existing which were already designed for industrial uses; by the standards of the densely populated city there was good availability of open spaces (Bassas de San Pere, Plaças de Marquilles and San Pere, the area around the gate of the Portal Nou); and, of course, the area had easy access to the zone outside the walls where the first bleaching meadows were set up. The Carrer de San Pere Mes Alt (three manufactures) had the advantage that the houses on one side of it had substantial gardens backing onto the city walls which could be converted for industrial use. It was space, too, which represented a principal attraction of the Raval. The area was lightly

---

[40] BC, JC, leg. 53, no. 40, fos. 4–11. The two unidentified streets are Natzaret and Corralet.
[41] Molas Ribalta, *Los gremios*, p. 373.

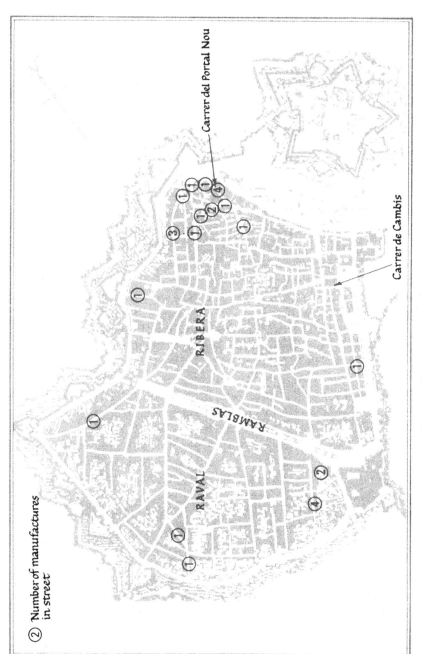

Carrer del Portal Nou

Carrer de Cambis

RIBERA

RAMBLAS

RAVAL

② Number of manufactures
in street

Map 3   The industry in 1768

populated and used at this stage principally for market gardens and institutional buildings (convents, hospitals, etc.). It was possible in this area to create the only manufactures with bleaching fields adjoining – those of Alegre and Guàrdia. Apart from these cases, bleaching meadows were concentrated principally in the village of Sant Martí de Provençals – fifteen out of twenty-two listed in 1768 – or slightly further east, on the river Besòs.

As will have been suggested by what has just been written about the distribution of calico-printing in the city, and as has already emerged from the description of the expansion of the Canals concern in chapters 3 and 4, the majority of the manufactures were created on the basis of a gradual accretion of buildings which were then consolidated into a single unit and converted to serve the requirements of calico-printing. Madalena Canet, after the splitting up of the Canals/Canet concern, purchased six different properties in the Carrer del Portal Nou which were then 'united and aggregated and a single house made from them with three doorways outside opening onto the said street of Portal Nou'. The cost of the conversion was 4,869 *libras* purely in builders' costs and the carpenters used a total of 42,984 nails.[42] Canaleta, on the other hand, building his concern on the north side of the Carrer de San Pere Mes Alt, was able to expand into the garden. He used the space to create an enormous building, described as 'quadras' in the notarial contract, some $32\frac{1}{2}$ by $7\frac{3}{4}$ metres: less adaptation of old buildings was required – only 9,731 nails used – but a great deal of earth shifting: 'a lot of earth has been moved', it was noted in the builder's accounts.[43] It was in the Raval that there was both the greatest possibility and the need (there was a lack of pre-existing buildings) for custom-built manufactures – Guàrdia's was one such: his royal privilege of 1748 describes what he had built: 'a house capable of containing more than 100 looms' with 'corresponding rooms for the Director of the manufacture, the painter and the head of the weavers, and the other offices and terraces necessary'. The bleaching meadow (about 1,000 square metres in size) was established next to the manufacture and its water supplies linked to the manufacture's to form a complex hydraulic system which is described in the privilege: two large tanks had been created 'into which the crystalline water to clean and bleach the pieces and woven cloth runs, and two large water wheels which communicate

[42] BC, JC, leg. 5, no. 8.   [43] AHPB, Josep Cols, 19 Aug. 1753, fos. 160–2.

Table 5.4. *Different rooms, spaces in the Canals manufacture in 1756*

Description of room/space	Its Purpose
Main manufacture between Carrer del Portal Nou and Cortines	
1. Warehouse	Storage of cotton
2. Room with furnace	For gluing warps
3. Patio	Containing well, space for folding cloth, storage space for old iron and space for mixing iron acetate for mordant, benches for relaxation
4. *Pintadors*	Engraving moulds, tables and equipment for burnishing calicoes before printing, sixteen printing tables
5. Room *de la gala*	For applying mordants
6. Room *de la pintura*	Eight copper vats for dyeing
7. Room *de la drogas*	Weighing scales, mortars, etc.: for mixing dyes and mordants
8. Room for calendering	Containing one large calender
9. Printing room	Containing four tables for painting
10. Carpentry room	Containing range of carpenter's equipment
11. *Los talers*	Containing 100 looms
12. Room of cotton-warpers and twisters	Containing four warping machines and seventy-six winding machines
13. Rooms of Marià Ferrusola	Living space for one of *fabricants*, containing collections of calico samples, and designs. 'Noble' rooms of the manufacture with five balconies facing onto the street
14. Rooms of *la obra nova*	Living space for two other *fabricants*, Pujol and Camarasa – the latter's with four balconies
15. Rooms of Francesc Soler	Living space; contains also equipment for measuring and packing calicoes and timber supplies for making printing moulds
Bleaching fields, Sant Martí de Provençals	
1. Total of *c.* 4,450 square metres of land	Bleaching area
2. Large gateway with rooms each side	Warehouse and workers' dormitory
3. Second building	Boiling operations
(a) Room of the pieces	For storing and measuring cloth
(b) Dyeing room	Containing two large vats
(c) Painting room	Containing two medium-sized vats, two shelves with printing moulds, six tables for beating cloth, range of equipment for use in the bleaching processes and for irrigation
(d) Small sitting room	Containing domestic furniture
4. Third house on second bleaching meadow	Containing tables for beating cloth and further equipment for servicing bleaching meadows
Canals's house in Carrer de Cambis	
1. Hall area	Containing wooden press for making up bales of calicoes

the water to all the sections of the manufacture and across the bleaching meadow'.[44] Campins's manufacture of Mataró likewise was custom-built at very great expense.[45]

The fullest idea of the use of space within a calico-printing concern is provided by the inventory which was drawn up for the Canals–Canet manufacture on Canals's death in 1756.[46] Above the manufacture's principal entry, as well as that of the warehouse in Canals's house where the manufacture's finished product was stored and the gateway to the manufacture's bleaching meadows in Sant Martí de Provençals, the royal arms, painted with oil paint on tin, had been placed. The interior details are set out in table 5.4.

Canals's was at this stage the largest manufacture in the industry and so his example should not be taken as representative from the point of view of the scale of production which it reveals but the actual character of the division of labour which it shows was representative. It is clear that the production process involved considering toing and froing between the manufacture and the bleaching meadows. Sizing, warping and weaving took place in the manufacture; boiling, bleaching and beating the cloth followed in Sant Martí de Provençals; burnishing, polishing, printing and some of the dyeing processes then took place in the manufacture; the cloth was returned to the bleaching fields for dyeing in madder, the final bleaching processes and the addition of extra colours (known as *sobrecolores*); it came back for a last time to the manufacture for calendering and packing before being delivered to Canals's warehouses in the Carrer de Cambis for baling and dispatch to customers. A requirement for the weaving and printing processes was good light and the inventory reveals how this was obtained: there were ten windows in the paint-shop and twenty-one 'which give light to the looms'. Canaleta's manufacture had been similarly equipped with 'many windows' in a south-facing wall. Also of interest is the evidence concerning the chemical side of the manufacture's activities – the mixing of mordants and colours – and that concerning the accommodation arrangements for (and here the large Canals concern is clearly exceptional) no fewer than four managers. The inventory also illustrates – though the details have not been included in the table – the complexity of the bleaching processes: a long list of different tools and equipment were stocked for

[44] ACA, Intendencia, Registros de la Superintendencia, 1/26, fos. 214–21, 24 Feb. 1748.
[45] Full details of construction costs in AHPB, J. B. Fontana, Libro de concordias, 91.
[46] AHPB, Duran Quatrecases, Inventories and Auctions, fos. 247–65, 18 Nov. 1756.

use in connection with this, including 'long cloaks for carrying out the night watch (*fer la vetlla en la nit*)' – a garment which it seems likely was designed to protect those encharged with supervising the bleaching field during the night from the damp.

These unprecedentedly large manufactures already made a considerable impact on the areas of the city in which they were concentrated. In the Raval they represented the beginnings of the urbanization of the area. Guàrdia described the effect of the creation of his concern in the Carrer de Trentaclaus in his application for a privilege in 1747 – its construction, he insisted (he was emphasizing its positive effects) had 'resulted in ... the uprooting of harmful people and women of ill repute (*mal vivir*) who lived in that quarter as a result of employees of the manufacture having come to reside in it'.[47] The size of the manufactures, and the noise to which their concentration of manufacturing activities gave rise, could also, however, represent an unwelcome intrusion. This is shown by an attempt made by the Abbess of San Pere de Puellas, who ran a convent and a church in the area of greatest density of the new manufactures, to oppose extensions being made to that of Joan Pongem in 1752 on the grounds firstly that it would overlook a cloister in which her nuns 'could be recognized ... and strike up conversations with facility', and secondly that the production processes 'would cause such a noise that they would be heard from the church and would cause a disturbance to the functions in this'.[48]

Managerial structures

The description of the development of the industry which has been provided in this and previous chapters has revealed a variety of types of managerial structures – some in which duties were pooled, others characterized by family or nuclear family control, artisanal concerns in which it was labour as much managerial tasks which were being shared and finally that ideal arrangement both from the point of view of entrepreneurial efficiency and for that of the investment of commercial capital in the industry – a concentration of managerial functions in the hands of one individual, be he the owner of the concern or a salaried, or minority share-holding, *fabricant*. By the end of the 1760s it was the second variant of this last type of managerial structure which had become by far the predominant one. Of the

---

[47] *Ibid.*   [48] AHPB, Creus Llobateras, 1752, fos. 46–9.

twenty-nine concerns existing in February 1768, in fifteen there was a division between ownership and direction. The distinction between the two statuses is made quite clear in the documentation: owners are described as *dueños*, production managers as *fabricantes* and in cases where the roles were combined the title was *dueño y fabricante*.[49] A very similar structure to that which characterized the running of drapers' shops in the city had become the majority one in the industry – in these, too, there was generally a distinction between ownership and direction, the former being vested in a company and the latter being entrusted to a salaried *botiguer*, who might also have a small stake in the company. Canals, himself, it will be recalled, began his career in the city as such, as a minority share-holding administrator of a draper's shop. The extent to which the industry had been absorbed into the structures of commercial capitalism is thus illustrated.

In the majority of cases, *dueños* continued to administer their concerns and exercise some commercial duties, but in some even these responsibilities were delegated to managers. The relationship between owners and manufactures could thus become a distant one. The Canals concern itself provides a good example of this trend. On Esteve Canals's death in 1756 its administration passed to his widow rather than to his heir, Joan Pau, then aged twenty-six. The latter was more interested already in developing a career in the service of the state than in following his parental profession. In February 1756 he had been sent to Madrid to represent the family firm before the Junta General de Comercio in connection with renewal of its privilege, and this experience must have given him a taste for life in the capital as well as an insight into the advantages to be gained from contacts within the administration. In 1757 he founded a company in Madrid to promote the cultivation and trading of madder and in 1760 he was sufficiently well placed in the city to be the natural choice of his calico-printing colleagues to represent them in their attempts to reverse the 15 May 1760 lifting of the import ban on calicoes. In the same year his artistic merit, which had had its source in the design, drawing and colouring departments of his father's firm, gained him the nobility-conferring membership of the Academy of San Fernando and he was also made *ciutadà honrat* of Barcelona. In 1764 he obtained an administrative post in the royal service as Director General de Tintes del Reino. Finally, in 1780 his career

[49] BC, JC, leg. 53, no. 40, fos. 4–11.

climaxed with the conferment of the title of Baron of Vallroja. As all these details reveal, Joan Pau Canals was far from following his father in his commitment to his Barcelona draping and manufacturing interests, and when he finally inherited these on his mother's death in 1763 they were to experience a steady decline. The manufacture had become a 'rentier'-type source of income.[50] Nor was Canals's example untypical of the earlier participants in the industry. There was a fairly general process of ennoblement of the early promoters of the industry, and a consequent tendency to separation from active participation in business affairs during these years: Glòria, Guàrdia, Alegre, Seguí and Pongem all became *ciutadans honrats* between 1748 and 1774.[51]

The *fabricants*, both in the case of those who combined this role with ownership and those who were purely paid managers, had become the crucial, entrepreneurial group within the industry. It was on them that the industry was technically dependent. It was they who possessed the necessary skills for mixing colours and mordants – it was knowledge in this area which represented the qualification for attaining the status of *fabricant* – and it was they who were responsible for the design of cloth and choice of colours. The centrality of their role is illustrated by the conditions of work which were imposed on them when working in a dependent role – they were committed both to working full time for, and also to residing inside, their manufactures (again a practice inherited from the management of drapers' shops in which 'administrators' were obliged to live in the building containing the shop and to devote themselves totally to its affairs). It was they, thus, who conferred an identity to their concerns.

As has already been noted, the existence of 'professional' managers facilitated the participation of commercial capital in the industry. They were a mobile group prepared to work for anyone with the resources to back them: there is evidence of considerable professional mobility between different concerns. Managers had good long-term prospects for achieving independence. Among those working in the industry in 1768 were a number of later founders of important concerns, including Joan Pau Olsina, Ramon Vicens, Bernat Busquets, Segimon Mir and Erasme Gónima.

[50] Alier, 'La fábrica de Canals', pp. 76–91; also AHPB, Creus Llobateras, 19 Feb. 1756, fo. 19: naming Canals to represent manufacture; ACA, RA, Diversorum, reg. 879, 1763, fos. 274–5, records decision of Madrid Royal Academy concerning Canals's election as well as recording his representation of calico-printers' interests in 1760.
[51] Molas Ribalta, *Comerç i estructura social*, p. 284.

Labour organization

The large labour forces which worked for the calico-printing manufactures were organized on the basis of extensive division of labour – this will already have emerged from the description of the different 'spaces' in the Canals concern. A memorandum drawn up in 1780 identified eighteen different categories of individuals 'which regularly tend to form the total of workers which composes a manufacture of *indianas*'. The different types of roles that these played in the production process are what were to have been expected – *fabricants*, foremen (*mayordomos*) of the weavers, engravers, designers, foremen for the bleaching meadow, boys employed in the bleaching meadow, etc.[52] The ratio between the sexes, and also that between adult and child employment, in the manufactures was relatively uniform from one concern to another – approximately 55 per cent male, 20 per cent female and 25 per cent boys. The uniformity has its explanation in the rigidity which characterized the division of tasks in the manufactures on the basis of sex and age. Men held all the managerial positions, wove, engraved, designed, printed, burnished and polished cloth and carried out general manual work and all transport activities. Women warped and wound cotton and assisted in burnishing before printing. Boys worked in the capacity of assistants in the printing processes and in the bleaching meadows.[53]

There is an almost total lack of data about any other aspects of the organization of labour apart from these details concerning job specialization in the manufacture. The lack is a sign of the freedom which the calico-printers enjoyed from any form of control over their affairs. What was particularly striking about the manufactures when the context of the guild system and the predominantly artisanal characteristics of industrial activity at this stage is taken into consideration was the total lack of any form of structure which would have permitted employees to achieve economic independence. Workers in calico-printing manufactures were intended to be workers for life. This unusual characteristic gave rise to misunderstandings

[52] BC, JC, leg. 53, no. 25, fos. 16–29, report for Junta de Comercio.
[53] Details from three manufactures: Margarola's (BC, JC, reg. 83, 1 Feb. 1766); Pongem's (BC, JC, leg. 53, no. 1, 1761); Formentí's (AHCB, Arxiu comercial B 142, Copiador de cartes of manufacture, 6 May 1784) give average ratios of 55 per cent men, 25 per cent women and 20 per cent boys, but a survey for the entire industry carried out in 1784 gives the ratios 53 per cent men, 20 per cent women and 27 per cent boys (BC, JC, leg. 53, no. 29, fos. 2–21, report of directors of Royal Spinning Company on the industry, 15 Dec. 1784).

among observers of the industry as well as to tensions within the industry itself. In response to these, members of the Junta de Comercio gave a clear exposition, and defence, of the system which was operating. Unlike guilds, they stressed: 'apprentices, and journeymen are not known nor, consequently, masterships'. There was no path to achieving economic independence and so workers must content themselves with achieving technical expertise:

> Technical knowledge ... is not a sufficient disposition to reach the status of *fabricant.* The assistant of the printer can aspire to attain this occupation; the printer to execute his production process with exactness; the weaver to be a good weaver, and the same applies to all the other respective destinies, but ... few, or none, to advance to arriving to direct the manufacture.

The attainment of the status of *fabricant,* the only position of independence available within the industry, was conditional on the one hand on the possession of 'the secret of the composition and application of the colours' – control over the diffusion of this remained throughout an important limit to social mobility within the industry – and on the other hand on access to sufficient resources to establish a manufacture on some scale.[54]

The signs are that monetary rewards took the place which was provided by the possibility of gaining economic independence in the city's guilds as the principal incentive within the industry. Alejandro Sánchez, in his study of the Rull manufacture, shows that the concern had a complex, hierarchical system of salaries with the highest rates of pay, and the greatest number of subdivisions, within the painting and printing section of the concern followed by the bleaching departments – the most skill-intensive sectors. The existence of such incentives contributed to stabilizing labour forces: a study on salaries in the calico-printing manufactures in the last third of the century shows that while rates of labour turnover in the industry were generally very high – it is based principally on documentation from the 1790s when market conditions were unstable – those for engraving and painting, for which salary differentials were greatest, were the lowest.[55]

---

[54] As n. 52.
[55] Sánchez, 'Los fabricantes de indianas', pp. 142–3; P. M. Antón, 'Salarios en las fábricas de indianas de Barcelona en el último tercio del siglo XVIII' (Tesis de licenciatura, Barcelona, 1972), pp. 21–27. See also B. L. Ayala, 'Condiciones de trabajo en las fábricas de indianas

Table 5.5. *Situation of Canals/Canet manufacture in March 1758*

Break-down of capital stock	Libras	%
1. 6,443.5 pieces of calicoes in the white or printed	61,950– 6–10	39.6
2. Spun cotton	14,343–11– 3 ⎫	
3. Drugs, glues, dyestuffs, etc.	4,607– 8–10 ⎭	12.1
4. Tools	4,861– 9– 8	3.1
5. Buildings, meadows, etc.	24,335–11– 4	15.6
6. Owed by drapers	46,349–17– 3	29.6
Total	156,449–17– 3	

Table 5.6. *Situation of French manufacture in 1752*

Break-down of capital stock	Libras	%
1. Fixed capital (manufacture, bleaching meadow, etc.)	3,500– 0– 9	11.8
2. Tools (moulds, looms, vats, etc.)	2,337– 9– 6	7.9
3. Calicoes (painted and in white)	18,722– 9– 3 ⎫	
4. Spun cotton	1,774–12– 8 ⎭	69.0
5. Drugs, chemicals, mordants, etc.	3,357–13– 9	11.3
Total	29,692– 5– 2	

Capital accumulation

The initial investment for founding manufactures was relatively small, it was noted in the second section of this chapter. Table 5.3 also recorded though, it will be recalled, substantial capital accumulation by several concerns over these years. Detailed inventories exist for three concerns – those of French, Guàrdia and Canals.[56] The contents of these have been summarized in tables 5.5–5.7.

The tables firstly reveal that fixed capital proportions, at about 20 per cent in the case of both the French and Canals/Canet concerns

de Barcelona durante el último tercio del siglo XVIII ', *Manuscrits, Revista d'Història Moderna*, 6 (1987), pp. 121–34.

[56] French and Guàrdia: AHPB, Sebastià Prats, 3rd and 4th books of statutes and agreements, acts of 8 June 1752, fos. 50–7, and 7 Sept. 1756, fos. 211–25; Canals and Canet, AHPB, Duran Quatrecases, act of 1 Sept. 1759, fos. 147–86.

Table 5.7. *Situation of Guàrdia manufacture in 1756*

Break-down of capital stock	Libras	%
1. 1,665 pieces either finished or in process of manufacture	18,918– 0– 0	16.4
2. 7,001 pieces at drapers	86,322– 0– 0	74.6
3. Spun cotton	4,850– 0– 0	4.2
4. Drugs, glues, dyestuffs, etc.	2,388–15– 0	2.1
5. Estimate of tools	3,176–10– 0	2.7
Total	115,655– 5– 0	

(no details exist for Guàrdia's manufacture), were comparatively large. As has been seen, the establishment of manufactures required a significant initial investment in building and equipment and this was added to as manufactures expanded. The dimensions of Canaleta's new buildings will be recalled – $32\frac{1}{2}$ by $7\frac{3}{4}$ metres – and Canals's manufacture contained, and Guàrdia's was built to contain, 100 looms – these were extremely large concerns and the extent of fixed capital investment in them represented, as has been stressed earlier, a major discontinuity with respect to contemporary investment practices. Grau and López, while they emphasize the relatively low initial investment required in the industry, concede this point: 'Within the textile sector...the *indiana* manufactures demand a large investment, above all in buildings, which supposes a rupture with other forms reigning during the period: guild artisanry, merchant-manufacturer and domestic system.'[57]

It was the case, though, and the tables demonstrate this, that 'circulating capital' far exceeded fixed in the case of all three manufactures. This circulating capital was committed above all to stocks of finished calicoes either kept at the manufacture (the case of the majority of that of Canals/Canet) or at drapers (the case of the majority of that of Guàrdia). The latter location demonstrates that an important part of the 'accumulated capital' effectively took the form of advances to drapers. The calico-printers were financing distribution as well as production. This, of course, represented for a lot of printers – whose origins were in cloth-draping – a continuance of their traditional practices.

The inventory of 1758 for the Canals/Canet concern on which

[57] Grau and López, 'Empresari i capitalista', p. 28.

table 5.5 is based contains an estimate of profits – 'the profits which God our Lord has been so good to give us' from 1 January 1757 to 28 February 1758 are declared to be 39,725 *libras* 18 *sols* and 2 *denarios*. The method of calculation of the profits appears, though, to have been an unconventional one for it is explained that in this figure 'are included the tools, tackle and equipment of the manufacture, in addition to the houses'. The ambiguity has been eliminated and the true profit margin calculated in table 5.8. The rate of return had been a relatively modest one. The most comparable type of investment was that in drapers' shops, and Pierre Vilar's calculations for those of Alegre and Amat between 1717 and 1735 and 1765 and 1789 show respectively average profit margins of 10.7 per cent and 9.4 per cent.[58] The calculation, though, is for a short period only, and perhaps, in view of the impending division, a not especially favourable one.

Technique

It will be recalled from chapter 3 that, although before the prohibition of 1728 both madder and indigo-dyed calicoes had been imported, the industry had initially been limited to the use of the first and simpler of these two techniques. This continued to be the case for the majority of concerns during the 1740s: inventories show calicoes with the normal colour range obtained with madder dyes – various shades of reds, lilacs, violets, browns and blacks. Indigo-dyeing was first introduced at Campins's Mataró manufacture. In its privilege it was claimed that it was producing the 'until now not discovered "blauet"' and details of its equipment support this claim – the existence of 'a very large vat for the blue' is recorded.[59]

During the 1750s, indigo-dyeing clearly spread among the principal printers – in the inventory of Guàrdia's concern 'printed calicoes with blue silhouettes (*blau de perfil*)' are listed, in that of Canals and Canet in 1758 20 out of 460 printing moulds were for 'the blue and white', and there were copper vats 'for the blues' both at the main manufacture and the bleaching fields,[60] and Joan Pongem's concern in 1761 contained two tables 'to give the colour dark blue'.[61] It was a different printing and dyeing process and it needed separate

---

[58] Vilar, *La Catalogne*, III, pp. 145, 150.
[59] AHPB, J. B. Fontana, Libro de concordias, 91.   [60] Sources as n. 56.
[61] BC, JC, leg. 53, no. 1.

Table 5.8. *Calculation of profits made in the Canals/Canet concern,*
1 January 1757–28 February 1758 (in libras)

1. Sales, stock of finished calicoes, raw materials, sales credits, tools, buildings, bleaching meadows, etc. (i.e. balance as at 28 Feb. 1758)	187,385–16– 6
2. Raw materials bought, wages and salaries paid, taxes, extraordinary expenses between 1 Jan. 1757 and 28 Feb. 1758 + stock as at 31 Dec. 1756	147,659–18– 4
3. (1) minus (2): i.e. profits including tools and buildings	39,726–18– 2
4. Value of tools and buildings	27,997– 1– 0
5. True profits: (3) − (4)	11,729–17– 2
6. Rate of return on total capital (= (2) + (4)) over fourteen months	6.68%

equipment. Its introduction, like that of madder-dyeing, had involved some cost and its diffusion was controlled. This is illustrated by a contract in which Josep Sala promised a gift of 56 *libras* and an annual salary of 250 *libras* to a silk-stocking-maker in return for instruction in 'dark blue in silhouette'. The secret was not to be passed on to anyone else under a penalty of 400 *libras* and the return of the 56 *libras* present.[62] In addition to the introduction of indigo-printing, Formentí, working in Pongem's manufacture in 1751, claimed to be attempting to 'obtain the secret for the permanence of the colours green, and yellow, which up to now have not been obtainable'.[63] This, too, would have involved the use of indigo. This process had been mastered by the 1760s.[64]

The two basic calico-printing processes – the printing with mordants followed by madder-dyeing and resist process, requiring waxing and then dyeing with indigo – were therefore introduced at different stages in the industry's development – the gap between Sala's introduction to the two techniques was nearly twenty years.

In addition to mastering these two processes, it should be emphasized that all *fabricants* constantly attempted to vary and

---

[62] AHPB, Duran Quatrecases, 2nd book of statutes and agreements, act of 8 April 1755, fos. 144–5: cancellation of the agreement.
[63] ACA, RA, Diversorum, reg. 494, 22 Sept. 1751, fos. 273–82.
[64] Thus these colours, and this method of obtaining them, are mentioned in the regulations drawn up for the industry in 1768 (BC, JC, 53, no. 3, fos. 2–7).

improve their colours – this was the essence of their art. As the Junta de Comercio recorded in 1783 'there is no *fabricant*... who does not believe himself to be the possessor of some secret thanks to which he obtains colours with greater economy or greater perfection than the others'.[65] Secrets for new formulas were carefully guarded and passed on to heirs: Francesc Ribas referred to his in 1772 as his 'only patrimony'. A report on the industry prepared in 1784 by a doctor Masdevall reported that the colouring ingredients and mordants were in all the manufactures prepared by 'one man alone shut in a room in order to conserve the secret which each manufacture has'.[66] From a mechanical point of view the industry was static – the only change during these years was the development of copper-plate printing in 1770 – the inventive effort was concentrated on colour and design. The manufacturing side of the industry continued to lag behind the progress achieved in the colouring and printing techniques. Regulations adopted for the industry included a clause entitling the printers to import fine cloth in the white for printing on as there was no manufacture in the kingdom capable of producing 'fine cloth of linen, nor of cotton, which equal those which come from foreign kingdoms'.[67]

Guilds and the industry

The industry managed for the most part to escape any interference in its affairs from the guilds. It was able to do this because it was a new industry, producing new types of cloth, and its raw material was little used by other guilds in the city. Theoretically, consequently, it was not subject to any existing guild monopolies. It experienced disputes, however, with three guilds – the silk-weavers, silk-dyers and linen-weavers. That with the first was occasioned by the fact that the silk-weavers, shortly after the prohibition on cotton imports of 1728, had obtained approval for newly registered statutes which conferred on them the right to produce muslins, *indianas* and other cotton cloths. In view of the existence of these, the early calico-printers, as has been

---

[65] BC, JC, reg. 87, letter of Junta of 30 July 1784.
[66] BC, JC, leg. 53, no. 7 and J. Masdevall, *Relación de las epidemias de calenturas putridas y malignas que en estos últimos años se han padecido en el Principado de Cataluña; y principalmente de la que se descubrió el año pasado de 1783 en la ciudad de Lleida, Llano de Urgel* (Madrid, 1786): this contains an appendix containing his 'verdict about if the cotton and woollen manufactures are pernicious or not to the public health of the cities in which they are established', written in 1784. The citation is from p. 6 of this appendix. [67] As n. 64.

noted, tended to entrust their weaving activities to silk-weavers, but the practice was not universally followed: Canals in 1746 was using a linen-weaver instead and it was this which led to a dispute.[68] The right to work with cotton extended to the silk-dyers too, and it was actions by their guild which gave rise to the most important guild conflict in which the industry became involved. In 1763, silk-dyers had cotton cloth dyed in the calico-printing manufactures seized on the grounds that the dyeing of cotton was their *privativo* or monopoly.[69] The linen-weavers' guild's dispute was not so much with the calico-printing manufactures but with some small-scale concerns which, with the return to prohibition in 1770, specialized in the production of cloth for printing or in the imitation of the new-style cotton cloths and cotton linen mixtures which had been developed in France and England during these years – stripes, checks, velvets, etc. During 1774 the guild had such cloth seized from a range of these small-scale manufactures.[70]

None of these guild challenges was successful. The industry owed its success to surmounting them to two principal types of argument. The first was legal. As the cloths which it was producing, and the dyeing techniques which it was using, were new, it could claim that the various guild statutes on the basis of which these rival groups of workers claimed monopolies over parts of their production process were not applicable to them. The second argument was a practical one – in the interests of quality, it was held, the printers needed to exercise control over the entire production process. In view of the importance which was being attached to the industry's role in import-substitution, this was a view which carried weight. The Barcelona Junta de Comercio argued against the silk-dyers' claims on these grounds saying that to give in to them would involve conceding similar claims to other guilds resulting in a breaking up of the manufactures when 'for the progress of the industry and perfection of its manufactures it is convenient that the manufactures can carry out all the processes which their cloth requires for themselves'. They added, emphasizing the principal entrepreneurial advantages to be gained from centralization, that in this way 'they achieve the prompt completion of them [the processes] and that each thing is carried out at that instant which is necessary on which success

---

[68] Molas Ribalta, *Los gremios*, p. 522.
[69] BC, JC, reg. 1, Acuerdos of 10 Sept. 1764, 15 March 1765.
[70] BC, JC, reg. 5, Acuerdos of 10 Jan., 3 Feb., 28 April 1774, and leg. 53, no. 14, fos. 3–7.

very often depends'.[71] To this argument of the need for direct
entrepreneurial control over the entire production process there
came to be added, too, that of the unsuitability of fixed guild
regulations on production methods for an industry experiencing
regular technical progress. This point was emphasized by Joan Pau
Canals, in his capacity of Director General of Dyeing, in a
memorandum of 1772: 'for dyeing a multitude of colours is presented
every day which were not known when the ordinances were drawn
up', he wrote in connection with claims of one of the dyers' guilds;
'these and other new establishments', he added with reference to the
calico-printing concerns, 'cannot sustain themselves without the
liberty to dye their cloths; it being the only way of preventing a
multitude of legal cases which are harmful to the public and to the
progress of industry'.[72]

The adoption of regulations

The dispute between the silk-dyers and the calico-printers brought to
the notice of the Junta General the fact that the calico-printers
possessed no guild, and some of the legal inconveniences which
resulted from this. In consequence, they ordered the Barcelona
Junta de Comercio on 7 March 1765, in accordance with its
constitution by which it was authorized to draw up regulations for
those trades which did not possess them, to set about composing
ordenanzas for the calico-printers. In June of the following year Joan
Pongem, a leading manufacture in the industry since 1747, was
named to consult with members of the industry concerning the
necessary contents of such statutes.[73]

The proposal which resulted from this consultation consisted of
twenty-five statutes. Some of these took a form that was to have been
exepected – would be *fabricants* were to be tested in their skills, and
thus a type of mastership in calico-printing was to be created, the
sorts of cloth which the printers were allowed to produce were listed
and their sizes and qualities prescribed and similar requirements
were laid down for the printing processes, and a system of marking
and inspecting laid down – but others did not. The very first statute
proposed, which was used as the epigraph for this chapter,

[71] BC, JC, reg. 83, letter of 13 Nov. 1764.
[72] BC, JC, leg. 54, no. 20, fos. 5–6, report of 11 Jan. 1772.
[73] BC, JC, reg. 1, Acuerdo of 18 March 1765.

demonstrated that the industry, which had benefited itself from so much 'freedom' in its growth, was not going to exercise a similar liberality with respect to potential competitors now it had achieved maturity. Other clauses were equally restrictive: the existence of cotton-weaving 'outside the manufactures' was defined as an abuse as it would serve 'as a cover for the frauds which the principal manufactures suffer'. It was to be prevented by the imposition of fines on, and the threat of confiscation of the equipment of, offending parties. In addition, the practice of printing and painting 'without having the form of a manufacture, or the departments (*oficinas*) necessary for its perfection', was to be similarly restricted.[74]

The intention, it is clear, was that the type of organization of production which predominated in the industry – the large, consolidated *fábrica* – one which owed, we have seen, as much to political as to economic or technical requirements, should be imposed on all potential participants in the industry.[75]

[74] BC, JC, leg. 53, no. 3, fos. 2–7.   [75] See above pp. 87–8.

CHAPTER 6

The industry at its height, 1768–86, with investment in it as common as in drapers' shops

There is every appearance as you walk the streets of great and active industry
(Comment on Barcelona made by Arthur Young in his 'Tour in Catalonia', *Annals of Agriculture*, 8 (1787), p. 238)

The regulations for the industry which received royal approval in 1768 were at no stage properly enforced. There were a variety of reasons for this which include initial jurisdictional conflicts between the Junta de Comercio (who had responsibility for their enforcement) and the Real Audiencia (which had previously monopolized this sphere of administration), the limited resources at the disposal of the Junta de Comercio[1] for controlling so large an industry (the body possessed a secretary and treasurer – virtually full-time appointments – but otherwise depended on the voluntary services of *comerciantes matriculados*),[2] the fact that 'regulating' was a policy which clashed with the principal ideological currents of Spanish economic policy in the second half of the eighteenth century[3] and the opposition to regulation experienced from leading firms in the industry itself which were long accustomed to freedom and only interested in its enforcement if this served their partial interests. The consequences of

[1] Molas Ribalta, 'La Junta de Comerç de Barcelona', pp. 263–77.
[2] *Comerciantes matriculados* were the leading members of the city's wholesaling community who were selected to be inscribed on a 'list' to serve as magistrates either on the Junta de Comercio or the consulate. The three organizations – *matrícula*, consulate and Junta de Comercio were created at the same time, in 1758, to start functioning in 1760. The first two represented near exact replicas of the *matrícula de mercaders* and consulate which had existed before the decree of Nueva Planta since medieval times. Considerable prestige was attached to the status of *comerciante matriculado* and candidates for the position were subjected to having their backgrounds carefully vetted (Molas Ribalta, 'La Junta de Comerç de Barcelona', pp. 263–7; see also Vilar, *La Catalogne*, I, p. 433).
[3] On economic policy during these years, see J. Rodríguez Labandeira, 'La política económica de los Borbones', in M. Artola (ed.), *La economía española al final del Antiguo Régimen* (4 vols., Madrid, 1982), IV, 148–54; on opposition of large-scale calico-printers to regulation, see BC, JC, leg. 53, no. 24, fos. 28–9, opposition expressed by Magarola brothers, 12 Jan. 1779, no. 26, fos. 7–12, opposition of Canals.

185

the failure are of importance. On the one hand, it had the result that existing manufactures continued to be run with virtually no interference from outside – better circumstances could hardly have been imagined for creating an independent, bourgeois group with its own ideology – and on the other, a technically illegal sector of the industry, composed of smaller manufactures, was able to develop.

The regulations, however, were observed informally by the majority of concerns in the industry. In administrative reports on the industry, too, a distinction was generally made between 'regulated' and 'unregulated' concerns, and as late as the 1790s there was still talk of formulating new regulations and ensuring their proper enforcement.[4] In view of this, largely for analytical convenience, I shall consider the two sectors of the industry – the regulated and unregulated – separately in this chapter.

The chapter's structure will follow the pattern of the previous two. In different sub-sections of the first part I shall document the growth in the industry with details on the number of regulated and unregulated calico-printing concerns founded in Barcelona, the origins of their founders, the industry's production and its diffusion outside Barcelona and I shall conclude with an assessment of the industry's growth pattern. In a second section I shall discuss the contribution of four different influences to this growth – government policy, the availability of calico-printing skills and capital and rising demand in the home and export markets. I shall conclude the chapter with descriptions of the characteristics of manufactures in the two halves of the industry, documentation of the industry's further diffusion within the city and details of an 'urbanization' controversy to which this diffusion gave rise.

THE GROWTH IN THE INDUSTRY

'Regulated' manufactures

The number of manufactures

As is the case throughout its history, documentation on the industry is inadequate for plotting its development precisely. The extent of administrative control over it was erratic. There are, however, three points during these years for which information is relatively abun-

[4] Reference to in a letter of the Junta de Comercio of 27 Jan. 1791 (BC, JC, reg. 89, fos. 374–5).

dant. The first is for the year 1770 when a control was exercised over all possessing calico-printing skills which led to a full enumeration of manufactures.[5] The second is for 1778–80 and was a consequence firstly of attempts to restrict contraband, involving listing and registering the marks of all exporting manufactures, in connection with the 1778 'Regulation of Free Trade', and secondly of the Junta de Comercio finally having its jurisdictional quarrel with the Audiencia settled in its favour which gave it an opportunity to try to assert its authority over the industry.[6] The third is for the years 1785–6 when two surveys of the industry were carried out, one by a 'Royal Spinning Company', founded in 1773, about which more will be said in the next chapter, and the other, by far the more thorough, on the orders of the Bishop of Barcelona, who, in an attempt to ensure proper religious education for the children employed in the calico-printing manufactures, ordered the preparation of a full list of all the manufactures in the industry.[7] The significance of the most thorough survey ever carried out on the industry having this source was pointed out in the introduction.

Table 6.1 summarizes the information available from these and other sources (the other sources being notarial acts, recording the foundations of calico companies, and the records of the cadaster principally).[8] It is not as precise a table as would be desirable and is particularly deficient from the point of view of the exact dates of manufactures' foundations – its dependence principally on the information drawn from the three points in the twenty-year period just

[5] BC, JC, leg. 53, no. 40, fos. 2–13, survey undertaken in 1770.
[6] BC, JC, leg. 53, nos. 21–6, extensive documentation including lists of manufactures and a range of other material relating to the years 1778–80.
[7] BC, JC, leg. 51, no. 13, fo. 2, Relación de las fábricas de indianas, 30 Sept. 1785; a copy of the 1786 diocesan survey (which was printed) is held in the Museo de Estampació Textil of Premià de Mar.
[8] The other sources for this table are BC, JC, leg. 53, no. 9, fo. 6, and leg. 51, no. 9, fo. 3, lists of manufacturers for 1772 and 1774; Grau and López, 'Empresari i capitalista', pp. 49–57, for information on Noguera, Gramatges, Ortells, Formentí, Espalter, Carrera, Armet & Salgado, Olsina, Pedra, Bruguera, Roig, and their 'Barcelona entre el urbanismo barroco y la revoluión industrial', *Cuadernos de Arquitectura y Urbanismo*, 80 (1971), p. 40, for information on Vermell, Busquets, Perich, Gónima; M.Prat i Canals, 'La manufactura cotonera a Catalunya: l'exemple de la fábrica de Magí Pujadas y Cia' (Tesis de licenciatura, Barcelona, 1976), p. 34, for Pujadas and Carrera; Molas Ribalta, *Los gremios*, pp. 527–8 for Prat; Sánchez, 'Los orígenes sociales', p. 782, for Anglès Rull; AHPB, Font Alier, fos. 237–40, act of 1 June 1778, for Noguera's bankruptcy, though Molas Ribalta (*Los gremios*, p. 528) gives 1775 as the date; Arxiu de la parròquia de Santa Maria del Mar for foundation date of Llorens manufacture. AHCB, cadastre for 1784–7, for foundation dates of several manufactures.

Table 6.1. The expansion in the number of regulated manufactures in Barcelona, 1768–86

Year	New manufactures	Manufactures which cease	Running total	Names of new manufactures	Names of manufactures which cease
Feb. 1768			25		
1768/70	4	2	27	Sala, Pujol, Alabau, Marí	Esteve, Alegre
1772	3	2	28	**Soler**, Vermell, Pujadas	**Guàrdia, Illa**
1773	1		29	Noguera	
1774	2	2	29	Busquets, **Aribau**	**Glòria, Ferrà**
1777	2	2	29	Gramatges, Ortells	Formentí, Noguera
1778	5	2	32	**Espalter, J. Costa, Rovira, Aguilar,** Carrera	**Soler, Pujol**
1779	7		39	**Vicens, Capalà, Illa and Crosi,** Formentí, Castañer, **Castelló,** Gallissà	
1781	4		43	Pedra, Olsina, Bruguera, Armet & Salgado	
1783	4		47	Roig, Prat, Gónima, Vehils	
1784	2		49	Anglès Rull, Perich and Janer	
1785	17	1	65	**Ramon, Masvidal, Font, Parellada, Henrich, Demestre, P. Costa, Clarós, Bertrán, Aimar, Riera,** Barbara,* Marimon,* Rolandi, Fontseré,* Llorens, Casas	Igual

| 1786 | 8 | 73 | **Muños, Gelabert, Bosch, Cantarell, Deparés, Margenedes, Bonaplata, P. Olsina** |

* 'Promotions' from the 'unregulated' industry, see table 6.2 below.

Notes: 1. In order to provide as clear as possible a view of the growth in substantial manufactures I have subtracted four manufactures from the 1768 figure (those of Crous, Pallarés, Pagès and Rigalt) the last of these was never accepted as an 'approved manufacture' and the first three would not have been either had they survived long enough to be subjected to the rigours of the 1778–80 survey.

The names of manufactures whose exact date of foundation is not known appear in bold type.

3. The 1786 survey by the diocese does not distinguish between 'regulated' and 'unregulated' manufactures. For most concerns this information is provided by the 1785 survey carried out by the Royal Spinning Company. In the case of those for which it is not I have distinguished between manufactures employing ten or more children, which I have included in this list; and those employing less than ten, which I have included in the list of unregulated concerns. Ten children would represent a total labour force of some forty which would have placed these concerns safely within the regulated category (on ratios of children to other types of employees in manufactures see p. 175n).

mentioned for which sources are adequate means that there is a bunching of concerns under these years. However, it does document the majority, if not all, the regulated concerns founded during these years and gives, too, an approximate idea of the stages of the industry's growth. As can be seen, a total of fifty-nine new manufactures were founded and the 'regulated' industry nearly tripled in size, from a total of twenty-five manufactures in 1768 to one of seventy-three in 1786.

The identity of founders

An initial distinction will be made between manufactures founded by individuals who involved themselves in manual work in the pro-duction processes, acting as *fabricants* for their concerns, and those founded by individuals who did not, employing managers to play this role.

The procedure assumes that the persons in whose names the manufactures were founded were the key agents in their foundations. This can be justified. In most cases, in contrast to the practice with draping shops, manufactures adopted the names of the individual or individuals who played the principal role in their foundations. There are, indeed, cases of concerns being renamed to reflect shifts in the relative size of the investments of different associates in them which demonstrates the priority given to this principle.[9]

The distinction can be established for fifty-six of the fifty-nine additions to this sector of the industry during these years – twenty-six were founded by individuals who involved themselves in manual work in the production processes, acting as *fabricants* for their concerns, five were joint foundations of *fabricants* with capitalist backers, and twenty-five were founded by merchants, or individuals of merchant status, who employed managers.

Of the twenty-six in the first of these three categories it is possible to identify the social origin of fifteen. Of these eight were *fabricants* and seven came from the guilds. The former included Bernat Busquets, Ramon Vicens, Joan Gallissà and Erasme Gónima, who had previously worked as *fabricants* for Josep Igual, Joan Batista Sirés, Josep Ribas, and the Magarola brothers respectively, Bernat Llorens,

[9] As may be recalled (see pp. 75–6), this was not the practice when the industry started. An example of a concern which changed its name in this way is that of Joan Pau Olsina called successively Joan Pau Olsina i fill, Tomba, Olsina i Cia and Francesc Tomàs i Pi (Grau and López, 'Empresari i capitalista', pp. 51–7).

son of Eudalt founder of the manufacture taken over by Isidro Cathalà in 1762, who was approved as a *fabricant* in 1779 and Ramon Soler, Antoni Carrera and Miquel Formentí, who had all temporarily withdrawn from the industry.[10] The seven ex-guild members were Josep Alabau, silk-weaver, and son of Francesc, who had established a manufacture in 1766, Pere Noguera and Lluís Cantarell, cloth-dyers, and four members of the linen-weavers' guilds – Josep Gelabert, who had relations in the ribbon-makers' guild and who had been involved in making stuffs and experimenting with spinning machinery since the early 1770s, Joan Aribau, Joan Barbara and Pau Fontseré – the last two had been working in the 'unapproved' sector of the industry.[11]

The five 'mixed' concerns were those of Illa and Crosi, Joan Pau Olsina, Anglès Rull, Pau Ramon and son and Esteve Gramatges. Illa, whose early experiences have been mentioned in the previous chapter, had, like Ramon Vicens, been associated with Francesc Ribas before establishing a new manufacture in his own name with commercial backing.[12] Olsina had served for eighteen years as *fabricant* for Antoni Buch and Manuel Armengol when he set up his own concern in 1781.[13] Rull, who associated himself with the wholesale merchant Geronim Anglès in 1784 to form Anglès Rull & Cia, was by origin a silk-weaver and had been working as *fabricant* for Manuel Ortells since at least 1779.[14] Pau Ramon and son and Esteve Gramatges were unusual examples of families which made use of a son, who had clearly been sent out to serve a form of apprenticeship in an established concern (in the case of Jacint Ramon with Joaquim Espalter & Rosàs), as a basis for establishing a family-run business.[15]

[10] BC, JC, leg. 53, nos. 40, fos. 2–13, survey undertaken in 1770, lists all these *fabricants*. For Llorens, see leg. 53, no. 21, fo. 2, list of printers examined according to 1767 regulations, and Arxiu de la parròquia de Santa Maria del Mar, Cathalà papers.
[11] For Alabau, Noguera and Cantarell, see Molas Ribalta, *Los gremios*, pp. 424, 528, 537; for Gelabert, see AHCB, cadastre for 1801, list of members of linen-weavers' guild, and BC, JC, leg. 23, no. 3, fos. 2–8, for inventing activities in connection with which a J. Gelabert, braid-maker, was mentioned – this, rather than the J. Gelabert linen-weaver, may have been our man: Gelabert was a common name in the silk and linen-weaving guilds; for Aribau, again there is some doubt: a Joan Aribau is listed among the linen-weavers between the 1740s and 1770s (AHCB, cadastre), and certainly Aribau entered the industry through the textile manufacturing end: in 1774 he is described as a *fabricante de encotonadas* and he was operating nineteen looms (BC, JC, reg. 5, Acuerdos, 3 Feb. 1774); for Fontseré, see BC, JC, leg. 51, no. 4, petition of 26 April 1774; for Barbara, see BC, JC, leg. 53, no. 24, fo. 88, letter of 10 March 1779.   [12] Vázquez de Prada, 'Un modelo', p. 636.
[13] BC, JC, leg. 53, no. 40, survey of 1770.
[14] Sánchez, 'Los orígenes sociales', p. 782.
[15] Grau and López, 'Empresari i capitalista', pp. 38, 51.

Of the twenty-five 'merchant' concerns, it is possible to identify the professional background of the founders of thirteen, and to these details I shall add those relating to the three merchant participants in the mixed concerns just discussed whose identities can be established in order to gain as full a view as possible of the character of merchant involvement in the industry. Half of the sixteen were from the guilds and the others were *comerciantes* without guild affiliations.

The guild members included Magí Pujadas, Manuel Ortells, Joaquim Espalter, Josep Deparés, Francesc Tomàs, Francesc Bruguera, Ignasi Masvidal and Magí Henrich. Pujadas was a wealthy shoe-maker, who had been involved in tax-farming and contracting for the city's bread supply. For his calico-printing he associated with Gil Grau, a commercial broker who had been involved in a previous manufacture.[16] Ortells came from a family of cloth-dressers and shearers who were among the principal members of the city's declining cloth industry.[17] Espalter was a maker of esparto whose family, Molas Ribalta records, were listed in the records of the cadaster as being involved in trades outside their own for a period of over fifty years.[18] Deparés was a silk-weaver[19] and both Tomàs (the backer of Olsina) and Bruguera were silk-braiders – the former had previously been an associate of Josep Capelino and both had further associates from their guild for their calico involvement, Antoni Tomba in Tomàs's case and Bonaventura Xuriach in that of Bruguera.[20] Masvidal was a silk-weaver[21] and Henrich, a carpenter, initially associated with Antoni Carrera, who established his own concern in 1785. It had been Henrich's father, or a close relation, Jacint Henrich, who had carried out all the carpentry work in the building of both the Canals and Canaleta manufactures.[22]

Of the eight *comerciante* participators, the social situation of two was nearly identical to that of the guild capitalists just described – Esteve Demestre was an ex-tailor and ex-associate with Bacardit in the first Carrera concern, who had renounced his guild mastership in 1767,[23] and Esteve Gramatges was involved in tax farming in the 1760s.[24] The six others – Francesc Capalà i Vidal, Fèlix Prat, Llorens Clarós, Marià Font, Geronim Anglès and Fèlix Vehils – were all from the top

---

[16] Molas Ribalta, *Los gremios*, p. 529; Vilar, *La Catalogne*, III, pp. 22–3; and Prat i Canals, 'La manufactura cotonera', p. 34.   [17] Molas Ribalta, *Los gremios*, p. 393.
[18] *Ibid.*, pp. 202, 482.   [19] *Ibid.*, p. 482.   [20] *Ibid.*, pp. 504–5.
[21] *Ibid.*, p. 527.
[22] BC, JC, reg. 92, 1 Dec. 1804, 'adds to the trade of carpenter that of manufacturer of cloth and printed calicoes'.   [23] Molas Ribalta, *Los gremios*, p. 528.
[24] Vilar, *La Catalogne*, III, p. 22.

levels of the city's wholesaling trades. Capalà had been a member of the select Compañía de Barcelona, was involved in insurance activities and from 1787 played a prominent part in the Junta de Comercio.[25] Prat began his career as a journeyman merchant (*mancebo de comercio*) working for Jaume Guàrdia, accumulated capital exporting eau-de-vie to Havana and became a *comerciante matriculado* in 1762: 'His life constitutes', Molas writes, 'a perfect model of social mobility in a single generation.'[26] Font was a carpenter's son who had made a vast fortune most rapidly, like Prat, in the American trade: he had joined the *matrícula* of merchants of Cádiz and spent time in Havana where he had acted as the contractor for the colonial army. Clarós was the son of a Figueras wholesaler who had established himself in Barcelona in 1781.[27] Anglès, Joan Rull's partner, had run an important commercial house for a number of years[28] and Vehils was a commercial broker.[29]

'*Unregulated*' *manufactures*

The number of manufactures
The difficulties involved in tracing the expansion in the number of manufactures in this sector of the industry are yet greater than with 'regulated' concerns. Generally the 'unregulated' manufactures were not established by companies and if they were it was normally on the basis of private agreements – the consequence is that they have left few traces of their activities in the notaries' registers. It is only as a consequence of the surveys carried out in 1770 and between 1778 and 1780 that the existence of the majority of them is recorded at all. Table 6.2's overwhelming reliance on these two sources leads to even more acute bunching of manufactures around the dates to which they relate than in table 6.1. The thoroughness of these two surveys, however, means that it includes most of the small concerns founded during the 1770s, and the existence of the 1786 survey carried out by

[25] Molas Ribalta, 'La junta de comerç de Barcelona', p. 270; Oliva, *Cataluña y el comercio privilegiado*, pp. 82–5; *Almanak Mercantil o guía de comerciantes para el año de 1802*, p. 251.
[26] Molas Ribalta, 'La junta de comerç de Barcelona', p. 290.
[27] BC, JC, leg. 45, no. 55, documentation concerning Font's election as *comerciante matriculado*. See also Fernández, 'La burguesía barcelonesa', p. 45: Font acted for Glòria in the American trade.
[28] Sánchez, 'Los orígenes sociales', p. 782.
[29] BC, JC, leg. 45, no. 42, a witness in connection with election of Busquets as *comerciante matriculado*.

Table 6.2. *The expansion in the number of unregulated manufactures in Barcelona, 1768–86*

Year	New manufactures	Manufactures which cease	Running total	Names of new manufactures	Names of manufactures which cease
Feb. 1768			4		
1768/70	11		15	Brusosa, Rafael, Sayol, Richelme, Daufí, Barruel, Casacuberta, Lorenzo, Francisco, Andarion, Gatell	
1772	2		17	González, Carrés	
1773	1		18	Prat	
1774	2		20	Fontseré, Marimon	
1777	1		21	Pérez	
1778	18	8	31	Barbara, Barro, Bassas, Baus, Cantarell, Corominas, Gatell, Estop, Jorge, Maleras, Baus & Rius, Mir, Nadal, Pla, Rovira, Salvadó, Serra, Solemon	Barruel, Crous, Andarion, Francisco, Lorenzo, Pagès, Rafael, Daufí

Year					
1779	7	36	Buscallà, Rodellas, F. Torras, J. Torras, Uger, Govatell, Moncunill	2	Estop, Cantarell
1780	2	34	Sala, Marsal	2	Govatell, Moncunill
1783		36			
1784	2	38	Illaca, F. Olsina		
1785	1	35	Feu & Pi	4	Marimon*, Fontseré,* Rovira, Barbara*
1786	19	40	Abeya, Xarau, Iglesias, Esteva, Millà, Ciriñach, Arqués, Ferrer, Grané, Carrera, Artés, Mayolas, Barjomé, Carafí, Figuerola, Estalich, S. Perich, Crous, Serralach	14	Sayol, Richelme, González, Carrés, Pérez, Barro, Corominas, Jorge, Nadal, Serra, Solemon, Torras, Uger, F. Olsina

* Included from this date among 'regulated' manufactures.

Notes: 1. Existing manufactures in Feb. 1768 were: Rigalt, Pagès, Pallarès and Crous.

2. The grounds for distinguishing between 'regulated' and 'unregulated' manufactures for those listed in the diocesan survey of 1786 are explained under table 6.1 above. They only serve as a rough guideline and some of the manufactures included here, for example that of Serralach, would probably be more aptly included in table 6.1.

the Bishop of Barcelona,[30] and other data for the 1790s,[31] makes it possible to work out which of these small manufactures survived. The table shows that 66 manufactures were founded during the period and that the sector grew from a minimal size in 1768 to a substantial one by 1786, with some 40 manufactures.

The identity of founders

Of the forty-seven founders of concerns established before 1783[32] it has been possible to identify the origins of twenty-seven. There were two principal sources: from within the large calico-printing manufactures – eighteen were founded by calico-printers, generally ex-employees of the manufactures[33] – and from the textile guilds – five were founded by linen-weavers, one by a cotton-weaver, one by a braid-maker associated with a linen-weaver, one by a linen-weaver qualified as a printer and one by two silk-weavers in association with other artisans.[34]

[30] See nn. 5–7 for details on sources for 1770, 1778–80 and 1785–6.

[31] The sources for the 1790s used are BC, JC, leg. 51, no. 20, list of manufactures with vacant looms, 1790 (only of use in a few cases as manufactures are not fully named); BC, JC, reg. 12, Acuerdos for 28 Jan., 1 and 15 Feb. 1790, listing attendance of printers at meetings concerning introduction of spinning machinery; Carrera Pujal, *Historia política*, IV, pp. 164–5, list of printers contributing to 1793 war loan; *Almanak Mercantil* for 1797; BC, JC, leg. 51, no. 22, list of attendance at meeting establishing a *cuerpo* of *fabricantes de tejidos e hilados* (cotton cloth and spun yarn). The other sources on which table 6.2 is based are as follows: Grau and López, 'Empresari i capitalista', pp. 49–57, for information on Pérez, Sala, Marsal, Olsina, Feu & Pi and Bausà; BC, JC, leg. 51, no. 4, 26 April 1774 on Fontseré, and reg. 5, Acuerdo of 10 Jan. 1774, on Marimon; AHCB, cadastre for 1784, on Illaca; BC, JC, leg. 51, no. 13, list of approved manufactures for promotions to this status of Marimon, Fontseré and Barbara, and for Rovira's employment as dependent *fabricant* by Castañer (and thus departure from the sector).

[32] I have not included concerns founded after 1783 because, as noted under the table, the question of the attribution of regulated or unregulated status to these is not in all cases clear.

[33] See BC, JC, leg. 53, no. 40. fos. 2–13, survey undertaken in 1770, for details on printing activities of the following (on the basis of which I have assumed origins in the printing industry) – Pagès, Pallarès, Rigalt, Crous, Dauff, Andarion, Barruel, Brusosa, Francisco, Lorenzo, Richelme and Sayol; BC, JC, leg. 53, no. 25, fo. 2, petition of 9 April 1779, for information on González, Prats, Pérez, Maleras and Serra and confirmatory evidence on Sayol.

[34] Linen-weavers (Gatell, Casacuberta, Fontseré, Carrés, Mir, respectively): BC, JC, leg. 53, no. 24, fos. 48–50, petition of 10 March 1779, fo. 58, petition of 17 April 1780, BC, JC, leg. 51, no. 4, petition of 26 April 1774 (Fontseré and Carrés described as '*fabricantes* of cotton cloth and linen-masters'), AHCB, cadastre, list of linen-weavers for 1801; cotton-weaver (Marimon): BC, JC, leg. 53, no. 25, fo. 2, petition of 9 April 1780; linen-weaver braid-maker association (Buscallà/Servià): BC, JC, leg. 53, no. 23, fo. 50; linen-weaver–printer (Barbara): BC, JC, leg. 53, no. 24, fo. 88, petition of 10 March 1779; silk-weavers (Marsal and others): Grau and López, 'Empresari i capitalista', p. 52.

Table 6.3. *Figures for production of* indianas *and other types of manufactured cloth and number of looms 1775–93*

	Production of *indianas* and other types of manufactured cloth (metres)		Number of looms		
	Regulated concerns only	Regulated and unregulated concerns	Regulated concerns	Unregulated concerns	Total
1775	1,240,000–1,395,000		950–1,000		
1779			1,299		
1784		3,119,811–4,254,480*	2,102	350	2,452
1789					2,730
1793		4,648,760*			

* The higher figure for 1784 seems wrong. It is an estimate made by the Royal Spinning Company and it does not concord with figures for cotton imports. The lower figure for 1784, and the figure for 1793, are based on the conversion of cotton import figures into metres of cloth on the following basis: (i) to get figures for spun yarn, those for unginned cotton have been reduced firstly by $\frac{2}{3}$, to account for losses in weight during the ginning process, and then by $\frac{1}{8}$, to account for losses in spinning, and those for ginned cotton have purely been reduced by the second of these amounts (ii) to convert spun yarn into pieces of calicoes the contemporary estimate of 8.4lbs of yarn to the piece has been used (iii) to convert to metres the figures for pieces have been multiplied by 15.55 (pieces were *c.* 10 *canas* long and there are 1.55 metres to the *cana*). (For losses in weight in the ginning and spinning processes and for the ratio between spun cotton and pieces of calico, see BC, JC, leg. 51, no. 12, fos. 7–14, report of Guàrdia and Duran on behalf of the Junta de Comercio, 13 March 1783, and no. 8, report of Junta de Comercio, 22 June 1775.)
Sources: 1775: BC, JC, leg. 51, nos. 8 and 10, reports of 22 June and 8 Oct.; 1779: BC, JC, leg. 53, no. 24, fos. 8–11, report of 11 June; 1784: BC, JC, leg. 53, no. 29, fos. 2–21, report of 15 Dec. 1784, and Maixé, 'El mercado algodonero', p. 376; 1789: BC, JC, leg. 51, no. 20, report of 16 June 1790; 1793: Vilar, *La Catalogne*, III, p. 122.

Production figures

Evidence concerning these questions is most limited. What there is has been included in table 6.3. In addition, the 1778 Regulation of Free Trade permitted the export of prints on imported calicoes and linens. These were called *pintados* and relatively complete figures for their export to America exist. As their production for internal use was not allowed, the export figures serve as an approximate guide to the quantity produced. The figures have been summarized in table 6.4.

Table 6.4. *Production of* pintados (*in metres*) *calculated on the basis of American exports, 1778–87*

1778	249,010
1779	330,558
1780	none
1781	52,881
1782	71,123
1783	228,321
1784	131,358
1785	1,116,091
1786	612,155
1787	733,444

Source: Delgado, 'La industria alogodonera catalana', p. 111.

Allowance has to be made, it should be noted, for the gap between manufacturing and exporting which could be large if the *pintados* were kept in stock because of difficulties in selling – the export figures thus refer to the production of a slightly earlier period. There may have been exports to other markets or some illegal sales of *pintados* in national markets. The table can thus only be used as a rough guideline to the total production of *pintados*, though it probably reflects fluctuations in the trade quite well.

Manufactures outside Barcelona

The industry throughout its history was to be concentrated to an extraordinary extent within Barcelona; however, there were some manufactures founded outside the city, and the diffusion was at its most rapid during these years. The details are included in table 6.5. Three principal stages in the industry's diffusion can be identified from the table. The first, up until about 1770, was limited to towns close to Barcelona and principally to Mataró. This town owed its industry, it will be recalled, to Campins's manufacture: a port, like Barcelona, it enjoyed similar advantages for the establishment of the industry in terms of ease of importing raw materials and the existence of commercial capital. It was also sufficiently close to the capital to be able to draw on it for equipment and expertise. The second phase began in the late 1770s with a wider diffusion of the industry in Catalonia – to Manlleu, close to Vic, to the town of Valls, in the *comarca* of the Alt Camp, and above all to Olot and the Garrotxa –

Table 6.5. *The establishment of calico-printing concerns outside Barcelona,*
1746–96

	Catalonia		Rest of Spain	
1746	Campins	Mataró		
	Peramás	Mataró		
1759	Sala	Manresa		
1764	Roca & Serralt	Madrid		
1768	Cantallops	Mataró		
	Casanovas	Mataró		
1769	Marxuach	Mataró		
1773			Lagoaniere	Corunna
1777	Gou	Olot		
1778	Illes	Manlleu		
1779	Amat/Gallissà	Valls		
1781	?	Banyoles		
1784	?	Tortellà	Font	Cádiz
	?	Les Preses		
	Mulleras	Besalú		
1785	Arenys	Manresa		
1788			Royal Table Linen Manufacture	Corunna
			Royal Cotton Manufacture	Avila
1789			?	Sanlúcar
			?	Puerto de Santa María
1792	Ausich	Mataró		
1796	Santmartí	Manresa		

Sources: see p. 97; also Llovet, *Mataró*, II, pp. 68–9; Ferrer, *Pagesos, rabassaires i industrials*, pp. 357–62; Enciso Recio, *Los establecimientos*, pp. 133–7; F. Ferrer, *L'economia del set-cents a les comarques gironines* (Gerona, 1989), pp. 149–54; Nadal, 'Los abortos', pp. 401–3; Larruga, *Memorias políticas y económicas*, II, pp. 391–2; Puig, *Les primeres companyies*, p. 27; Molas Ribalta, *Los gremios*, p. 528.

four manufactures were established in Olot itself and further ones in the neighbouring villages of Les Preses and Tortellà and small towns of Besalú and Banyoles. Finally, from the mid-1780s there was some growth of the industry around Cádiz – in Cádiz itself, where Marià Font founded a second large manufacture during these years, and in Sanlúcar – and the growing interest of the State in securing the diffusion of the industry outside Catalonia is apparent from the diversification of the Royal Table Linen Manufacture into printing and the foundation of the Royal Cotton Manufacture at Avila. A single manufacture was also established in Madrid in 1764 and there were attempts made in 1779 to encourage further growth there by granting more favourable conditions for production than those applying to the Barcelona industry.[35]

Concluding on the pattern of growth

The data presented in the first four sub-sections of this chapter permit an assessment of the pattern of the industry's growth during this period. It is clear that it grew at an unprecedented pace from the mid-1770s to 1786 – 49 regulated and 50 unregulated concerns were founded during these years, the first significant diffusion of the industry within and beyond Catalonia occurred, production of *indianas* was multiplied by approximately two and a half times and a very large trade in *pintados* was developed. The growth was achieved above all, it is clear, in two expansive phases – the first from 1777 to 1779, which witnessed a sharp rise in the number of calico-printing concerns established and the reestablishment of the trade in *pintados* and the second from the end of the American war to 1786, with an unprecedentedly rapid expansion in the number of manufactures in the industry. The bulk of the growth was in 1784. A report on the regulated industry recorded the existence of fifty-four manufactures already for this year, which would suggest that most of the concerns for which I have no record of foundation dates had their origins then, and it is for this year that a colossal increase in the production of *pintados* is recorded.[36] A report of 1785 recording 'the large number of manufactures which have been established in this city and other villages of the Principality since the beginning of the previous year' provides further evidence of what was clearly a massive industrial expansion during these years throughout Catalonia.[37] It is clear that these years represented a second major turning-point for the industry, and in this case, as has been noted by other historians, it was one which was shared by industrial activity throughout the Principality.

The part played by the founding of new manufactures in this great expansion is evident. As important to it, however, was the fact that so

---

[35] A royal edict of 19 May 1779 granted a number of largely fiscal exemptions to calico-printers in Madrid (E. Larruga, *Memorias políticas y económicas, sobre los frutas, comercio, fabricas y minas de España* (44 vols., Madrid, 1785–1800), II, p. 392).

[36] BC, JC, leg. 53, no. 29, fos. 2–21, report of 15 Dec. 1784.

[37] Report of directors of Royal Spinning Company of 30 Sept. 1785 (reproduced in Torrella Niubó, *El moderno resurgir*, pp. 133–46).

few manufactures were lost during these years. The industry's 'shake-out rate' was exceptionally low – a loss of 15 per cent of regulated manufactures was experienced against one of 35 per cent of all manufactures in the period analysed in the previous chapter. What is more, the disappearance of several firms from the list was occasioned not by insolvency but, on the contrary, by their owners having had sufficient resources to sell out and invest in land or other easily administered sources of income.[38] Even among unregulated manu-factures there was a reasonable chance of survival – of the thirty-four concerns existing in 1780 there is evidence for at least twenty still having been in existence in 1786.[39] The industry, it is clear, was exceptionally stable during this period. This was not to have been anticipated in view of the commercial disruptions occasioned by the American war and represents a sharp contrast with the experience of other centres of calico-printing in Europe during these years – it was, for example, a period of severe crisis for the London printing trade which lost several of its principal concerns and there was a resulting shift of the centre of the trade to Lancashire.[40] The stability also presents a sharp contrast, as will be seen, with what were to be the experiences of the industry from the 1790s through to the 1830s.

THE CAUSES OF THE EXPANSION

The question, as was that of the causes of the first major turning-point in the industry's development in the 1740s, is a particularly important one. The industry experienced, we have seen, a period of virtually uninterrupted prosperity, with very few failures, even during the period of the American wars; it had two phases of unprecedentedly rapid expansion and it achieved dimensions beyond which it was not going to grow very much further. It provides the principal example of that general industrialization which took place in Catalonia during these years, removing incipient signs of Malthusian crisis

[38] On the withdrawal of the Glòria family, see Fernández, 'La burguesía barcelonesa', pp. 74–5. Other withdrawals by distinguished participants in the industry include those of Guàrdia and Alegre.

[39] In addition to the three previously unapproved concerns which graduated to approved status during these years the following 1780 manufactures still existed in 1786 – Bassas, Baus & Rius, Brusosa, Buscallà & Servià, Casacuberta, Daufí, Gatell, Maleras, Mir, Pallarès, Pla, Prats, Rigalt, Rodellas, Salvadó and Torras. These concerns are either listed in the 1786 diocesan survey or appear in other lists of the 1790s as in n. 31.

[40] S. D. Chapman, 'David Evans & Co. The Last of the Old London Textile Printers', *Textile History*, 14 (1983), p. 32; P. Caspard, *La Fabrique-Neuve de Cortaillod. Entreprise et profit pendant la Révolution Industrielle, 1752–1854* (Paris, 1979), p. 111.

which had been emerging between 1750 and 1770. This general industrialization represents, within Vilar's argument, the turning-point in the region's movement towards industrial capitalism.

Government

From approximately the mid-century policy became more liberal. By this is meant that in place of a piecemeal approach to achieving industrial growth on the basis of individual privileges and founding state manufactures, in which agriculture had little place, there began to develop a sense of the interconnectedness of economic change and general policies were devised of a type to benefit all producers. The extent of 'liberalism' was limited at all stages. There was generally no question of opening frontiers to allow foreign producers to compete on equal terms. It was the national and imperial economy which it was intended should benefit and there was no abolition of, only reforms to, the guild system and other central institutions of the traditional, corporative economy. Of the general direction of change being in a liberal direction, however, there can be no doubt. The causes for the shift were various – the practical difficulties with, and lack of success of, the previous policies, contact with the liberal economic thought being espoused in northern Europe and also the pressing need occasioned by population growth and poverty to give priority to industrial development. The English example was clearly particularly important – the success of its version of mercantilism, with its emphasis on ensuring the monopolization of all the advantages to be obtained both from its American possessions and the home market for domestic producers, was clearly a particularly relevant one for the other major European imperial power.[41]

Some of the early influences of this policy change on the development of the Catalan cotton industry were noted in the last chapter. It was argued that the edict of 24 June 1752, which had provided a general procedure for obtaining privileges which had previously only been granted on an individual basis, lay behind a concentration in the movement into the industry during the years 1753–6, and it was also shown that the policy could have more mixed effects – the 25 May 1760 replacement of the import ban by a 20 per

---

[41] On economic policy during these years, see Rodríguez Labandeira, 'La política económica de los Borbónes', pp. 107–81; Herr, *Eighteenth Century Revolution*, pp. 120–53; J. Lynch, *Bourbon Spain, 1700–1808* (Oxford, 1989), pp. 208–25.

cent duty, we saw, increased instability while on the other hand having the salutary effect of exposing the industry to competition and providing it with the opportunity to carry out printing on higher-quality cloth. In the period covered by this chapter the movement towards liberalism within a protectionist framework was carried further and in this case there were no obvious ways in which policies can be construed as having been disadvantageous to the industry.

There were three principal axes to the policy – the extent of protection was increased, measures were taken to increase the efficiency of the functioning of this better protected national market and there was some promotion of change on the supply side. I shall provide information on each with specific reference to that relating to the cotton industry.

As noted in the previous chapter a first step in the return to a system of total prohibition of cotton imports was taken with the edict of 8 July 1768 which renewed the ban on the import of printed calicoes. A further measure of 19 January 1770, in response to demands from the Barcelona industry, extended the ban to cotton cloth in the white. The import of muslins was prohibited by an edict of 24 June 1770 and finally the Royal Pragmatic of 14 November 1771 extended the ban to the import and use of any type of foreign cloth made wholly or partly of cotton. The import restrictions were renewed at various points and also extended to made-up goods, such as hats and gloves, in 1778. The only divergence from this total prohibition of cotton imports was an edict of 30 September 1771 permitting the import of cloth in the white on payment of a 20 per cent duty. The background to this concession will be discussed in the next chapter. It was reversed by a further edict of 7 July 1773 which restored full prohibition. The other side of this protectionist policy was the favouring of the domestic producer from the point of view of access to national raw material supplies – silk, cotton, dyestuffs, wool. In the case of our industry the principal measures taken were edicts of 1766 and 1773 which, respectively, granted exemption from import dues, and the right of *tanteo* (first option to buy), on cotton imports.[42]

The principal barriers to national producers taking full advantage of these measures were firstly physical, transport difficulties, and

---

[42] See González Enciso, *Estado e industria*, pp. 243–56, on these and other fiscal measures summarized below. See also Izard, *Industrialización*, pp. 18–23, for a summary of this legislation.

secondly institutional, the existence of internal customs dues, high sales taxes or, in the case of the American market, the continued existence of restrictions on the freedom of trade. Some priority during these years was given to road and canal building but difficulties here were not easily or rapidly soluble. The principal changes thus consisted in the removal of institutional and fiscal barriers to commercial growth as follows. Firstly, access to interior markets was improved by an article in the fiscal reform of 4 June 1770 which granted complete freedom to all internal trades and reductions on duties on nationally produced goods while retaining those on imported goods: thus internal customs came to represent a second series of protective duties in favour of the national producer. Secondly, the *alcabala*, a sales tax, was reduced in Castile and the Catalan *bolla*, a tax confined to textiles, was replaced by an import tax on foreign goods – a direct transfer of tax liability onto the foreign product.[43] Thirdly, the rules surrounding participation in the American trade which had already been relaxed in 1765, it was noted in the last chapter, when nine Spanish ports, including Barcelona, were permitted to trade with the islands of the Caribbean (but not the mainland colonies), were liberalized further in 1778 with the 'Reglamento de Comercio Libre': this measure extended the permission to participate in the trade to a total of thirteen ports in the peninsula and twenty-two in the colonies, though New Spain and Venezuela continued to be excluded from the free trading area. Included in the regulation were, again, a variety of measures designed to favour national over imported products: the export of a number of these was banned (including various items of clothing, furniture, wines, spirits and oil) and those items whose export was permitted were subjected to over double the duty of national products – 7 per cent to 3 per cent.[44] Finally, a series of measures (royal edicts in 1778, 1786 and 1789) were taken to restrict contraband. It was to the fulfilment of one of these, it will be recalled, that we are indebted for one of the few accurate surveys of the Barcelona industry.

The promoting of changes on the supply side in the case of cotton included encouragements given to the cultivation of cotton in the American colonies and within Spain and backing given in 1773 to a Barcelona spinning company which became the Real Compañia de

---

[43] Herr, *Eighteenth Century Revolution*, pp. 128–33.
[44] Fisher, *Commercial Relations between Spain and Spanish America*, pp. 13–15.

Hilados de Barcelona.[45] Later, in 1802, a total ban was placed on the import of spun cotton and this was to enforce a rapid incorporation of the spinning processes into the industry which will be documented in the following chapter. The cotton industry also benefited, as other industries did, from a series of measures designed to increase the social prestige attached to manufacturing and to remove guild restrictions on the right to make certain types of cloth, on the carrying out of industrial work by women and concerning the number of looms used in individual concerns.[46]

Skills

At various points in this study it has been demonstrated that restrictions on the availability of calico-printing skills were significant influences on the industry's diffusion. This was particularly the case in the 1730s and 1740s but continued to be so into the 1760s – as late as 1768 a thorough survey of the industry revealed only twenty-nine individuals possessing calico-printing skills.[47]

That restrictions in the availability of the printing skills continued to act as a restraint on the growth of the industry in the 1760s is suggested by a comparison of the timing of the foundation of manufactures by those possessing printing skills with that of those investing from outside the industry. This is done in table 6.6. As can be seen, although for the period as a whole there was a near equality in the number of concerns from the two different sources, the first group dominated in the 1770s (sixteen foundations of manufactures to six). Now there could be various explanations for this predominance but that one was probably the existence still of a relative shortage of skills, which placed those possessing them at an advantage in the founding of new concerns, is suggested on the one hand by evidence of efforts made by the government to ensure wider diffusion of the calico-printing techniques and on the other by the efforts of calico-printers to limit the impact of these measures.

Examples of both these tendencies is provided by the case of Francesc Ribas who was granted a royal privilege in 1769 in return for a commitment to teach 'the secret to make the colours with the qualities of consistency, fastness and beauty, with their manner of composition, mixture and designs' to two individuals every three

---

[45] Izard, *Industrialización*, p. 24.   [46] *Ibid.*, pp. 22–3.
[47] BC, JC, leg. 53, no. 40, fos. 3–4, 'Noticia de los qe se hallavan actuales fabricantes de colores de Indianas en ... 1768'.

Table 6.6. *Founders of manufactures in the regulated industry 1768–87*

	Printers and other workers	Printers associated with merchants	Outsiders to the industry	Unknown	Total
1768–70	4				4
1772–7	5	1	2		8
1778	4		1		5
1779	3	1	3		7
1781–3	1	1	6		8
1784–7	5	2	13	7	27

years. Ribas, while benefiting from the fiscal advantages conferred by the privilege, ensured that its impact on the extent of availability of colouring and printing skills should be minimal by confining his tuition principally to his own and close associates' sons. Of the six individuals whom he trained in ten years two were his own sons, Miquel and Francesc, two were sons of one his calico-printing associates (Marià and Pau Illa), a fifth was the son of an existing printer (this was Josep Olsina whose father worked for Buch & Armengol) and a sixth, Jaume Verges, was the only one for whom there is no evidence of prior involvement in the industry. His own sons and those of the other printers would already have had access to the calico-printing 'secrets' from their own fathers and so the privilege had only served to enlarge the pool of *fabricants* by one.[48]

By the 1780s, however, despite attempts like these to slow the pace of technical diffusion, the industry's scale, the failure to impose regulations and thus the development of an unregulated sector within it, and also possibly the existence of published manuals on calico-printing techniques – the French work *L'Art de faire l'indienne a l'instar d'Angleterre* published in Paris in 1770 was translated and published a year later in Spain at the orders of the Junta General – had had the consequence that calico-printing skills were abundant in the city. The archives of Barcelona's Junta de Comercio record that twenty-two new printers had their skills examined and approved during the 1770s and a further three between 1780 and 1784,[49] and the survey of the industry undertaken by the Royal Spinning

[48] BC, JC, leg. 53, no. 7.   [49] BC, JC, leg. 53, no. 21, fo. 2.

Company in 1785 showed the existence of thirty-two professional managers in the industry – *fabricants* working in a dependent status for generally merchant employers – in addition to the numerous *fabricants* who possessed their own concerns.[50] Isidro Cathalà, who worked in both the printed silk and printed calico industries, and who like Ribas had been instructing would-be printers in the silk-printing techniques, reported in 1779 that no applicants for instruction had presented themselves to him recently 'because the secret of the colours is already very well known'.[51] The supply of skills was not only adequate, it is clear, for the expanding industry within Barcelona but also to meet the requirements of those founding manufactures in other parts of the Principality and of the peninsula. Technical transfer from the capital was behind the introduction of the industry to the Garrotxa, and during the late 1780s and early 1790s the Royal Manufacture of Table Linen of Corunna and the Royal Cotton Manufacture of Avila both called on the Barcelona industry for the provision of colourists, engravers and other skilled workers.[52]

Capital

The details provided in the first section of this chapter concerning the origins of the founders of the new manufactures serve to give an approximate idea of the areas of the city's economy which financed the expansion. It can be seen that there were four principal sources of new concerns during this period – from within the industry itself (from among former managerial *fabricants* in the case of the regulated industry and from among the labour force for the unregulated), from the guilds (principally textile ones) which provided individuals with manual skills which could be used in the industry, from among what may be termed 'guild' capitalists (members of the guilds who were involved in a range of investments outside their own trades) and finally from among large-scale wholesale merchants.

From certain points of view there was thus continuity – all four categories had played an important role in the previous period of expansion. We are reminded that the industry itself was a significant source of social mobility, that the importance of the cotton

[50] BC, JC, leg. 51, no. 13, fo. 2.
[51] BC, JC, leg. 54, no. 17, fo. 41, letter of 28 July 1779.
[52] L. M. Enciso Recio, *Los establecimientos industriales españoles en el siglo XVIII. La mantelería de La Coruña* (Madrid, 1963), p. 137; E. Herrera Oria, *La real fábrica de Ávila*, pp. 16–17.

manufacturing processes within it had the consequence that it provided opportunities for individuals from the textile guilds – this was now particularly apparent in the unregulated sector in which the most successful concerns were those founded by individuals with weaving skills and particularly linen-weavers – and that the tradition established in the 1740s of merchant investment in the industry had become established practice. However, the extent of involvement of merchant capital in the expansion, and in particular in the two phases of rapid growth – 1777–9 and 1784–6 – does represent, it is clear, a discontinuity. This becomes even more evident when the size of these 'merchant capital' concerns is considered: the twenty-seven merchant or co-*fabricant*/merchant concerns founded between 1777 and 1786 for which evidence exists employed a labour force of some 2,411 in 1786, or an average of 89 each, and there are some cases of very large concerns being founded, rivalling those which had been in the industry for many years – Fèlix Prat's approximate labour force was 296, that of Anglès Rull 185, those of Espalter and Roig, Feu & Martí 140 and those of Marià Font, Manuel Ortells and Josep Castañer some 133. The second turning-point in the industry's history, like the first, had behind it a significant increase in the extent of investment of merchant capital.[53]

Our data on the source of this capital is not complete but it can at least be seen that quite a wide range of trades was represented among the new merchant participants in the industry – 'guild capitalists', the roots of whose fortunes lay in the textile trades, tax farmers, insurers, commercial brokers, participants in the American trade. The explanation at a general level for such widespread existence of funds for investment lies in the long prosperity which the Catalan economy had been experiencing since its recovery began in the late 1720s. Pierre Vilar's description of this process up until the 1740s was summarized at the beginning of chapter 4. There had been no interruption in it since this decade with further progress registered in the already established trades – the farming of taxes and seigneurial dues, the export of eau-de-vie, the import of foodstuffs and foreign textiles – and with the emergence of new trades – insurance from the 1760s, ship-building and the provision of shipping services (Vilar writes of 'An Atlantic navigation passed largely into Catalan hands') and an expansion of trading with America, particularly after the first

---

[53] These figures have been calculated on the basis of the number of children recorded as working for these concerns in the diocesan survey of 1786 using the ratio (see p. 175n) of 27 per cent with respect to these and the total labour forces.

liberalization measure of 1765 which opened the West Indies trade to Barcelona. The number of ships plying this trade grew spectacularly from three in 1768 to fourteen in 1770, twenty-two in 1773 and twenty-eight in 1777. Agricultural prosperity had paralleled the commercial – Vilar writes of the years 1760–80 as 'the "happy" period of the century for seigneurial revenue'. The same families in many cases were involved in these trades but they were richer: 'a great concentration of accumulated capital has taken place', Vilar writes, 'the evident increase in the global figure of affairs having profited quite a small number if not of individuals, at least of families'.[54]

The case of a participant in the industry, Nicolau Sivilla, partner of Isidro Cathalà, can be used as an example for what was a general process. Sivilla was one of the wealthiest members of the silk-weavers' guild, with seventeen looms under his control in 1753. His initial investment in the Cathalà concern in 1762 was 5,000 *libras*. This share had grown to 35,879 *libras* by 1777 and meanwhile he had branched out to participating in the American trade: in 1772, in conjunction with three others, he had invested 60,000 *libras* in an Atlantic general trading company, which made connections with Galicia, England, Hamburg, America and Canada, achieved a turnover of over 200,000 *libras* within a year, and profits of over 15,000 *libras* or a clear 25 per cent on the original investment. In 1781 he branched out into yet another commercial sphere, founding an insurance company with three others with an initial investment of 20,000 *libras*.[55]

If, though, there is abundant evidence of a massive commercial enrichment having taken place in Catalonia which was clearly the source for the capital which was transferred into the industry during these years, there remains the problems of explaining firstly what had caused industrial investment to become so generally acceptable to merchant capital and secondly why the transfer into the industry took place at a particular moment of time. With respect to the first of these questions it should be noted that a change of scale was involved. Precedents for industrial investment by commercial capital clearly existed by this stage but from this period the holding of capital in manufactures became nearly universal practice for Barcelona merchants. The process was wider than our analysis of the industry in terms of individual firms implies – most of the firms had three or four

---

[54] Vilar, *La Catalogne*, III, pp. 338–68 and 464–86, especially pp. 479–85.
[55] Arxiu de la parròquia de Santa Maria del Mar, details among the Cathalà papers.

210 A distinctive industrialization

backers. The second of these two questions will only be answerable
when an analysis of the industry's markets and profitability has been
undertaken in the next section, but the first can be dealt with here.
A first, important explanation of the extent of merchant participation in the industry was that it had become a very safe
investment. As we have noted, the industry was remarkably stable
during these years. There were very few failures. The risk element
was clearly minimal. A second explanation has been touched upon in
the previous chapter – an organizational structure had been adopted
in the industry which made possible a variety of forms of merchant
participation. The company system had become virtually universal
and this permitted the merchant participation to be a relatively
active one, with the merchant administering the concern and paying
salaries to managers, or of a more passive nature, limited to the
advance of capital at interest. As was noted in the previous chapter,
the type of structure adopted was almost identical to that which
operated with respect to drapers' shops and it proved equally
amenable to the investment of commercial capital. Finally, the social
values which operated in the city had adjusted to the emergence of
calico-printing and other large-scale industrial activities by attributing high status to industrial investment: for election onto the
matrícula of *comerciantes*, proof had to be provided by the individual
concerned that he confined his activities to wholesale trading – one of
the questions to be asked of witnesses concerning applications was
whether they knew if the candidate 'is involved in commerce, and is
known as a wholesaler, and not as a shopkeeper, or retailer' – but, as
a further question reveals, investment in manufactures had been
defined as wholesaling activity: witnesses, once they had established
the wholesaler's credentials, were to be asked what type of wholesale
activities he was involved in, 'if in letters of exchange, in the import
or export of goods or primary products, promotion of manufactures
or other similar branches of trade'. Manufacturing had been placed
on a par with wholesaling and success in it was a possible path to
nobility by the conferment of the status of *ciutadà honrat*.[56]

---

[56] BC, JC, leg. 45, no. 41, has details of the manner in which would-be *commerciantes matriculados*
were vetted. On the nobility conferring status of *ciutadà honrat*, see J. Amelang, *Honored
Citizens of Barcelona. Patrician Culture and Class Relations, 1490–1714* (Princeton, NJ, 1985).

Table 6.7. *Exports of* indianas *(in metres), 1778–95*

1778	47,074	1788	13,173
1779	23,820	1789	12,514
1782	8,630	1790	57,474
1783	16,652	1791	60,415
1784	15,790	1792	469,542
1785	38,546	1793	83,716
1786	63,029	1794	97,740
1787	74,951	1795	119,312

Source: Delgado, 'La industria algodonera catalana', p. 111.

Markets

In the two previous chapters we have traced the development of the industry's market network since the 1740s. Initially, we showed, sales were concentrated principally in Catalonia, regions immediately adjacent to the Principality, Madrid and Andalusia. It was our argument that the 1750s and 1760s witnessed a widening of the peninsular market and the effective completion of the process of import-substitution which had been initiated in 1728. The American market's importance, it was held, had been secondary up to this point. From the late 1770s and into the early nineteenth century, it is clear that the American market increased in importance for the industry – the large increase in the production of *pintados* for export there was documented in table 6.4 – but this is not to say that the industry became 'export-driven', as will be seen.

The expansion in American exports' coincidence with the two phases of particularly rapid growth in the industry would appear to support the argument for their having represented the principal cause of the industry's experiencing a turning-point with respect to both its size and the extent to which it attracted commercial capital during these years. The first phase coincides with the 1778 Regulation of Free Trade and the rapid rise in the export of *pintados* to which this gave rise, and the second phase with that second boom in the export of *pintados* which occurred during 1784 and 1785. The colonies' isolation from the metropolitan economy during the war had led to a depletion of stocks and thus to the building up of a strong demand for when peace ensued. The industry benefited from this – 'in the years [17]83 and [17]84, there were so many requests...from America to this city for consignments of *indianas* to those Dominions...whose stocks of this product were exhausted because of the previous war', a contemporary recorded in 1785.[57] In addition, the identity of some of the new recruits to the industry suggests that the production for the American market was the paramount explanation for their involvement – two of the founders of the largest new concerns, Prat and Font, had made their fortunes during the recent growth in the Catalan American trade, and Font, it was noted, had founded a second manufacture in Cádiz itself in 1784.

However, despite these coincidences, by no means all the growth can be attributed to the rise in American demand. This has been demonstrated by recent research by Josep Maria Delgado, showing that although there was a massive expansion in the sales of *pintados* for America, production of *indianas*, which was the industry's principal product, representing the most value added, continued to be almost exclusively for the home market.[58] The predominance is demonstrated in table 6.7. Production of *indianas* in 1784, it will be recalled, was over 3 million metres: the exports for that year to America thus represented a mere 0.5 per cent of the total product. The details of *indiana* exports for 1778, which are lower than those for 1777 despite the opening of the American trade, suggest, indeed, that the export of *pintados* was partly at the expense of the small trade in *indianas* to America which existed. The predominance of the home market as the outlet for the production of *indianas* continued, it is clear, into the 1790s. If the 1784 production figures for *indianas* are taken as representative for these years then the following export/production ratios emerge – in 1792, the maximal year, 15 per cent, and if the average of the twelve years from 1784 to 1795 is calculated, a mere 2.95 per cent.

If the export market, therefore, had introduced a speculative element which contributes to explaining the extent of the growth achieved in the industry between 1777 and 1778 and 1783 to 1785, it is to the home market almost entirely that the more than doubling in the production of *indianas* and the number of looms during these years is accountable, and which provided the stability which represented one of the principal attractions of the industry, we have noted, to merchant investors.

The causes for the buoyancy of the home market for printed

---

[57] BC, JC, leg. 32, no. 5, fo. 145.

[58] Delgado, 'La industria algodonera catalana', p. 112. Since this was written, A. García-Baquero, in 'La industria algodonera catalana y el libre comercio. Otra reconsideración', *Manuscrits. Revista d'Història Moderna*, 9 (1991), pp. 13–40, has disputed Delgado's views concerning the low level of *indianas* exported after 1784.

calicoes are relatively clear. In addition to the favourable influence of the governmental measures designed to promote production for the national market, to which reference was made above, the industry was benefiting, as it was elsewhere in Europe, from a general change in clothing habits and a switch in demand from wool and silk to cotton, which was causing it to be the principal gainer from the rising population and incomes which characterized this stage in Spanish and European history. Cotton goods had definite advantages over the traditional products and these, and the nature of the general trend over these years, could not have been better summarized than they were by delegates of the industry in 1784:

> Printed manufactured calicoes... are the most convenient product for the regular use of people which has been invented up to now. They are suitable for all the seasons of the year, for all climates and regions: they clothe the rich and adorn the poor, they are the most hard-wearing, they adorn most and cost least.
>
> They are not susceptible to moths, in the same way as silk, and act as a substitute for the popularity of this material, exceeding it in the convenience of their use consequent upon their renovation when they are washed. It is as a consequence of these precious qualities that the consumption of our *indianas* has become so general, that despite the number of these manufactures having increased by half, they can scarcely meet the demand. A few years ago the use of *indianas* was only known in coastal areas and populous cities of the kingdom and in the Americas. Nowadays its use has spread into the bowels of the kingdom, and the most unknown people and remote villages wear it.[59]

The process received an extra stimulus from the war itself. There are signs that the break which this gave rise to in the supply of English woollens acted as a catalyst to this process of import-substitution. Evidence of this is provided by a report of the Junta de Comercio of March 1783 in which it pointed out that despite the interruptions of the war 'the demand for this type of textiles has been no less strong because the interior of the kingdom has substituted its use for that which it made previously of light woollen goods imported from England' and they anticipated that the growth achieved on this basis would be sustained after the war 'as people have become used to having this material which clothes them with so much cleanliness, comfort and low price, it will not be easy for them to abandon its use'.[60] This increased Catalan penetration of the peninsula's markets

[59] BC, JC, leg. 53, no. 29, fos. 1–21, report of directors of Royal Spinning Company, 15 Dec. 1784.
[60] BC, JC, leg. 51, no. 12, fos. 7–14, report of Junta de Comercio, 13 March 1783.

Table 6.8. *Rates of profit in Isidro Cathalà's manufacture, 1777–89*

Year	Capital invested at beginning of year (*libras*)	Profit (%)
1777	106,210	7.00
1778	113,677	−6.18
1779	100,981	8.15
1780	100,213	8.43
1781	108,663	8.39
1782	114,000	12.80
1783	120,000	10.05
1784	120,000	16.73
1785	120,000	8.79
1786	130,548	2.10
1787	120,000	6.20
1788	120,000	8.90
1789	129,717	10.68

Note: the negative profits for 1778 were a consequence of a discounting of some 23,000 *libras* of bad debts incurred since the company's foundation.
Source: Arxiu de la parròquia de Santa Maria del Mar, Cathalà papers.

was recorded at the receiving end. Xan Carmona, in a study on the linen industry in Galicia, notes the growing impact of Catalan textiles before and after the American war and cites a contemporary who estimated in 1788 that more than 4 million *reales* were being spent on '*indianas*, stockings, handkerchieves and other products from Catalonia by means of merchants from that country established in this'.[61]

The steady growth in the home market, it is clear, not only sustained the industry, preventing bankruptices, but caused the years of warfare to be ones of high profit. The returns on Isidro Cathalà's investment in his calico-printing manufacture are summarized in table 6.8 – as can be seen, profits were at record levels between 1782 and 1784. The high returns available on the well-tried enterprise of production for the home market must have been as powerful an, if not a more powerful, incentive to investment in the industry as the prospect of achieving sales in America.

[61] X. Carmona, 'Clases sociales, estructuras agrarias e industria rural doméstica en la Galicia dels siglo XVIII', *Revista de Historia Económica*, 2 (1984), p. 49, n. 6.

An interpretation

It is now possible to draw some conclusions. It is clear, firstly, that the turning-point in the development of Barcelona's cotton industry during this period needs to be related to the general expansion of the city's and the region's economy since the late 1720s. There is ample evidence for the fact that year after year of good trading conditions and the opening up of a succession of new areas of commercial activity had generated by this period an impressive accumulation of capital. There was a confidence and optimism among the leading merchants of the city which it is clear had this at its source. This in itself encouraged the undertaking of new types of investment – and involvement in calico-printing was far from the only innovation of these years. The commercial expansion had achieved a momentum which was such that even the more difficult economic circumstances which were to prevail after 1790 were to take many years to bring it to a halt.

The expansion, however, cannot purely be accounted for in terms of an accumulation of capital. There had been previous periods in the principality's history, we have noted, in which capital had been accumulated, but this had not invariably given rise to industrial investment on a large scale. The interest of these years lies precisely in the fact that the movement into industry was on an unprecedented scale, giving rise to something very much like an industrialization process, and removing, apparently, any Malthusian threat. Our analysis has shown that various fairly long-term developments had combined to create circumstances which favoured this movement. Firstly, we have seen, some forty years of steady growth in the calico-printing industry had resulted in the availability of sufficient skills and managerial expertise to furnish the basis for rapid industrial expansion. Just as Catalonia's achievement of predominance in the provision of shipping services in the Atlantic trade served, according to Pierre Vilar, to prepare Barcelona for 'le commerce libre' so its prior, gradual establishment of its calico-printing industry, and other industries, provided the basis for so firm and prompt a response to the exceptional opportunities available after 1780. Secondly, over the same period, an extensive market network had been developed in the peninsula for commercializing the product of the industry. As was noted in the previous chapter in the discussion on investment in the industry, a high percentage of the capital in the calico-printing concerns was devoted to this national distribution of their product. Nor were the calico-printers alone in this, as we have also seen – similar networks had been established by woollen cloth producers. The existence of this network made it possible to benefit from the various forces – population growth, rising incomes, a change in taste in favour of cotton goods, a cutting off of English supplies during the American war – which transformed the demand situation in the peninsula during these years. Pierre Vilar noted this dramatic turn in the strength of the internal market from approximately 1780.[62] The expansion of the American market represented an additional attraction, but it was the existence of the more established and stable market connections in the peninsula which must have represented the stronger incentive to merchant investors to commit their resources on a long-term basis to industrial investment. Finally, we have noted, the manner in which the industry was organized, and social attitudes to industrial investment, were both favourable to large-scale merchant involvement.

A background permissive influence throughout, and one also which affected business expectations at specific moments in time, thus contributing to conferring to the expansion an occasional precipitate quality, was state policy. No longer was there any question of the state's commitment to the future of the industry and during these years a favourable framework was provided both for production for the interior and export markets with a particularly sharp stimulus being given to the latter by the free trade legislation of 1778. The importance of stimuli offered to the supply side is less easily identifiable – to a certain extent it is the limitations in the government's ability to enforce guild and other regulations rather than the various measures which it passed to moderate them which were significant (for example it permitted the development of the unregulated sector) – but the importance of a pro-industry ideology on participants in industry of all social classes is not to be underestimated.

[62] Vilar, *La Catalogne*, III, pp. 58, 481–4.

THE INDUSTRY IN THE 1780s

A regulated manufacture: Isidro Cathalà & Cia

Much of what characterized a regulated manufacture was revealed in the last chapter. Details were provided on physical characteristics, use of internal spaces, managerial structures, the division between fixed and circulating capital, the labour forces, techniques and relationships to the guilds. The purpose of this section will be different: it will be to look at a manufacture's management over the comparatively long term in order to obtain insights concerning financial and managerial practices and any developments of a dynamic kind, such an increase in the investment in fixed capital or the achievement of technological progress. The survival of the annual balances of Isidro Cathalà's manufacture for the years 1777 to 1797 makes such an assessment possible.[63]

The concern, it will be recalled, was initially called Cathalà Llorens, having developed out of a smaller manufacture founded by the silk-dyer Eudalt Llorens. Something has already been said about the associates in it and the collaborative managerial structure which they adopted.[64] It may be helpful, though, in view of our attempt in the previous section of the chapter to place the expansion of calico-printing within the general dynamic of the Catalan expansion, to say a little bit more about Isidro Cathalà, the leading member of the company. He was a second-generation inhabitant of the city. His father, also called Isidro, had moved to Barcelona from the village of San Feliu de Cabrera, near Mataró, in 1709, had married into an established family of ribbon-weavers (the Vives) and obtained a mastership in the silk-weavers' guild in 1720. Our Isidro obtained his silk-weaver's mastership in 1745, and in 1747, as has already been mentioned, he obtained a royal privilege for a manufacture which he had founded to paint silk in liquid colours in the Chinese style.[65] To place him in the series of generations which presided over the various

[63] In addition, the accounts of the successor concern to Cathalà's, that of Nicolau Sivilla & Cia, for 1794–1801, are held in the library of Barcelona's Chamber of Commerce.

[64] See above pp. 160–1.

[65] On Cathalà, see Molas Ribalta, *Los gremios*, p. 463; L. Camós, 'Historia industrial. Los Catalá y las sedas pintadas a la chinesca', *Boletín de Divulgación Histórica del Archivo Histórico de la Ciudad de Barcelona*, 6 (1945), pp. 117–21; AHPB, Josep Ponsico, book of wills for 1786–7, copy of Cathalà's will of 23 Jan. 1780; ACA, RA, Diversorum, reg. 492, fos. 18–22, copy of Cathalà's privilege for silk-painting.

A distinctive industrialization

Table 6.9. *Capital accumulation and profits in Isidro Cathalà's manufacture, 1762–89*

Year	Capital invested at beginning of year (*libras*)	Capital accumulated at end of year (*libras*)	Profit (*libras*)	Profit (%)	Profit shared out (*libras*)
1762	26,000				
1768	53,381				
1777	106,210	113,677	7,467	7.00	0
1778	113,677	106,646	−7,031	−6.18	5,665*
1779	100,981	109,213	8,232	8.15	9,000
1780	100,213	108,663	8,450	8.43	0
1781	108,663	117,780	9,117	8.39	3,780
1782	114,000	128,596	14,596	12.80	8,596
1783	120,000	132,065	12,065	10.05	12,065
1784	120,000	140,079	20,079	16.73	20,079
1785	120,000	130,548	10,548	8.79	0
1786	130,548	133,301	2,753	2.10	13,301
1787	120,000	127,486	7,486	6.20	7,486
1788	120,000	129,717	9,717	8.90	0
1789	129,717	143,565	13,848	10.68	0

* Capital repayment to Joan Aran who left the company in this year.
Source: Arxiu de la parròquia de Santa Maria del Mar, Cathalà papers.

stages of the growth of the Catalan economy, he was considerably younger than Bernat Glòria, Esteve Canals, Jaume Guàrdia, Francesc de Clota and Bonaventura Canet, who played the central role in the expansion of the industry in the 1740s, and slightly older than Joan Pau Canals and Jaume Canet, sons of this first generation. He was one of several individuals the basis of whose fortune was made in the silk industry between approximately 1730 and 1760 before he joined the calico-printing industry. His fortune, unlike that of Canals, Guàrdia or Glòria, had an industrial origin. The origin of his technique for painting silk is not known. He maintained a total secrecy about it for over twenty years and on the basis of the monopoly which this secrecy gave him he built up a large silk-painting manufacture before he became involved in calico-printing.[66]

[66] A substantial documentation on Cathalà exists in BC, JC, leg. 54, and it is from this that these details are drawn. I have written at greater length on Cathalà in the unpublished paper 'The State and Technological Progress in Eighteenth-Century Barcelona: The Experience of Isidro Cathalà i Vives, Silk-Painter in the Chinese Style' which was delivered

Table 6.10. *Fixed and circulating capital invested in Isidro Cathalà & Cia,
1777–84*

	Circulating capital (*libras*)	Fixed capital (*libras*)
1777	102,314	11,363
1778	88,815	17,831
1779	90,731	18,282
1780	90,381	18,282
1781	100,285	17,496
1782	111,394	17,201
1783	115,083	16,981
1784	123,144	16,935

Source: Arxiu de la parròquia de Santa Maria del Mar, Cathalà papers.

In Cathalà's case, thus, not only had capital been accumulated in the silk industry but experience had been obtained in it in running a large concern.

The association with Llorens's widow came to an end in 1768 – she was bought out by the other associates – and the manufacture from this point became known simply as Isidro Cathalà & Cia. Table 6.9 above serves to chart the progress of the company from its foundation in 1762 through to 1789. Various points emerge. Firstly, it is clear that a steady accumulation of capital, and growth in the size of the manufacture, took place from 1762 until approximately the early 1770s. From this point, however, it is clear that its size and the investment in it were maintained at a fairly constant level. There were slight fluctuations in the concern's circulating capital – for example, with the general expansion in the industry which has been commented on in the last section between 1781 and 1784 – but when profits caused the company's capital value to rise above a certain point the practice seems to have been to distribute them. Probably growth beyond the point which was reached in the early 1770s would have required a significant increase in fixed capital investment – for new bleaching space for example – as well as entailing additional managerial burdens. That the latter consideration, in particular, had weight is suggested by the use of profits in 1785 to establish what was effectively a satellite company, in the name of Bernat Llorens. Rather

to the workshop on Work and Family in Pre-Industrial Europe held at the European University Institute, Florence in December 1987.

than expand the parent comany, it was felt to be a better investment to participate in a smaller concern.[67] Similar practices have been noted in the case of the Glòria family by Roberto Fernández though in its case the investing in smaller companies was a substitute for direct participation in the industry.[68] Català's case shows that a rentier attitude to the industry could exist whilst participation within it was still continuing.

The details on the division between fixed and circulating capital in table 6.10 also give the impression of a nearly totally static organization: the only significant increase in fixed capital investment was occasioned by the purchase of a house for the manufacture in 1778 which had previously belonged to the Llorens widow. The only regular fixed capital expenditure was for printing moulds – each year a number of new designs were either made by the manufacture's engraver or purchased from freelance operators. The introduction of new designs as well as colours was essential for market success. The number of such new moulds made or purchased is one of the few clues which the accounts reveal of the prosperity of the trade. During the years 1781 to 1784 there was a steady increase – from thirteen to twenty-one – paralleling the slight rise in circulating capital commented on.

The accounts reveal continuity with respect to managerial practices. Català acted as administrator until 1778 when his deteriorating health forced him to hand over to one Josep Dalmau. From this point, Català's company's connection with the concern was purely a financial one – no direct role in either administration or production was being taken by any of its members. A succession of *fabricants* worked to the orders first of Català and later of Dalmau. A managerial technique which the company practised in order to increase the commitment of these was to grant them a share of the profits. In 1785, for example, Jaume Verges was paid a small amount for interest on 'the fictitious capital of 1,000 *libras* which the company has provided him with'.

There are, of course, dangers from generalizing from the case of a single manufacture. It may be, too, that the caution which we have detected in the investment practices of the Català company has something to do with the age of its associates – Català was approaching sixty when he handed over the administration of his

---

[67] Details of the investment in the Llorens concern are contained in the Català accounts.
[68] Fernández 'La burguesía barcelonesa', pp. 74–5.

concern to Dalmau. It would seem, though, that the manufacture provides a representative example of the firms in that sector of the industry in which there was a division between ownership and direction – those run by merchant capital making use of the services of a *fabricant* in a managerial capacity. In such concerns the priority must have been on the obtaining of a good and safe return on investment. Risks must have been avoided and fixed capital investment kept to a minimum. The division between ownership and organization of production would seem to be a contributory factor to what was to emerge increasingly as characteristic of the industry – having reached a certain technological level it showed few signs of moving beyond it.[69]

Unregulated manufactures

As already noted, the small scale of the majority of these concerns in this sector of the industry, and the fact that they were generally founded without the formal establishment of a company, have the consequence that documentation concerning them is sparse. The attempt to enforce regulations between 1778 and 1780, however, gave rise to a number of protests from participants in this sector which provide insights into the character of their concerns. As it is one of the rare occasions for which such information exists, and as also the type of concern which existed in this sector was not only going to survive but also to prove, as will be shown, far more resilient than the 'regulated' manufacture when crisis came, I shall take this opportunity to summarize information drawn from these protests. I shall firstly deal with what these sources reveal about manufactures founded by printers, and secondly with what they reveal concerning those founded by members of the textile guilds, and principally by linen-weavers.

The ex-employees of the calico-printing manufactures who were responsible for the majority of these small concerns would in some cases have been working in the industry in a dependent status since childhood. The calico-printing manufactures were large-scale employers of child labour. Such was the case, for example, of Rafel Prat – 'since childhood', he recorded in a petition of January 1779, 'he has always up to now exercised the art of painting *indianas*, and linens, having worked as apprentice, journeyman and master in the

---

[69] On the backwardness of the industry in international terms in the 1790s there is a report of the Junta de Comercio of 8 May 1797 (BC, JC, leg. 53, no. 34, fo. 5).

manufactures of the most creditworthy manufacturers of this commodity'.[70]

Clearly, the barriers to independent production by employees of the manufactures were considerable: as waged employees they would have had no experience of indpendent economic activity and they had to face not only the difficulty of securing sufficient resources to buy tools and raw materials but also that of traversing the psychological, social and political barriers to free industrial activity which existed in a city whose industrial life was overwhelmingly dominated by regulation, be it within the guild system or the generally privileged manufactures. This, in addition to the attempts at maintaining secrecy about colours and mordants, is probably the principal explanation of the relative lateness of the emergence of this rival sector to the established manufactures. It is consistent, too, with something which has already been observed from table 6.2 – the movement to establish these small manufactures was a fairly sudden and large-scale one. The timing may be partly explained by an awareness of the government's increased commitment to achieving technical diffusion which became public in the period immediately preceding the expansion – two privileges were granted in Barcelona, to Isidro Cathalà and Francesc Ribas in 1767 and 1769, with the intention of attaining a wider diffusion of colouring and printing skills – and the scale suggests that strength was experienced in numbers: 'in the year 1771', explained Bonaventura Sayol, '*in imitation of others* I set up a small manufacture of *indianas*'.[71] There are signs, too, that an element of solidarity was conserved among these small-scale producers: when the new industry was threatened during the attempted imposition of the regulations between 1778 and 1780 no less than eleven of them united to protect their right to carry on producing.[72].

It seems likely that some support was received from merchant capital in establishing these independent concerns. One of the rare notarially registered terms of a company to exist for these small concerns reveals that the printer Francesc Casacuberta benefited from such: he possessed, it is recorded, 'a small workshop with looms, tables, moulds and other tools for painting cloths', and his merchant backer was to provide him with all the raw materials and circulating

---

[70] BC, JC, leg. 53, no. 24, fos. 70–1, petition of 15 Jan. 1779.

[71] BC, JC, leg. 53, no. 24, fo. 68, petition of 15 March 1779.

[72] BC, JC, leg. 53, no. 24, fos. 6–7, petition of 15 March 1780.

capital necessary for running his concern.[73] Such assistance, though, was not totally assured – Pau Rovira, prevented from manufacturing in 1779 for lack of looms, explained that there were difficulties involved in finding an associate as a source of finance 'as there are so many who at this moment want to find associates'.[74] Several printers would appear to have led only a semi-independent existence. Such was the case, for example, of a Frenchman, Geronim Richelme, who explained in March 1779 that he had arrived in the city ten years previously and 'has supported himself in it manufacturing and painting linen and cotton cloth' for a range of different manufactures, though recently he had been carrying out some work on his own account. Richelme was clearly what was known in the English trade as a job-printer living principally from commission work.[75] In one case, at least, a printer was successfully retailing all his production which would have ensured the rapid circulation of his working capital: this was Francesc Brusosa who claimed in 1775 that he could not 'meet the demand from his shop, as there were so many buyers who want to provide themselves with, and take advantage of, his cloth.[76]

It is of relevance to explaining the resilience of this 'unapproved' sector of the industry, and it is a sign of the impracticality of the 1768 regulations, with their requirement that all printers should possess or hire bleaching fields, that the setting up of printing concerns had been eased slightly by technological developments – as noted in the previous chapter indigo-dyeing, using the 'resist' process, had been introduced to the city during the 1750s and an initial specialization in this was one easy way into the industry as no bleaching meadow was required. This was the course which Francesc Casacuberta and Joan Gatell had adopted – the latter explaining 'that he specializes in the dyeing of blue and white, for which no bleaching meadow is necessary' – as had several of the approved manufactures in their first years of producing.[77]

As noted, the ex-employees were new to entrepreneurial activity; their small-scale printing industry was also novel in its lack of a corporative framework. Lacking precedents, the painters would seem to have adopted guild practices as their model. The description,

[73] Grau and López, 'Empresari i capitalista', p. 52.
[74] BC, JC, leg. 53, no. 24, fos. 189–90, petition of 15 March 1779.
[75] BC, JC, leg. 53, no. 24, fo. 51, petition of 10 March 1779.
[76] BC, JC, leg. 53, no. 14, fos. 3–7, petition of 19 May 1775.
[77] BC, JC, leg. 53, no. 24, fo. 63, petition of 21 Jan. 1779.

provided by Rafel Prat above, of his career within the calico-printing manufactures in terms of apprenticeship, service as journeyman and mastership, despite the fact that these categories, as we have shown in the last chapter, did not in fact officially exist, will have been noted. In addition, seven other printers described themselves in a petition as 'Approved master manufacturer painters of *indianas*' after passing their examinations as printers in 1779.[78] The description which the eleven, mentioned in the penultimate paragraph, gave of their concerns also shows a respect for guild traditions as well as providing a description of the type of calico-printing arrangements which, as we shall show, were coming to be predominant in the city:

they have had their public workshop in this city for the expressed purpose with moulds, tables for printing, vats for boiling and the other tools necessary to paint and dye the referred to products and a public display [of their trade] in their houses and on the walls of these which face the street so that the public might be aware of the operations which were being conducted there.[79]

The linen-weavers and members of the silk guild who involved themselves in the making and in some cases the printing of calicoes during these years did not face the same legal and psychological barriers to involvement in the industry as the ex-employees of the manufactures. Indeed, as noted in the previous chapter, the linen-weavers' guild was one of the privileged institutions which actually obstructed the carrying out of independent production by the printers on several occasions, claiming to have the monopoly in the production of cotton and linen mixtures. This group's participation in the industry represented a resumption of that experimentation in the use of the new fibre which had been occurring before the 25 May 1760 lifting of the prohibition on imports (the loss of small-scale producers of cotton cloth as a consequence of this measure was mentioned in the last chapter). The greater strength of their position explains a more strident reaction to the attempts of 1778–80 to check their printing activities and impose the 1767 regulations. Agustí Gatell pointed out that he had been a 'master weaver of linen and cotton' since 1749, that he possessed all that was required by the regulations, had some 200 pieces of calicoes in the process of production and was working 'with much greater resources than others who publicly hold themselves to be *fabricantes*'.[80] Joan Gatell

---

[78] BC, JC, leg. 53, no. 25, fo. 2, petition of 9 April 1780.   [79] As n. 72.
[80] BC, JC, leg. 53, no. 24, fos. 48–50, petition of 10 March 1779.

was to make similar claims – 'That for the last fifteen years he has been a manufacturer, directing his manufacture in the present city, to the total satisfaction of the public, and in the same way as all the old manufacturers.'[81]

As has emerged, the 'unapproved' sector of the industry was a broad one grouping a wide range of different types of manufacture and its top end overlapping with the approved sector. The regulations prescribed a variety of different qualifications for approved status – the passing of an examination in the colouring techniques and the possession of twelve looms in a single building and of a bleaching meadow being the principal ones – which did not purely relate to manufactures' size. There were several other substantial concerns like Agustí Gatell's: the linen-weavers Joan Carrés and Pau Fontseré possessed respectively twelve and thirteen looms in 1774 and the latter was having cotton spun by a *paraire* of Berga;[82] Pau Rovira, whose manufacture had been stopped in March 1779 for a default in its number of looms, claimed to have four printing tables in operation, a calender and a rented bleaching meadow and to be investing 22,000 *libras* a year in cloth for printing; Joan Barbara claimed to have 250 pieces of calicoes in the process of painting in 1779[83] and Francesc Salvadó, who only possessed six looms, claimed in the same year that he had invested 9,000 *libras* in the purchase of linens for printing.[84]

Some concerns were distinguished, too, for the quality of their production. Francesc Rigalt, father and son, came near to obtaining a royal privilege for their production of *lanquins*, a yellow-coloured cotton cloth, in 1778.[85] Francesc Brusosa distinguished himself both in the field of introducing new types of cotton cloth and cotton mixtures – 'cotton-linens, stripes, checks… with linen and cotton and others with linen and silk', and also with respect to his skills as printer and colourist – he was the first to pass the exam prescribed by the regulations and in 1779 he himself served as the examiner of a number of other would-be printers. Brusosa's inclusion still on a list of unapproved manufactures at the end of 1779 must be explicable in terms of his lacking the resources to maintain the prescribed number

---

[81] BC, JC, leg. 53, no. 24, fo. 64, petition of 9 April 1779.
[82] BC, JC, leg. 51, nos. 6 and 7, reports of 18 June and 26 Sept. 1774.
[83] BC, JC, leg. 53, no. 24, fos. 89–90, petition of 15 March 1779.
[84] BC, JC, leg. 53, no. 24, fo. 91, petition of 15 March 1779.
[85] BC, JC, leg. 53, no. 20, fos. 6–7, report of Junta de Comercio of 16 May 1778.

of looms and a bleaching meadow.[86] At the other extreme were the cases of Francesc Torras y Cia, with just four looms, and who was working 'for whoever gave him work', Aleix Buscallà and Francesc Servià, 'who produce cloth in the white with six looms for sale', and Miquel Pérez, with three looms, to whose request to be allowed to manufacture the delegate of the Junta de Comercio responded that 'although he imagines himself to be a *fabricant* of *indianas*... he is not such on the grounds of lacking all the qualifications required in the royal orders'.[87]

The fate of the manufactures in this sector has been touched upon in the first section of the chapter. A great number disappear from the records. Some were clearly only ephemeral concerns in the first place – in two cases it is only by the printers' first names that they were known. Some went out of business actually during the 1778–80 survey, a fate which was partly due to the interference which they experienced in the course of their business during these years. A certain number of manufacturers from this sector chose the less perilous if less profitable option of working for others – this was the destiny of Pere Dauff, Pau Rovira and Joan Carrió (who had been one of Joan Gatell's associates), who in 1785 were working as *fabricants* for Ignasi Masvidal, Josep Castañer and Josep Francesc Seguí respectively.[88] A solid core progressed, though – three, Fontseré, Barbara and Marimon, as already noted, into the approved category by 1785 and ten others, including Brusosa, Casacuberta, a Gatell and Francesc Torras are to be found among lists of manufactures drawn up in 1790.

With respect to the longer-term development of the industry, of the two groups discussed in this section – ex-members of calico-printing concerns' labour forces and individuals drawn from the textile guilds, and in particular from that of the linen-weavers – it was the contribution of the latter which was to be the more important. The manufactures established by the former group tended to be the less substantial – few lasted long – whereas some of those founded by the latter were, as some of the evidence presented above has shown, not only of some size but also played an important role as introducers to Barcelona of the new types of cotton cloths which were being developed in England and France during these years – principally

[86] BC, JC, leg. 53, no. 14, fos. 6–7, report of Junta de Comercio of May 1775, and no. 24, fo. 18, for his position as inspector of local manaufactures.
[87] BC, JC, leg. 23, no. 52.
[88] BC, JC, leg. 51, no. 13, industrial survey of 30 Sept. 1784.

stripes, checks and cotton velvets. They were the Barcelona equivalent, clearly on a very small scale, of the fustian-makers of Lancashire whose progress from the 1720s through to the 1760s provided a basis for the take-off of the cotton industry there as well as being the cause of the attraction of the calico-printing trades from London. Their expertise in the use of cotton, as will be seen, was to stand them in equally good stead with the expansion of cotton-spinning, and the growth in demand for a wide range of different types of cotton products, which were beginning to occur in the Catalan industry.[89]

The industry and the city

The survey of the industry undertaken at the orders of the Bishop of Barcelona in 1786 permits the establishment of the distribution of the industry in that year. The majority of manufactures were still situated in the older, eastern half of the city – fifty-eight of the ninety-eight sites which it has been possible to locate – and of these, the great majority, forty-five, with a labour force of approximately 3,289, were concentrated in that north-eastern corner of the city which had been the site of its medieval cloth industry and where, as noted in the previous chapter, the majority of the early manufactures had been built. Some streets must have virtually been given over to the industry – Portal Nou with seven manufactures and a labour force of some 678, San Pere Més Baix and San Pere Més Alt with seven and eight manufactures and labour forces of some 259 and 955 respectively must have been cases in point. Of the two concentrations of manufactures which had existed in the western half of the city in 1768, it was the northern one which had progressed most – a number of connecting streets contained one or several manufactures – Tailers (two manufactures and 326 workers), Valldonzella (four manufactures and 144 workers), Montealegre (four manufactures and 267 workers), Carme (four manufactures and 237 workers), Hospital (eight manufactures and 174 workers), de la Cera (three manufactures and 522 workers), Sant Llàtzer (two manufactures and 259 workers). The southern half contained fewer but larger manufactures – Trentaclaus, (four manufactures and 470 workers), Sant Pau

[89] On the early development of the Lancashire industry and the shift of calico-printing away from London, see Wadsworth and Mann, *The Cotton Trade*, pp. 4–53, 72–96, 170–92; Chapman and Chassagne, *European Textile Printers*, pp. 10, 25–33; Lévy Leboyer, *Les Banques européennes*, pp. 32–49.

⑤ Number of manufactures in street

RAVAL

RAMBLAS

RIBERA

Map 4   Manufactures in 1786

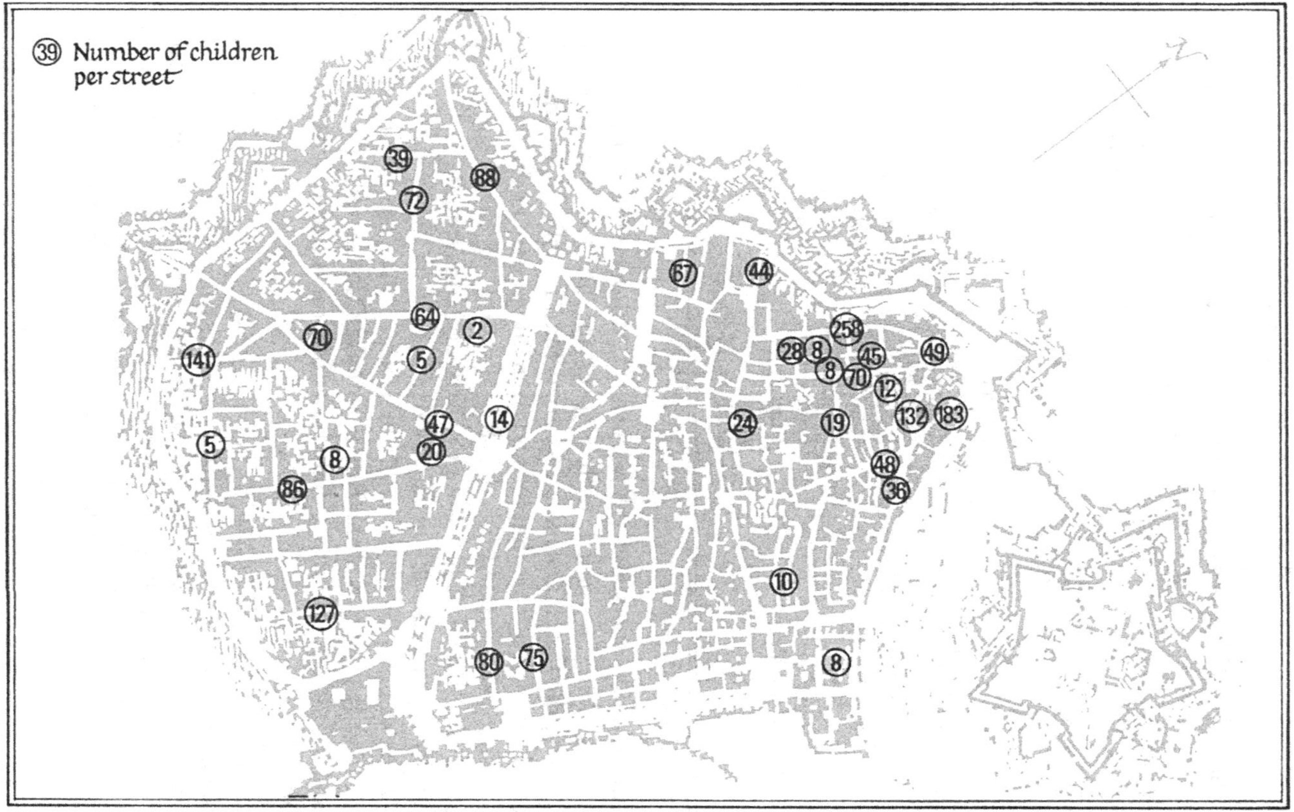

Number of children per street

39 Number of children
   per street

Map 5   Children employed in 1786

Table 6.11. *Principal large manufactures established in the Raval between 1779 and 1786*

Street	Name	Estimated number of workers
Voltes de San Agustin	Vicens	74
de la Cera	Font	133
Carme	Bruguera	55
Hospital	Deparés	48
Sant Pau	Castelló	74
	Espalter	140
	Ramon	103
Sant Llàtzer	Gónima	185
	Masvidal	74
Valldonzella	Gelabert	81
Montealegre	Clarós	56
	Roig	140
	Gallissà	51

(three manufactures and 318 workers).[90] Although the eastern half of the city still dominated with respect to the distribution of the industry, the dominance was less great than in 1768. A trend in the period covered by this chapter had been an increase in the number of manufactures founded in the Raval, most of them substantial concerns. Table 6.11 lists the principal, large manufactures founded between 1779 and 1786 in this quarter.

The extent of the diffusion of the industry gave rise to complaints. In 1785 the directors of the Royal Spinning Company reported that the multiplication of unregulated manufactures had reached such a point that

the street or alleyway of this city and its suburbs in which signs of calico-printing are not to be seen or heard is rare. The hallways, second, third and fourth floors of the smallest of houses which one or two printing tables totally fill have become workshops of this noble and important industry and these days its vulgarization and degradation going beyond this one sees the painting tables, inn-keepers' barrels and gardeners' filthy buckets mixed up in the same place.[91]

[90] Again, I have used the number of children listed in the 1786 diocesan survey of the industry as a basis for estimating total labour forces (see above p. 175n).
[91] Report of directors of Royal Spinning Company of 30 Sept. 1785 which is reprinted in Torrella Niubó, *El moderno resurgir*, pp. 133–46.

The report provides a valuable, additional insight into the character of the unregulated industry which was described above, but apart from that it has to be treated with care. It reflects the hostility of the Royal Company, composed entirely of large manufactures, to the unregulated concerns which represented competition for labour and for customers. As our analysis has just shown it was the larger concerns as much as the small which were putting pressure on space in the city – so much so that an attempt was made by the Real Audiencia to prevent the building of any more manufactures.

The attempt took the form of two edicts which were made public by Barcelona's Town Hall in March 1784 for all building of either woollen or cotton manufactures to be temporarily forbidden within the city walls until new regulations about urban development had been decided upon. The Junta de Comercio was quick to defend the industrial interests threatened by this measure. In a meeting held on 11 June 1784 they defended the practice of concentrating manufactures in cities:

all public order policies attempt to keep the inhabitants of cities and villages grouped together and such has been the case of the workshops of the principal manufacturers and artisans...To remove now such manufactures to outside the city walls or to uninhabited areas would be to suffocate them in their growth and care. It amounts to removing them from the attention of buyers, and from competition between each other and to placing them at a distance from the control of those investing in them and from the visits of the Junta Particular; finally it involves separating them from urban society, which gives life to them, stimulates them [and] situating them outside must cause difficulties for the lodging of workers, make difficult the provisioning [with raw materials] while easing fraud and providing poor prospects either for the construction of the manufacture, its progress or its survival.[92]

The Junta de Comercio's defence of urban manufactures is a curious mixture of medieval, guild ideas – control over quality and the carrying out of industrial activities under the public eye – and more recent ones – competition, invention, the need to provide housing for the labour force (implying a separation of place of work and home) – but it was responded to by the Junta General. On 15 July the Count of Floridablanca ordered the Audiencia to withdraw its March ban.

[92] BC, JC, reg 87, copiador de cartas, letter to Junta General of 11 June 1784.

In response to this command the Audiencia composed a long petition to the king expressing its hostility to the new industry.[93] This provides an outstanding expression of the attitude of the city's administrative and landed elite to the economic changes – foremost among which was the development of the new industry – which were undermining their social and political position. The petition makes five principal types of criticism of the industry – its contribution to a housing problem, the threat which it presented to health, its endangering of 'social control', the lack of respect shown by its leaders to the city's political hierarchy and the corrupting effects of the type of work to which it gave rise – and I shall deal with these in turn.

The housing problem was a general one. Rents in the city had doubled in the space of ten years, the Ministers of the Audiencia recorded. The aspect of it which which clearly irked this body most, however, was the fact that it was the largest, most prestigious buildings which were being occupied by the manufactures, depriving its members of the possibility of finding lodgings which accorded to their status.

> As the cotton manufacturers make such large profits [they complained], it is easy for them to buy the best houses, in the principal streets and sites of the city, using them for this trade, leaving, on account of the large areas which they occupy, a large number of those in the army, legal profession or working for the fisc, who have to live within the city walls, not only without housing but also without any space to build houses, on account of the large areas which they occupy

and they cited both an example of two of their most distinguished colleagues who had been made 'homeless' – the treasurer Blas González and the retired colonel Miguel Abreu – and also a particular case of one of the city's finest houses which had fallen into the rapacious hands of a printer. The 'magnificent' house had belonged to Dona Eulalia Sampere, and had been a 'dwelling worthy of any person of mark'; it had been rented by Miquel Formentí and ruined as a consequence: 'it has already been split up for the processes necessary for his pieces of cloth', the authors of the petition recorded, 'causing universal regret to the many who see it because its beautiful garden, perhaps the best of this city, and which

---

[93] Reprinted in Torrella Niubó, *El moderno resurgir*, pp. 220–5, but dated uncorrectly by him as 1785 whereas it was clearly written shortly after the receipt by the Audiencia of a letter of 15 July from the Count de Floridablanca which reversed the ban on the building of new manufactures.

has already been relegated for the most part into an area for staking out *indianas*, gives onto the much frequented landward city wall'. In support of its argument that the density in the concentration of manufactures in the city represented a health risk the Audiencia had called on the services of doctors from the Junta de Sanidad. They summarized the view of these that the manufactures could give rise to a

> general contagion with such a multitude of people conglomerated in poorly ventilated and cramped sites, working with raw materials and drugs which all give off noxious and venomous particles in quantity...for whose purification a draught of air to blow and scatter them is required, and which can in no way be achieved with the encirclement of so many houses, walls and other fortifications such as surround the manufactures established within the walls.

The concern over 'social control' in the city had existed since the 1760s – it had represented a local justification for that general tightening of the institutional role of the guilds which occurred in Spain in the second half of the century.[94] 'No one is capable of anticipating the consequences which there might be of the existence of so many thousands of men, shut in by the walls, all of the lowest of origins, and who would be difficult to contain in a moment of crisis', it was noted in the petition.

The relative freedom of the principal calico-printers from any type of administrative control was referred to at the beginning of this chapter. It was clearly irksome to those members of the city's population whose livelihood came from the exercise of this control, and this shows up strongly in the petition.

> The directors [referring to the directors of the Royal Spinning Company who had been leading the opposition of the industry to any attempt to restrict building in the city] and manufacturers have never had other political objectives than their own interests, profits and personal comfort. They complain instantly about whichever royal measure appears to be in opposition to these with intolerable arrogance; there is no adequate dyke to contain the pride which money gives to common people.

An ideological as well as a social and political conflict existed, it is clear, and the members of the Audiencia defended themselves against the criticism (made by the Spinning Company) of their being

[94] On this, see R. Grau, 'Barcelona ante el reformismo ilustrado. Un estudio sobre la inestabilidad ciudadana y los orígines de la reformisma municipal barcelonesa en los ãnos 1766–70' (Tesis de licenciatura, Barcelona 1969), esp. pp. 62–102.

'wicked destroyers of national felicity... and downright ignoramuses of the political principles most accepted in Spain and foreign countries' – clearly it was the principles of Adam Smith about which they were being accused of ignorance – and defended the traditional founts of authority – 'the most sacred of the laws and of the magistrature'.

The Audiencia was prepared to concede that the expansion in manufactures had given rise to great prosperity. 'It cannot be denied that nowadays the cotton manufactures of Catalonia are in a highly flourishing state', it was noted in the petition. It claimed, though, that the gains were 'ephemeral and impermanent' and at the cost of both the Principality's traditional wool manufactures and the morals of the labour forces involved. On this latter question, its feelings were strong.

As the manufacturing operations do not require excessive strength or great intelligence [it noted], all devote themselves to live from this superficial (*ligera*) trade which provides an excessive daily wage in few hours, without depriving those who earn it from contracting its vices and being corrupted and harmful members of the Republic. Vagabonds are welcomed... and thus conceal themselves from the view of Justice. Customs are corrupted daily with the participation of members of both sexes and grave harm is occasioned to the most sublime in religion.

CHAPTER 7

Spinning

The disposition of this province is inclined to imitate that which
comes from abroad.

(BC, JC, leg. 23, no. 3, fos. 18–21, report of Junta de
Comercio on textile machine, 4 Oct. 1775)

The Catalan industry incorporated the spinning processes at a late
stage. In 1784 it was still only carrying out some 25 per cent of its own
spinning, relying on imported Maltese yarn for the rest of its needs.[1]
From this date, however, manual spinning spread rapidly and, a
curiosity of the Catalan case, mechanical spinning was introduced
very soon after. In 1802 a royal edict was passed banning the import
of spun yarn. This enforced the completion of the introduction of the
spinning processes. In this chapter the three principal stages of the
development of this new sector of the industry will be described – a
gradual expansion in manual spinning up to approximately 1790, the
first stage of the introduction of mechanical spinning during the
1790s and the completion of the nationalization of spinning between
the imposition of the 1802 ban on yarn imports and the outbreak of
the War of Independence.

THE GRADUAL SPREAD OF MANUAL SPINNING UNTIL 1790

The reasons for the lateness in moving into spinning are relatively
clear: the advantages to be obtained from doing so were not
particularly great. The principal one would have been the possibility
of exercising greater control over the quality of yarn and thus
producing higher-quality calicoes and obtaining better results from
the printing processes. The cloth which was produced with imported

---

[1] Calculation based on the cotton import figures for this year which distinguish between
imports of spun and raw cotton (J. C. Maixé, 'El mercado algodonero y la producción
industrial en Cataluña (1780–1790)', Segon Congrès d'Història Moderna de Catalunya, Pedralbes,
Revista d'Història Moderna, 8, i (1988), p. 376).

235

Maltese yarn did not match the best *toiles* available on the European market but which protective legislation, with rare exceptions, prevented the industry from importing. This was noted both in chapter 3, in connection with the early development of the industry, and in chapter 5, in the context of tariff policy in the 1760s. Against this potential advantage from introducing spinning had to be set the costs involved in terms of the initial training of a labour force and the increased requirements of working capital to which it would give rise. The latter was an important consideration as the Maltese cottons were available on credit.[2]

The growing possibility of drawing on the American colonies for raw cotton increased the incentives to introducing spinning, for its quality was higher than that available in Mediterranean markets and Spanish producers were given privileged access to it.[3] On the other hand, its supply was not regular until the late 1780s as its cultivation and marketing at the American end were little developed (a large share of it reached Barcelona unginned) and direct trading links between Catalonia and America were still relatively undeveloped. In contrast, the trade in Mediterranean spun and raw cotton was well established. One of the reasons for the long dependence on Maltese yarn, Catalan historians have concluded, was its competitiveness with respect to alternatives.[4]

The first sustained efforts to introduce spinning date from the 1760s. Before then the only documented attempt had been that of Bernat Glòria who in 1750 had had some 8,400 lbs of American cotton, imported from Vera Cruz, via Cádiz, on a Catalan organized shipment, spun on an experimental basis in Barcelona with the assistance of a foreign worker. The trial had been successful and Glòria had followed it up firstly by obtaining a royal privilege, conferring both fiscal advantages and the promise of transport facilities for raw cotton on royal warships, and secondly by extending his spinning activities to the town of Terrassa and its hinterland.[5] The pioneer in the 1760s was Josep Canaleta, whose role in the Canals concern had been so prominent and whose manufacture, founded in 1753, had emerged to become one of the leading ones in the industry

---

[2] On this question, see especially Grau and López, 'Empresari i capitalista', pp. 32–3.

[3] It was 'softer and fills the warp with less material' according to delegates of the Junta de Comercio reporting in 1775 (BC, JC, leg. 51, no. 10, fo. 4, 9 Oct. 1775).

[4] Maixé, 'El mercado algodonero', pp. 366–70; on the availability of credit on cotton supplies, see also Sánchez, 'L'estructura comercial', pp. 15–16.

[5] Martínez Shaw, 'Los orígenes', pp. 265–6, and ACA, RA, Diversorum, reg. 499, fos. 129–36, copy of Glòria's privilege.

– it was the eighth largest in terms of looms in 1768.[6] To establish spinning in his concern he had recruited a German spinning 'mistress' from the town of Konstanz, the centre of the Swiss muslin industry, who had brought with her a new type of spinning wheel which was capable of producing finer yarn than that imported from Malta. By September 1765 Canaleta had fifty-five of these wheels functioning, operated by fifty-five spinners, forty-five of whom were 'experienced and skilled' and ten still being trained.[7]

The background influence on Canaleta's attempt was, it would seem, the change in tariff legislation of May 1760. This, it will be recalled, had permitted the import of both printed and unprinted calicoes on payment of a 20 per cent duty. The measure had threatened the survival of the industry for initially the 20 per cent import due was charged on the import of Maltese spun yarns as well – Catalan printers were thus having to produce on very nearly equal terms with their competitors (the latter were having to pay import dues on the cloth they imported but the Catalan producer was having to pay the same dues on his yarn, the cost of which represented a high proportion of the value of the cloth which he produced). After strong protest, concessions were granted to these import dues in the form of permission to import a certain fixed quantity of spun Maltese cotton duty free, and this must have enabled the Catalan producer to retain his dominance of the lower- and medium-quality markets,[8] but the situation with respect to the market for higher-quality printed calicoes must have continued to be the same: the industry's own cloth was not of sufficient quality to enable it to compete, and with respect to the alternative, the printing on imported cloth, the industry was forced to operate on similar terms to its competitors – the imported cloth in the white, like the imported printed calicoes, being liable to the full 20 per cent import dues. Canaleta, it is clear, was trying to equip his company to compete at an advantage in this the most profitable sector of the market – the raw cotton which he imported from America would pay a lower rate of duty than the 20 per cent charged on imported textiles, and the existence of Glòria's precedent

---

[6] Relación de fábricas de indianas en 1768, reproduced in Fernández, 'La burguesía barcelonesa', p. 67.

[7] BC, JC, regs. 1 and 83, Acuerdo of 26 Sept. and letter of Junta de Comercio to Junta General of 5 Oct. 1765. Also Albareda and Sancho, 'Catalunya el 1765', p. 293.

[8] The details of the pressure applied to obtain concessions with respect to the duties charged on imported Maltese yarn are in BC, JC, regs. 81–2, copies of Junta's correspondence for 1760–4.

meant that the prospects of obtaining a royal privilege conferring additional fiscal advantages were good.

Having established his spinning activities, Canaleta did indeed apply for a royal privilege during 1765. The Junta de Comercio, after inspecting his efforts, advised acceptance of the application on the grounds firstly that Canaleta 'merited a reward for having succeeded in establishing a previously unknown skill in Spain', and secondly that to reward him would contribute to others making similar efforts to introduce new techniques. The terms of the privilege, they recommended, should include exemption of import duties for five years on American cotton and the granting to Canaleta of a once-off permission to import 3,000 pieces of cloth in the white free of the 20 per cent import due – the latter rather curious recommendation (the aim of introducing fine spinning was to decrease not to increase imports of foreign calicoes in the white) is a further demonstration of the relevance of the desire to obtain a supply of high-quality calicoes at advantageous prices to Canaleta's interest in fine spinning. The Junta's advice was not followed by the Junta General, however, and the privilege granted in 1766 was not a personal one for Canaleta but a general one for the whole Barcelona industry. Its terms included the exemption of duty on the import of American cottons and on the export of calicoes made with this cotton.[9]

With the benefit of Canaleta's example, and the granting of this general privilege in 1766, the movement into spinning was generalized. In 1768 the Junta de Comercio reported on the progress: 'they have had some wheels or appliances built', it noted of the printers, 'with which spinning can be carried out perfectly and yarn can be reduced to the fineness necessary to make fine calicoes equal to the foreign ones'; some 800 to 1,000 of these 'wheels' had been built – nearly twenty times as many as were being operated by Canaleta in 1765. Spinning had been extended to country areas outside Barcelona, and the Caracas and Barcelona trading companies had collaborated in promoting the import trade in American cotton by transporting cotton-ginning machinery to the provinces of Caracas and Cumana in Venezuela.[10] The registration of the cotton imports in Cádiz for the purpose of claiming the fiscal exemptions granted reveals the identity of some of the printers involved – Joan

[9] BC, JC, reg. 83, letters of Junta de Comercio of 5 Oct. 1765, 6 and 13 Dec. 1766.
[10] BC, JC, leg. 53, no. 4, report of delegates of Junta of 6 July 1768.

Pongem, Miquel Formentí, Pujol and Cantarell and Jaume Canet.[11] Other sources provide other names – the Magarola brothers (who were spinning in 1765 and presented a rival privilege request to Canaleta's),[12] Canaleta himself (he had persisted with his spinning efforts and in July 1768, as again was noted in chapter 5, he presented a request to the Junta General for the use of two ships to export the city's calicoes to Vera Cruz and bring back raw cotton), Josep Igual (his son Ramon Igual recorded that he established various spinning schools in different parts of the Principality from 1770)[13] and Isidro Català (an inventory of whose manufacture in 1778 revealed his ownership of ninety-three spinning wheels).[14]

The 'Real Compañia de Hilados de América', which has been mentioned at several points in the previous chapter, was founded in Barcelona on 24 August 1772. It obtained its royal privilege on 30 June 1773. It consisted in a collectivization of these previous, individual spinning activities. Membership of the company was confined to owners of regulated manufactures who, from the day of its foundation, committed themselves to surrendering to it all their spinning equipment and spinning areas. The initial investment made in it was slightly over 30,000 *libras* (contributions in the form of existing cotton stocks and spinning equipment were permitted) though the directors of the company were entitled to raise an extra 100,000 *libras* by borrowing. The associating printers committed themselves firstly to not carrying out any spinning on their own account during the company's existence, and secondly to accepting their share of any yarn spun.[15]

---

[11] A. M. Bernal, 'Cotó americà per a Catalunya (1767–1777)', in Comissió Catalana del Cinquè Centenari del Descobriment d'Americà, *Segones Jornades d'Estudis Catalano-Americans* (Barcelona, 1986), p. 214.

[12] On the Magarolas' unjustified privilege request, see BC, JC, reg. 83, letters of Junta de Comercio of 1 and 22 Feb. and 1 May 1766.

[13] Herrera Oria, *La real fábrica*, p. 56 n. b.

[14] Existence of recorded in the inventory of Català's manufacture made in 1778 (Arxiu de la parròquia de Santa Maria del Mar, Cathalá papers).

[15] BC, JC, leg. 51, no. 2, fos. 2–11, terms of the Royal Spinning Company, 24 Aug. 1772. Since carrying out the research on which this section is based in the course of 1985, an article by A. Sánchez, 'Los inicios del asociacionismo empresarial en España: La Real Compañia de Hilados de Algodon de Barcelona, 1772–1820', *Hacienda Pública Española*, 108–9 (1987), pp. 253–68, based on similar sources and reaching similar conclusions with respect to the causes of the foundation of this company, has appeared. I shall, therefore, be going over some already covered ground in this section. On the other hand, my version of events contains some minor differences of interpretation from Sánchez's and is also more concerned with the technological side of spinning developments rather than the institutional significance of the formation of the spinning company.

It was rather an exceptional organization. In a period when the development of spinning in Europe represented the cutting edge of the advance towards industrialization, and was subject to the most ferocious competition, a corporative basis had been adopted for the activity in the Catalan industry. The reasons for this apparent regression were various. That on which most emphasis has been placed by historians was the need to create a strong organization to confront the Maltese yarn suppliers who on frequent occasions took advantage of their position as virtual monopoly suppliers to the industry. The principal evidence for this view is provided by one of the clauses of the company's founding charter: in this it was noted that as the foundation of the company would have the consequence that the Maltese would be obliged to supply their yarn more cheaply, and as, consequently, the imported yarn would be cheaper than that produced by the company, founders of new calico-printing concerns would have to be obliged to join the company in order to shoulder their part of the burden of supporting probable running losses.[16] That the desire to exercise pressure on Maltese yarn suppliers was one consideration behind the company's foundation is certain but it was not the only one and the question of whether it was the most important will probably have to be left open.

Additional factors which would need to be taken into consideration to provide a full explanation include the following. Firstly, as has been made clear, the attempts to foment spinning since 1765 had been in the interest of obtaining a higher-quality yarn than that provided by the Maltese industry: in other words the foundation of the company could be argued to represent a continuation of the previous individual efforts to achieve technical improvement in the industry. Secondly, it is clear that the immediate cause of the foundation of the company – like so many other developments in the industry – lay in the complex political negotiations in which the printers had been involved virtually continuously since the 1760 removal of prohibition demonstrated the industry's vulnerability to changes in tariff systems.[17] The need which the industry was under to import the majority of its raw materials in a semi-manufactured form had the consequence that protectionist arguments in its respect were weaker than was the case with the wool industry. Why should the state forgo customs revenue, it could be posited, on the imported spun

---

[16] Grau and López, 'Empresari i capitalista', p. 32.
[17] This has now been clarified by Sánchez, 'Los inicios del asociacionismo empresarial en España', pp. 254–7.

yarn, or for that matter on cloth which might have been imported in the white had such imports been permitted, when only Barcelona's manufacturers and no agricultural interests benefited from these measures Such thinking must have been behind a decision taken on 30 September 1771 to return to a position close to that established by the May 1760 edict – the concessions relating to the import of spun cotton were removed and the import of cotton cloth in the white once again allowed.[18] The establishment of the Royal Company, it can be shown, was the final episode of a series of measures taken by the Catalan industry firstly to ensure the reversing of this decision and secondly to reinforce its position with respect to the ideology which was guiding government policy. The details are as follows.

In response to the decision, 'commissioners' of the printers sent a petition to the Junta de Comercio of 31 October 1771 warning of the loss of their manufacturing activities to which it could give rise – they would be reduced, they lamented, to 'mere painters', and they emphasized the serious social consequences of this in view of the large number of families dependent on these branches of the industry for employment. (They estimated that 18,000 to 20,000 people would be affected and added that 'had the spinning branch been entirely established those continuously occupied in spinning, weaving and bleaching would soon have exceeded 30,000': the petition thus provides further evidence for the extent of spinning undertaken on a private basis before the establishment of the spinning company, as well as of an apparent intention of promoting this activity further.)[19] The Junta de Comercio backed the commissioners' request for a reversal of the decision to admit calicoes in the white but was more reticent about the removal of the 20 per cent duty on the import of spun yarns as its existence, it argued, would serve as a stimulus to an extension in the spinning of American yarn 'which is so necessary in order not to depend on foreign hands for everything relating to these manufactures'. Its concern about this issue led it to appoint two of its delegates to investigate how the spinning of American cotton might be promoted in the industry.[20] These reported back on 14 December with several suggestions amongst which was one to found a spinning company in Catalonia to give 'impulse' to the movement.[21] The Junta de Comercio itself, however, in the report which it submitted

[18] *Ibid.*, p. 256.
[19] BC, JC, leg. 53, no. 8, petition of 'comisionados de las fábricas de indianas', 31 Oct. 1771.
[20] BC, JC, reg. 84, letter to Junta General of 5 Nov. 1771.
[21] BC, JC, leg. 51, no. 1, fos. 1–8, report of 19 Dec. 1771.

to the Junta General in February 1772, while accepting the majority of its delegates' suggestions, rejected this particular one – 'it does not consider it advisable because of companies being liable to the expenses of their managers'; its spun cotton would be 'more expensive to the public', it noted.[22]

The nature of the government's response to the pressure being applied with respect to reversing its September 1771 edict reflected its growing interest firstly in promoting the American cotton trade and secondly in establishing cotton-spinning in Spain on a widespread basis. Cotton-spinning had the characteristics of the 'popular industry' favoured by Campomanes – its promotion could take place within traditional structures promoting social stability.[23] The priorities are apparent in the royal edict which was passed on 12 May 1772. The measure restored the concessions with respect to import duties on imported spun yarn from Malta for a further three years but also extended the application of the 1766 privilege which had withdrawn import levies on American cotton for Catalan manufacturers to all such cotton imported through ports permitted to trade with America and expressed the royal desire that Catalan printers should carry out the spinning of this cotton outside as well as within Catalonia. The royal aim, it stated, to promote the consumption of American cotton could be achieved 'by the cotton manufacturers of Catalonia dedicating themselves, as His Majesty hopes they will, to promoting the establishment of the spinning of American cotton, which they need for their manufactures, not only in the Principality, but also in the other northern provinces to which it will be imported directly'.[24]

The wording of the edict shows that a response to the further concession concerning the import of Maltese cottons was expected from the printers. The foundation of the Spinning Company was this response. The preamble to its founding charter states specifically that it had been founded to respond to this royal desire to promote spinning activities. That it was the right sort of response is suggested firstly by the fact that the company, despite the reservations which the Junta de Comercio had about it, was given royal status on 30

[22] BC, JC, reg. 85, letter of 8 Feb. 1772.
[23] Pedro Rodríguez de Campomanes, count, fiscal and then president of the Council of Castile, was the propagator of the ideas of the Physiocrats in Spain, particularly by means of two pamphlets which he wrote, and had circulated widely throughout Spain in 1774 and 1775, *Discurso sobre el fomento de la industria popular* and *Discurso sobre la educación popular de los artesanos y su fomento* (Herr, *Eighteenth Century Revolution*, pp. 50–2).
[24] AHN, Consejos, libro 1514, copy of edict of 12 May 1772.

June 1773 and secondly by the fact that a week later the ban on the import of calicoes in the white was renewed.²⁵

The Royal Spinning Company initiated its spinning activities immediately. Its output between 1772 and 1774 is recorded in table 7.1 below. Its efforts, however, ended abruptly. No evidence has been found of any spinning by it after September 1774. The causes of the failure were given in a report prepared by representatives of the calico-printers in 1783 when the company's revival was being discussed: its establishment had resulted, it was noted, in the Maltese lowering their prices causing the company's production to become uncompetitive. Irregularity in the supply of American cotton was another difficulty, and in addition, if the analysis undertaken up to this point concerning the influences on the movement into spinning has been correct, then the restoration of full protection to the industry by the 7 July 1773 measure removed what throughout had been a principal stimulus for promoting spinning – the competition to the industry's product from higher-quality imported *toiles*. Finally, it seems unlikely that the organization of spinning on a collective basis could have been efficient – the Junta de Comercio's reservations in this respect would seem to have been justifiable.²⁶

The foundation of the Barcelona Spinning Company would appear thus to have had some negative consequences for the introduction of spinning to Catalonia. It had led, we have seen, to the abandonment of some promising, individual promotion of spinning by calico-printers and the clause in its charter forbidding such activities may have been a disincentive to these being resumed. Certainly the abandonment of spinning by the company represented a temporary ending for the involvement of the industry as a whole – the movement into spinning came to a virtual halt for seven or eight years – the paralysis being contributed to by the severing of trading links with America between 1779 and 1783 and a further refusal of an individual privilege to the Canaleta concern for the production of muslins in 1774. To the company's credit, however, was the introduction of cotton-spinning techniques to several parts of Catalonia where they had previously been unknown and the establishment thus of a technical basis for the expansion in the sector which took place some ten years later.²⁷

If the Royal Company had failed largely as an industrial

²⁵ Izard, *Industrialización*, pp. 21–24.
²⁶ BC, JC, leg. 51, no. 13, fos. 3–10, report of directors of Royal Spinning Company, 4 June 1783. ²⁷ See below, p. 246.

Table 7.1. *Spinning by the Royal Spinning Company, 1772–4*

24 Aug. 1772–3 Jan. 1773	20,714 lbs
4 Jan. 1773–4 Jan. 1774	98,873 lbs
5 Jan. 1774–30 Sept. 1774	59,533 lbs

Source: BC, JC, leg. 51, no. 8, report of directors of Royal Spinning Company of 22 June 1775.

organization, however, it had succeeded as a political one – not surprisingly, given the circumstances of its coming into existence. The industry's interests, or at least the interests of the majority of its 'regulated' manufactures, was from this point promoted by elected directors of the Royal Company, rather than by 'commissioners', such as those who had opposed the 1771 relaxation in tariff legislation. This was to be the case into the nineteenth century, long after the company had ceased to play any commercial role.[28]

With peace in 1783, the question of the industry's extending its spinning activities was raised again. Once more, it was the question of what should be done about the import of Maltese cottons – which had been permitted because of the shortage of American supplies – which led to the reopening of the issue: there were suggestions made again that these imports should be restricted and greater use of American cottons made. With peace, it was clear, a more regular supply of these could be assured. In addition, some printers were again anxious to ensure independence with respect to their yarn supplies – Miquel Formentí wrote to a customer in 1784 that 'the manufacture of *indianas* was a fruitless activity' and predicted that this would last until 'the raw cottons from our Americas arrive in quantity at reasonable prices and the spinning of the said cottons which we are promoting with utmost effort is in a position to meet the demand'.[29]

The majority of concerns in the regulated sector of the industry, however, again favoured the delegation of responsibility for the extension of spinning to the Royal Spinning Company. During 1783, their representatives recommended that the company should be reestablished and strengthened, supporting their request with the types of argument which they knew from their past negotiation over

[28] On this, see Grau and López, 'Empresari i capitalista', p. 32, and Sánchez, 'Los inicios del asociacionismo empresarial en España', *passim*.

[29] Cited by Sánchez, 'Los fabricantes de indianas', p. 72 n. 126.

the issue would appeal to the Junta General – the spread of spinning could contribute to resolving 'the recent excesses and disorders [referring to popular protest] which cause so much concern… to Your Majesty', and by collaboration with the Sociedades de Amigos del Pais these benefits could be extended beyond the Principality.[30] During 1783 more precise demands were formulated, including that the company should be granted a monopoly in the buying and spinning of cotton in the Principality, and in addition that the sale and purchase of cotton cloth in the white should be made illegal. In other words, it was not only foreign competition which they now wanted eliminated but also that of local small-scale producers of calicoes within the Principality.[31] This hardening of their position clearly represented a reaction to the great expansion in the industry which had been occurring since the end of the war and to that consequent multiplying of smaller manufactures to which reference was made in the previous chapter. The character of the reaction of the Junta de Comercio, between whose opinions and those of the representatives of the industry a deepening rift had been developing, was not to be doubted: it pointed out that to accept the printers' proposals would result in the victimization of both the cotton-growers, forced to sell to a single buyer, and the cotton-spinners, forced to work for a single employer, while the ban on the sale of locally produced calicoes in the white 'was no less odious' and clearly intended as a means whereby 'the manufacturers would secure an abundant supply of weavers in order to contract them at low wage rates'.[32]

The extremity of the Royal Company's proposal was a sign in fact that the expansion of the industry, both with respect to spinning and other processes, was beginning to slip from the control of the oligarchy of regulated manufactures whose interests it represented. Industrial change was beginning to move at too fast a pace for it to be checked by political negotiations and, while these were going on, spinning, to a great extent on an independent basis, was spreading. During 1784 a succession of complaints was made to the Junta General from woollen production centres around Sabadell and

[30] BC, JC, leg. 51, no. 13, fos 3–10, report of directors of Royal Spinning Company, 4 June 1783.
[31] These demands of the Royal Spinning Company are summarized in a letter of the Junta to the Junta General of 20 March 1784 (BC, JC, reg. 87).
[32] BC, JC, reg. 87, letter of Junta of 20 March 1784. See also leg. 51, no. 13, fos 19–46, extensive documentation on the affair, including a copy of this letter.

Table 7.2. *Yarn spun with American cotton, 1772–93*

1772	20,714 lbs
1773	98,873 lbs
1774	59,533 lbs
1783	228,500 lbs
1784	131,480 lbs
1785	273,183 lbs
1786	52,916 lbs
1787	54,066 lbs
1788	226,275 lbs
1789	374,500 lbs
1790	769,475 lbs
1793	1,098,600 lbs

Source: Maixé, 'El mercado algodonero', p. 377, and Vilar, *La Catalogne*, III, pp. 117, 123 (for 1793).

Terrassa whose working areas were being invaded by cotton (including the towns and villages of Sant Quirze, Castellar, Sentmenat, Monistrol, Castellbell, Vacarisses, Olesa, Esparreguera and Sant Vicenç de Castellet)[33] and there is evidence of the spread of activity in a number of other localities too – in villages in the *comarcas* of Cervera, Noguera, Anoia and Urgell (where the activity had its source in the expansion in the Royal Company's activities in the 1770s),[34] in Berga,[35] in Ripoll (where the Barcelona printer Serralach was having spinning carried out in 1784),[36] in Manresa (the royal Company had been the agent for the introduction here too),[37] in Vic[38] and in the *comarcas* of the Garrotxa and Cerdanya where cotton stocking-makers, using mechanical looms, had been spinning with American cotton since the early 1770s.[39] The figures for the number of pounds of yarn spun in the principality with American cotton during these years (summarized in table 7.2) attest to this growth. A rapid expansion at the end of the American war is apparent, with

[33] BC, JC, reg. 87, letters of Junta of 7 May and 21 July 1784.
[34] E. Tello, 'La filatura domèstica del cotó a l'interior de Catalunya. L'exemple de la Segarra (1770–1824)', *Estudis d'Història Econòmica*, 1 (1987), p. 101.
[35] BC, JC, leg. 51, no. 7, report of June 1774.
[36] BC, JC. leg. 51, no. 15, fo. 2, petition of 2 April 1785.
[37] J. Oliveras, 'El agua y el vapor en la formación del paisaje industrial de Manresa en el siglo XIX', *Primeras jornadas sobre la protección y revalorización del patrimonio industrial* (Bilbao, 1982), p. 402.   [38] J. Albareda, *La industrialització a la plana de Vic* (Vic, 1981), pp. 32–3.
[39] M. Puig, *Les primeres companyies per a la fabricació de gènere de punt a Olot (1774–1780)* (Olot, 1988), pp. 39–40.

production levels reaching two to three times those achieved by the Royal Company during the 1770s, a sharp decline followed in 1786 to 1787 – the sector sharing in the general crisis of these years – and then, from 1788, continuous growth to 1793 by which time nearly half of the industry's yarn was being spun in the Principality.

As significant as the growth itself was the manner in which the new sector of the industry was being organized. From approximately 1770, rural Catalonia had begun to be involved in the cotton industry but now this involvement was becoming autonomous. Some printers were continuing to control their rural spinning directly – the cases of Serralach and Formentí have just been referred to – but increasingly rural spinning was being carried out by independent agents who were then selling their yarn in the capital: a provincial yarn market was developing. The change was noted by the administrator of Barcelona's customs in 1790: 'The production of yarn with cottons from our Americas is on the increase', he noted, 'and this manufacture has spread in many villages of this Principality.' He added that originally this spinning had been run by the Spinning Company in Barcelona but that 'now it has increased so much that they buy the said cottons, and spin them or have them spun on their own account, and sell them later to the manufacturers'.[40]

Concluding on this first stage of the movement of the Catalan industry into spinning, up to the early 1780s efforts made were discontinuous and insubstantial, but after that date greater commitment was shown. The reasons for the early lethargy were the limited advantages to be obtained from the introduction of spinning. The ability to produce higher-quality cloth was the principal one, but this only became of paramount importance during the short period when the prohibition on foreign cloth imports was withdrawn. The principal stimulus to early attempts at spinning was provided by such withdrawals. The existence of protection has thus been shown to have been another of the causes of that conservatism in the investment policies of the industry which was identified in the last chapter. Protection also played a major contribution to that corporativism which became an increasingly marked characteristic of the industry – the sharing by calico-printers in a general privileged position was one unifying factor and the other was the growing need to act

[40] Maixé, 'El mercado algodonero', p. 369.

collectively to defend this position.[41] The greater commitment to spinning after 1780 had, it is clear, a variety of explanations: firstly the supply of imported American cotton became more regular, secondly there was both a massive growth in the industry and a considerable widening in the range of cotton production in the Principality which greatly increased demand for yarn and thirdly there was a structural change in the spinning branches – spinners achieved autonomy and a yarn market (and a cloth one, too) developed in the Principality. The last change was the fundamental one – whereas the printers' interest in spinning had been predominantly instrumentalist, a class of cotton-spinners was emerging during these years for which the activity had become essential to its livelihood.

THE INTRODUCTION OF SPINNING MACHINERY IN THE 1790S

A first mechanical spinning device was introduced in Barcelona in 1785. It was described in a report of the Junta de Comercio as a 'machine with which a single person can spin 36 threads of cotton yarn'. This description makes it clear that it was a version of Samuel Hargreaves's spinning jenny.

Its introducer was not a calico-printer but, it seems, one Pontet, described by the Junta de Comercio as 'a subject of distinction inspired by his generous desire for the advancement of the arts and the public good'. Pontet had had the machine constructed in a house in the Carrer Escudillers, in the heart of the commercial area of the town (some way from the majority of calico-printing concerns), by two foreign machine-makers whom he had recruited in October of the previous year. Their expertise had not extended to making the machine function properly and in view of this Pontet himself had had to make a visit to France to recruit someone with skills in the use of the machine. The difficulty had consisted in preparing the cotton rovings for spinning. Eight other machines had been built and six started on and Pontet was offering to pass these on as well as their secret, 'of which he is the sole holder not having communicated it to anyone else', in return for the refunding of the approximately 6,000 *libras* in costs which he had sustained.[42]

---

[41] This is the central argument of Sánchez in his article cited in n. 15 above.
[42] BC, JC, leg. 23, no. 14, fos 1–2 (undated). The individual is not named in this document; however, the name of Pontet is recorded in the accounts for the expenses involved in

On 10 November the Junta de Comercio called on two directors of the Royal Spinning Company to inspect the machine. Their report was most favourable: the individual who had introduced it (about whose identity secrecy was still apparently being maintained) was 'most worthy of attention', they informed the Junta, and his machine, with which a single woman could spin eight times as much fine yarn as with the normal wheel, they described as 'an object worthy of all admiration and respect'. As directors of the organization 'whose purpose is to promote, extend and perfect the spinning of this kind to the point of enabling the manufactures to be independent of foreign supplies', they offered to enter into negotiations to buy the machine and its secret provided that the Junta contributed at least a third of the cost, offering in return to instruct anyone whom the Junta proposed in its manner of operation once it had been in use for two years.[43]

Arkwright's roller spinning machine was to reach Barcelona soon after the spinning jenny. Again the introduction was independent of the actions of either the Royal Spinning Company or of those of any individual printers. Its source was two English machine-makers, John Waddle and Joseph Caldwell, who had first sought their fortunes in France but who, frustrated no doubt by the economic crises and changes of ministry which preceded the Revolution, had offered their services to the Spanish Ambassador in Paris who had sent them to Madrid. There they had been maintained for nearly a year but the government had finally decided, in view of its prior involvement in establishing cotton manufactures at Avila and in Madrid, to respond to their wish to be allowed to try their chances in Barcelona. A letter of 20 October 1789 from the Count of Florida-blanca to Barcelona's Intendant, Juan Miguel de Indart, informed him of this decision and the Intendant in turn instructed the Junta de Comercio to check, on the arrival of the English 'artisans', whether their 'skills... in the practice of spinning and carding cotton, and in machine-making... exceeded the progress which has been made here'.

On 24 October Waddle and Caldwell left Madrid, laden with over

introducing the jenny (no. 14, fo. 4), even though he is not precisely identified as the machine's introducer, and J. Townsend, in his *A Journey through Spain in the years 1786 and 1787* (3 vols., London, 1791), I, p. 138, states that it was a M. Pontet who had introduced what he takes, mistakenly it seems, to be a machine like Arkwright's to the city.
[43] BC, JC, leg. 23, no. 14, fos. 6–7, report of Pongem and Prat, 23 Feb. 1786.

120 kilograms of baggage – they were bringing with them a small version of their spinning machine – and preceded by a reputation for being difficult individuals with whom to negotiate: exact details of the sums which they had been advanced for their travel were passed on with the explanation that this was a necessary precaution in view of 'what these men might allege, for those of their class and nation are generally difficult to satisfy and nearly always ungrateful'. Their arrival in Barcelona from the 'Court' was reported to the Junta de Comercio on 11 November. In reply to an interpreter who had asked them to detail their skills they had said that they 'knew how to card and spin cotton by means of a machine which they had brought' which, if enlarged, would be capable of driving 4,000 spindles. They presented samples of the yarn which could be produced with the machine.

The claims were put to the test by a demonstration of the machine in the Stock Exchange, which was where the Junta had its offices, attended by a delegate of the Junta with expertise in cotton-spinning. His report was favourable – the yarn was finer and much cheaper than both that produced by the regular means and that imported. With Waddle's and Caldwell's credentials thus established the Junta instructed four of its delegates to take the necessary measures to secure the commercial exploitation of the invention.

The first step taken was to convince members of the industry of the utility of the machine. For this purpose, a further demonstration of it was arranged on 21 January 1790: a range of American cottons were spun in front of a group of muslin-spinners. The reaction again was highly favourable: the machine, it was calculated, was capable of producing fine yarn at half the cost of that which was being imported from Switzerland.

With all doubts thus removed, the introduction of the spinning machinery could be initiated. An initial difficulty was the negotiation of terms with the English machine-makers – the taking place of 'many and long discussions with them, with the interpreter showing a lot of patience and flexibility' was recorded by the Junta – but their basic proposal was a very simple one. It was recorded in written form: they intended, they declared, 'to be supply'd with Proper Persons Money and all necessary Materials to erect a House for Carding, Drawing, Roving and Spinning Machines Containing 1000 Spindles Drove by Water or as many more as may be found necessary to supply this country with Cotton Yarn'. What they were planning, it is clear, was to build as many mills as were required to service the industry's yarn requirements on the basis of the standard model used in the English industry (1,000 spindles) – mills of this type have been referred to as the 'Arkwright proto-type mill'. More profound difficulties, however, were to be encountered firstly with respect to working out the form in which the calico-printers would participate in the enterprise, and secondly in obtaining ministerial approval for the project – the fact that the machine-makers had reached Barcelona via the Court meant that such approval was essential.

The former difficulties emerged after a meeting had been organized by the Intendant to arrange for the funding of the enterprise – some 70,000 *libras* was required. It was attended by fifty-four printers, showing the wide interest which the project had attracted, who agreed that the investment should be divided into a hundred shares. Sixty of these were immediately subscribed. After the meeting, however, the precise defining of the company's terms led to a renewal of a conflict of principles between members of the Junta and the majority of calico-printers which had existed since the foundation of the Royal Spinning Company. The majority of printers were only prepared to participate in the company if it were granted a ten-year monopoly in the use of the new machinery but this demand clashed with the Junta's desire to ensure rapid diffusion of the machinery: 'the machine must be generally available, and instruction in spinning public as this is what is necessary for its promotion', one of its delegates claimed.

In view of this disagreement a representative of the Junta prepared an alternative proposal for establishing the spinning machinery, designed to ensure its rapid diffusion, and this was put to a second meeting of the calico-printers which was held on 15 February 1790. It was emphatically rejected by the printers. Of the fifty-one who attended this second meeting, forty-six backed the original idea of a company with a ten-year monopoly, three refused to back either the original or the Junta's scheme and there were only two individuals who showed partial support for the Junta's position. One of these was Erasme Gónima, who voted to accept the idea of a company but without a monopoly, recording his agreement with the Junta de Comercio's views on liberty, and asserting that his opposition to a monopoly was such that he would freely cede the five shares which he had bidded for in the company should this principle be adopted. Gónima was to emerge during the decade as a leading spirit in the

industry and he showed here foresight both in his awareness of the
inequity and probable impracticality of a monopolistic solution and
of the need to reach a rapid decision in order to take advantage of the
opportunity which had been presented to the industry.

In view of the rejection of its proposal, the Junta de Comercio
devised another plan – to buy the secret itself from the English
machine-makers, to manufacture the machinery and to pass it on in
small units of fifty-six spindles, and with the provision of instruction
in its use, at a price of 200 *pesos* to anyone requiring it. This proposal,
together with that of the calico-printers for a monopolistic company,
and a third option, for the dismissal of the English machine-makers
and the abandonment of the project, were then, on 25 February
1790, passed on to Floridablanca with a request that he should decide
between them. No reply, though, was to be received to this request,
nor to a succession of reminders which were sent about it. In October
1790 the two Englishmen, no doubt frustrated by the long delay, and
who themselves had received no replies to letters which they had sent
to the Junta General de Comercio requesting a decision on the
matter, asked the Junta whether it still wanted to continue with the
project and, if it did not, whether they might have permission to put
the machinery into operation in association with 'some individuals'.
In May 1791 the Junta backed this proposal, explaining to the Junta
General that the original company was not practicable 'because of
their [the Englishmen's] excessive demands and incomplete explanations' but that 'a separate organization could contribute to the
development of manufactures'. The long silence of the Junta General
was only finally broken in June 1791 : it was explained that the papers
connected with the case had been mislaid. Copies of the correspondence were then sent from Barcelona, and shortly after these
were received a decision of a sort was finally reached – the Junta was
instructed to send the Englishmen's machine to the Royal Cotton
Manufacture of Avila for comparison with those in operation there.
When, though, an attempt was made to locate the Englishmen in
order to obtain their machine it was found that they had left the city.
One of them was later to find employment in what was described as
'a most sumptuous cotton manufacture' established by the Duke of
Infantado near Santander.

The opportunity was thus lost, for the Englishmen had retained
secrecy over their machine until the end. As the Junta pointed out to
the Intendant, its members had witnessed the experiments which had

been carried out with the machine but the Englishmen had carried them out

in a wary manner so that the good results achievable by the machine should be seen, without its manner of construction or operation being understood, and they never would allow a model of it to be made – requests to do this were made many times – for if it had been possible to obtain one all that was desired would have been achieved insofar as there would have been no lack of artisans here who would have constructed it with the assistance of a model.

The blame for the failure was put on Waddle and Caldwell – 'the Junta is very disturbed that the said Englishmen by the secrecy with which they have disappeared should have caused the many steps, measures, projects and expenses... which it has undertaken for the achievement of this public good to be fruitless', it was recorded – but it is clear that the fault was not confined to them. Carrera Pujal was closer to the mark – the Junta and the printers, he recorded, had let slip a 'magnificent opportunity... the first because of its platonism and the second because of egoism'.[44]

There was to be one other new spinning machine introduced during this period and, in connection with it, one other attempt to gain monopolistic advantages from controlling the process of technological diffusion. The machine was an improvement on the spinning jenny and it had been introduced, in conjunction with carding and ginning machinery, to the town of Cardona by two associated merchants, Manuel Flotats, from Cardona, and Salvador Pallerolas, from Seu d'Urgell, in collaboration with an 'English machine-maker' from Manchester, one Bernard Young. The improvements consisted in the ability to drive a larger number of spindles (Young had constructed a machine with seventy-eight), and resultant higher productivity, and an easier mode of operation – a larger wheel was used, the spinner was situated at the centre of the machine rather than at the side, as was the case with the original jenny, facilitating control of the machine and the mending of broken threads, and the releasing of yarn for winding on the bobbins was apparently automatic, not requiring 'backing off'. It is clear that the

---

[44] The principal documentation concerning the introduction of Arkwright's roller-spinning techniques is contained in BC, JC, leg. 23, no. 19, fos. 1–69; reg. 12, Acuerdos of 26 Oct., 11 Nov. 1789, 21, 28 Jan., 1, 15, 25 Feb., 22 April, 29 July, 18 Oct. 1790; reg. 89, letter of 10 Jan. 1790. Carrera Pujal includes a description of these events as well as this comment in his *Historia política*, IV, pp. 240–3.

machine incorporated the improvements made to the jenny shortly after it had been invented by Haley, who was responsible for replacing Hargreaves's awkward horizontal wheel by a vertical one and developing a roller system for driving spindles which greatly increased the maximal size of jennies (machines with up to 130 spindles were recorded), and possibly those of Thomas Highs – who also had used the roller or cylinder principle for driving the spindles, enlarging the potential size of the machines, and was the inventor of an automatic method of winding spun thread onto the bobbins.[45]

The existence of the machine came to public notice as a consequence of a request made by Flotats and Pallerolas during 1792 to the Junta General de Comercio for various fiscal privileges and the right for six years to charge a substantial licensing fee on anyone wanting to use the new spinning device and the other machines which they had introduced. The request was referred to Barcelona's Junta which arranged for the testing of the machines in the presence of two printers with specialized knowledge of spinning, Jacint Ramon and Ramon Bosch. The machines were found to represent, indeed, a considerable improvement on those already in use in the industry, but the delegates of the Junta encharged with assessing the terms which Flotats and Pallerolas were requesting for their privilege advised against their acceptance. Their grounds were firstly that what they had achieved were improvements rather than inventions, secondly that a number of other people were involved in the developing of spinning machinery and there existed already machines in the Principality very similar to those of Flotats and Pallerolas and thirdly that to impose the licensing fees would result in a near doubling of the cost of the machines, slowing their diffusion, to which the Junta, as during the Waddle and Caldwell affair, attached much importance.

In view of the opinion of its delegates, the Junta de Comercio submitted strong advice against conceding Flotats's and Pallerolas's demands – 'in view of the concession being opposed to the good of the state and the development of the national industry which it desires and seeks' – and recommended instead the making of a one-off payment from central funds. Surprisingly, however, in view of this advice, the Junta General granted a six-year exclusive privilege to Flotats and Pallerolas on 25 October 1792 for the construction and

[45] R. L. Hills, *Power in the Industrial Revolution* (Manchester, 1970), pp. 54–9.

sale of the machines in question, which was intended to apply retrospectively to similar machines which were already in operation.

The individuals who had introduced spinning and carding machinery of very similar types to those for which Flotats and Pallerolas were requesting their privileges were Ramon Farguell and Francesc Angerill, cotton manufacturers of Berga, who in July 1792 had offered to make public a machine with sixty-four spindles in return for a reward and who had also developed a new carding engine; Josep Serraima, a Barcelona manufacturer, who had mounted a machine with sixty spindles in the Barceloneta, apparently of identical design to that of Flotats and Pallerolas; and Simeon Lebret, a Frenchman, who was operating thirty spinning machines in Barcelona (of the traditional Hargreaves type it seems), and had also developed a new carding machine. The speculations of the delegates of the Junta de Comercio as to the reasons for these cases of near simultaneous innovation in the industry are instructive as to the state of interest in technical change at this stage and the methods by which it was probably achieved: the new machine, and they were referring in particular to the spinning one,

is not completely secret ... either because of the indiscretion of the workmen whom Pallerolas and Flotats used for the construction of the pieces [of the machine]; or of that of the workers who have spun with their machines, or by the indulgence or carelessness of the associates themselves in offering to show the machines to people who while claiming to be merely curious about them, perhaps tried to copy them; or maybe because some have known how to get information by other means which were perfectly regular and honest and have built one which approximates to the nature and advantages of this.[46]

These new machines represented the cutting edge of a general movement towards a mechanization of spinning which took the form principally, it is clear, of diffusion of the Hargreaves machine introduced in 1786. 'The progress...which has been made in machinery for cotton during the last four years is notorious' the Junta's delegates had recorded in their response to the Flotats privilege request, and they predicted that the branch of the industry

---

[46] Documentation concerning this case and also the privilege requests of Farguell, Angerill and Lebret is contained in BC, JC, leg. 23, no. 21, fos. 1–19 (especially valuable is the letter containing the report of the delegates of the Junta of 9 Aug. 1792 (fos. 6–11)), and reg. 13, Acuerdos of 23 July, 11 Oct., 8 Nov. 1792, and 18 July, 4 Aug. 1793.

'would carry on improving...the multitude of people interested in developing it making them think this way'.[47] The progress was sustained throughout the 1790s. In 1796 Flotats and Pallerolas reported that they themselves were operating thirty of the improved spinning jennies in Cardona and that there were a total of 250 such machines operating in the Principality, but they complained that their licensing rights were being ignored and that their version of the jenny had not achieved predominance because inaccurately copied versions of it which had been done on an illegal basis had led to its losing its reputation.[48]

In practice, it is clear that the mechanization of spinning in this period took the form above all of a rapid diffusion of the traditional Hargreaves jenny. It was a machine which could be produced in a variety of different sizes, its cost was low and its use was compatible with the traditional domestic organization of production. These qualities of the improved version of the jenny introduced by Flotats were pointed out by the members of the Junta de Comercio encharged with vetting the Flotats privilege request:

To these and to other useful characteristics, the machine adds the qualities of very easy construction and operation, low costs hardly attaining 500 copper *reales*, transportability and easy mounting, with the result that the mother of a family, without abandoning her domestic chores, and however meagre her resources, can own and use this machine in her house. It is perhaps more useful in these respects than other more perfect machines, more complex and with higher productivity, but very costly, which have been established in Avila, and in other areas outside Spain.[49]

They held even more strongly for the simple jenny and were among the principal causes for its rapid diffusion.

By 1797, there were said to be 333 machines in use in Reus, spinning 350 lb of cotton a day (they could not have been very large ones as a hand-spinner was capable of spinning 6 oz of yarn in a day) and 4,000 in the plain of Vic.[50] It is clear that, as had been the case in Lancashire during the early years of the diffusion of the jenny, machines of all sizes were introduced, both for carding and

---

[47] BC, JC. leg. 23, no. 21, fos. 6–11, letter of delegates of Junta of 9 Aug. 1792.
[48] BC, JC, leg. 51, no. 21, report of Pallerolas and Flotats of 25 Sept. 1796.
[49] *Ibid.*
[50] *Almanak Mercantil* (1797), p. 482, for Reus; for Vic, see J. M. Delgado, 'Las transformaciones de la manufactura al segle XVIII', in J. Nadal Farreras (ed.), vol. IV of J. Salvat and J. M. Salrach (directed), *Història de Catalunya* (6 vols., Barcelona, 1978–80), p. 254.

spinning.[51] In the Sabadell area, which experienced a rapid movement into cotton towards the end of the decade, the use of 'many machines, of all types, more or less simplified and operable by a girl' was noted.[52]

If one explanation for the rapidity with which mechanical spinning was taken up was the machinery's cheapness and its compatibility with the domestic unit of production, others were, on the one hand, the growing poverty of these years – there were several periods of high grain prices and impending Malthusian crisis, the first, the years 1788 to 1789, being described as 'of extraordinary poverty' in one of the areas which moved quickly into spinning[53] – and, on the other hand, the crisis being experienced in wool and silk production. The latter was caused both by competition from the new fibre and also by the market interruptions occasioned by the wars of these years. The wool centre Sabadell, where there were reported to be 800 people working in cotton in 1800, is one case of such a transfer.[54] In both the cases of movement into the industry, for reasons of agrarian crisis and for depression in other industrial sectors, the 'freedom' of cotton from any form of guild restrictions was a crucial consideration.

Despite this progress, the Catalan industry had not become completely self-reliant for yarn by the turn of the century. It continued to import considerable quantities of spun yarn, particularly, it would seem, for warp thread for the production of which the jenny and its variants were not suitable.[55] It was the Arkwright machinery which could have supplied this warp thread but, although M. M. Gutiérrez in a generally reliable work published in 1837 on the industry claimed that warp-spinning with the Arkwright 'continuous' machinery was introduced into Catalonia in 1791, no evidence of use of this machine during the 1790s has been found.[56] Its cost and power requirements were considerably greater than those of

[51] 'Being only the size of an armchair, they easily fitted into the cottages of the domestic spinners who quickly realized that here was a golden opportunity to augment their incomes' (Hills, *Power in the Industrial Revolution*, p. 58).
[52] Cited by Torras, 'Especialización agrícola e industria rural', p. 124 n. 25.
[53] Albareda, *La industrialització de Vic*, p. 34.   [54] As n. 52.
[55] On the unsuitability of jenny thread for warps, see Hills, *Power in the Industrial Revolution*, pp. 60–1. On a large company which continued to import considerable quantities of spun yarn into the nineteenth century, see Sánchez, 'L'estructura comercial', pp. 14–15.
[56] M. M. Gutiérrez, *Impugnación de las cinco proposiciones de Pebrer sobre los grandes males que causa la ley de aranceles a la nación en general, a la Cataluña en particular, y a las mismas fábricas catalanas* (Madrid, 1837), p. 143. There is no mention of a pre-1800 introduction of roller-spinning in Sánchez's accurate account of the mechanization process in his paper 'La era de la manufactura', pp. 34–9.

the jenny and these considerations, as well as lack of technical expertise (Waddle and Caldwell had not passed on their secrets, we noted above), a broadening in the range of European suppliers of spun yarn and the availability of this yarn on credit, may explain the lateness of its introduction.

Concluding on this second stage in the incorporation of spinning, and the first stage in its mechanization, it is clear that it represents a key period in the industry's development. The industry entered the decade with the virtual monopoly of the position of the large Barcelona calico-printers within it largely intact but by the end of it significant changes had occurred both with respect to its geographical distribution and its organizational structure.

The only conceivable way in which the dominance of the printers could have been conserved was if the Arkwright mode of spinning had been adopted on a large scale as it was in England. The details of the efforts of Waddle and Caldwell to introduce this method of spinning into Barcelona in the early 1790s suggest, however, that there was never really any likelihood that this could have taken place. The printers throughout showed an extraordinary lack of interest in the new technology which, they would have known, was revolutionizing the industry in England and in France. Both the jenny and the Arkwright machinery reached Barcelona not through their efforts, it was noted, but through those of outsiders to the industry – Pontet, in the case of the jenny, and the Junta General de Comercio, in the case of roller-spinning. The opportunity provided by Waddle and Caldwell was lost but this should not have prevented printers attempting to introduce the new machinery on their own account. The consequence of the failure, as has been noted, was that despite its many years of involvement in cotton production, Barcelona lagged with respect to Avila and manufactures in Andalusia in the industry's mechanization.[57] Rather than profiting from the new opportunities provided by the existence of the spinning machinery the printers, as has been seen in part in this chapter, and as will be demonstrated more fully in the next, gradually decreased their commitment to cotton manufacturing processes during the decade, becoming, as they had predicted might happen some twenty years earlier, 'mere painters of cloth'.

[57] J. Nadal, 'Los abortos de la revolución industrial en Andalucía', in A. M. Bernal (ed.), *Historia de Andalucía* vi, *La Andalucía liberal, 1778–1868* (Barcelona, 1984), pp. 402–3.

In the absence of the Arkwright spinning device, that of Hargreaves, in its original and improved form, dominated this stage of the mechanization of spinning and this was a form of mechanization which rather than threatening the small-scale unit of production actually favoured it. In England, too, the compatibility of the jenny with the domestic production unit was both noted and experienced – 'the Jenneys are in the Hands of the Poor, and the Patent Machines [Arkwright machinery] are generally in the Hands of the Rich', it was recorded, and jenny-spinning expanded there into the nineteenth century.[58] The dependence on this machine contributed to two trends which have been noted in this section. The first of these was the decentralization of the industry away from Barcelona: this trend began with the need to find cheap labour, and the fact of the suitability of the early spinning machinery to the domestic unit of production, even though later it was to be reinforced by the need for hydraulic power. The second, linked clearly to the first, was a process of structural change, both within and outside Barcelona, with a decline in the predominance of the large manufacture and the emergence of smaller units of production. More will be said about this, too, in the next chapter.

Two footnotes to these conclusions concern firstly the role of foreign expertise in the relatively rapid mechanization of spinning in Catalonia, and secondly the influence of government. In addition to the cases that we have cited there is evidence for the founding of at lest five other spinning concerns in Barcelona and one in Sallent by French workers during the 1790s.[59] The disruptions caused to French industry by the Revolution would appear to have provided an opportunity to the Catalan industry, precipitating considerable technological transfer not only of French workers but also of English machine-makers working in France – this was the cause of Waddle's and Caldwell's coming to Spain and it was also that of Bernard Young who had been in the employment of the French Controller General, Calonne, before arriving in Catalonia.[60] With respect to

---

[58] Wadsworth and Mann, *The Cotton Trade*, p. 499.
[59] Reverdy & Co (1788), Turpin Gramond (1789), Simeon Lebret (1791), Paul Durand (1799), Jean Bordas (1799), Blas & Barrera (1799), Antoine Despren (1799) in Barcelona (Grau and López, 'Empresari i capitalista', p. 54, and Sánchez, 'La era de la manufactura', p. 73 n. 128, for the first three; AHCB, cadastre, lists of 'personas vagos' for 1799 for others), and Llorens Claret with Francesc Enrich in Sallent (1796) (A. Benet, 'La industrialització d'un poble de la Catalunya central: Sallent (1750–1808)' *Segon Congrès d'Història Moderna de Catalunya, Pedralbes, Revista d'Història Moderna*, 8, i (1988), p. 343).
[60] BC, JC leg. 23, no. 21, fos. 1–4, petition of Flotats and Pallerolas of 10 March 1792.

government a plus and a minus seem to be attachable to its role. If cotton-spinning spread in the way that it did during this decade an important contribution to this had been made by some of the liberal legislation mentioned in the previous chapter. It was the fact that cotton was a new material, and the fact, too, that several edicts had been passed universalizing the right to work with it, which facilitated the transfer of resources into the new industry, thus breaking down the rigid divisions which had existed between different trades and the production of different towns. However, the evidence presented of lack of collaboration between the Junta General de Comercio and the Junta de Comercio in the handling of both the Waddle and Caldwell and the Flotats cases suggests that the government's position from the late 1780s as an entrepreneur in the cotton industry, with the foundation of the Avila mill, caused its attitude to the modern-izing of the Catalan industry to be ambivalent.

ACCELERATED DIFFUSION OF MACHINERY AFTER THE 1802
PROHIBITION ON THE IMPORT OF SPUN YARN

The banning of the import of spun yarn which was combined with a measure prohibiting the export of American cotton represented the logical outcome of the economic policy of the government towards the industry since the 1760s. To the last, the measure was opposed by Catalan manufacturers – both by a newly founded *cuerpo de fabricantes de tejidos e hilados* as well as by the guild of linen and cotton weavers.[61] It gave, however, the necessary impulse to completing the process of incorporating the spinning processes and accelerated the process of mechanization. The sources are quite clear about this – the Junta de Comercio, referring back in 1808 to the rapid expansion in the consumption of raw cotton in the previous years, referred to 'its conversion to yarn, which *patriotism introduced first* and self-interest has promoted since'.[62]

The stage is thus firstly characterized by a rise in the number of spinning concerns founded. In Barcelona, for example, records exist of at least ten new spinning undertakings between 1800 and 1807.[63]

---

[61] Carrera Pujal, *Historia política*, IV, p. 165.
[62] Letter of 9 April 1808, reproduced by Torrella Niubó, *El moderno resurgir*, pp. 195–7. My emphasis.
[63] The names of promoters of new spinning activities during these years in Barcelona include (i) Francesc Arolas (1800), (ii) Jayme Viguier (French) (1801), (iii) Sebastià Esprest (1802), (iv) Llorens Clarós and Manuel Torner (1803), (v) Agustí Deltort (in Sant Andreu

As significant, however, were three other types of change in the
sector. Firstly, there was a great growth in the use of hydraulic power
for spinning, with a consequent further shift in the centre of gravity
of the industry away from Barcelona. Secondly, there was a
considerable refinement in the technology of the industry. Finally,
there were the first signs of considerable capital accumulation within
the sector, and also of investment in it from outside, and the
appearance thus of some substantial concerns which, if they did not
rival the larger calico-printing concerns, certainly dwarfed the
family-scale units discussed in the previous section.

The first of these developments – the further shift away from
Barcelona and the growing reliance on hydraulic power – is illustrated partly by records of the demands for the tapping of rivers for
the purpose of spinning machinery. Fifteen such requests were
acceded to between 1803 and 1807, of which eight were in Manresa
(on the Cardener), three in Sallent (on the Llobregat), two in
Barcelona (on the Rech Condal) and the others in Pobla de Lillet
(also on the Llobregat) and Ripoll (on the Ter).[64] The Cardener, the
Llobregat and the Ter were to be the principal sources of energy for
the industry which was to exploit hydraulic resources more
thoroughly than anywhere else in Europe, well into the second half of
the twentieth century. So we have here the source of a decisive
change in the industry's development. The details of such water
concessions are far from complete, however, and do not give a full
idea of the extent of the geographical shift which was occurring –
seven cotton-spinning concerns, for example, were established in
Sallent during these years,[65] twenty-two cotton-spinning and weaving concerns were established in Berga between 1803 and 1808 and a
random search in the archives of this town for the years 1815–16
revealed a hundred names of 'makers of pieces of cotton cloth' and a
further hundred of 'cotton-weavers',[66] Vic's cotton industry was
composed of twenty-eight spinning and weaving manufacturers by

del Palomar, 1804), (vi) Esteve Barnadell (1804), (vii) Magí Pujadas (in Clot, 1804), (viii)
Jaume Puig (1805, in Sant Martí de Provençals) (ix) Jacques Joumart (1805), (x) Antoni
Cabaner (1806). (Sources for (i), (iv), (v), (ix) and (x): Grau and López, 'Empresari i
capitalista', pp. 42, 57; for (ii), (iii), (vi): AHCB, cadastre, lists of 'vagos'; for (vii) and
(viii), Sánchez, 'La era de la manufactura', pp. 37 and 74 n. 149). See also p. 262 for
activities in this area of Jacint Ramon.
[64] Sánchez, 'La era de la manufactura', p. 37.
[65] Benet, 'La industrialització de Sallent', pp. 343–7.
[66] Vicens Vives, *Industrials i polítics*, p. 46; E. Moreu Rey, 'Una dinastia industrial: els Rosal
de Berga', in *Homenaje a Vicens Vives* (2 vols., Barcelona, 1967), II, p. 450.

1806.[67] By 1808, according to M. M. Gutiérrez, cotton-spinning had extended to Manresa, Reus, Valls, Igualada, Vic, Olot, Mataró, Sallent, Berga, Ripoll, Roda and Manlleu and was employing a labour force of some 80,000 and a circulating capital of 200 million *reales* or 20 million *libras*.[68]

The principal refinements in the industry's technology consisted in the diffusion, at last, of Arkwright's water-frame, the introduction of Crompton's spinning mule and the first application of steam-power to spinning.

The exact date of the adoption of the first of these devices is not known. The lack of evidence for its use in Catalonia during the 1790s was noted in the previous section. It seems to have been the 1802 ban on the import of yarn which represented the decisive incentive. From this date the industry had to supply its own warp yarn. Jacint Ramon, who was to be responsible for the first application of steam-power to spinning, is also held to have played an important role in the perfecting of this process. He was owner of one of the largest calico-printing concerns in the city and showed an early interest in the promotion of spinning – it was he, it may be recalled, who was called upon by the Junta de Comercio to act as one of the experts to assess the Flotats machine in 1792 together with Ramon Bosch – the choice was justified in terms of their being 'the most suitable individuals for judging the merit of these machines'.[69] The evidence for his involvement in the introduction of roller-spinning is provided by the memoir written by Francesc Sanponts, Director of Statics and Hydrostatics, in the Real Academia de Ciencias Naturales y Artes of Barcelona, in connection with his later involvement in the introduction of the steam engine: in this Santponts makes reference to Ramon having 'established various important branches of industry, particularly the introduction and perfection of the method of spinning cotton with English machines which he discovered at the cost of much application, expense and trouble'. (The Arkwright machine was generally referred to as the 'English spinning machine'.)[70]

If the protectionist measure was not the cause for the initial adoption of the machine, it certainly was for an increase in the pace of its diffusion. There is abundant evidence of this. The Arkwright

[67] Albareda, *La industrialització de Vic*, p. 51.   [68] Gutiérrez, *Impugnación*, p. 144.
[69] BC, JC, leg. 23, no. 21, fo. 5, letter of 9 Aug. 1792.
[70] Cited in J. Agustí, *Ciència i tècnica a Catalunya en el segle XVIII o la introducció de la màquina de vapor* (Barcelona, 1983), pp. 145–6.

118

spinning machine needed far more power than the jenny, or indeed the spinning mule, to be driven – it was this need, and the high cost of satisfying it, which, it was noted above, was one of the reasons for its late adoption – and the large number of requests for the use of hydraulic power to which reference has been made were thus largely in connection with its adoption. Ramon was using horses to drive his machines before attempting to introduce steam-power (the situation of his manufacture in the Carrer Sant Pau prevented any resort to water-power). The cost of the roller-spinning machines was also significantly higher – some eight times the price – than that of jennies. This discrepancy facilitates the tracing of its diffusion by the analysis of manufactures' inventories. Its need of water-power had the consequence that it spread principally to areas outside Barcelona: Joan Vilaregut & Cia was operating the simple jenny-type 'spinning machines' in Barcelona in 1807, but 'English machines' in Martorell where it could tap the water resources of either the Llobregat or Anoia.[71] Other cases of early use of the machines outside Barcelona include those of Codina, Dalmau, Martí and Serrano in Manresa,[72] and of Josep Font in Vic in 1806.[73]

There is some confusion about who introduced the spinning mule to the Catalan industry. The appearances are that it was the achievement of an ambitious cotton-spinning company formed by Jacques Joumart, a merchant, the Marquis of Sabran, a French marshall, and Jean de Cramp, a French *fabricant* from Toulouse in 1805, most probably with the protection of the Conde de Cabarrús, whose purpose was described as being to 'establish... twenty-four cotton-spinning machines operated either by water-power or by steam or by horses... according to the most modern and perfect method which is known'.[74] The most modern and perfect method which was known was certainly Samuel Crompton's spinning mule, and a letter from the Junta de Comercio written in 1815 provides further support for this concern being the introducer of the mule – it attributed the introduction of 'French machines', whose method of functioning was 'initially... a mystery' to the Conde de Cabarrús between 1806 and 1807 at a cost of some 30,000 to 40,000 *pesetas* – 'French machines' was the name which came to be given to the mules and the fact that their method of functioning was initially a mystery

[71] Grau and López, 'Empresari i capitalista', p. 41 n. 29 – also gives prices for 'English' and normal jennies. For other prices, see Sánchez, 'La era de la manufactura', p. 38.
[72] Sánchez, 'La era de la manufactura', p. 38.
[73] Albareda, *La industrialització de Vic*, p. 51.
[74] Grau and López, 'Empresari i capitalista', p. 41, n. 2.

suggests that this was their first introduction to Barcelona.[75] A report of three printers to the Junta in the same year gave a slightly different version of events – Cabarrús, it stated, had imported from England and France 'all the workers, machines and tools necessary for the establishment of a factory which included the different methods of spinning which other nations used, to discover from personal experience which was the most advantageous' – but not one which contradicts the view that Cabarrús was the source of the spinning mule.[76]

Other claims have been made for Jacint Ramon and other printers having been responsible for the mule's introduction in the years immediately prior to the establishment of the Cabarrús concern but it seems likely that these attributions are a consequence of confusion with the Arkwright machine which was, as we have just seen, widely diffused in the years immediately before the establishment of the Joumart concern.[77] The involvement of Cabarrús is another sign of the extent to which the mechanization of the Catalan industry was stimulated by individuals not directly involved in it – founder of the national bank of San Carlos in 1782, Cabarrús had been Spanish ambassador in Paris since 1797, which must have provided him with the opportunity to obtain machinery and technical assistance in putting it into operation.[78]

Jacint Ramon's attempt to apply steam-power to the spinning processes dated from 1804. Sanponts, in the memoir to which reference has just been made, provides full details of the sources of the initiative. Ramon had contacted him in the course of the year explaining 'the strong desire which he had had for many years that steam engines should be introduced into this country', and, more specifically, that 'a fire pump that he wanted to have in his house to card, spin, raise water and execute other operations in his manufacture in the same way that he had heard it said that the famous machine of Manchester carries out these processes' should be constructed. He had already made attempts at building such a machine but they had only served to show to him 'the hard work involved and the difficulty of such a project', Sanponts's appointment

---

[75] Also Sánchez, 'La era de la manufactura', p. 38, and Carrera Pujal, *La economía de Cataluña*, II, p. 200.

[76] BC, JC, leg. 33, no. 55, fos. 13–16, letter of Gónima, Rull and Clarós of 30 Sept. 1815.

[77] The attribution to Ramon is by R. N. Soler, *Ensaig sobre la màquina catalana de filar cotó coneguda per bergadana o maxerina* (Madrid, 1919), p. 13; to others, by Izard, *Industrialización*, p. 29, and Nadal, *El fracaso*, p. 190.   [78] Lynch, *Bourbon Spain*, pp. 326, 399.

as Director of Statics and Hydrostatics in the city's Real Academia de
Ciencias Naturales y Artes, however, had appeared to provide him
with the opportunity of obtaining proper technical assistance in the
attainment of his goal.

Sanponts responded warmly to the invitation and in the course of
a year he devised two steam engines for Ramon. The first was rejected
as its action was too irregular for the cotton machinery. The second
was a more complex 'double effect' machine whose simple and
economic design, Sanponts claimed, represented a distinct improvement on similar English machines. During 1805 this improved
machine was tested for the fulfilment of two purposes within the
Ramon manufacture. Firstly, it was used as a direct source of power
for an 'English machine' and found to be more effective than the use
of horse-power:

It was not so difficult to make the comparison between the smoothness of the
movement of this steam machine with that powered by horses [Sanponts
reported], both were in the same room and so near to each other that the
first was not further than a yard away from the second and it was only
necessary to listen for anyone to be convinced of the difference in the
smoothness of the movements of these spinning machines, for at the same
time that the noise of the wheels powered by the steam engine was smooth,
that which was the result of the repeated pushes of horses in the other
machines seemed undulatory.

Secondly, it was used for pumping water to provide 'a continuous fall
of water which landing on a mill wheel in this way kept a certain
number of machines in movement, the same water being used again'.
The second experiment was also successful.[79]

Jacint Ramon's steam-powered spinning was not persisted with
because of the high cost of coal. An 1815 report on spinning explained
that 'the profit which resulted from this source of power did not
compensate him', and that the scarcity of coal had forced him to
going back to depending on mules for power.[80] The effort is certainly
not without significance though. Firstly, it provides an exemplary
case of cooperation between industrialists and scientists in the
advance of the industry. Sanponts had provided the scientific
expertise, Ramon and his labour force the technological. This is
made clear in the former's report: Ramon had put under his

[79] Agustí, *Ciència i tècnica*, pp. 145–51.
[80] BC, JC, leg. 33, no. 55, fos. 13–16, letter of Gónima, Rull and Clarós of 30 Sept. 1815: 'as
it [coal] was scarce here he [Ramon] was forced to substitute it by mules'.

direction, he noted, 'Skilled artisans for the purpose of making the machine according to the plans and designs that I showed him.' Since the 1770s the Junta de Comercio had been giving priority to mechanical development in Catalonia and this is probably the most significant, if not the most long-lasting, achievement from this. Secondly, the effort, and the high cost which it represented, as well as the near contemporaneous introduction of the mule, is a good illustration of the high degree of confidence which existed in the future of the cotton industry at this point. A particular symbolism was attached to the introduction of steam-power because, as Sanponts's report reveals, it was regarded (mistakenly most historians today would argue), as the key feature characterizing the English advance over the rest of Europe: 'England', he wrote, 'owes most of its industrial wealth to the establishment of steam engines...,' by means of this machine ports are cleaned and deepened, navigational canals are dug, loaded boats are lifted into dry locks... extraordinary things which seem incredible are achieved.' The high expectations placed on the steam engine gave rise to the Ramon manufacture and Ramon himself acquiring considerable notoriety – 'The novelty of this invention', Sanponts reported, 'attracted a crowd of cultivated nationals and foreigners of different types to see the manufacture of Don Jacinto Ramon' including the Intendant who ordered a description of the introduction of the machine to be sent to the Minister of Hacienda.[81]

The emergence of larger, specialized spinning or spinning and weaving manufactures during these years will already have been picked up from what has been said about the introduction of the new spinning technology. Ramon's case appears to have been a relatively unusual one of an integrated manufacture. More generally, printers, if they carried out spinning, did it in a separate building. Among the members of the newly founded *cuerpo de fabricantes de tejidos e hilados* in 1802, there were four concerns of some size – those of Joan Serra (forty looms and forty-eight spinning machines), Joan Vilaregut (sixty-three looms and twenty spinning machines), Manuel Torruella (fifty-three looms and forty-six spinning machines) and Melchior Augé (fifty-one looms).[82] Joan Vilaregut's affairs expanded considerably after 1802: in 1807 he was operating one hundred and twenty-seven looms, forty-six spinning machines, twelve carding

[81] Agustí, *Ciència i tècnica*, pp. 143–51.
[82] Sánchez, 'La era de la manufactura', p. 72 n. 121.

engines, valued at 12,000 *libras*, in Barcelona and had also established a specialized spinning concern in Martorell which was equipped with eighteen 'English machines' and had equipment of a total value of 15,000 *libras*.[83]

Vilaregut may have been the Canals of the mechanization of the manufacturing processes. He had started on a relatively humble scale in the early 1790s – he had founded a company in association with two others in 1791 and specialized in the production of finer-quality plain cotton goods and cotton mixtures.[84] A year later he was reported to be one of only two manufacturers in the city of *lanquins*, a cotton cloth of yellow, egg-yolk colour, with which he was achieving good sales.[85] In 1799, when the cotton-weavers and spinners founded their *cuerpo* to represent their collective interests, he was appointed one of its twelve *comisionados*.[86] His manufacture was to expand yet further from its size in 1802 – by 1807 it was composed of a hundred looms and forty-six spinning machines.[87] As was noted in the previous chapter, opportunities in this period were good for men like Vilaregut with a background in specialized cotton manu-facturing, and it is to this that must be due the rapid expansion in the size of his concern. Like many others, however, he was brought down by the crisis occasioned by the War of Independence and went bankrupt in 1818.[88]

---

[83] Grau and López, 'Empresari i capitalista', p. 40 n. 29.   [84] *Ibid.*, p. 55.
[85] Report of delegates of Junta de Comercio of 15 May 1792, reproduced in Torrella Niubó, *El moderno resurgir*, pp. 168–70, stating that his product was 'being sold in considerable quantities'.   [86] BC, JC, leg. 51, no. 22, fos. 2–13, 10 May 1799.
[87] Sánchez, 'La era de la manufactura', p. 72 n. 121.
[88] AHCB, Arxiu comercial, B304.

CHAPTER 8

The crisis of the fábrica: the industry from 1787 to 1832

Those ostentatious manufactures which were then the envy of
foreigners... were reduced to ashes and piles of rubble.
(M. M. Gutiérrez in 1837, cited by Nadal, 'La
consolidación de la industria algodonera', p. 215)

The relatively uninterrupted prosperity which the industry had
enjoyed from the 1770s to the mid-1780s was not sustained into the
1790s and the new century. A period of great instability opened. One
of the causes for this has been noted in the last chapter – the
introduction first of manual and then of mechanical spinning
interrupted the status quo, representing a challenge to the calico-
printers if they wanted to sustain their dominance of the industry,
and providing an opportunity for small-scale producers. The other
causes were, on the one hand, self-generated within the industry –
expansion had been so rapid that overproduction became a threat –
and, on the other, imposed from outside: the French Revolution was
followed by a succession of wars – with France from 1793 to 1795,
with Britain between 1796 and 1801 and 1804 and 1808, with France
again from 1808 to 1814. These occasioned isolation from the
American market (particularly during the wars with England) and
direct disruption to manufacturing and marketing in the national
market (particularly during the War of Independence of 1808–14
during which Catalonia suffered first occupation by the French and
then incorporation into the Napoleonic empire). Peace in 1814
brought little respite and it was not until the 1830s that circumstances
which can be described as favourable returned.

In this chapter, I shall firstly outline with more precision the
economic circumstances which confronted the industry during these
years. This tracing in of the 'conjuncture' I shall follow in a second
section with a documentation of the response of the industry to these
circumstances. In a third, I shall attempt to explain this response.

268

THE 'CONJUNCTURE' FROM 1787 TO 1832

The period opened with what was the worst crisis in the industry's history up to this point. It was an overproduction crisis: the extremely rapid expansion in production following the American war, documented in the penultimate chapter, led to a saturation in markets and a consequent collapse in demand. It was distinct, thus, from the typical 'ancien régime'-type crisis, consequent upon harvest failures and demographic recession, and has been characterized by Catalan historians as the Principality's first 'modern', 'capitalist' crisis.[1] Recovery from it was relatively rapid, with conditions favourable in both the domestic and external markets until approximately 1793. This year represents a probable peak for Barcelona's and Catalonia's eighteenth-century expansion – Bonaventura Gassó, a well-placed observer as the recently appointed secretary to the Junta de Comercio, was to write later that it was then that 'Barcelona had experienced its greatest hopes, touched the peak of prosperity for the century' – but from this point circumstances deteriorated. Total collapse was prevented, however, by the fact that, although there was a relatively sharp downturn in the domestic market, the export trade continued to flourish, experiencing little check until the English war in 1797. Barcelona was benefiting from being one of the few continental European ports with an undisturbed Atlantic trade, and, indeed, demand for calicoes, which were among the most convenient exports for exchange for American colonial products on which very good profits could be obtained, was speculatively high throughout 1796. From 1797, however, with England soon gaining naval superiority at the battle of St Vincent (14 February) and thus barring the route to export markets, the depression became general: near total stagnation set in till 1801, Catalonia experiencing what Vilar categorizes as its worst crisis since the beginning of its eighteenth-century expansion.

Rapid but temporary recovery took place with the return of peace between 1802 and 1804 – Vilar writes of a 'new very brief phase of creative activity' – but the renewal of war with England in 1804 brought the expansive phase in export markets to a halt, and from 1806 there was depression, too, in national markets. From 1808, with

[1] J. M. Delgado, 'El impacto de las crisis coloniales en la economía catalana (1787–1807)', in J. Fontana (ed.), *La economía española al final del Antiguo Régimen*, III, *Comercio y colonias* (Madrid, 1982), pp. 99–118.

the outbreak of the War of Independence, the halt became complete. Many retrospective reports on the commerce and industry of the Principality written during the next thirty years were to refer to this as the moment when the great eighteenth-century expansion was finally halted. Vilar reaches the same conclusion:

Trafalgar occasioned a very hard blow to them, but one which was badly assessed initially. Only the French invasion was decisive. Between 1807 and 1815, while English trade was going to increase from a value of approximately £60 million one of approximately £90 million, Catalan maritime activity, reduced to the clandestine operations of blockade-busters, fell to nearly nothing. This is the real turning-point, the end of the great colonial and international expansion underway since 1760.[2]

Peace with the French in 1814 brought some relief – at least for a few years there was no fighting on Spanish soil – but it did not bring Spain's imperial problems to an end. The principles of the French Revolution had spread to its American possessions and a series of reverses had deprived it of all its colonies except the Philippines, Cuba and Puerto Rico by the 1820s. Gone were the sources of bullion and a range of valuable colonial products, as well as what had been the most dynamic market for the producers of the Principality since the late 1770s. Even those few imperial possessions which remained were of little service to the metropolitan economy as the years of interruption in the trade, in conjunction with unwise legislative decisions such as those of 12 October 1797 and 18 January 1798 which had opened American ports to other nations, had had the consequence that they had established new commercial links, principally with American and English suppliers, while the Spanish connections, in terms of individuals and shipping services, had been gradually eroded.[3]

In view of this curtailment of overseas economic possibilities Spanish producers were forced to focus their efforts on the domestic market, but the situation in this was barely more favourable. The

---

[2] My analysis of this period is drawn from Vilar, *La Catalogne*, II, pp. 410–18, III, pp. 20–8, 39–42, 59–66, 115–38, and Delgado, 'El impacto de las crisis coloniales', pp. 97–169. Gassó is cited by Vilar in II, p. 415, and the two quotations from Vilar's work are, respectively, from II, p. 418, and III, p. 138.

[3] Vicens Vives, *Manual*, pp. 555–6; on legislative decisions of 1797 and 1798, see Delgado, 'El impacto de las crisis coloniales', p. 131; on English moving into Spanish and American markets, see F. Crouzet, 'Vers une économie d'exportation', in his *De la supériorité de l'Angleterre sur la France* (Paris, 1985), pp. 186–7: 'exports to southern Europe and Latin America progress enormously'.

many years of occupation and warfare had occasioned massive disruption – famine conditions returned in some years, the agricultural progress of the eighteenth century had been reversed, commercial and industrial capital had either been lost or had shifted into land and state loans and a political struggle between progressive and reactionary forces in Spanish society, which was not to be finally settled until the 1970s, had opened. Economic recovery in these circumstances was to be very slow. A sign of the generally depressed level of economic activity is the gradual fall which was experienced in grain and wine prices which only touched their lowest levels in the late 1820s. There was some demographic recovery and there are some signs already in the 1820s of an expansion in grain production assisted probably by protectionist measures passed in 1820 forbidding the import of foreign grain. Recovery, however, was not to be marked until the political changes at the end of the reign of Fernando VII which marked the establishment of a new consensus between liberal and manufacturing interests, whose basis was described as the 'properly interpreted system of liberty (*libertad bien entendida*)', and which was the preliminary for the liberal reforms, freeing the land and labour markets, of the reign of Isabella II which provided a basis if not for unlimited growth at least for a period of sustained prosperity.[4]

As, or possibly more, damaging than the loss of the American market and the depressed state of the domestic economy for Catalan industrialists was the loss of what had been nearly, we have seen, a position of monopoly suppliers during the eighteenth century. This had been occasioned firstly by the same forces which had caused a *de facto* separation of Spain's West Indian colonies from their metropolitan suppliers during this period: invasion by French and English armies had not only disrupted national industries but had brought with it a flood of imports and stimulated new commercial links. Rebuilding the privileged position which the Catalan economy had built for itself in the eighteenth century was not to be easily achieved.[5] In addition, for a variety of reasons – the relative decline of the Catalan industry, the fiscal advantages to be obtained from

---

[4] Vicens Vives, *Manual*, pp. 556–9 (a summary of the politics) and pp. 560–2, 586–90 (demographic and agricultural development).

[5] Crouzet, 'Vers une économie d'exportation', p. 187: 'the "Peninsular War" created a broad opening in the markets of those countries and their American possessions for the British'.

permitting imports, the strength of exporting and importing trading interests were among them – the extent of the government's commitment to protecting national industry had declined. In theory, the two prohibitions on the import of spun cotton and cotton cloth of 1802 and 1804 held, but their effectiveness was undermined by widespread contraband and a series of concessions to them made to importing interests. The Philippines company, as in 1789, was allowed to import Asian textiles and similar privileges were conferred on other organizations and individuals. The Guadalquivir company was permitted in 1815 to import 3,200 tons of cotton goods, the company of José Aullon of Cartagena was permitted in 1816 to import 300 *fardos* (bales) of prohibited goods in return for services rendered during the war, Vicent Bertran de Lis was licensed in 1816 to import 150 tons of cotton goods and Félix Torres and Manuel Gómez licensed in 1825 to import similar loads. Finally Enrique Dollfuss, a French calico-printer from Mulhouse, was permitted to introduce up to 30,000 pieces of cotton cloth a year in 1829 in connection with a privilege granted to establish a cotton manufacture in the royal palace of San Fernando. The fact of these concessions made the enforcement of the 1802 prohibitions virtually impossible as cloth imported by means of them could not be distinguished from contraband goods. Consequently, as in the period of the first prohibitions a century earlier, continuous complaints were made about smuggling, and a variety of generally unsuccessful attempts were made to control the selling off of legally imported cloth in order that the prohibition might be properly enforced.[6]

The permission granted to Dollfuss was not the first attempt made by the state to introduce cotton manufactures in other parts of Spain. In 1815 two North Americans, Thorndike and Carroll, requested a ten-year monopoly in the use of imported cotton machinery and permission to import five cargo-loads of cotton cloth, in return for their commitment to establish a spinning manufacture in Valencia. Such requests were particularly worrying for participants in the Catalan industry for they were made, and the government was inclined to grant them, because of its perceived backwardness: Thorndike and Carroll in their request stated that 'it is proven that cotton cannot be spun perfectly with the means and machines used today in Catalonia for to achieve this water- or steam-power has to be

[6] Carrera Pujal, *La economía de Cataluña*, I, pp. 15–35, 73, 95–6; see also A. Sánchez, *Protecció, ordre i llibertat: El pensament i la política econòmica de la comissió de fàbriques de Barcelona (1820–1840)* (Barcelona, 1990), pp. 126–33.

used, and they do not use it.' The requests, in both cases, gave rise to reports stressing the modernity of the Catalan industry. There were, indeed, in the attempt to ensure a guaranteed position in the national market for the local industry, a series of public relations exercises designed to show its modernity, principally in the form of industrial exhibitions, the most celebrated of which was the tour arranged for the (apparently totally uninterested) visiting Fernando VII in March 1828 to visit seven manufactures in the space of two days.

The industry was in a slight dilemma – on the one hand, as was pointed out in reaction to the request of Thorndike and Carroll, capital would not move into it on a big scale until there was assurance of persistence with prohibition: 'All depends on this constancy on the government's part and that, assured of it, the artisan can see in the progress of the branch of industry increased individual property', it was recorded, but on the other, until capital had moved in, reversing the backwardness with respect to the foreign product and production methods, the extent of the government's commitment was likely to fluctuate.[7] The necessary commitment came, however, with the so-called 'libertad bien entendido' which has just been referred to. In the early years of the Restoration, after the Liberal Triennium of 1820–3, there had been some vacillating with respect to persisting with the prohibition on cotton imports which had been restored in 1820 as one of the first measures of the liberal government, but in 1828 new tariff legislation was passed banning the import of a range of cotton products, in 1830 stronger measures were introduced against contraband and finally a royal decree of 30 April 1832 confirmed the total prohibitions of 1802 and 1804 on the import of any sort of cotton cloth. As M. Izard writes, with this measure 'a new stage in tariff policy was decisively intitiated, one which lasted until the free-trading reform of Figuerola'.[8]

[7] Carrera Pujal, *La economía de Cataluña*, I, pp. 16–17 (on Thorndike and Carroll), 30, 55 (on exhibitions); BC, JC, leg. 33, no. 55, fos. 13–16, letter of opposition from Barcelona manufacturers of 30 Sept. 1815 (records and contradicts views on Catalan spinning capacity), and reg. 92, letter of 15 Nov. 1815, in support of the manufacturers' position from the Junta de Comercio (contains remark about 'constancia'). J. Fontana, *La fi de l'Antic Règim i la industrialització, 1787–1868*, vol. v of P. Vilar (directed), *Història de Catalunya* (8 vols., Barcelona, 1987–90), pp. 230–1 on the 1827 visit of Ferdinand VII.

[8] Izard, *Industrialización*, pp. 36–7. On tariff policy of these years see also Izard's thesis, *La revolución industrial en España*, p. 35.

Consumption of cotton

The simplest, and most generally used, way of recording progress in cotton industries is from the records of their cotton consumption. Figures for the Catalan industry are not complete for this period but they are full enough to inform on the general trends. They have been summarized in table 8.1, together with the percentage which they represent of the cotton used in the British industry.

What does the table show? Firstly, it demonstrates the impressive growth achieved in the industry after the American War and into the 1790s. It can be seen that it was during this period that the ratio of Catalonia's to Britain's consumption of cotton stood at its highest. Britain's industry had not yet reached the massive size it was to attain during the nineteenth century – these were the early stages of the Industrial Revolution – but its expansion had certainly started (cotton imports had risen from just over 3.5 million lbs in 1770 to between 19 and 35 million between 1790 and 1795), and so the table demonstrates something which it is important for us to record: up to and well into the 1790s the Catalan industry was experiencing an expansion which was comparable in its rapidity to that of the British. The figures for 1808 show that 1790s production levels had been sustained, but the comparison with Britain shows that a sharp relative deterioration had taken place. This is not surprising: it was British producers, primarily, who were occupying the place in American markets which had previously been held by the Catalan industry. By contrast, the period of the War of Independence, it can be seen, witnessed actual industrial regression: it was only three years after peace had been made that production levels reattained those of 1808. The recovery from then, though, was relatively rapid into the period of the Liberal Triennium, with some recuperation in relative performance with respect to Britain. Some wavering in the growth process is apparent with the return of absolutist role in 1823, demonstrating, possibly, the susceptibility of the industry to any sign of weakening in the commitment to the legislation prohibiting imports, but then a rapid spurt from 1827 to 1831. The table then informs us about the period beyond that with which this book is concerned: the outbreak of the Carlist war may have slowed growth down but between 1836 and 1845, it can be seen, there was renewed

Table 8.1. *Raw cotton used by the Catalan industry, 1784–1848*

	Raw cotton used (lbs)	British consumption (%)
1784	1,877,772	16.65
1792	4,743,008	14.19
1793	2,869,974	16.06
1808	2,535,769–3,042,923	6.00–7.25
1816	1,910,868	2.20
1817	2,444,236	2.10
1818	2,505,948	1.50
1819	4,399,184	3.30
1820	4,436,652	3.72
1824	5,833,988	3.50
1825	2,904,872	1.73
1826	5,327,068	3.50
1827	6,131,528	3.12
1831	8,600,008	3.27
1834	7,528,864	2.49
1835	6,418,048	2.02
1836	8,115,128	2.34
1837	9,567,564	2.61
1838	11,412,312	2.74
1839	8,242,960	2.16
1840	18,484,948	4.03
1841	18,621,596	4.24
1842	10,872,332	2.50
1843	5,889,088	1.13
1844	15,599,912	2.86
1845	33,883,476	5.60
1846	15,203,192	2.47
1847	16,366,904	3.71
1848	23,699,612	4.10

Note: I have converted eighteenth-century Catalan figures for spun yarn to raw cotton by adding the one eighth of weight lost in the spinning processes. Figures for unginned raw cotton have been reduced by two-thirds. Comparisons are with net British cotton imports up to 1819 and UK cotton consumption from this date. The figure for 1792 is for cotton imported in the whole of Spain. Catalonia was the principal, but not the only, importer and so it represents a slight overstatement of the quantity used.

Sources: Maixé, 'El mercado algodonero', p. 376; Nadal and Ribas, 'Una empresa cotonera catalana', p. 50, and *El fracaso*, appendix 7; the figure for 1808 is taken from an estimate of the Junta de Comercio for this year (Torrella Niubó, *El moderno resurgir*, p. 195). British figures are taken from B. R. Mitchell and P. Deane, *Abstract of British Historical Statistics* (Cambridge, 1962), pp. 177–81, and B. R. Mitchell, *European Historical Statistics, 1750–1975* (2nd edn, London, 1981), pp. 449–50.

276 A distinctive industrialization

and rapid expansion, the ratio with respect to the British industry reaching its highest point since 1808 in 1845. Albert Carreras, who has recently compiled a similar table for the period 1816–61, concludes that growth was at its most rapid between 1835 and 1855 and that within this period the years 1835–41 were the most dynamic. The speed of the growth are his grounds, we have noted in our introduction, for his following a number of other Catalan historians in baptizing this period 'the industrial revolution in Catalonia'.[9]

Numbers and types of manufactures

Documentation on the industry during these crucial phases in its development is particularly inadequate. There are no industrial surveys of the type that were used in the penultimate chapter – or, at least, I have found none – until the 1830s, and I have been forced instead to pool the information obtainable from a variety of different types of incomplete documentation. I have divided the period into two – pre- and post-1814. For the first phase, it is possible to reconstruct the development of the industry with some precision until approximately 1806. For the second period, virtually no detailed sources exist but some idea of the dimensions of the industry, in terms of number of concerns and the sizes of its different sectors (spinning, weaving and printing), can be obtained from a levy which was raised on industry and commerce in Barcelona in 1823, and analysis of the distribution of this loan among the participants in the industry provides some insights concerning industrial structure at this point.[10]

Sources

Three principal sources have been used for the reconstruction of this phase. The first of these consists in lists of printers and other participants in the industry published in the *Almanak Mercantil*, a merchants' handbook, for the years 1797, 1798, 1802, 1805 and 1806, and also drawn up on the following three occasions: 1790, in connection with the meetings held for organizing a company to finance the introduction of Arkwright's spinning machinery,[11] 1793, in connection with donations made for the war against France,[12] and

[9] Carreras, 'Cataluña, primera región industrial de España', pp. 268–71.
[10] AHCB, cadastre, VIII, 3, Contribución extraordinaria de guerra aplicada al comercio e industria en al año 1823.
[11] BC, JC, reg. 12, Acuerdos, 28 Jan., 1 and 15 Feb. 1790.
[12] Details recorded by Carrera Pujal, *Historia política*, IV, pp. 164–5.

1804, in connection with complaints about contraband and the loss of sales in the American market.[13] The second is the records of the cadaster and in particular (1) the lists of larger calico-printing concerns which paid tax separately from the guilds in conjunction with wholesale merchants and (2) lists of what were referred to as *individuos vagos* (literally, 'indistinct individuals'), non-guild members, giving their places of residence, which include a large number of participants in the industry – both owners and *fabricants* of calico-printing concerns.[14] Finally, recourse has been made to bankruptcy records and any other scattered sources available (such as the few studies which have been made on individual concerns).[15]

There are problems in the use of all these sources. We do not know how complete the various lists of printers are. Those compiled for the *Almanak Mercantil* firstly fail to include a number of minor calico-printing concerns founded during these years, whose existence can be traced from the lists of *individuos vagos*, and secondly do not appear to have been kept completely up to date, with the consequence that whereas the first list, prepared for the 1797 edition, may be relatively accurate, the succeeding ones became progressively less so (although a few modifications were made). For example, we know from four different sources that the Isidro Cathalà concern, which was run by Nicolau Sivilla after Cathalà's death, ceased production in 1801: the manufacture was sold in 1802; its accounts, which have survived, come to an end in 1801; the concern was withdrawn from the list of those playing the cadaster on an independent basis in 1801 with the note 'nulo' being placed against it; and finally the manufacture's *fabricant*, Josep Mané, disappears from the list of *individuos vagos* for the Plaça Marquilles, where the manufacture was situated, in 1801, and yet Sivilla is listed in the *Almanak* as a member of the Royal Spinning Company in 1802, 1805 and 1806.[16] Similarly, it would appear that the Canals concern was finally wound up in 1802 when Antoni Nadal i Darrer, who had been directing it, is shown by the list of *individuos vagos* to have changed his residence from the manufacture to the Plaça del Borne and to have changed his description of his profession from that of *fabricant* to that of *comerciante* but the *Almanak*'s

[13] Document and list of names reproduced in Torrella Niubó, *El moderno resurgir*, pp. 184–8.
[14] Held in AHCB. I have used the cadastral records for 1783–9 and 1794–1805.
[15] Bankruptcy records are recorded by Delgado, 'El impacto de las crisis coloniales'.
[16] Sources as explained in the previous paragraph except for the terminating Sivilla accounts held in the library of the Barcelona Chamber of Commerce.

lists, as in the case of Sivilla, continue to record his membership of the Royal Spinning Company. Listing as a member of the company in the *Almanak* thus does not serve as firm evidence of involvement in calico-printing for the period after 1802.

The problems with the cadaster as a source are various. Firstly, it is not complete for these years. There are no records for 1790–4, nor, for obvious reasons, for the crucial period of French occupation between 1807 and 1814. Secondly, the separate lists for the payment of the cadaster by the larger calico-printing concerns – an invaluable source for tracing the progress of the industry – either ceased to be made after 1802 or, if they were made, have been lost. Thirdly, disappearance from these lists cannot be used as evidence for withdrawal from the industry. It can also mean, it is clear, a decline in the scale of production of the resources of the individual concerned, disqualifying them from being taxed any longer on the same basis. This, it would seem, was the case of Joan Canaleta whose annual cadastral payments experienced a gradual decline – 400 *libras* in 1786, 300 *libras* in 1787–94, 200 *libras* in 1795–6, 150 *libras* in 1797 – before he finally disappeared from the list in 1798; however, we know that he did continue with some manufacturing activities even though these were greatly reduced.[17] Fourthly, while the lists of *individuos vagos* provide information on a large number of individuals involved in the industry, and are particularly useful, as we shall see, in tracing shifts in the locus of the industry from one part of the town to the other, they are by no means complete and cannot thus be used as a basis for assessing the industry's total size.

The records of bankruptcies present a range of problems. Firstly, the fact of bankruptcy did not necessarily cause a concern to cease production – the case of Joan Rull, involved in two bankruptcies, but who survived to be one of the leaders in the industry in the 1820s and 1830s, provides a good illustration of this,[18] and others are those of

---

[17] See below p. 295. Canaleta had reduced his manufacture to a skeleton labour force because of the crisis occasioned by the war with England. Its revival with peace in 1802 was noted by the Barcelona chronicler Rafael d'Amat 'In proof of the fact that the cotton and painted calico manufactures are already begin to pick up, in addition to the many knocks of its printers within, at midday great quantities of handkerchieves, for export to the Indies, could be seen extended on the pieces of wood, or frames, on those patios of the land orientated city wall, from Canaleta's manufacture to the market garden of Fabà, all of which makes everyone happy at not having to be molested by all those needy workers, harassing us and after our money, and some of them fairly annoying' (cited by Duran Sanpere, *Barcelona*, II, p. 298).

[18] Sánchez, 'Los fabricantes de indianas', pp. 208–11; the bankruptcy records for Rull are held in AHCB, Arxiu comercial, B988–91, 992–7, 1004.

Magí Pujadas, bankrupt in 1797, but who appears on the *Almanak*'s lists through to 1802 and who was involved in mechanical cotton-spinning in 1804, and Joan Costa, bankrupt in 1791, and whose manufacture continued producing, it would seem, beyond 1806.[19] Secondly, if there were both bankruptcy and withdrawal from the industry, the two events did not necessarily coincide. The abandonment of production might precede the bankruptcy – representing a cutting back on investments by a commercial company in difficulty – and such, it would seem, was the case of the important calico-printing concern of Pujol and Cantarell: its withdrawal from production appears to have preceded 1793 whereas the bankruptcy of its leading associate, Ramon Pujol i Prunés, took place in 1795;[20] or it might follow it: apparently the case of another important calico-printing concern, Formentí's, which went bankrupt in 1787 but which ceased production in 1796.[21]

More general difficulties relating to all the sources is the identification of concerns in the case of changes in their names on account of inheritance or the opening of new partnerships. All care has been taken to avoid mistakes in this area by cross-checking between sources but it would certainly be difficult to avoid all error as a very large number of concerns were operating at some stage of this period – in addition to the 113 manufactures whose existence in the city in 1786 we recorded in chapter 6, over 131 new calico-printing concerns were founded and there was a most rapid growth in the number of specialized spinning and weaving establishments to a figure of about 130 in 1802/4.[22] Failure to identify changes in name of companies has the result both of increasing my figures for concerns which went out of production and also of increasing those for new firms founded, whereas a mistaken identification of a new concern with an old has the opposite consequences.

The question of the completeness of the records which have been used is another problem. Some shorter-term involvements in the industry may have left no record of their existence. In addition, as the

[19] Bankruptcy records of both held by AHCB; for Pujadas's (bankrupt in 1797) spinning in 1804 see above p. 260n, though his name is withdrawn from the *Almanak*'s lists after 1802. Costa's (bankrupt in 1791) name continues to appear in the lists of the *Almanak Mercantil* till 1805 when its place is taken by that of Rafael Costa, possibly his successor.

[20] Delgado, 'El impacto de las crisis coloniales', p. 124, for the bankruptcy. There is no evidence for calico production after 1790.

[21] *Ibid.*, p. 110; his production accounts continue till 1796 (AHCB, Arxiu comercial, B141–7).

[22] Sánchez, 'La era de la manufactura', p. 28.

case of the decline in the Canaleta concern illustrates, continuity in the existence of a company may conceal considerable changes in its dimensions. It would have been useful to have been able to have supplemented the lists of manufactures with production figures but these do not exist. Overall, though, the sources which have been used, and the tables which have resulted from them, can be defended. A good start is provided by the completeness of the details, analysed in the penultimate chapter, for the beginning of the period: it seems likely that we possess near complete records of the state of the industry in 1786 and the use of a wide range of sources for the period 1790–1807 makes it likely that the overwhelming majority of printing concerns founded during these years has been identified – the survey is thus relatively complete up to this point. The lack of any documentation for the period of most acute crisis, 1808–15, however, is particularly unfortunate – it would have been good to have been able to follow the destiny of the industry in as much detail as is possible up to this point – and this deficiency in the sources will enforce considerable reliance on the analysis of the loan document for 1823, mentioned above, for an assessment of the changes wrought by the most severe crisis of them all.

The charting of the industry's progress in this way, in terms of manufactures coming into it and withdrawing from it, is, I would argue, although a poor means of assessing production trends, useful from the point of view of assessing some of the principal issues with which this book is concerned: the extent of stability of the industry at various stages in its development; the extent of disruption occasioned by the wars and crises of this period and, therefore, of continuity between its eighteenth-century expansion and its renewed growth from the 1820s and, particularly, the 1830s; the extent of social mobility that existed in the industry; and finally the issue of whether the hold of 'commercial capital' on the industry gave way to one of 'industrial'.

The fate of the 1786 industry

Table 8.2 has been drawn up in order to isolate the experiences during this period of the established industry, of the 114 concerns operating in the two halves of the industry, the regulated and unregulated, in 1786. A word of warning about the principal

Table 8.2. *The fate of the 1786 industry: number of concerns withdrawing from the industry during various phases*[23]

Pre-1790	1790–3	1793–1800	1800–8	1808–18	Survivors
32	12	5	10	11	44

deficiencies in the table is a first preliminary. Two particular gaps in the sources at the end of the period surveyed make it likely that the number of survivors was in fact considerably less than the forty-four recorded. Firstly, extensive reliance has had to be placed on the lists in the *Almanak Mercantil* for establishing which concerns were still running before the outbreak of the War of Independence. For eight different concerns this is the only reference for production after 1801 which exists. As this source's principal weakness is its failure to record the disappearance of concerns, the consequence is that the table's record of a number of manufactures still existing in 1808 is likely to be too high. Secondly, the records for the period 1808–15 are, as pointed out, most deficient of all, and it is certain that more concerns than the ten recorded here were lost during these years. Thirdly, the records throughout are at their worst for smaller concerns – the shake-out rate of these may be overstated by the table as a consequence: I may have categorized such firms as having withdrawn from production when no mention is found of them when in fact it is their smallness which is the cause of non-mention.

With these qualifications, the table is of some use in interpreting aspects of the industry's experience during these years. Firstly, it shows the extent of the first overproduction crisis which the industry

[23] The withdrawing concerns from the 'regulated' section of the industry (see table 6.1) were as follows: before 1790, A. Aimar, Bertran, Capalà, Carrera, P. Costa, Font, Iglesias, Margenedes, Marí, P. Olsina, Perich, Pongem, Vehils; 1790–3, Bruguera, Cantarell & Pujol, Gallissà, Gramatges, Pedra, Seguí, Rovira; 1793–1800, Buch/Armengol, Demestre Vidal, Formentí; 1800–8, Canals, Cathalà (by then Sivilla), Costa, Ribas, Riera Albanell, Roig, Rolandi, Soler, Vicens, Pujadas; 1808–18, Aymar/Ribas, Alabau, Aribau, Espalter, Magarola, Ortells, Sirés, Soler, Canaleta, Busquets; possibly survivors: Aguilar, an Alabau, Armet & Salgado, Barbara, Bonaplata, Bosch, Canet, Cantarell, Capelino & Tomàs, Casas, Castañer, Castelló, Clarós, Deparés, Fontseré, Gelabert, Gónima, Illa & Crosi, Henrich, Llorens, Marimon, Masvidal, Muños, Olsina/Tomàs & Pi/Tomba & Olsina, Parellada, Prat, Ramon, Rull, Sala/Bosch, Sala, Vermell. Additional sources used to those described above are as follows: Sánchez, 'La era de la manufactura', p. 77 n. 177, for losses of Canaleta, Magarola, Sirés, Soler, Alabau, Ortells, Espalter, Costa, Busquets and Aribau.

282   *A distinctive industrialization*

Table 8.3. *Substantial manufactures which withdrew before 1793, with details of numbers of children employed and estimates of total labour forces in 1786*[24]

Bertran	10	(37)	Pongem	60	(222)
Capalà	18	(66)	Vehils	10	(37)
Carrera	12	(44)	Bruguera	15	(55)
P. Costa	24	(88)	Gallissà	17	(63)
Font	36	(133)	Gramatges	20	(74)
Iglesias	16	(59)	Pujol & Cantarell	131	(485)
Margenedes	58	(215)	Seguí	14	(52)
P. Olsina	10	(37)	Rovira	30	(111)
Total children 481			Estimated total labour force 1,778		

underwent following the post-American war expansion – over a quarter of concerns were lost by 1790. A further twelve disappeared before 1793 bringing the total losses to over 37 per cent. A contemporary recorded in 1787 a reduction of the size of the industry from 100 manufactures to only 30 or 40 and commented on the melancholy sight of the manufactures' bleaching fields 'with only 40 or 50 pieces, instead of the 1,500 or the 3,000 which we used to see extended in them continuously':[25] while this account is shown to be exaggerated, the crisis was, it is clear, very severe, and to contemporaries must have appeared all the more so in that it followed so many years of near total stability in the industry. As was to have been expected, the toll was greatest among smaller manufactures – those which had perhaps been founded with principally speculative motives: of the thirty-five concerns for which the details exist twenty-one were employing less than ten children and thus would have been likely to have had labour forces of thirty or less; however, among the fourteen employing ten or over there were some very substantial concerns including those of Pujol and Cantarell, Pongem, Font and Marià Rovira with labour forces of 485, 222, 133 and 111 respectively.[26]

[24] I have included in this table the manufacture of Pere Margenedes which was included in the 1786 diocesan survey but about which there is no other information.

[25] The contemporary was Josep Francesc Vila and the occasion of the statement was an emergency meeting held to discuss the crisis by the cities' *comerciantes matriculados*. The document in question is reproduced but misdated (11 Dec. 1786 rather than, as it should be, 11 Dec. 1787) by Torrella Niubó, *El moderno resurgir*, pp. 150–3. On this meeting, see BC, JC, leg. 32, no. 1.

[26] For ratios for conversion of number of child employees to total labour forces, see p. 175n.

Table 8.4. *New calico-printing manufactures founded, 1788–1806*[27]

1788–90	1791–3	1794–7	1798–1801	1802–6
18	33	21	24	36

The sample of calico-printing concerns isolated in table 8.2 clearly becomes progressively less useful for judging the extent of prosperity of the industry as a whole, as it was depleted by losses and new concerns were founded, but an initial assessment can be made from it about the extent of discontinuity occasioned by the crisis of these years. A reduction in the 1786 industry to at the very most slightly over a third of its size (and this, as has just been noted, would be a maximal figure) in the space of some thirty years clearly represents a great discontinuity. What is more, the crisis had been selective – the older concerns had been hit in particular: of manufactures founded before 1775 the only ones possibly surviving (and question marks have been put against the most doubtful) were those of Alabau (?), Canet (?), Capelino & Tomàs (?), Illa, Marimon (?), Sala and Vermell (?). The list of the pre-1775 concerns lost during the period is more definite and includes the principal manufactures of the early years – those of Canals, Formentí, Pongem, Canaleta, Seguí, the Magarola brothers, Cantarell and Pujol, Buch & Armengol, Isidro Cathalà, Ribas, Soler, Sirés, Vicens, Alabau, Aribau and Busquets.

[27] The new manufactures were as follows (dates = year of first documented mention): 1788, Rovira; 1789, Sarriera, Dot, Artigas, Scherrer; 1790, Jordà, Agell, J. Puig, Igual, J. Alabau, J. Canals, Rosas i Casas, Bruguière, P. Sala, Trias, Durdal, Llobet-Xipell, Cuyas; 1792: Casas-Ricart; 1793: J. Amat, J. Mach, Olivet, Monjó, Tarascó, Subiellos, Giol, Martís, Gabriel Bonaplata, L. Margenedes, Viñals, Dalmau, Guell, Roca, Aurich, Carranca, Rialp, Jacas, Domech, Claret, Xuriach, Fresas, Figuerola, Roca, Cornet, Coll & Viladomiu, Eliàs, Solà, Roger, Carrió, Mir; 1794: Flotats, A. Sala; 1795: Alabau, Tresserras; 1796: Mataró; 1797: Puig Torras, Puig Julià, M. Ribas, Valentí, Anglora, J. & P. Alabau, Buxó, Dot–Bulena, Lletjós Batlle, J. Mauri, J. Riera, Santaló & Cia, Xampané, Teplí, Mayner–Amat, Batlle; 1798: Molas, Fresca, Puig & Bas, Championet, Espina, Parell, Puchot, Mató, J. Pla; 1799: F. Sala, A. Rivera, Jermen; 1800: A. Font, E. Amigó; 1801: Blanch, Bringas, Chavas, Codina, Crespió, Minech, Vigo, Arolas, Prats, Pujols; 1802: Casas, Puig, Torras; 1803: Amat, Biquet, Fàbregas, Parella, Sala, Sandehi, Sirchent, Nadal; 1804: Gebelly, Parset, Tirigall, Keittinger, Arís, Planas, Batlle, J. Estrada, Geroni Bonaplata, P. Estrada, Calafell, Calmó, Bracon Bricfeus, Franquesa, Puig Major, J. Amigó, Millá, Orell, R. Costa, Planas & Aguilar, Santalona; 1805: Martí; 1806: Archel, Cardoch, Comte.

Table 8.5. *Fate of new calico-printing concerns up to 1806: numbers withdrawing from the industry, surviving at certain dates*

Pre-1793	Pre-1800	Pre-1806	Survivors
8	21	22	80

Survivors were concentrated in particular in the new generation of manufactures founded immediately before or following the American war, in that great expansion in the industry which was described in the penultimate chapter – Castañer and Castelló, founded in 1779, Armet & Salgado (?), founded in 1781, Barbara (?), founded in c. 1778, Gónima, founded in 1783, Rull, founded (as Anglès Rull) in 1784, Henrich (?), Llorens (?), Masvidal (?), Parellada, Clarós and Ramon founded in 1785, Deparés (?), Gelabert and Bonaplata founded between 1785 and 1786.

New calico-printing manufactures founded up to 1806
The first tables thus demonstrate an undoubted crisis in the industry as it had existed at the beginning of this period; however, an interpretation of the period as a whole clearly requires consideration of data on the establishment, and success, of new manufactures. The available data on these is summarized in tables 8.4 and 8.5 above. Again, a word of warning about the limitations of these tables is necessary. In addition to the problems mentioned above concerning completeness of evidence and the difficulties resulting from manufactures changing their names, problems were encountered in drawing up these tables on account of sparsity of data for the period after 1793 – the *Almanak*'s lists and the protest of the printers of 1804, mentioned above, being the only substantial sources, though they have been supplemented by information drawn from the cadaster. An attempt to avoid one consequence of this, the grouping of manufactures' foundations of disappearances for the few years for which there is adequate information on the industry, has been made by dividing the period into blocks of several years, though this, clearly, has the consequence that the relating of the development of the industry to commercial expansion or crisis is rendered less precise. More serious from the point of view of what is a central aim of the chapter – the establishment of the extent of discontinuity which was

experienced by the industry during these years – is the near total lack of data for the period after 1806. The tables provide no basis for judging the impact of the most severe crisis of all, and as noted this task will have to be left until the state of the industry in 1823 has been analysed.

Despite their failings the tables serve some purposes. They show firstly, that the industry – with 132 new printing concerns founded, and we are going to provide details on the expansion in the number of weaving concerns below – was certainly far from inert during these years. On the contrary, levels of activity were unprecedentedly high – in the period studied in the previous chapter, which was active enough, it will be recalled, there were 115 approved and unapproved calico-printing concerns founded, but no similar expansion in the number of spinning and cotton-weaving concerns. It is clear that, though there were crises during these years, the momentum of the eighteenth-century expansion was being more than maintained from the point of view of the establishment of new commercial and industrial concerns. Restrictions on industrial development in terms of guild rules or the calico-printers' regulations seem to have been completely disregarded and the combination of population growth, high expectations, capital accumulated during the long years of prosperity, wide availability of skills, favourable governmental policy with this fairly total institutional freedom was making possible rapid industrial change.

Analysing the tables more closely to relate them to particular stages in the commercial development of these years, the large number of new calico-printing concerns founded up to 1793 is clearly related to the commercial expansion of these years described in the opening section of this chapter. The more mixed character of the industry's performance from this point – forty-five new concerns founded between 1794 and 1801 but twenty-one concerns withdrawing from the industry before 1800 – is consistent with what we have shown was the character of the 'conjuncture' of these years, with continued prosperity in export markets up to 1797 but then a collapse in these and difficulties in the domestic market from this point. The founding of twenty-four new concerns between 1798 and 1801, the years of maximal crisis for the whole century (ten, admittedly, in 1801), is surprising – its significance will be returned to – but the large number founded between 1800 and 1806 is clearly related to the return to favourable trading circumstances which we noted with the signing of peace with England in 1802. The period of prosperity, however, was short, it was noted, with the renewal of warfare with Britain in 1804: the majority of the failures of new calico-printing concerns recorded in table 8.4 was concentrated in the years following the outbreak of war – seven bankruptcies are recorded between 1805 and 1807.[28]

Our final judgement on the extent of discontinuity occasioned by the crises to the industry is going to have to wait, we have emphasized, until the 1823 information on it has been analysed. A contribution to assessing this question can be made at this point, however, by considering the evidence which exists concerning the types of new calico-printing concerns which were filling the gaps left by the departure of the old, documented in tables 8.2 and 8.3. Were they equivalents to the old manufactures, in which case continuity with the old industry will have been shown, or were they smaller concerns, in which case, though the number of manufactures may have been stable, the industry's productive capacity will have been shown to have decreased and its character to have changed? These will be the questions that will concern us.

The only major source relating to this question is the cadaster with its separate listing of larger calico-printing concerns for the in- dependent (from the guilds) payment of taxes. This source only exists up to 1801, we have noted, but a total of twenty-two of the ninety- four new concerns founded up to this point do appear in it, and their inclusion in the lists can be taken as a sign that they were substantial manufactures. They would not have been as large as the principal concerns in the industry – in only six cases was the tax imposed upon them above the minimal rate of 100 *libras* charged on the list (those of Joan Coll i Viladomiu, Segimon Mir, Manuel Flotats, Llorens Roger, Sarriera brothers and Bartomeu Jorda, taxed at 200, 125, 150, 115, 130 and 150 *libras* respectively), whereas rates paid by the largest calico-printers were up to 500 *libras* (this was the rate paid by Erasme Gónima from 1794, and in 1787, there were fourteen subscribers at the rate of 200 *libras*, seven at that of 150, five at 100, four at 300 and one at 350).[29]

We have the notarial contract by which one of these concerns was founded and this provides some idea of what it is likely was a representative investment in a concern of this type. The manufacture

---

[28] Delgado, 'El impacto de las crisis coloniales', pp. 161–2.
[29] AHCB, cadastre for these years.

is that of Amat, Mayner & Co., taxed at 100 *libras* in the cadaster, and founded by eight associates in 1797 with an initial investment of 68,000 *libras*.[30] In addition, there is other evidence available about some of the other new, substantial manufactures established and about their founders. Manuel Flotats we have encountered in the previous chapter – it is clear that he had extended his activities during these years from his cotton-spinning in Cardona to printing in Barcelona: this extension, and the substantial investment which he had made already in spinning machinery, shows that he possessed ample financial resources.[31] The brothers Josep and Antoni Sarriera, the first mention of whose manufacture is for the year 1789, were leading wholesale merchants in the city. The company Galup and Sarriera was taxed at 300 *libras* in the cadaster in 1783, and in 1796, Josep was elected to become a *comerciante matriculado*. Their manufacture, described as 'old and accredited' (its origin probably went back before 1789), specialized in particular in the manufacturing of high-quality cotton cloths – in 1797, it was one of the only makers of muslins in the city. It was clearly a leader in this sector of the industry and responsible for introducing new technologies from abroad – in 1793 it was employing a Frenchman, Xiera or Siera, as its majordomo or manager and experimenting with new bleaching techniques. Later, in 1803, when Antoni Sarriera was chosen to act as a delegate for the Junta de Comercio, the choice was justified in terms of the major contribution which he had made to the development of cotton-weaving via his participation firstly in Galup Sarriera and Co. and secondly in Sarriera brothers.[32]

Other evidence, too, can be compiled to show continued commitment of 'commercial' capital to the industry during these years – Ermengol Gener, one of the city's leading wholesale merchants, whose company's trading activities with America since the 1750s was referred to in chapter 5, founded a calico-printing concern between 1787 and 1790 (though it did not outlast his bankruptcy in 1794);[33] Joan Serra, a leading member of the elite guild of silver-smiths,

---

[30] Grau and López, 'Empresari i capitalista', p. 56.   [31] See above pp. 253–5.

[32] AHCB, cadastre for 1783; Molas Ribalta, 'La Junta de Comerç de Barcelona', p. 293; BC, JC. leg. 45, no. 77, fos. 3–5, election of Josep as *comerciante matriculado*; *Almanak Mercantil* (1797), p. 461, for muslin production; BC, JC, leg. 53, no. 33, fos. 2–4, for employment of Frenchman and experimentation in bleaching; BC, JC, reg. 91, 1803, records major contribution of Antoni Sarriera to the cotton-weaving sector of the industry.

[33] Gener's presence is recorded at the meetings held in 1790 to discuss the forming of a company to finance the introduction of Arkwright's roller-spinning and he also subscribed with other calico-printers to the war donation made in 1793 (see above p. 276).

founded a spinning, weaving and printing company during these
years which was employing a labour force of 300 in 1805, and was
equipped with forty looms and forty-eight spinning machines.[34]
Of course, the state of health of the industry cannot be assessed
purely on the basis of the number of concerns moving in and out of
it. There remains the central question of whether those manufactures
which remained in it expanded or contracted their level of activity.
The level of cadastral payments of the larger printing companies
provides us some clues about this. There was a fairly marked
distinction between a group of concerns which experienced a decline
in their rate of payment and another group which either experienced
an increase or began to be separately assessed for the cadaster for the
first time.[35] In the former, were the manufactures of Canaleta, whose
case has already been mentioned, and those of Alabau, Tomàs & Pi
(successor to Joan Pau Olsina), Costa i Merla, Bosch & Sala and Pere
Vermell, and in the latter were Rull, Gónima, Marià Casas,
Castañer, Castelló, Clarós, Deparés, Espalter, Gelabert, Prat and
Riera Albanell – predictably the principal 'survivors' among the
members of the 1786 industry. Gónima's cadastral payment rose
steadily from 300 *libras* in 1787 to 400 *libras* in 1788 and 500 *libras* in
1794, at which level it remained, Rull's and Castañer's from 200 *libras*
to 300 *libras*.[36]
The smallness of the share of new concerns taxed separately on the
cadaster shows that they represented a minority of the new additions
to the industry. Smaller manufactures predominated, it is clear.
Investment in this type of concern, as we already know, could be
minimal. Bartomeu Rovira founded his manufacture in 1788 with
three associates with an investment of 300 *libras* in cash. That may
have been an extreme: other investments recorded are the 12,000
libras invested in the company of Casas, Ricart and Amigó by five
associates in 1792, the 6,000 *libras* contributed by two associates for
the company of Jaume & Pau Alabau founded in 1795 (bankrupt in
1805) and the 9,000 *libras* invested by three associates in the company
of Josep Mató in 1798.[37] The exact balance between the different
sizes of the new concerns in the industry is impossible to establish.

[34] BC, JC, reg. 91, 16 Oct. 1805; Sánchez, 'La era de la manufactura', p. 72 n. 121.
[35] In the previous paragraph, we were considering new manufactures included on the
cadastral lists; here, we are considering manufactures existing in 1786 of which some,
because of an increase in the scale of their affairs (this is our assumption), are moved onto
the list for the first time.   [36] AHCB, cadastre for these years.
[37] Grau and López, 'Empresari i capitalista', pp. 54–6.

The expansion in the number of independent weaving concerns
Some weaving of cotton cloth outside the manufactures had taken place since the early years of the industry. It had been on a small scale and had suffered a reverse, it will be recalled, during the 1760s but expanded again in the 1770s and particularly in the 1780s, with some diffusion outside Barcelona. The particularly important role of linen-weavers in the development was stressed. The trend was initially opposed by the large manufactures, we have seen, as it represented both a threat to the maintenance of control over their labour forces – who might be encouraged by the trend to set up on their own – as well as to the quality of production in the industry (or at least this was their argument). It also, more significantly, was a challenge to their very existence as large, concentrated manufactures, as the existence of a market in locally produced calicoes made it possible for small-scale printing concerns to be established. For these reasons the early stages of the development of this sector had something of a submerged, black market economy about it. In 1786 the directors of the Royal Spinning Company reported that the 'traffickers' in these cotton cloths produced outside the manufactures 'circulate in bands in these streets...having difficulty in finding purchasers' in view of the opposition exercised by 'the owners of manufactures which attach importance to their good name'.[38]

By the 1790s, however, the development had become irreversible and was no longer opposed by the large manufactures. Its acceptance is demonstrated by the fact that the trade was being handled by, among others, one of the principal commercial brokers involved in the provision of the manufactures with raw cotton, spun yarn and imported linens for printing. Delgado has noted in his recent study on the affairs of Josep Just i Anglada, who handled the provisioning of thirty of the city's manufactures, a rapid increase in the sales of the locally produced calicoes from a figure of some 3,489 metres in 1789 to 70,688 metres by 1793.[39]

The source of these locally produced calicoes in the white was firstly within the city itself, and the growth in an independent weaving sector in the industry can be traced from a variety of sources. Between 1788 and 1797 there is evidence for the establishment, or

---

[38] For earlier discussions of this sector, see pp. 245–7; the quotation is from a report of the directors of the Royal Spinning Company of 30 Sept. 1785 (reproduced by Torrella Niubó, *El moderno resurgir*, pp. 133–46).
[39] Delgado, 'La industria algodonera catalana', p. 109.

existence, of a total of thirty-two such concerns.[40] There were also, it has been noted, a number of concerns run by cotton and linen weavers who carried out printing too – these have been counted in the previous enumerations of calico-printers. Growth in the new sector would appear to have been continuous. In 1799, forty-nine participants in it, describing themselves as 'manufacturers of cloth and spun yarn', attended a meeting to a form a *cuerpo* to represent their interests.[41] Again, some of those listed were also involved in calico-printing, and to avoid double-counting have had to be removed from this figure, but other names, drawn from other sources, have to be added to make a total of at least fifty-seven cotton-weavers and spinners operating in the city in this year.[42] By the years 1802 to 1804 the new sector, at least from the point of view of the number of functioning concerns, was rivalling that of the calico-printers in size – a count of 130 concerns has been made by Alejandro Sánchez on the basis of attendance at three meetings of the new *cuerpo de fabricantes de tejidos y hilados*.[43]

Almost certainly more significant quantitatively, however, was the expansion of such weaving activities outside the city. They tended to develop alongside spinning. The report of the directors of the Royal Company of Spinners referred to above noted what were the beginnings of this trend and of its importance, even at this early stage: 'the [disorder] which comes from outside [the walls] is of greater importance since the production of such cloth has spread to different parts of the Principality', they noted, and by the turn of the century the trade had become a very large one.[44] As noted in the previous chapter, one of the reasons for the rapidity with which it grew was the disturbances being occasioned to other trades by the warfare. Figures for the production of cotton cloth in the former

---

[40] As follows: Ermenter & Serra, Negrevernis, Camps, Conill, Curdal, Faboteu, Pujol, Sendra, Rosell, Verdaguer, March, Pons, Albafull, Blanch, Capdevila, Pujol, Torrens, Marangas (all listed in *Almanak Mercantil* (1797), which records concerns working in 1796; I have not included those specialist cotton workers who were also printing and have been included, thus, in the enumerations earlier in the chapter); Ermenter & Pere Camps, Comas, J. Vilaregut (Grau and López, 'Empresari i capitalista', pp. 54–6); S. Vilaregut, J. Rovira Casella, Baulenas, Viladoms, Amigó (listed by Sánchez, 'La era de manufactura', p. 72 n. 120); Domenech, Torda, Vila, Auger, Manresa (identifiable from list of concerns made in 1790, BC, JC, leg. 51, no. 20); Carlos Guàrdia (reported on by Junta de Comercio, 20 Dec. 1787, see Torrella Niubó, *El moderno resurgir*, pp. 158–9).

[41] BC, JC, leg. 51, no. 22, fos. 2–13, meeting of 10 May 1799.

[42] The other sources and names as in n. 40.

[43] Sánchez, 'La era de la manufactura', p. 28.   [44] As n. 38.

Table 8.6. *Barcelona's cotton industry in 1823: printers, weavers, spinners and others definitely identifiable in the* contribución extraordinaria *raised in this year*

Printers	65
Weavers	154
Spinners	56
Others (comb-makers, bleachers, chemical manufacturers, etc.)	11

Note: I have omitted those listed as *pintores* and *gravadores* among whose number there would have been some participants in calico-printing.

woollen cloth centre Sabadell give some idea of the extent of growth to which the disruptions in previous trades and the opportunities available in cotton was giving rise – a growth was recorded from 2,352 pieces of cotton cloth produced in 1794 to 14,876 pieces in 1803.[45] In 1804, it was estimated that 6,000 pieces of cotton cloth a week were entering Barcelona from other parts of the Principality.[46] An extra stimulus to the development had been provided by the legislation of 1802 banning the import of spun yarn which disfavoured the city's manufacturing interests, shifting the centre of gravity of the yarn market from the port (formerly the source of spun yarn) to the interior (where most spinning was done).

The industry in 1823
The document which I shall use for this description is the record of an 'Exceptional war tax imposed on commerce and industry'.[47] It lists the names of merchants and industrialists giving their places of work, in some cases the type of building in which they operated (a whole house, a *tienda*, or on different floors of buildings being the three variants) and the taxes which they paid. It has imperfections, the principal of which is that a number of individuals are simply listed as *fabricantes* or *tejedores* without specifying what industry they were involved in (totals of fifty-five and twenty-nine respectively). It

[45] Details in J. Nadal, 'La consolidación de la industria algodonera', in vol. VIII of P. Vilar (directed), *Història de Catalunya* (8 vols., Barcelona, 1987–90), p. 215 n. 106.
[46] BC, JC, leg. 53, no. 38, fo. 3, request from Josep Salvat to the Junta General of 13 October 1804 to be allowed to be measurer for cloth coming from outside the city.
[47] AHCB, cadastre, VIII, 3.

does serve, however, to give an approximate idea of the following – the numbers of concerns in different sectors of the industry, the geographical distribution of the industry in the city, the relation of the resources invested in the industry to those invested in commerce, the relative resources of different participants in the industry within and between its three sectors and organization of production.

Firstly, the number of concerns in the different sectors of the industry. The figures are shown in table 8.6. It may be, of course, that those listed simply as *fabricantes* included a disproportionate number of printers. This is likely as the majority of those involved in cotton manufacturing would have been members of the guild of *tejedores de lino & algodon* and are thus listed as *tejedores de algodon* rather than as *fabricantes* whereas, as there was no calico-printers' guild, it was more normal for them to be listed simply as *fabricantes*. With this reserve aside, however, the table shows that (judged purely in terms of numbers of concerns) since 1808 the cotton manufacturing sector of the city's industry had maintained its size, the spinning section had grown and the printing one had declined.

The document shows that there had been some spatial shifts in the distribution of the industry: its centre of gravity, which had been shifting gradually during the eighteenth century away from the area close to the Portal Nou, in the north-east of the city, where the industry was originally founded, towards the newly urbanized area of the Raval, had completed this transfer: 171 of the total of 286 concerns were located in the latter quarter. The predominance of the Raval in the spinning and weaving sectors was particularly striking – it contained 50 of the 56 spinning establishments and 98 of the 154 weaving ones. The older centre still predominated with respect to printing – there were twenty-three printing establishments still in the area surrounding the Carrer del Portal Nou.

The comparison of the quantity of taxes paid by those involved in the industry with that paid by *comerciantes* suggests that the industry had become very much a poor cousin to the city's trading activities. As can be seen from table 8.7, even if all the *fabricantes* are counted as forming a part of the industry, a total of only 27 'industrialists' subscribed at rates of above 100 *libras*: in contrast purely in the first of five *cuartels* (quarters), into which the city was divided for fiscal purposes, 97 of a total of 207 *comerciantes* were paying above this rate. Looking at the distribution of taxes within the industry, it can be seen that there were clearly some contrasts in the 'wealth' of the different

Table 8.7. *Rates of subscription to the* contribución extraordinaria *of 1823 (in* libras)

	Fabricantes	Printers	Weavers	Spinners
16 and below	26	19	62	38
17–49	20	20	59	13
50–99	5	14	22	4
100–49	2	2	4	
150–99	1	1	2	1
200–49	1	3	3	
250 and above		5	2	

Table 8.8. *Types of space containing printing, spinning and weaving manufactures in 1823*

	Printing	Spinning	Weaving
Basements		4	6
Entresols		2	2
Shops	13	19	54
1st floor	10	23	47
2nd floor	4	3	6
3rd floor	1	1	1
'Whole houses'	5	3	7

sectors, with the average payments made by printers exceeding that of weavers and, in particular, that of spinners, which was clearly the sector of the industry in which the scale of concerns was smallest – the divergent size of investments in the three sectors of the industry has been well established on the basis of studies on company formations[48] – but overall the predominance of small and very small concerns is notable in all three sectors. Large concerns, it is more than clear, were the exception.

This predominance of the small scale, and of what may be termed the familial unit of production over the *fábrica* which dominated in the eighteenth century, is further demonstrated by table 8.8, illustrating organization of production. The document provides information on the type of housing in which a total of 211 of the

[48] Sánchez, 'La era de la manufactura', p. 47.

printing and spinning manufactures were situated as shown in the table. It is clear that the small 'domestic' production unit predominated overwhelmingly. Again the extent of its predominance was slightly greater in the spinning and weaving sectors than in the printing but the table shows that in the latter sector, too, the *casa fábrica* (house/manufacture), dominant in the eighteenth century, had become very much a minority phenomenon. In 1785, it will be recalled, the directors of the Royal Spinning Company complained that 'The hallways, second, third, and fourth floors of the smallest of houses which one or two printing tables totally fill up, have become workshops for this noble and important industry' – such production units during the years of crisis had become, it is clear, virtually universal.[49]

AN INTERPRETATION

The data assembled in the previous section provides a reasonably adequate basis for interpreting what occurred to the industry during this period of some thirty-five years.

The overproduction crisis of 1787, we have seen, opened a far more difficult period for the industry, one which was in sharp contrast to the stable and prosperous epoch which had preceded it. It was not one, however, totally without possibilities of profit. Immense gains were to be made from the American trade, in particular, and some printers clearly benefited from this. Erasme Gónima in 1788 was said to be spending more than 2 million *reales* annually for the purchase of imported linens for export as *pintados*,[50] and Joan Canaleta, it was claimed, made over 100,000 *libras* on a single cargo to Vera Cruz in 1794.[51] The historian of Joan Rull's manufacture has calculated that this concern made a profit of 55.3 per cent between 1803 and 1805.[52] The prospects of such large profits caused the industry to continue to be an attractive outlet for commercial capital during these years. As late as 1806, for example, a year after the battle of Trafalgar, when prospects for the American trade must have been at their bleakest, the merchant Josep Ravella found a buyer for his 32,194 *libras* stake in the company of Esteve Bosch, the investment being justified as

[49] As n. 38.
[50] Francisco de Zamora, who wrote an important description of Catalonia during this year, is author of this statement.
[51] Delgado, 'El impacto de las crisis coloniales', p. 122.
[52] Sánchez, 'Los fabricantes de indianas', p. 200.

follows: 'that just as the perils and chances which trade encounters can cause enormous prejudices to the buyer, so it can also, war ceasing and even among the comings and goings of war, give rise to substantial profits'.[53]

At this late stage, too, we have noted in the last chapter, there was a rapid rise in investment in spinning activities in which large-scale as well as small-scale producers participated. Alexandre de Laborde, visiting the principality during these years, commented on the high level of activity which he had noted: 'They have increased by remarkable proportions since the coming to the throne of the grandson of Louis XIV', he reported, 'and have not been slowed down by the last war; on the contrary the capital which has been placed in this Province has served for some important investments with the coming of peace.'[54] It was on the basis of this considerable momentum that Bonaventura Gassó was to conclude later, when quite different economic prospects held, that 'without the naval war of 1804 and the execrable invasion of 1808, Catalonia's state of mechanization would already have been useful and promoting growth'.[55] Pierre Vilar has even argued that the extent of the crisis in the colonial and other trades had encouraged a transfer of investment into industry.[56]

This, however, would probably be too favourable a verdict to draw. If profits had been made in the American trade, big losses, too, had been registered. For nearly three years, between 1799 and 1801, all manufactures had been working on short time and had suspended the majority of their labour forces – those laid off had been dependent on the distribution of food by the city's Junta de Caridad and up to 30,000 weekly rations had been handed out.[57] Canaleta was to complain himself in 1805 that he had lost 2 million *reales* during the war of 1797–1801 and 80,000 already in that which had broken out in the previous year. It is clear that he had experienced a gradual process of impoverishment. His name, we have noted, dropped out of the registers of the cadaster and in 1805 he protested himself unable to pay the sum of 20,000 *reales* which had been imposed on him as part of a loan to finance the war against England on the grounds of

[53] Sánchez, 'La era de la manufactura', p. 41.
[54] Cited by Vilar, *La Catalogne*, III, p. 137.
[55] A. B. Gassó, *España con industria, fuerte y rica* (Barcelona, 1816), p. 70.
[56] Vilar, *La Catalogne*, III, p. 138.
[57] Delgado, 'El impacto de las crisis coloniales', p. 138.

his losses and the difficulties he was experiencing in supporting his eight children. He was relying on loans, he claimed, to 'support the few workers which I employ in my manufacture'.[58]

Commercial capital was still moving into the industry, we have seen, but the scale of the movement in did not match that of the movement out. The most obvious sign we have seen of the latter development is the withdrawal from the industry of so large a number of the predominantly commercially financed concerns which had existed in 1786 but it applied, too, to some of these concerns which remained in production, but from which resources were steadily withdrawn in a process of decapitalization. One example of this was the manufacture of Joan Aribau who was obliged to buy out his merchant associates one by one, the first in 1795, another in 1796 and the last between 1800 and 1803.[59] Another was that of Joan Rull whose company, Anglès Rull, was liquidated in 1797, Joan Rull retaining the buildings and bleaching fields in return for a commitment to pay back his capitalist backers.[60] The trend has been interpreted as having been favourable to the emergence of the genuine industrialist, enabled to pay off his capitalist backers at knock-down rates. There is no doubt that the period, as is generally the case of periods of rapid technological and commercial change, did see a sharp change in the identity of the dominating firms in the industry. The rise of Erasme Gónima's fortune, for example, is legendary.[61] The suddenness of these processes of disinvestment was a sign of crisis, however, and it put a strain on the resources of the companies concerned.

To a great extent, it is clear that the mixed character of the fortunes of different participants in the trade was a matter of generations. As we have seen, the survivors, and those whose cadastral payments rose, were concentrated above all among the new companies founded shortly before or after the American war. In contrast, we have seen that the withdrawals from the industry were concentrated principally among older manufactures. The big opportunity up until the mid-1790s was in the American trade and it was profited from most by new companies, some of which had been founded specifically with this trade in mind.

[58] BC, JC, leg. 2, no. 3, fos. 141–2, letter of 7 June 1805.
[59] Grau and López, 'Empresari i capitalista', p. 40.
[60] Sánchez, 'Los fabricantes de indianas', p. 115.
[61] See, for example, Duran Sanpere, *Barcelona*, II, pp. 307–8, and E. d'Imbert, *Erasmo de Gónima, 1746–1821. Apuntes para una biografía y estudio de su época* (Barcelona, 1952).

By the first decade of the nineteenth century, it is clear that a principal reason for commercial capital remaining in the industry had become speculative – the hope that during periods of peace speculative profits could be made. J. M. Delgado categorizes this investment strategy as being typical of commercial capital.[62] We have seen, however, from our survey of the industry in the 1770s and 1780s that 'commercial capital' was quite satisfied with stable trading conditions which provided a regular and respectable return. The speculative character of the commitment to the industry was a new attribute introduced by the instability and by the fact – and this was a significant change which forms another part of the changing character of the economic circumstances of these years – that the industry, and its manufacturers, had become traders as much as manufacturers on account of the importance of their participation in the American trade. This they had always been in part – from the beginning the large manufacturers had, we have seen, financed the commercialization of their production – but from the 1790s some of the markets for which they had been producing (they did not drop the internal trade, we have noted) had become far more distant, requiring a greater commitment in terms of circulating capital, and they were disposing of their calicoes against colonial goods for resale when these were imported to Barcelona.[63]

Crisis and the American trade had, thus, contributed to the commitment to the trade becoming more speculative and, consequently, when circumstances became hopeless, with the English war being followed by that of the French, had contributed to the factor which caused the industry to be abandoned so totally to its fate. Delgado has documented the general disinvestment from the colonial trade which occurred during these years and, contrary to Vilar's comment, there are no signs of this disinvestment having been in

---

[62] Delgado, 'El impacto de las crisis coloniales', pp. 128, 152: his interpretation of the 1802–4 expansion in the American trade is that it was as much an attempt at liquidation as speculation.

[63] Sánchez notes the change in his study on Rull, who during the 1790s widened his range of commercial activities and from 1800 referred to himself as *comerciante* rather than as *fabricante* ('Los fabricantes de indianas', p. 203). It would seem that the predominating production of calicoes for the interior had been largely a cash trade, whereas that with America in a number of cases involved the printers in receiving colonial products in return for their calicoes. A witness used for vetting the application of one of the Magarola brothers (owners of an important calico-printing concern) for promotion to the status of *comerciante matriculado* in 1792 recorded that most of what he produced in his manufacture 'they direct on their own account from the manufacture, in Cádiz, and to America, whence in return they receive the fruits and other products of these countries' (BC, JC, leg. 45, no. 73, fo. 13, 1792).

favour of manufacturing in any other than the very short term. On the contrary, the evidence which we have presented both on the fate of the industry of 1786 and of the state of the industry in 1823 shows clearly that the disinvestment extended to manufacturing activities too. That the extent of the disinvestment may have provided an opportunity for a different type of production system based on the domestic unit of production is, of course, another question.

On the other hand, if the hopes that had been placed on the American trade proved in the end to have been misplaced because of British naval power, the domestic market continued to exist, and was to recover relatively rapidly after 1814, we have seen, and in addition there were legislative and technological changes in this period which clearly favoured the manufacturing, as opposed to the printing, side of the industry – in particular the ban on the import of yarn, which provided a new, protected sector into which the industry could expand, and the mechanization of spinning, which provided a satisfactory technical basis for this expansion as well as the chance of a lowering of costs which gave the prospect of a steady expansion in the sales of cotton goods. The crisis of the Catalan manufacture can only be fully understood if the failure to take advantage of these alternative opportunities is explained.

In addition to the cyclical and war-caused difficulties from which the industry was suffering during these years, it was suffering too, it is clear, from a structural crisis. The type of industrial organization which predominated in the industry – large, concentrated manufactures combining weaving with printing – had its explanation, we have shown, not in any particular economies of scale which resulted from such a form, but in government policy and the existence of guilds. In addition, as we have noted, the industry adopted regulations in 1767 in order to protect its industrial structure.[64] By the late 1780s and 1790s, however, a number of forces were now working against the centralized manufacture – government measures were now favouring the domestic production unit and skills were widely diffused; in addition, population growth, and increasing Malthusian pressures, had had the consequence that there was surplus labour ready to move into the new industry. Initially, as we saw in the penultimate chapter, the established manufactures, with the assistance of their collective organization, the Royal Spinning company, had attempted to defend their position as virtual

[64] See above, pp. 87–8, 183–4.

monopoly producers but from the 1790s it is clear that the struggle was abandoned and, on the contrary, that the large printing concerns gradually began to conform to the trend, cutting down or abandoning their manufacturing activities and buying cotton cloth for printing from small-scale producers. This was certainly an important contributory explanation for their relative lack of interest in promoting mechanical spinning which was noted in the last chapter. When the opportunities for mechanization presented themselves, the signs are that the manufactures were already beginning to become primarily printing establishments. The vast trade in *pintados* may well have encouraged the trend: the large profits, Gónima's purchase of *toiles* suggests, were obtained by the achievement of maximal throughput rather than through maximal value added.[65]

A first sign of the slackening of interest by the printers in manufacturing is provided by the response to the measure of 1789 permitting the Philippines company to introduce cotton cloth in the white from Asia. As had been the case with similar concessions, it imposed a threat to the manufacturing interests of the industry, but the mobilization of opposition to it was organized not, as had all previous such mobilization, by the printers but, curiously, by two weavers, Emeteri Serra and Josep Subirana, 'weavers of the *indiana* manufactures... in the name of the majority of individuals involved in these processes in the manufactures'. In their protest against the measure they complained that the *fabricants* were abandoning the weaving processes – the lack of protest by the *fabricants* themselves, as well as the additional evidence which we presented of the development of a flourishing market in locally produced cloth in the white during these years, suggest that they were already none too strongly committed to these activities.[66] As the decade proceeded, the evidence for this change of approach becomes more abundant – on the one hand, we have the details of the growth of the number of independent cotton-weavers, inside and outside Barcelona, on the other hand, we have that which is available from the records left by the *fábricas*: in the case of the Rull concern, Sánchez shows that whereas in 1800 30 per cent of wage payments were to weavers, by 1805 the figure had declined to a mere 6 per cent, and in the case of that of Joan Batista Sirés there is evidence of its supplying itself with

---

[65] Sánchez has also shown how Joan Rull, another of the successes of the decade, rapidly shifted from manufacturing his own cloth to buying it in the white, 76 per cent of his manufacture's costs during the years 1791–1808 consisting in this item ('L'estructura comercial', pp. 13–20).   [66] BC, JC. leg. 51, no. 20, fo. 2, 16 June 1790.

its cotton cloth predominantly from a wide range of Barcelona cotton *fabricants* from 1796.[67] By the end of the decade, the emerging independent cotton-weaving and spinning sector of the industry had achieved full autonomy, creating its own *cuerpo* to represent its interests in 1799, we have noted. Significantly, in 1802, when the import of spun yarn was prohibited, this *cuerpo* and the guild of linen- and cotton-weavers protested but not a murmur was heard from the calico-printers.[68]

The fundamental reason for the failure of the manufacture to take advantage of the new spinning and weaving opportunities which presented themselves to the industry during these years is reasonably easily identifiable. It was an unnatural type of industrial organization, liable to high running costs and could not compete with smaller-scale production units. The dominance of the small-scale producer is not surprising – there was a similar predominance in the English industry with respect to weaving, and there was a survival there, too, to a late stage of an important sector in the cotton-spinning industry using the domestic production unit and the jenny and its variations. The English example suggests that the only way in which the Catalan manufacture could have dominated the cotton manufacturing sectors of the industry at this early stage would have been by the creation of large-scale Arkwright mills and mass production – this possibility existed in 1790, we have seen, but the industry's investment record and the distraction of high profits obtainable in the American market at this stage made it unlikely that it would be taken advantage of.

So it was the combination of the cyclical and wartime crises with the structural one which made the decline of the Catalan manufacture so sudden and total. We have seen the extent of the losses in the 1786 industry (pp. 280–4), and the details provided on the state of the industry in 1823 (see pp. 291–4) shows that the large concerns which were founded during these years fared no better. The large manufacture was already severely 'damaged' by 1808. The War of Independence brought near total destruction. M. M. Gutiérrez's quotation, with which this chapter opens, describes the collapse. The property market was flooded with unneeded industrial buildings: 'for months past advertisements of the sale of manufactures had been appearing frequently', wrote Carrera Pujal of the period following

---

[67] Sánchez, 'La era de la manufactura', pp. 71–2 nn. 118, 120.
[68] Carrera Pujal, *Historia Política*, IV, p. 165.

the War of Independence. One of those whose disposal was attempted in 1818, by means of a royally authorized and municipally organized lottery, was that of the Magarolas – a last survivor from the formative period of the industry. The lottery had to be annulled as insufficient subscribers to it were found to satisfy the manufacture's creditors.[69]

But if the period witnessed the crisis of the manufacture, it also saw, it is clear, the birth of a new industry. It was perhaps not a total coincidence that the years in which this new industry emerged and made its presence felt were those of greatest difficulty for the manufacture. The years 1799–1801 were those of short time for the manufactures, and of soup-kitchens for their labour forces, we have noted, and it was during these years that the cotton-weavers founded their independent *cuerpo* and also that no less than twenty-four new, predominantly small-scale, printing, weaving, bleaching and spinning concerns were established in Barcelona's Raval – the strangeness of this development in this period of depression was mentioned in the previous section. The signs are that some of those who had waited in the queues for food distribution had finally lost faith with the manufacture and decided to ensure their own destiny. A new and this time 'popular' industry was being born.[70]

[69] Carrera Pujal, *La economía de Cataluña*, I, p. 26, and II, p. 207.
[70] AHCB, cadastre, the lists of *individuos vagos* record this large number of new concerns founded in the Arrabal during these years.

CHAPTER 9

The Bonaplata mill and Catalan industrialization

The smoke of the chimney of the Bonaplata manufacture...
marked the beginning of a new industrial era and indicated the
future of Catalan manufacturing.

(Madoz, *Diccionario geográfico-estadístico*, III, p. 48)

The enormous capital sums invested in royal bonds and other
public issues in the Barcelona capital market during the first
quarter of this century were cashed up... and... a large part of
their cash product, assembled by the spirit of association, was
devoted to industrial enterprises, for which the country possesses
the most important ingredient – the capacity for hard work of its
inhabitants.

(Bonaventura Carlos Aribau, *c.* 1860, cited by Fontana,
Aribau, p. 49)

THE EVENTS

As was apparent from the figures for cotton imports recorded in the
last chapter, the transformed industry was capable of growth. There
was a gradual expansion in the number of concerns in Barcelona, as
table 9.1 below demonstrates, and that spread of the industry to
other parts of the Principality, whose beginnings have been traced in
the last two chapters, continued. Progress in spinning was particularly rapid in Igualada, which developed into the second most
important Catalan spinning centre after Barcelona,[1] and in and
around Manresa: this town contained eleven water-driven spinning
mills by 1831 and there were other concerns in the surrounding
villages of Navarcles, Rajadell, Artés, Súria and, especially, Sallent.[2]

---

[1] J. M. Torras Ribé, 'Trajectòria d'un procés d'industrialització frustrat', *Miscellània
Agualatensia*, 2 (Igualada, 1974), p. 173; and see also P. Madoz, *Diccionario geográfico-
estadístico-histórico de España y sus posesiones de Ultramar* (16 vols., Madrid, 1845–50), III, p. 457.
[2] J. Vilá, 'La aparición y las primeras fases de la industria algodonera en la comarca de
Bagés', in *Primer simposio nacional sobre la industria textil*, Nov. 1971, *Ponencias y Comunicaciones*
(Terrassa, 1976), pp. 187–9; J. Oliveras, *Desenvolupament industrial: evolució urbana de Manresa*

302

Table 9.1. *The Barcelona industry in the 1820s*

	1823	1829
Printing manufactures	65*	56
Spinning manufactures	56	74
Spinning and weaving manufactures		15
Weaving manufactures	154	199
Total	275*	344

* These are minimal figures (see notes under table 8.6).
Sources: AHCB, cadastre, vIII, 3; Padrón General of industry, 2 July 1829, reproduced by G. Graell, *Historia del Fomento del Trabajo Nacional* (Barcelona, 1929), pp. 421–30.

Cotton-weaving was more widely diffused, with significant concentrations (in descending order of importance) in Mataró, Berga, Igualada, Reus, Vic, Manresa, Terrassa and Valls. Printing continued to be overwhelmingly concentrated in Barcelona.[3]

There was some technological progress in the industry. In 1817, Joan Rull introduced the cylindrical printing process in return for which, against the advice of the Junta de Comercio, he was granted a six-year monopoly in its use.[4] By 1829, its use had spread to just one other printer, Josep Giralt.[5] There was a gradual improvement in spinning techniques. In 1815, Barcelona manufacturers claimed that with the ending of the Napoleonic wars some reequipping of manufactures had taken place – they cited the case of Josep Martí, who had just established a new spinning concern in Súria, and there is further evidence for such reequipping in Manresa, Sallent, Terrassa and in Barcelona itself. The number of manufactures using new equipment – meaning either Arkwright's continuous spinning device or Crompton's spinning mule – was calculated at over forty and hydraulic power was being used to drive machinery in Manresa, Vic, Cardona, Martorell, Berga, Sabadell, Ripoll, Súria, Castellar and

---

(*1800–1870*) (Manresa, 1985), p. 44; L. Ferrer, *Pagesos, rabassaires i industrials a la Catalunya Central (segles XVIII–XIX)* (Montserrat, 1987), pp. 379–87.
[3] Madoz, *Diccionario geográfico-estadístico*, III, pp. 462–3.
[4] BC, JC, reg. 93, letter of Junta of 31 Oct. 1817; Carrera Pujal, *La economía de Cataluña*, II, pp. 205–6; Sánchez, 'Los fabricantes de indianas', pp. 211–12.
[5] Padrón General of industry, 2 July 1829, reproduced by G. Graell, *Historia del fomento del trabajo nacional* (Barcelona, 1929), p. 429.

other centres.[6] Leading Barcelona manufacturers resumed the practice of investing in manufactures outside the city with access to water-power, Joan Rull establishing a spinning concern on the Ter, near Gerona, in 1818.[7]

The gradual progress was sustained. As table 9.1 shows, there was an increase in the number of spinning concerns in Barcelona between 1823 and 1829. There was also, it is clear, a steady improvement in the quality of their equipment. If in 1816 there were some forty manufacturers in the whole of Catalonia using either the Arkwright spinning technique or the mule, a census of production taken in 1829 shows that in Barcelona alone there were some fifty users of the mule, with a total of 410 machines between them.[8] By 1833, according to the protectionist writer M. M. Gutiérrez, there were thirty-six spinning concerns with continuous or mule jenny spinning devices driven by water-power in the Principality.[9]

Both in terms of the industry's own history (thinking back to the hectic expansion in calico-printing in the 1780s and the promising beginning made to the mechanization of spinning between 1802 and 1807), and the performance of other European textile centres, the progress appeared slow. Vicens Vives wrote of 'the freeze which from the War of Independence seemed to delay the manufacturing progress of Catalonia'.[10] However, it must be remembered, as was shown in the last chapter, that this was a new industry largely that was developing. The discontinuity with the rich calico-printing industry of the eighteenth century was nearly total. When this optic is adopted, then the period takes on another hue – as one of widespread, if small-scale, capital accumulation and of general diffusion of cotton manufacturing and entrepreneurial skills throughout the Principality. This was the true period of 'proto-industrialization' for the industry.

What made such a process possible was the flexibility of the new machinery. In its early stages, mechanization of textiles offered opportunities for all types of producers. There were multiple reports of the proliferation of small-scale production units in which use was

---

[6] BC, JC, leg. 33, no. 55, fos. 13–16, report of Gónima, Rull and Clarós of 30 Sept. 1815; Carrera Pujal, *La economía de Cataluña*, II, p. 200.
[7] Sánchez, 'Los fabricantes de indianas', pp. 211–12.   [8] As n. 5, pp. 422–3.
[9] Gutiérrez, *Impugnación*, p. 174: 'The most economic and powerful motive force which Catalonia uses is water; there are thirty-six large mechanical spinning and weaving establishments which use this force.'   [10] Vicens Vives, *Industrials i polítics*, p. 50.

made of all types of variation on the jenny in its simple form or the locally developed *bergadana*, the name given to the local adaptation of the jenny described in chapter 7. A report of 1815 mentions this general proliferation of smaller machines, compatible with the domestic production unit. In it, it is noted that where water-power did not exist for driving spinning machinery, 'mules or horses are used', and that there were 'other machines which although they can receive motion from one of the sources indicated [water- or animal-power] have been calculated to be more profitable when it [motion] is provided by the women who spin with them, because in this way popular industry is maintained'.[11]

The democratic or 'popular' nature of the spreading industry was used by protectionist writers to support their case for the prohibition of cotton imports. M. M. Gutiérrez, for example, in a detailed defence of the industry against free-trading critics, published in 1837, provided a full description of the types of production units which predominated, and of their social advantages. In many villages, he explained, carding mills had been set up which carried out the pre-spinning processes on behalf of small-scale, female spinners, who consequently simply needed to acquire a jenny or *bergadana* in order to spin, at a cost of some 600–800 *reales*, in order to provide employment for themselves and their children – 'even for boys of eight years of age' – while their husbands carried out their agricultural tasks. He asked whether it was not the cotton industry 'which with least investment occasions most circulation, and gives work and a livelihood to the greatest number of workers of both sexes and of all ages'.[12] Cotton-weaving was even more of a 'cottage industry'. In a report of the Barcelona Comisión de Fábricas of 1832, it was noted that

As the manufacture is an entirely free craft there are in the villages of the interior many workers who devote themselves in certain seasons of the year, with one, two or more looms, to the weaving of pieces of cotton cloth, receiving for this raw material, with part of the labour costs advanced to them by speculators who without being manufacturers make them work on their account.[13]

The parallels with the industrialization process of the English cotton industry are clear. There, too, progress was achieved on the

---

[11] As n. 6.   [12] Gutiérrez, *Impugnación*, pp. 152–3.
[13] Cited by Sánchez, 'La era de la manufactura', p. 50.

basis of using the new spinning technology in small units within the domestic economy, as well as by centralization of production. There, too, the mechanization of spinning multiplied the demand for handloom-weavers and gave rise to a massive cottage industry.[14]

There were contrasts, too, however. The first of these was that this stage of domination by the small-scale production unit was exceptionally prolonged in the Catalan case. In 1833, only two Catalan manufactures were using mechanical looms at a time when 100,000 were at work in the English industry,[15] and as late as 1841, the dominance of traditional technology in the spinning industry in Barcelona is apparent from this break-down in its energy sources – it was using 10 h.p. of water-power, 229 of steam, 659 horses and 203 operator-driven machines – a literal predominance of horse-power.[16] The second contrast was that the predominance of the small-scale production unit was nearly total. In the English case, from an early stage, the jenny-spinners were exposed to harsh competition from large-scale Arkwright-spinners. The early machine-breaking riots of 1779 in Lancashire attest to this, and it was fear of such a reaction which was an important reason for the process having been first developed in Nottingham rather than in Lancashire.[17] In the Catalan case, as can be seen from the slow uptake in the use of hydraulic power, large-scale investment in the sector, and thus the extent of competition, was limited until the 1830s.

The timing of the Catalan movement into spinning may itself have influenced this factor. As was seen in chapter 7, it was only from the mid-1790s that this occurred, and by this stage Crompton's spinning mule was available – though it was not introduced into Catalonia until approximately 1805, we have shown. It was a machine of great flexibility. It could spin all types of yarn. A witness before a Parliamentary Select Committee in 1812, considering an application from Crompton for a reward for his invention, stated in reply to a query concerning the fineness of thread which it could produce that 'It may be made hard for warp superior to anything that can be produced by Mr. Arkwright's Machine or it may be made soft for weft which Mr. Arkwright's can not at all produce'. It was also adaptable to all types of production unit because of its low energy

---

[14] See Hills, *Power in the Industrial Revolution*, p. 58; P. Mathias, *The First Industrial Nation* (2nd edn, London, 1983), pp. 184–5.

[15] Gutiérrez, *Impugnación*, p. 155; D. Landes, *The Unbound Prometheus* (Cambridge, 1972), p. 86.　　[16] Madoz, *Diccionario geográfico-estadístico*, III, p. 462.

[17] Wadsworth and Mann, *The Cotton Trade*, pp. 478–80, 496–503.

demands. In other words, as much as lack of competition the extent of dominance of the small-scale production unit in spinning in Catalonia during these years was explicable by the fact that the possibilities of competing with it by mechanization of production were limited. In England, too, the mechanization of mule-spinning, which was both more complex than that of continuous spinning, and less urgent in view of the machine's lower energy requirements, was gradual.[18]

The final contrast was the extent of the rupture which occurred when large-scale investment did begin to be made in the Catalan industry. In the English case, that of the pioneer, the modernization of textile technology had been gradual, and consequently the erosion of the position of the small-scale producer using hand or simpler mechanical processes had been slow. In the Catalan case, in common with other later industrializers, and Alexander Gerschenkron's paradigms are clearly of relevance to this phenomenon,[19] the confrontation with the fully mechanized production system was to be more violent, both because of the relative lack of precursors, and the resultant long reign of the artisanal production unit, and also because it was equipment of the most advanced kinds which were imported.

The agent for the first introduction of the new machinery was the company of Bonaplata, Vilaregut and Rull. The company in fact consisted in a grouping of two existing manufactures – the spinning and weaving mill of Vilaregut in Sallent, which had been the first in Spain to introduce mechanical weaving in 1828, and the printing works of Joan Rull, a pioneer, too, we have just noted, with respect to the introduction of roller-printing – with a new steam-driven mill established in the Carrer Tallers in Barcelona, which included within it a foundry and a machine-making workshop.[20] It thus represented an alliance between the most dynamic representatives of the different sectors of the industry.

As was noted in the introduction, despite the fact that the company did not last long – it was brought to an end when the Tallers manufacture was burnt down in 1835 – great importance has been attached to its establishment: '"El Vapor" of 1832 [the name given

---

[18] Hills, *Power in the Industrial Revolution*, pp. 125–31; the whole questions of the different power demands of Arkwright's roller-spinning and Crompton's mule, and other questions relating to the costs of the two processes, are fully covered in N. Von Tunzelmann, *Steam Power and British Industrialization* (Oxford, 1978).

[19] A. Gerschenkron, *Economic Backwardness in Historical Perspective* (Cambridge, MA, 1966).

[20] Nadal, 'Los Bonaplata', pp. 79–95.

to the Tallers concern]', Vicens Vives wrote, 'constitutes the point of departure for Catalan industry.'[21] The reasons for this are clear. Firstly, it was the first successful application of steam-power to the industry in the city (barring Jacint Ramon's short-term use of this source of energy in 1805 to which reference was made in chapter 7) – as such it was both the symbol and initiator of a new age. Secondly, its establishment, and its receipt of a generous royal privilege, marked a milestone in the policy of the state towards Catalan manufacturing – like the privilege granted to the Canals manufacture just under 100 years earlier, or perhaps more precisely like the renewal of the Canals privilege in 1746, which was a prelude, it was noted in chapter 4, for an inrush of capital into the calico-printing industry, the favour shown to the Bonaplata concern, and the actual content of the privilege, were the final proof of the governmental commitment to domestic manufacturing interest of which earlier signs had been the provisional and then definitive prohibition of imports imposed in 1828 and 1832.[22] Finally, it was not purely a cotton manufacturing concern but also an iron-working and machine-building one. The possession of these facilities was as significant as its steam engine. Its foundation was intended to be a means for reequipping the local industry, the terms of its privilege including the obligation to manufacture 200 mechanical looms and 40 spinning machines a year. It was this combination of the role of spinning with that of machine-making which made the factory the target of smaller-scale producers in the city in 1835[23] – it was not only competing directly with them in the production of yarn, but was also producing the means for others to do so.

More than for its direct economic role, therefore, the Bonaplata mill was important as an example, as a sign of modernity and of the type of organization of production which was going to become universal, and as a symbol of the state's commitment to national manufacturing interests. This is what Pascual Madoz expressed in the statement at the heading of this chapter. Its foundation was the preliminary for an inrush of capital into the industry. Within a year of its foundation, five other Barcelona manufacturers were mounting steam engines in the city and a sixth steam-driven concern had been

---

[21] Vicens Vives, *Industrials i polítics*, p. 50. [22] *Ibid.*, pp. 48–9.
[23] M. Izard, 'Inversión de capitales en la primera etapa de la industrialización catalana', in *Primer simposio nacional sobre la industria textil*, Nov. 1971, *Catalogo y estudios complementarios de la exposición documental y bibliografica sobre la industria textil catalana* (Terrassa, 1973), n. 7.

established at Vilanova i La Geltrú, a coastal town some 60 kilometres to the south of Barcelona.[24]

English and French assistance was provided in the mounting of these manufactures but significantly the domestic machine-making and iron-working industry participated – Barcelona contained eighteen machine-making workshops by this date (another example of the type of preparatory progress which had been made in the city's industries during the years of apparent stagnation). Of two larger steam-powered plants established in the city in 1833 (with 24 horse-power steam engines, whereas others introduced were as small as 6 horse-power), one was constructed by Cockerills of Liège but the other by the Barcelona-based French concern of Louis Perrenod. An imported steam engine was used by the latter concern in the mill which it set up but it was on the point of initiating the building of steam engines itself during 1833, when the outbreak of the Carlist war brought the development to a halt.[25]

These prestige projects were paralleled by a general rise in levels of industrial investment. The Commisió de Fàbricas reported in 1833 that 'Barcelona is turning into a universal workshop, a new city is being built in its furthest suburbs which were occupied by extensive market gardens'; 'all was movement and all foretold wealth and abundance', it was noted two years later.[26] The boom was not confined to the city. As Gutiérrez wrote, 'the activity was no less throughout the Principality' and he mentioned 'similar establishments' to that founded at Vilanova being established in Martorell, Navarcles, other villages on the Llobregat, along the coast from Badalona to Malgrat and in the interior in Gerona, Banyoles, Olot and other villages.[27]

The extensive disruptions occasioned by the Carlist wars slowed down the pace of industrial expansion. The burning of the Bonaplata mill and the failure to compensate its owners was a particularly great blow to confidence. Pascual Madoz recorded 'the terrible impression which the burning of the manufacture produced'.[28] The progress was not, though, brought to a complete halt: the new commitment to mechanization had not been totally eradicated. As Alejandro

[24] Gutiérrez, *Impugnación*, p. 171; J. Nadal and E. Ribas, 'Una empresa cotonera catalana: la fàbrica "de la Rambla", de Vilanova, 1841–1861', *Recerques*, 3 (1974), p. 53.
[25] Gutiérrez, *Impugnación*, pp. 171–2.
[26] Cited by Sánchez, 'La era de la manufactura', p. 54.
[27] Gutiérrez, *Impugnación*, p. 268.
[28] Madoz, *Diccionario geográfico-estadístico*, III, p. 458.

Sánchez has noted, the larger manufacturers during the years of civil disturbances were acquiring steam engines and new spinning equipment, very often in secrecy in view of the fate of the Bonaplata concern.[29] Between 1836 and 1840, 1,229 machines were imported to Barcelona, including 23 steam engines, 92 spinning machines and 966 Jacquard looms.[30] Progress in the metallurgical industry had also been sustained – the manager of 'El Vapor', Valentí Esparó, had continued his iron-founding activities in the street in front of his ruined manufacture; in 1836 the 'Nuevo Vulcano' was founded in Barceloneta for the production of iron bars, largely for the naval industry; in 1837 the Bonaplatas founded a new iron-founding and machine-making concern in Madrid, Bonaplata Sandford and Company, and in 1839 extended the family activities to Seville with a new branch – possibly this was the equivalent of the movement made by James Hargreaves and Richard Arkwright to Nottingham in the late 1760s to escape industrial Luddism; finally in June 1839 the iron-founding company of Pau Llovera, later called La Compañía Barcelonesa de Fundición y Construcción de Máquinas or La Barcelonesa, was founded in Barcelona.[31]

The pace of the advance accelerated with the ending of the Civil War in 1840. Within six years there were eighty steam engines functioning in the Province of Barcelona, according to Madoz, and he recorded that 'in Barcelona alone fifty chimneys parade imposingly',[32] and the 1840s, like the 1740s, was to be the decade of major investment of predominantly commercial capital in the industry with the founding of 'El Vapor Vell' of Joan Güell in 1840, the 'Fabril Igualidina' in 1842, the spinning company of Ferran Puig, later Fabra & Coats, in 1843, 'La España Industrial' in 1847, Güell, Ramis and Co. in 1848 and Batlló Hermanos in 1849.[33]

Expansion in the 1850s continued, but had two new characteristics. Firstly, concerns were larger and were financed by companies grouping greater numbers of investors: eighteen associates founded the 'Fabril Algodonera' in 1851, seventeen founded 'La Auxiliar de la Industria' in 1852, there were thirty-five associates in 'La Industria Lano-Algodonera' founded in 1853, eighteen in 'El Porvenir de la Industria' and sixteen in 'La Progresiva Industrial' of 1854.

[29] Sánchez, 'La era de la manufactura', p. 55.
[30] Vicens Vives, *Industrials i polítics*, p. 51.
[31] *Ibid.*, pp. 56–7; Nadal, 'Los Bonaplata', pp. 75–95.
[32] Madoz, *Diccionario geográfico-estadístico*, III, p. 316.
[33] Vicens Vives, *Industrials i polítics*, p. 52.

Secondly, companies were being founded for longer periods. Five years had been the normal span in the eighteenth century, though companies were frequently renewed and often lasted far longer than this – the first Bonaplata company followed this tradition, the company of Achón, Puigmartí founded in 1838 was to run for seven years, La Fabril Algodonera of 1851 for twenty and La Industria Lano-Algodonera of 1853 and El Porvenir de la Industria of 1854 for thirty.[34] The lengthening of the period for companies' durations demonstrated both the greater commitment of capital which the large fixed capital investments in these concerns made necessary as well as the confidence which now existed in the industry's future (a message which the positivist titles of the manufactures also gave). The growth in the number of investors in these concerns – one which was paralleled in other trades – was a sign that, once again, as in the 1780s, industrial investment was becoming universal among the city's proprietary class. The change was noted by Bonaventura Carles Aribau, the contemporary economist and writer, in the second of the quotations which head this chapter. He went on to note that the switch in investment practices changed the character of the regional capital market. 'Thus it is', he wrote, 'that commerce, which previously was stock-exchange orientated (*borsista*) *par excellence*, has adopted a new orientation.[35]

AN INTERPRETATION

Looking at Catalan industry, as I have done, over the very long term one is struck by two factors. The first of these is the extent of repetition apparent in its fortunes. There have been periods of intense industrialization, with industry proliferating both in urban and rural areas – the fourteenth, sixteenth, eighteenth and, as just seen, nineteenth centuries – and there have been periods of industrial decadence – the fifteenth and seventeenth centuries and, it is clear, the period 1808–32, even though we have argued that a basis for recovery was being created during these years. The second factor concerns the type of industry which flourished during these different phases. During the periods of expansion urban industries did well, their influence extending into the countryside, and the large production unit became common; during the periods of decline it was

[34] Izard, 'Inversión de capitales', notes to tables 2 and 3.
[35] Cited by Sánchez, 'La era de la manufactura', p. 48; see also Fontana, *Aribau*, p. 49.

the smaller towns and countryside which fared better, urban production being hit most severely, and production tended to be dominated by the smaller-scale domestic unit. There was, thus, industrial continuity in Catalonia but it was only ensured by rural and small-town production – the urban commitment was discontinuous.

Now the existence of similar, cyclical fluctuations in the experiences of other major textile centres is well established. The extent of the polarization between periods of expansion and urban concentration, and others when industry was confined principally to small towns and rural areas producing cloth of a relatively simple kind, was particularly marked in the Catalan case, however. Nor did other centres show the same powers of recuperation. The shifting of industry in the pre-industrial period from one major centre to another has been frequently noted, but this meant generally permanent decline – one thinks of the examples of Florence, Venice, Hondschoote, East Anglia, England's West Country or Languedoc[36] – but in the Catalan case decline was invariably followed later by recovery, the industrial buildings which had been deserted, and unsaleable, finding again new occupants prepared to pay high rents. The houses in Barcelona's textile centre grouped around the Plaça San Pere and the Portal Nou must have been occupied by successions of different manufacturing groups in the various cycles of the city's industrial development.

The explanation for this originality lies first of all in an often noted dualism in the Catalan economy. Catalonia was, and is, as Pierre Vilar has shown, on the one hand, a functioning, market economy, with well-integrated agricultural and industrial sectors, reasonable natural resources, a healthy demographic structure, good communications and a type of land-holding and inheritance system which is highly favourable for agricultural and industrial development, and, on the other hand, a uniquely well-situated and equipped area for participation in international trading activities and for serving as a point of access to Spain from other parts of Europe. This dualism explains both the endurance and the instability which characterize different sections of its industry. The continuity shown by its rural and small-town production is explicable in terms of the natural advantages enjoyed by its market economy; the unstable element is

[36] On the question of industrial decline and the cyclical character of the fortunes of cloth-making centres, see my 'Variations in Industrial Structure', pp. 78–83.

explicable in terms of the more irregular involvement of its commercial capital in the area's industrial development.

This dualism, this possession of an economy with more than one set of characteristics, clarifies the reasons for the contrasts with both other industrial centres, such as those mentioned, as well as with other major trading areas. As Pierre Vilar is careful to emphasize, Barcelona was neither a city state like Venice, dependent for its prosperity on cornering the spice trade, nor a manufacturing centre like Florence, whose fortunes were a consequence of attaining a European leadership in the techniques of cloth-making, rather it was the capital of a coherent and balanced market economy which experienced a precocious development of autonomous political institutions and a sense of nation – he argues, indeed, that it was the first of Europe's 'national economies'.[37] These qualities gave its industrial development, on the one hand, a depth and resilience lacking in centres whose fortunes were dependent on the more transitory forces of technological skill or the monopolization of trade routes and, on the other, via a combination of its political influence with either the international orientation of its economy or its favourable position with respect to the rest of the peninsula, occasional, exceptional opportunities for industrial specialization. One thinks of Braudel's division of European pre-industrial life into three tiers – the material, the market and the capitalist. Catalonia was an uncommonly successful synthesis of all three layers, though the latter was subject to marked fluctuations.[38]

Our study makes it possible to identify with a reasonable degree of precision what it was that caused Catalan commercial capital both to involve and to disinvolve itself from industrial investment, thus occasioning both the periods of industrial glory as well as those of decadence. In no case, it is clear, was technological leadership behind the successes. Politics, rather, represented the source. The fourteenth-century expansion in the cloth industry had its origin, we have noted, in the curtailment of French textile imports because of warfare between the kingdom of Aragon and the Capetian dynasty, which enabled Catalan producers, rather than Languedocian, to benefit

[37] Vilar, *La Catalogne*, I, p. 452: 'This achievement remains remarkable above all for its *precociousness*, then: language, territory, economic life, psychic formation, cultural community – the fundamental conditions of the nation – are already present, perfectly assembled, from the thirteenth century.'
[38] F. Braudel, *Civilisation matérielle, économie et capitalisme, XVe–XVIIIe siècle* (3 vols., Paris, 1979), I, pp. 7–10, for an exposition of his three layers.

from the market possibilities available in both the areas forming part
of the Aragonese empire (particularly Sicily and Southern Italy) and
in the Levant trade in which Barcelona had secured itself a strong
position. Decline and disinvestment were a consequence not only of
the Black Death and the demographic crises of the fourteenth and
fifteenth centuries – a degree of immunity from these for the
exporting trades was noted – but also of the decline of the Aragonese
empire and the shift of the Levant trade to Marseilles. The sixteenth-
century expansion was a consequence not of Catalan political power
but Castilian, we have noted, with Catalan industrial producers
benefiting from the pronounced, but short-lived, economic vitality to
which Castilian political power and its dominance of the American
trade gave rise. As this source of stimulus began to ebb, a new basis
for growth was found in monopolistic production for the Sicilian
market. The decline which followed in the seventeenth century had
its sources, we noted, on the one hand, in Catalonia's sharing to a
degree in the general Spanish process of decadence and, on the other
hand, in its economic and, for some years, political domination by
France. The beginnings of industrial revival in the late seventeenth
century had, too, more than one explanation. On the one hand, it
was noted, mercantilism was involved – Narcís Feliu de la Penya
was representative of a general desire of the local bourgeoisie to attain
greater political power and autonomy, and the importance for this of
achieving industrial growth was coming to be realized to be
paramount. On the other hand, and this factor was to be of growing
importance and thus needs emphasizing, it was a consequence, we
have seen, of the fact that technological progress in other parts of
Europe was beginning to have implications for the organization of
production, making merchant participation in industrial investment
both more practical and also attractive in view of the possibility of
significant profits in the early stages of technological diffusion.

   From the eighteenth century, the material presented in this book
permits the question to be assessed in greater detail. In the case of the
movement into calico-printing investment in the 1740s, we saw in
chapter 4 that a prior recovery in the economy, permitting a
substantial accumulation of commercial capital, was an important
pre-condition, but that the extent of involvement was influenced by
two other factors. The first of these was political measures – the 1728
prohibition of calico imports which provided a monopoly in the
national and imperial market and the granting of privileges which

both confirmed royal commitment to the industry and gave their recipients most important and advantageous concessions with respect to the guild system. The second, again, was the types of technological factors which had favoured merchant involvement in industrial investment in the 1680s and 1690s – the existence of new technologies, whose introduction provided the prospect of exceptional profits in the short- and medium-term, and for whose introduction wholesale merchants were best placed.

Following the course of the eighteenth-century expansion, we have noted (in chapters 5 and 6) an additional characteristic of the city's commercial capitalism which contributed to the extent of the industrial expansion even if, too, it may have undermined its momentum: if the industry was founded by wholesale merchants whose role can be categorized as 'entrepreneurial', the industry soon, once it had been established, and a managerial industrial structure had been imposed upon it, attracted large investments of 'rentier' capital from Barcelona's and the Principality's proprietary class. The extent of this development is to be explained by certain characteristics of the Catalan elite and its investment practices – since the Middle Ages, when Catalonia developed Europe's first major public bank, the so-called 'Taula de Canvi', the practice of holding wealth in forms other than land had existed, and group investment, of a kind that emerged, too, in the 1850s, we have just noted, was common.[39]

The extent of the disinvestment from the industry which, we have seen, occurred at the end of the eighteenth century cannot, however, purely be explained in terms of previous such industrial declines. As was shown in chapters 7 and 8, although the 1793–1814 period was much disturbed by warfare and political instability, there were new investment opportunities opening, particularly in the spinning sector, in which the possibility of introducing new technology – a process in which merchant investors were well practised – offered the possibility of large profits. In addition to suffering from the disruptions occasioned to markets, our study has shown that there was a crisis of the Catalan manufacture during these years occasioned above all by an excessive size caused by non-economic factors – government legislation and the existence of the guild system.

[39] On this, see Renouard, 'Les principaux aspects économiques', pp. 251, 258. Renouard states his belief that Barcelona contained more holders of current accounts with money-changers/bankers in the thirteenth century than any other Mediterranean town. See also on this, Amelang, *Honored Citizens of Barcelona, passim.*

The revival of commercial investment in industry from the 1830s was, we have seen, linked to factors which are by now familiar to us: state backing in the form of new guarantees concerning freedom from competition in the domestic market and the granting of a royal privilege to the Bonaplata manufacture; the existence of surplus capital both in state bonds, on which returns were unsure and low, and as a consequence of repatriation of funds from America (the Vilanova manufacture of 1833 and Güell's 'Vapor Vell' of 1840 had this latter source);[40] the return of more favourable circumstances in the domestic market, to which a stimulus was to be given by the building of railways from the 1850s; and finally, once again, the possibility of gaining from privileged access to foreign technology. The beginning of the expansion coincides with the removal of English bans on the export of skilled workers (1825) (crucial for the establishment of the Bonaplata mill) and the acceleration with the ending to restrictions on the export of machinery (1842)[41] and with the beginning of a vigorous export drive by English machine-makers who began marketing 'packages' of technology, involving information, machines, skilled labour and management expertise.[42]

The instability of Catalonia's industrial past up to the nineteenth century, therefore, has its source in fluctuations in the extent of commitment of commercial capital to industrial investment. Barcelona and its wholesale merchants were traders primarily rather than industrialists – in their trading activities, and above all in their importing ones, there was continuity.[43] This is not meant to imply a criticism of them. The continuity apparent in the strength of the Catalan economy just as it owes something to the stability and solidity of its market economy owes something, too, to its mercantile

[40] Vicens Vives, *Industrials i polítics*, pp. 326–32; Nadal and Ribas, 'Una empresa cotonera catalana', p. 53.

[41] W. O. Henderson, *Britain and Industrial Europe, 1750–1870* (Leicester, 1965), p. 7; Landes, *Unbound Prometheus*, p. 148.

[42] On this, see K. Bruland, *British Technology and European Industrialization. The Norwegian Textile Industry in the Mid-Nineteenth Century* (Cambridge, 1989). I owe this reference to G. P. C. Thomson, 'Continuity and Change in Mexican Manufacturing, 1800–1870' (paper delivered at conference on 'Precocious Attempts at Industrialization of the Periphery, 1800–1870', Centre d'Histoire Economique Internationale, University of Geneva, 10 June 1989). For the precisely contemporaneous modernization of the Mexican cotton industry, initially by the introduction of hydraulic power, under similar influences, see this author's *Puebla de los Angeles. Industry and Society in a Mexican City, 1700–1850* (Boulder, CO, 1989).

[43] See, for example, Vilar, *La Catalogne*, I, p. 592: with reference to the early seventeenth century: 'the Principality imports more than it exports. It is what the Royal Counsel…underlined in 1615, contrasting the feebleness and the monotony of the exports to the diversity of needs in products from outside.'

tradition. Even by their importing activities, they ensured that the Principality was never a backwater, and it was they who, when the opportunities offered themselves, had the means, the knowledge and the contacts to introduce the technology necessary to exploit them. The Catalan economy may be characterized as 'dualistic' but it is a dualism characterized by a strong degree of mutuality. The basis of this is suggested by the citation from Aribau which heads this chapter – an alliance of capital with the capacity for work of the Catalan population.

Where does this leave the various major controversies which were raised in the opening chapter of this book? Even though, as was shown there, there is common ground between them, I shall refer to them briefly one by one.

When and why was there a movement from commercial to industrial capitalism?

Our study suggests that Vilar was right in emphasizing that the change began in the 1770s and 1780s. It was during these decades that a combination of factors, including population growth, capital accumulation, technological change and a relaxing of the guild system, caused something like a 'take-off' – a continuous, self-reinforcing process of growth which caused the corporative system to begin to take on the appearance of a relic. However, he was probably wrong if he believed that the expansion in the number of large *indiana* manufactures, the principal beneficiaries from these structural changes initially, was a progressive development. These concerns, as we have seen, were not to enjoy a long future. More significant was the emergence during these years of a small-scale 'free' industry, which, my last three chapters have demonstrated, was to be the principal agency for the industry's mechanization, surviving the crises of the French and English wars, and providing the basis for a steady expansion of the industry through to the 1830s. This, then, to use Marx's distinction, was the period during which Catalan industrialization took 'the really revolutionary way', with a section of the producers themselves accumulating capital and beginning to trade. However, a complete explanation of the movement from commercial to industrial capital in the area also has to take into account the second turning-point, that represented by the establishment of the Bonaplata mill in 1832, which marks the return of merchant capital to industrial investment on the basis of importing the new textile machinery.

Proto-industrialization?

Hopefully this study will have contributed to throwing light on why proto-factories were so large. It should also have served to demonstrate whey their existence in the Catalan case at least (it is possible that in other countries their survival rate was higher) was probably only indirectly important to the process of industrialization insofar as they served both as agents for the introduction of techniques which were later used on a smaller scale and as catalysts for occasioning structural change in the local economy.

On the other hand, a more crucial phase in Catalan development has been identified (though it has not been studied in depth) which does relate well to the proto-industrialization theory – that is the growth in small-scale cotton production from the 1770s through to the 1830s. Enriqueta Camps, in her important thesis on labour migration in the mid-nineteenth century, has documented the links between the 'proto-industry' which resulted from this growth, as well as a woollen 'proto-industry' whose sources went further back, and the later development of a factory labour force.

Finally, in its emphasis on the importance to the Catalan case of another type of industrialization process, consisting in the import of technology from abroad by traditional social groups, this study has, it is hoped, identified one area of investigation which is necessary if proto-industrialization theories are to be made more complete and their rural bias compensated for.

Industrial Revolution in 1832?

This question has been made an issue by those – including Vicens Vives – who have tended to regard the period 1808 to 1832 as one of stagnation and who have thus attached greatest importance to the second of the two turning-points which we have discussed, that represented by the foundation of the Bonaplata mill. Whilst they are right, we have argued, to attach significance to this foundation, by their effective exclusion from consideration of the earlier turning-point they are contributing to neglecting what was probably the most interesting aspect of the Catalan experience – its following the 'really revolutionary' path to industrialization between the 1790s and 1830s on the basis of a gradual accumulation of capital on a small-scale basis. The importance of the lack of guild restrictions attached to cotton-working to this development, I would add, was probably crucial. From the point of view of those participating in this process, we have seen, the foundation of the Bonaplata mill was more like counterrevolution than revolution.

The region and Spanish industrialization

The dualism which, it has been argued, characterized Catalan industrial growth has relevance to Pollard's theory concerning the regional basis of the early stages of European industrialization. If the behaviour of Catalonia's market economy, and also the early development of its cotton-spinning and weaving industry between 1790 and 1830, conform to his model – the similarities with the English experience were noted – that of its 'capitalist economy', and its movement in and out of industrial investment in the 1790s and 1830s, clearly does not, and in explaining the latter the nature of the Catalan relationship to the Spanish state and to other Spanish regions, as well as the question of the availability of foreign technology suitable for use on a large scale, need to be taken into account.

Bibliography

MANUSCRIPT SOURCES

ARCHIVO GENERAL DE SIMANCAS

1 *Consejo Supremo de Hacienda*

Registros 213, 248 (indices of transactions of Junta General de Comercio y Moneda)

2 *Dirección General de Rentas, Segunda Remesa*

Legajos 438 (letter of 1737) and 4907 (survey of stocks of imported calicoes in Spain, 1732)

3 *Superintendencia de Hacienda*

Legajo 1103, correspondence

ARCHIVO HISTÓRICO NACIONAL

Consejos, libros 1476, 1477, 1514 (copies of royal edicts)

ARXIU HISTÒRIC DE LA CIUTAT DE BARCELONA

Arxiu comercial, B141–7, 298, 300, 304
Cadastre personal: 1759, 1764, 1783–9, 1794–1805
Cadastre VIII, 3: Contribución extraordinaria de guerra aplicada al comercio e industria en el año 1823

ARXIU DE LA CORONA DE ARAGON

1 *Batllia General (Administration of the Royal Patrimony in Catalonia)*

Aa 51, 52 (requests concerning use of irrigation facilities, 1738–40)
Indice del llevador general de concesiones de agua desde el año 1752 hasta 1768
Cabreo del corregimiento de Barcelona, 1748–62

2 *Intendencia*

Registros de la Superintendencia, 1/26, 1746–8, 1/47, 1769

3 *Real Audiencia*

Cartas acordadas, registro 16
Diversorum, registros 491–4, 499, 879
Papeles de su excelencia, legajo 249

ARXIU HISTÒRIC DE PROTOCOLS DE BARCELONA

Registros of the following notaries for the period 1745–60: Francesc Albìa, Josep Bosom, Miquel Cabrer, Josep Cols, Creus Llobateras, Duran Quatrecases, J. B. Fontana, Olzina Cabanes, Sebastià Prats, Severo Pujol and Rojas Albaret. Also those of Font Alier for 1778 and Josep Ponsico's book of wills for 1786–7

ARXIU DE LA PARRÒQUIA DE SANTA MARIA DEL MAR

Papers of Isidro Cathalà, consisting principally in annual balances of his manufacture for 1778–97

BIBLIOTECA DE CATALUNYA

Junta de Comercio
Acuerdos, registros 1, 5, 12, 13
Legajos 5, 23, 45, 51, 53, 54
Libros de cartas, registros 81–93

MUSEO DE ESTAMPACIÓ TEXTIL DE PREMIÀ DE MAR

Copy of diocesan survey of the calico-printing industry of 1786

PRINTED SOURCES AND CONTEMPORARY PUBLICATIONS

Almanak Mercantil o guía de comerciantes para el año de ... (Madrid, 1798–1806)
Gassó, A. B., *España con industria, fuerte y rica* (Barcelona, 1816)
Graell, G., *Historia del fomento del trabajo nacional* (Barcelona, 1929)
Gutiérrez, M. M., *Impugnación de las cinco proposiciones de Pebrer sobre los grandes males que causa la ley de aranceles a la nación en general, a la Cataluña en particular, y a las mismas fábricas catalanas* (Madrid, 1837)
Larruga, E., *Memorias políticas y económicas, sobre los frutos, comercio, fábricas y minas de España* (44 vols., Madrid, 1785–1800)
Madoz, P., *Diccionario geográfico-estadístico-histórico de España y sus posesiones de Ultramar* (16 vols., Madrid, 1845–50)
Masdevall, J., *Relación de las epidemias de calenturas pútridas y malignas que en estos últimos años se han padecido en el Principado de Cataluña; y principalmente de la que se descubrió el año pasado de 1783 en la ciudad de Lleida, Llano de Urgel*

(Madrid, 1786) (containing appendix with Masdevall's 'Dictamen sobre si las fábricas de algodon y lana son perniciosas o no a la salud pública de las ciudades donde estan establecidas')

Mitchell, B. R., *European Historical Statistics, 1750–1975* (2nd edn, London, 1981)

Posthumus, N, W., *Inquiry into the History of Prices in Holland* (2 vols., Leiden, 1946–65)

Rhyiner, J., 'Traité sur la fabrication et le commerce des toiles peintes', in D. Dollfuss-Ausset, *Matériaux pour la coloration des étoffes* (2 vols., Paris, 1865), II

Torrella Niubó, F., *El moderno resurgir textil de Barcelona (siglos XVIII y XIX)* (Barcelona, 1961)

Townsend, J., *A Journey through Spain in the Years 1786 and 1787* (3 vols., London, 1791)

Young, A., 'Tour in Catalonia', *Annals of Agriculture*, 8 (1787)

SECONDARY WORKS

Agustí, J., *Ciència i tècnica a Catalunya en el segle XVIII o la introducció de la màquina de vapor* (Barcelona, 1983)

Albareda, J., *La industrialització a la plana de Vic* (Vic, 1981)

Albareda, J., and Sancho, S., 'Catalunya el 1765: un informe econòmic i polític', *Segon Congrès d'Història Moderna de Catalunya, Pedralbes, Revista d'Història Moderna*, 8, i (1988)

Alier, R., 'La fàbrica d'indianes de la família Canals', *Recerques*, 4 (1974)

'Juan Pablo Canals. Un "ilustrado" catalán del siglo XVIII' (Tesis de licenciatura, Barcelona, 1971)

Amelang, J., *Honored Citizens of Barcelona. Patrician Culture and Class Relations, 1490–1714* (Princeton, NJ, 1985)

Andreu, M., 'Catalunya i els mercats espanyols al segle XVIII. La casa Ermengol Gener', *Primer Congrès d'Història Moderna de Catalunya* (Barcelona, 1984), I

Antón, P. M., 'Salarios en las fábricas de indianas de Barcelona en el último tercio del siglo XVIII' (Tesis de licenciatura, Barcelona, 1972)

Arranz, M., 'Demanda estatal i activitat econòmica a Catalunya sota els primers Borbons (1714–1808)', *Primer Congrès d'Història Moderna de Catalunya* (Barcelona, 1984), II

Artola, M., 'Campillo y las reformas de Carlos III', *Revista de Indias*, 12 (1952)

Ashtor, E., 'Catalan Cloth on the Late Medieval Mediterranean Markets', *Journal of European Economic History*, 17 (1988)

Ayala, B. L., 'Condiciones de trabajo en las fábricas de indianas de Barcelona durante el último tercio del siglo XVIII', *Manuscrits, Revista d'Història Moderna*, 6 (1987)

Batlle, C., *L'expansió baixmedieval (segles XIII–XV)*, vol. III of P. Vilar (directed) *Història de Catalunya* (8 vols., Barcelona, 1987–90)

Benaul, J. M., 'La comercialització dels teixits de llana en la cruïlla del XVIII i XIX. L'exemple de la fàbrica de Terrassa Anton i Joaquim Sagrera, 1792–1807', *Arrahona*. *Revista d'història*, 2 (1988)

Benet, A., 'La industrialització d'un poble de la Catalunya central: Sallent (1750–1808)', *Segon Congrès d'Història Moderna de Catalunya*, *Pedralbes*, *Revista d'Història Moderna*, 8, i (1988)

Bergeron, L., *Banquiers, négociants et manufacturiers parisiens. Du directoire à l'Empire* (2 vols., Paris, 1975)

Bernal, A. M., 'Cotó americà per a Catalunya (1767–1777)', Comissió Catalana del Cinquè Centenari del Descobriment d'Americà, *Segones Jornades d'Estudis Catalano-Americans* (Barcelona, 1986)

Bonnassié, P., *La organización del trabajo en Barcelona a fines del siglo XV* (Barcelona, 1975)

Braudel, F., *Civilisation matérielle, économie et capitalisme, XVe–XVIIIe siècle* (3 vols., Paris, 1979)

Brenner, R., 'Agrarian Class Structure and Economic Development in Pre-Industrial Europe', *Past and Present*, 70 (1976)

'Dobb on the Transition from Feudalism to Capitalism', *Cambridge Journal of Economics*, 2 (1978)

Bruland, K., *British Technology and European Industrialization. The Norwegian Textile Industry in the Mid-Nineteenth Century* (Cambridge, 1989)

Callahan, W., 'A note on the Real and General Junta de Comercio', *Economic History Review*, 3 (1968)

Camós, L., 'Historia industrial. Los Català y las sedas pintadas a la chinesca', *Boletín de Divulgación Histórica del Archivo Histórico de la Ciudad de Barcelona*, 6 (1945)

Camps, E., 'Migraciones internas y formación del mercado de trabajo en la Cataluña industrial en el siglo XIX', (D. Phil thesis, University Institute of Florence, 1990)

Carmona, X., 'Clases sociales, estructuras agrarias e industria rural doméstica en la Galicia del siglo XVIII', *Revista de Historia Económica*, 2 (1984)

Carrera Pujal, J., *La economía de Cataluña en el siglo XIX* (4 vols., Barcelona, 1960)

Historia de la economía española (5 vols., Barcelona, 1943–7)

Historia política y económica de Cataluña (4 vols., Barcelona, 1943–7)

Carreras, A., 'Cataluña, primera región industrial de España', in J. Nadal and A. Carreras (eds.), *Pautas regionales de la industrialización española (siglos XIX y XX)* (Barcelona, 1990)

Carrère, C., *Barcelone, centre économique à l'époque des difficultés, 1380–1462* (2 vols., Paris, 1967)

'Structures et évolution des entreprises pré-industrielles: le cas de Barcelone au bas Moyen-Age', in *Studi in Memoria di Federigo Melis* (Naples, 1978), III

Caspard, P., *La Fabrique-Neuve de Cortaillod. Entreprise et profit pendant la Révolution Industrielle, 1752–1854* (Paris, 1979)

Chapman, S. D., 'David Evans & Co. The Last of the Old London Textile Printers', *Textile History*, 14 (1983)

'The Textile Factory before Arkwright: A Typology of Factory Development', *Business History Review*, 48 (1974)

Chapman, S. D., and Chassagne, S., *European Textile Printers in the Eighteenth Century* (London, 1981)

Chassagne, S., *La Manufacture de toiles imprimées de Tournemine-lès-Angers (1752–1820), étude d'une entreprise et d'une industrie au XVIIIe siècle* (Paris, 1971)

Chaunu, P., and Gascon, R. (eds.), *Histoire économique et sociale de la France* (4 vols., Paris, 1970–80)

Chobaut, H., 'L'Industrie des indiennes à Marseille avant 1680', Institut Historique de Provence, Marseille, *Mémoires et bulletins*, 1 (1939)

Clarà, J., 'Les Fàbriques gironines del segle XVIII', *Primer Congrès d'Història Moderna de Catalunya* (Barcelona, 1984), 1

Crouzet, F., 'Vers une économie d'exportation', in his *De la supériorité de l'Angleterre sur la France* (Paris, 1985)

Crouzet, F., Gascon, R., and Leon, P. (eds.), *L'Industrialisation en Europe au XIXe siècle. Cartographie et typologie* (Paris, 1972)

Davis, R., 'English Foreign Trade, 1660–1700', in W. E. Minchinton (ed.), *The Growth of English Overseas Trade in the Seventeenth and Eighteenth Centuries* (London, 1969)

Delgado, J. M., 'El impacto de las crisis coloniales en la economía catalana (1787–1807)', in J. Fontana (ed.), *La economía española al final del Antiguo Régimen*, III, *Comercio y colonias* (Madrid, 1982)

'La industria algodonera catalana (1776–96) y el mercado americano. Una reconsideración', *Manuscrits, Revista d'Història Moderna*, 7 (1988)

'Las transformaciones de la manufactura al segle XVIII', in J. Nadal Farreras (ed.), vol. IV of J. Salvat and J. M. Salrach (directed), *Història de Catalunya* (6 vols., Barcelona, 1978–80)

Dermigny, L., *Cargaisons indiennes, Solier et Cie, 1781–1793* (2 vols., Paris, 1960)

d'Imbert, E., *Erasmo de Gónima, 1746–1821. Apuntes para una biografía y estudio de su epoca* (Barcelona, 1952)

Dobb, M., *Studies in the Development of Capitalism* (revised edn, London, 1963)

Doncel, J., 'Els adroguers i sucrers de Barcelona, 1700–1820. Un exemple d'élite gremial', *Primer Congrès d'Història Moderna de Catalunya* (Barcelona, 1984), 1

Douglas, A. W., 'Cotton Textiles in England: The East India Company's Attempt to Exploit Developments in Fashion, 1660–1721', *Journal of British Studies*, 8 (1969)

Duran Sanpere, A., *Barcelona i la seva història* (3 vols., Barcelona, 1972–5)

Elliot, J. H., 'The Decline of Spain', in C. M. Cipolla (ed.), *The Economic Decline of Empires* (London, 1970)

Enciso Recio, L. M., *Los establecimientos industriales españoles en el siglo XVIII. La mantelería de La Coruña* (Madrid, 1963)

Feliu, G., 'El comercio catalan con Oriente', *Revista de Historia Económica*, 6 (1988)

Fernández, R., 'La burguesía barcelonesa en el siglo XVIII: la familia Glòria', in P. Tedde (ed.), *La economía española al final del Antiguo Régimen*, II, *Manufacturas* (Madrid, 1982)

Ferrer, F., *L'economia del set-cents a les comarques gironines* (Gerona, 1989)

Ferrer, L., *Pagesos, rabassaires i industrials a la Catalunya Central (segles XVIII–XIX)* (Montserrat, 1987)

Fisher, J., *Commercial Relations between Spain and Spanish America in the Era of Free Trade, 1778–1796* (Liverpool, 1985)

Florensa, N., 'Política industrial a Castella sota el regnat de Carles II: 1680–1700' (Tesis de licenciatura, Barcelona, 1981)

Floud, P. C., 'The English Contribution to the Early History of Indigo-Printing', *Journal of the Society of Dyers and Colorists*, 76 (1960)

'The Origins of English Calico-Printing', *Journal of the Society of Dyers and Colorists*, 76 (1960)

Fontana, J., *Aribau i la indústria cotonera a Catalunya* (Barcelona, 1963)

'Comercio colonial e industrialización: una reflexión sobre los orígenes de la industria moderna en Cataluña', in J. Nadal and G. Tortella (eds.), *Agricultura, comercio colonial y crecimiento económico en la España contemporánea* (Barcelona, 1974)

La fi de l'Antic Règim i la industrialització, 1787–1868, vol. V of P. Vilar (directed), *Història de Catalunya* (8 vols., Barcelona, 1987–90)

'La primera etapa de la formació del mercat nacional a Espanya', in *Homenaje a Vicens Vives* (2 vols., Barcelona, 1967), II

'Sobre el comercio exterior de Barcelona en la segunda mitad del siglo XVII: Notas para una interpretación de la coyuntura catalana', *Estudios de Historia Moderna* 5 (1955)

Gerschenkron, A., *Economic Backwardness in Historical Perspective* (Cambridge, MA, 1966)

Giralt, E., 'La colonia mercantil francesa de Barcelona a mediados del siglo XVII', *Estudios de Historia Moderna*, 6 (1956–9)

'La viticultura y el comercio catalan del siglo XVIII', *Estudios de Historia Moderna*, 2 (1952)

Gómez, J. I., 'La burguesía mercantil catalana y su presencia en Aragón (1770–1808)', *Segon Congrès d'Història Moderna de Catalunya, Pedralbes, Revista d'Història Moderna*, 8, i (1988)

González Enciso, A., *Estado e industria en el siglo XVIII. La Fábrica de Guadalajara* (Madrid, 1980)

Grau, R., 'Barcelona ante el reformismo ilustrado. Un estudio sobre la inestabilidad ciudadana y los orígenes de la reformisma muncipal barcelonesa en los años 1766–70', (Tesis de licenciatura, Barcelona, 1969)

'Cambio y continuidad en los orígenes de la Barcelona moderna (1814–1860)', *Revista de la Universidad Complutense*, 28 (1979)

'La metamorfosi de la ciutat emmurallada: Barcelona, de Felip V a

Ildefons Cerdá', in M. Taradell, *Evolució urbana de Catalunya* (Barcelona, 1983)

Grau, R., and López, M., 'Barcelona entre el urbanismo barroco y la revolución industrial', *Cuadernos de Arquitectura y Urbanismo*, 80 (1971) 'Empresari i capitalista a la manufactura catalana del segle XVIII. Introducció a l'estudi de les fàbriques d'indianes', *Recerques*, 4 (1974) 'Revolució industrial i urbanització. Barcelona en la construcció de la Catalunya moderna (1714–1860)', *L'Avenç*, 88 (1985)

Gual, M., 'Para una mapa de la industria textil hispana en la Edad Media', *Anuario de Estudios Medievales*, 4 (1967) 'Origenes y expansión de la industria textil lanera catalana en la edad media', in *Produzione, commercio e consumo dei panni di lana. Atti della seconda settimana di studio* (10–16 April 1970) (Florence, 1976)

Henderson, W. O., *Britain and Industrial Europe, 1750–1870* (Leicester, 1965)

Herr, R., *The Eighteenth Century Revolution in Spain* (Princeton, NJ, 1973)

Herrera Oria, E., 'Ideas de Ramón Igual sobre la organización en España de la industria de tejidos', *Revista Histórica: Investigaciones, Bibliografia, Metodologia y Enseñanza* (Valladolid) (1924) *La real fábrica de tejidos de algodón estampados de Avila y la reorganización nacional de esta industria en el siglo XVIII* (Valladolid, 1922)

Hills, R. L., *Power in the Industrial Revolution* (Manchester, 1970)

Izard, M., *Industrialiación y obrerismo* (Barcelona, 1973) 'Inversión de capitales en la primera etapa de la industrialización catalana', in *Primer simposio nacional sobre la industria textil*, Nov. 1971, *Catalogo y estudios complementarios de la exposición documental y bibliografica sobre la industria textil catalana* (Terrassa, 1973) *La revolución industrial en España. Expansión de la industria algodonera catalana, 1832–1861*, (photocopied edition, Mérida, 1969)

Jover Zamora, J. M., *Historia de España*, XXIX, *La época de los primeros borbones* (Barcelona, 1985), I

Kamen, H., 'Narcís Feliu de la Penya i el "Fènix de Cataluña"', introductory essay to new edition of *Fénix de Cataluña* (Barcelona, 1983) *Spain in the Later Seventeenth Century, 1665–1700* (London, 1980)

Kerridge, E., *Textile Manufactures in Early Modern England* (Manchester, 1985)

Kriedte, P., 'La ciudad en el proceso de protoindustrialización europea', *Manuscrits, Revista d'Història Moderna*, 4–5 (1987)

Kriedte, P., Medick, H., and Schlumbohm, J., *Industrialization before Industrialization* (Cambridge, 1981)

La Force, J. C., *The Development of the Spanish Textile Industry* (Berkeley, CA, 1965)

Landes, D., *The Unbound Prometheus* (Cambridge, 1972)

Lévy Leboyer, M., *Les Banques européennes et l'industrialisation internationale dans la première moitié du XIXe siècle* (Paris, 1964) 'Le processus d'industrialisation: le cas de l'Angleterre et de la France', *Revue historique*, 239 (1968)

Llovet, J., *La ciutat de Mataró* (2 vols., Barcelona, 1959–61)

López, M., and Grau, R., 'Barcelona entre el urbanismo barroco y la revolución industrial', *Cuadernos de Arquitectura y Urbanismo*, 80 (1971)

Lynch, J., *Bourbon Spain, 1700–1808* (Oxford, 1989)

Maixé, J. C., 'El mercado algodonero y la producción industrial en Cataluña (1780–1790)', *Segon Congrès d'Història Moderna de Catalunya, Pedralbes, Revista d'Història Moderna*, 8, i (1988)

Maluquer, J., 'The Industrial Revolution in Catalonia', in N. Sánchez-Albornoz (ed.), *The Economic Modernization of Spain, 1830–1930* (New York, 1987)

Martínez Shaw, C., *Cataluña en la carrera de las Indias* (Barcelona, 1981)

'El comercio maritimo de Barcelona, 1675–1712. Aproximación a partir de las escrituras de seguros', *Estudios Históricos y Documentos de los Archivos de Protocolos*, 6 (1978)

'Los orígenes de la industria algodonera catalana y el comercio colonial', in J. Nadal and G. Tortella (eds.), *Agricultura, comercio colonial y crecimiento económico en la España contemporánea* (Barcelona, 1974)

Mathias, P., *The First Industrial Nation* (2nd edn, London, 1983)

Matilla Quizá, M. J., 'Las compañias privilegiadas en la España del Antiguo Régimen', in M. Artola (ed.), *La economía española al final del Antiguo Régimen* (4 vols., Madrid, 1982), IV

Mendels, F. F., 'Proto-Industrialization: First Stage of the Industrialization Process', *Journal of Economic History*, 32 (1972)

Mercader Riba, F., *Felip V y Catalunya* (Barcelona, 1968)

Meuvret, J., 'Circulation monétaire et utilisation économique de la monnaie dans la France du XVIe et du XVIIe siècle', *Etudes d'Histoire Moderne et Contemporaine*, 1 (1947)

Mitchell, B. R., *European Historical Statistics, 1750–1975* (2nd edn, London, 1981)

Mitchell, B. R., and Deane, P., *Abstract of British Historical Statistics* (Cambridge, 1962)

Molas Ribalta, P., 'La companyia Feu-Feliu de la Penya (1676–1708). Comerç de teixits vers el 1700', 'La Junta de Comerç de Barcelona. Els seus precedents i la seva base social', 'La represa catalana de 1680–1700. Narcís Feliu de la Penya' and 'La represa econòmica de 1680. Economia i política a finals del segle XVII', in his *Comerç i estructura social a Catalunya i València als segles XVII i XVIII* (Barcelona, 1977)

'Los gremios de Barcelona en el siglo XVIII' (4 vols., DPhil thesis, Barcelona, 1968)

Los gremios barceloneses del siglo XVIII (Madrid, 1970)

Societat i poder política a Mataró, 1718–1808 (Mataró, 1973)

Monjonell Pardas, M., 'La real fábrica de indianas de Mataró de Jaime Campins y Compañía', (Tesis de licenciatura, Barcelona, 1956)

Moreu Rey, E., 'Una dinastia industrial: els Rosal de Berga', in *Homenaje a Vicens Vives* (2 vols., Barcelona, 1967), II

Muñoz, J. M., 'La contribució de la indústria rural a la industrialització: el cas de Sabadell i Terrassa al segle XVIII', *Primer Congrès d'Història Moderna de Catalunya* (Barcelona, 1984), 1

Muset, A., 'La conquesta del mercat peninsular durant la segona meitat del segle XVIII: l'exemple de la casa Francesc Ribas i Cia (1766–1783)', *Segon Congrès d'Història Moderna de Catalunya, Pedralbes, Revista d'Història Moderna*, 8, i (1988)

'Protoindústria e indústria dispersa en la Cataluña del siglo XVIII. La pañeria de Esparreguera y Olesa de Montserrat', *Revista de Historia Económica*, 7 (1989)

Nadal, J., 'Los abortos de la revolución industrial en Andalucía', in A. M. Bernal (ed.), *Historia de Andalucía*, VI *La Andalucía liberal, 1778–1868* (Barcelona, 1984)

'Los Bonaplata: tres generaciones de industriales en la España del siglo XIX', *Revista de Historia Económica*, 1 (1983)

'Bonaplata, pretext i símbol', in Ajuntament de Barcelona, *Catalunya, la fàbrica d'Espanya. Un segle d'industrialització catalana, 1833–1936* (Barcelona, 1985)

'La consolidación de la industria algodonera', in vol. VIII of P. Vilar (directed), *Història de Catalunya* (8 vols., Barcelona, 1987–90)

'The Failure of the Industrial Revolution in Spain, 1830–1914', *The Fontana Economic History of Europe* (London, 1973), IV, pt 2

El fracaso de la Revolución Industrial en España, 1814–1913 (Barcelona, 1975)

Nadal, J., and Giralt, E., 'Barcelona en 1717–1718. Un modelo de sociedad pre-industrial', in *Homenaje a don Ramón Carande* (2 vols., Madrid, 1963), II

Nadal, J., and Ribas, E., 'Una empresa cotonera catalana: la fàbrica "de la Rambla" de Vilanova, 1841–1861', *Recerques*, 3 (1974)

Oliva, J. M., *Cataluña y el comercio privilegiado con América* (Barcelona, 1987)

Oliveras, J., 'El agua y el vapor en la formación del paisaje industrial de Manresa en el siglo XIX', *Primeras jornadas sobre la protección y revalorización del patrimonio industrial* (Bilbao, 1982)

Desenvolupament industrial: evolució urbana de Manresa (1800–1870) (Manresa, 1985)

Ormrod, D., 'English Re-Exports and the Dutch Staple Market in the Eighteenth Century', in D. C. Coleman and P. Mathias (eds.), *Enterprise and History: Essays in Honour of Charles Wilson* (Cambridge, 1984)

Pascual, P., *Agricultura i industrialització a la Catalunya del segle XIX* (Barcelona, 1990)

Perkin, H., *The Origins of Modern English Society (1780–1880)* (London, 1969)

Pollard, S., *The Genesis of Modern Management* (London, 1968)

Peaceful Conquest (Oxford, 1981)

'Regional Markets and National Development', in M. Berg (ed.), *Markets and Manufactures in Early Industrial Europe* (London, 1991)

Prat i Canals, M., 'La manufactura cotonera a Catalunya: l'exemple de la fàbrica de Magí Pujades y Cia' (Tesis de licenciatura, Barcelona, 1976)

Puig, M., *Les primeres companyies per a la fabricació de gènere de punt a Olot (1774–1780)* (Olot, 1988)

Rapp, R. T., 'The Unmaking of the Mediterranean Trade Hegemony: International Trade Rivalry and the Commercial Revolution', *Journal of Economic History*, 35 (1975)

Reglà, J., 'El comercio entre Francia y la Corona de Aragón en los siglos XIII y XIV, y sus relaciones con el desenvolvimiento de la industria textil catalana', in his *Temas medievales* (Valencia, 1972)

Renouard, Y., 'Les Principaux Aspects économiques et sociaux de l'histoire des pays de la couronne d'Aragon aux XIIe, XIIIe et XIVe siècles', *VII Congreso d'Historia de la Corona d'Aragón* (Barcelona, 1962)

Riu, M., 'The Woollen Industry in Catalonia in the Later Middle Ages', in N. B. Harte and K. G. Ponting (eds.), *Cloth and Clothing in Medieval Europe: Essays in Memory of E. M. Carus Wilson* (London, 1983)

Rodríguez Labandeira, J., 'La política económica de los Borbónes', in M. Artola (ed.), *La economía española al final del Antiguo Régimen* (4 vols., Madrid, 1982), IV

Ruíz Pablo, A., *Historia de la Real Junta Particular de Comercio de Barcelona, 1758–1847* (Barcelona, 1919)

Sales, N., *Els segles de la decadència (segles XVI–XVIII)*, vol IV of P. Vilar (directed), *Història de Catalunya* (8 vols., Barcelona, 1987–90)

Sánchez, A., 'De la Compañia de Hilados a la Comisión de Fábricas. El asociacionismo empresarial en Cataluña durante la crisis del Antiguo Régimen (1771–1820)', *Segon Congrès d'Història Moderna de Catalunya, Pedralbes, Revista d'Història Moderna*, 8, i (1988)

'La era de la manufactura algodonera en Barcelona, 1736–1839' (photocopied text now to be published in *Estudios de Historia Social*)

'L'estructura comercial d'una fàbrica d'indianes barcelonina: Joan Rull i Cia (1790–1821)', *Recerques*, 22 (1989)

'Los fabricantes de indianas de Barcelona a finales del siglo XVIII y principios del XIX: la familia Rull' (Tesis de licenciatura, Barcelona, 1981)

'Los fabricantes de algodón de Barcelona, 1772–1839', (3 vols., DPhil thesis, Barcelona, 1987)

'La formación de una política económica prohibicionista en Cataluña, 1760–1840', *Quaderns del Departament de Geografia i Història i l'Estudi General de Lleida* (1988)

'Los inicios del asociacionismo empresarial en España: la Real Compañia de Hilados de Algodon de Barcelona, 1772–1820', *Hacienda Pública Española*, 108–9 (1987)

'Los orígenes sociales de los fabricantes de indianas. La familia Rull', *Primer Congrès d'Història Moderna de Catalunya* (Barcelona, 1984), I

(ed.), *Protecció, ordre i llibertat: El pensament i la política econòmica de la comissió de fàbriques de Barcelona (1820–1840)* (Barcelona, 1990)

Schwarz, P. R., 'La coloration partielle des étoffes', in M. Daumas (ed.), *Histoire générale des techniques* (3 vols., Paris, 1962–8), III

'Contribution à l'histoire de l'application du bleu d'indigo (bleu anglais) dans l'indiennage européen', *Bulletin de la Société Industrielle de Mulhouse*, 2 (1953)

Soler, R. N., *Ensaig sobre la màquina catalana de filar cotó coneguda per bergadana o maxerina* (Madrid, 1919)

Tello, F., 'La filatura domèstica del cotó a l'interior de Catalunya. L'exemple de la Segarra (1770–1824)', *Estudis d'Història Econòmica*, 1 (1987)

Thomson, G. P. C., 'Continuity and Change in Mexican Manufacturing, 1800–1870' (paper delivered at conference on 'Precocious Attempts at Industrialization of the Periphery, 1800–1870', Centre d'Histoire Economique Internationale, University of Geneva, 10 June 1989)

Puebla de los Angeles. Industry and Society in a Mexican City, 1700–1850 (Boulder, CO 1989)

Thomson, J. K. J., 'The Catalan Calico-Printing Industry Compared Internationally', Societat Catalana d'Economia, *Anuari*, 7 (1989)

Clermont-de-Lodève, 1633–1789: Fluctuations in the Prosperity of a Languedocian Cloth-Making Town (Cambridge, 1982)

La indústria d'indianes a la Barcelona del segle XVIII (Barcelona, 1990)

'State Intervention in Catalan Calico-Printing', in M. Berg (ed.), *Markets and Manufactures in Early Industrial Europe* (London, 1991)

'The State and Technological Progress in Eighteenth-Century Barcelona: The Experience of Isidro Català i Vives, Silk-Painter in the Chinese Style' (unpublished paper delivered at Workshop on Work and Family in Pre-Industrial Europe, European University Institute, Florence, December, 1987)

'Variations in Industrial Structure in Pre-Industrial Languedoc', in M. Berg, P. Hudson and M. Sonenscher (eds.), *Manufacture in Town and Country before the Factory* (Cambridge, 1983)

Torras, J., 'Early Manufacturing and Proto-Industry in Spain' (unpublished paper given at workshop held at Warwick University on 'Manufacture and Trade in the Mediterranean in the 18th and 19th centuries', April 1989)

'Especialización agrícola e industria rural en Cataluña en el siglo XVIII', *Revista de Historia Económica*, 2 (1984)

'Estructura de la indústria pre-capitalista. La draperia', *Recerques*, 11 (1981)

'Mercados españoles y auge textil en Cataluña en el siglo XVIII. Un ejemplo', in *Haciendo historia: Homenaje al Profesor Carlos Seco* (Madrid, 1989)

'The Old and the New. Marketing Networks and Textile Growth in Eighteenth Century Spain', in M. Berg (ed.), *Markets and Manufactures in Early Industrial Europe* (London, 1991)

Torras Ribé, J. M., 'Trajectòria d'un procés d'industrialitzció frustrat', *Miscel·lània Aqualatensià*, 2 (Igualada, 1974)

Vázquez Montalbán, M., *Barcelones* (Barcelona, 1990)

Vázquez de Prada, V., 'Las fábricas de indianas y estampados de Barcelona en el siglo XVIII', *Third International Conference of Economic History* (Paris, 1965), v
'Un modelo de empresa catalana de estampados en el siglo XVIII: la firma Francisco Ribas', *Primer Congrès d'Història Moderna de Catalunya* (Barcelona, 1984), 1
Vicens Vives, J., *Cataluña a mediados del siglo XV* (Barcelona, 1956)
Industrials i polítics del segle XIX (Barcelona, 1958)
Manual de historia económica de España (6th edn, Barcelona, 1972)
Noticia de Catalunya (Barcelona, 1954)
Vilá, J., 'La aparición y las primeras fases de la industria algodonera en la comarca de Bagés', in *Primer simposio nacional sobre la industria textil*, Nov. 1971, *Ponencias y Comunicaciones* (Terrassa, 1976)
Vilar, P., *La Catalogne dans l'Espagne moderne. Recherches sur les fondements économiques des structures nationales* (3 vols., Paris, 1962)
'La Catalunya industrial: reflexions sobre una arrencada i sobre un destí', *Recerques*, 3 (1974) (first published as 'La Catalogne industrielle. Réflexions sur un démarrage et sur un déstin', in F. Crouzet, R. Gascon and P. Léon (eds.), *L'Industrialisation en Europe au XIXe siècle* (Paris, 1972))
Von Tunzelmann, N., *Steam Power and British Industrialization* (Oxford, 1978)
Vries, J. de, *The Economy of Europe in an Age of Crisis, 1600–1750* (Cambridge, 1976)
Wadsworth, A. P., and Mann, J. L., *The Cotton Trade and Industrial Lancashire* (Manchester, 1931)
Walker, G. J., 'Algunes repercussiós sobre el comerç d'Amèrica de l'Aliança Anglo-Catalana durant la Guerra de Successió Espanyola', in Comissió Catalana del Cinqué Centenari del Descobriment d'Amèrica, *Segones Jornades d'Estudis Catalano-Americans* (Barcelona, 1987)
Spanish Politics and Imperial Trade, 1700–1789 (London, 1979)
Wolff, P., 'Esquisse d'une histoire de la draperie en Languedoc du XIIe au début du XVIIIe siècle', in *Produzione, commercio e consumo dei panni di lana. Atti della seconda settimana di studio* (10–16 April 1970) (Florence, 1976)

Index

Corregimientos of Catalan place-names, and provinces of non-Catalan, have been indicated.

Vallroja, etc., 166, 183; manufacture of
ceases, 277; summary of career, 173–4

Canals, Sebastià, silk-weaver, 152n; founds
manufacture, 97, 114; granted privilege,
137; summary of career of, 112;
withdraws from industry, 150

de Canaveras, Julián, sub-delegate of
Hacienda, 54

Canet, Bonaventura, commercial broker:
origins of, 78; and Serra/Canals
company, 77–8, 86–7; *see also* Canals,
Esteve

Canet, family of, 94–5

Canet, Pere, cloth-draper, 94; marriage of,
94

Canet, Tomàs, peasant/*fabricant*, works for
Canals and Canet, 139

Canet i Ferrusola, Jaume, wholesale
merchant: close links of with Anglí and
Sabater, 153; manufacture of,
construction of, 169, foundation of, 149,
151, spinning by, 239

Canet de Mar (Gerona), calico sales in, 58,
126

Cantallops, Josep (Mataró), founds
manufacture, 199

Cantarell, F., manufacture of, 194

Cantarell, Lluís, wool-dyer: manufacture of,
ceases, 279, 282, founds with Ramon
Pujol, 150, spinning by, 239; origins of
152; *see also* Pujol i Prunés, Ramon

Cantarell, Lluís, cloth-dyer, founds
manufacture, 189, 191

Capalà i Vidal, Francesc, wholesaler:
manufacture of, ceases, 282, foundation
of, 188; origins of, 192–3

Capelino, Josep, silk-weaver: associate in
manufacture, 114; copper-plate printing
by, 166; founds manufacture, 150, 154;
origins of, 152

capital: accumulation of, favourable
circumstances for, 102–3, between
1750–80, 208–9, by Cathalà, 218–20; in
buildings, 99; in calico-printing, 75,
80–1, 100–1, 114, 120–1, 138, 155–6, 161,
209, 218–20, 287, 288; cooperative basis
for provision of, 121, 302; fixed and
circulating, 177–8, 219; returns on,
100–1, 179, 214; in Royal Spinning
Company, 239; in small manufactures,
222–3; sources of, agricultural, 103, from
America, 316, Andalusian, 120–1,
between 1770 and 1787, 207–9, overseas
trade, 104–5, rentier/proprietary, 160,
220, from silk industry, 159–60, state

affairs, 103–4, 108, from state bonds, 302,
316; *see also* commercial capital;
company

Capmany, Antoni de, Catalan philosophe, 32

Caracas Company, 162

Carafí, Josep, manufacture of, 194

carding mills, 305

Cardona (Cervera): cloth industry at, 30;
hydraulic power in, 303; introduction of
cotton machinery to, 253

Caresmar, Jaume, eighteenth-century
Catalan historian, 49

Carlist Wars, 309

Carnisser, Miquel, merchant, Reus, 114

Carrera, Antoni, *fabricant* of *indianas*, 152;
associated with Henrich, 192; *fabricant* to
Pongem, 151; manufacture of, 150, 188,
191, 282

Carrera, Francesc, manufacture of, 195

Carreras, Albert, historian, on growth in
cotton industry, 276

Carrère, Claude, historian: on cloth
industry, 29, 32; on commercial capital,
47–8

Carrés, Joan, linen-weaver, manufacture of,
194, 225

Carrió, Joan, becomes *fabricant*, 226

Cartagena, 112; as market, 124, 126, 127,
179, 180, 183

Carvajal, José, Secretary of State and
President of the Junta General de
Comercio, 137

Casacuberta, Francesc, linen-weaver,
manufacture of, 194, 222, 223

Casanovas, Antoni, cloth-draper, 62

Casanovas, Jacint, Mataró, founds
manufacture, 199

Casas, Marià: founds manufacture, 188;
manufacture expands, 288

Casas, Ricart and Amigó, company of,
investment by in manufacture, 288

Castañer, Josep, manufacture of: expansion
of in 1790s, 288; foundation of, 188;
labour employed in, 208; survival of crisis
by, 284

Castelló, Miquel, manufacture of:
foundation of, 188; survives crisis and
expands in 1790s, 284, 288

Castelló d'Empúries (Gerona): calico sales
in, 125; cloth industry of, 30

Castile: calicoes for, 164, 165; cloth
production for, 34, 163

Cathalà i Vives, Isidro, silk-weaver, 166,
207, 222; a capitalist investor in industry,
160; career of, 217–18; manufacture of,

Sabater, Josep, silk stocking-knitter:
associations, with Formentí, 155, with
Pongem, 116; expands commercial
activities in Cádiz, 153n, 155
Sabater, Pau, merchant: 153n; *see also*
Anglí and Sabater
Sabran, Marquis of, France, and spinning
mule, 263
Sala, Geroni, manufacture of, 195
Sala, Jaume (Manresa), manufacture of,
199
Sala, Josep, glass-maker, 100–1, 139;
associations, with Esteve, 73–6, with
French, 142, with Glòria, 80–2, (and
dispute with) 142–3; career of, 89–90;
manufacture of, foundation of, 114, 115
indigo-dyeing in, 180
Sala, Josep, manufacture of, 188, 288
Sala i Millàs, Jaime, merchant, associated
to Campins, 121n, 130
Salamó, Agustí, cloth-draper: manufacture
of, 150, 152n; origins of, 152
Salamó, Sebastià, cloth-draper/*fabricant* of
indianas, 97; links of with Agustí Salamó,
152n; manufacture of, 150; origins, 152
salaries, 75, 81, 116, 141–2
Sallent (Manresa): hydraulic power in, 261,
302; mechanical loom in, 307
Salou (Tarragona), 111, 122; port of, 105
Salvadó, Francesc, manufacture of, 194, 225
Sanaüja, Pau, manufacture of, 150
Sánchez, Alejandro, historian, 21, 239n;
interpretation of, of 1740s expansion, 101,
109, 134
San Francisco de Paula, ship, voyage of to
America, 111, 112
Sanlúcar (Seville), calico-printing in, 199
Sanponts, Francesc, Director of Statics and
Hydrostatics, Royal Academy of Natural
Sciences and Arts of Barcelona, 262; and
introduction of steam-power, 264–6
Santa Coloma de Queralt (Cervera): calico
stocks in, 58; cloth industry of, 30
Santa María, port of, calico-printing in,
199
Sant Feliu de Codines (Mataró), calico sales
in, 126
Sant Feliu de Guixols (Gerona), calico
stocks in, in 1732, 58
Sant Joan de les Abadesses (Vic), woollen
industry of, 28, 30
Sant Llorenç de Morunys (Manresa), cloth
industry of, 30
Santamartí, Josep, Manresa, manufacture
of, 199

Sant Martí de Provençals (Barcelona),
bleaching meadows in, 77, 79, 80, 169
Saragossa: centre for calico trade, 62–3; as
market, 124, 126
Sarriera, Antoni and Josep: found
manufacture, 286–7; resources of, 287
Sartine, Antonio, Intendant of Catalonia
(1727–44), 55
Sayol, Bonaventura, worker in industry,
manufacture of, 194, 222
Seguí, Anton, wholesale merchant, 112
Seguí, Josep Francesc, wholesale merchant:
career of, 149, 174; manufacture of, 150,
282
Serra, Antoni, merchant: death of, 89, 139;
manufacture of, description of, 83–4,
foundation of, 77–80, 139, privilege of,
77, 82–4; origins of, 78–9
Serra, Joan, silver-smith, spinning by, 266,
287
Serraima, Josep, cotton manufacturer,
introduces cotton machinery, 255
Serralach, Josep: manufacture of, 195;
spinning by, 246
Seu d'Urgell (Puigcerdà): calico stocks in,
58; cloth industry of, 30
Seville: foundation of company in, 136;
sales to, 34, 124, 127, 129, 130, 131
shipping in industry, 208–9, 215
Sicily, as market, 34, 36
silk industry: and calico-printing,
contributions to, 159–60, 217, friction
with respect to, 52, 181–2; in seventeenth
century, 42, 43, 44, 45; silk-printing, 217
Sirés, Joan Batista, dry-salter: manufacture
of, decline and cessation of, 283, 299,
foundation of, 150, takes over that of
Alegre, 154; origins of, 152
Sitges (Vilafranca), calico stocks in, 58
Sivilla, Nicolau, silk-weaver, 217n, 277;
associate of Cathalà, 154, 161;
enrichment of, 209–10
social structure: high status of
manufacturing, 210; social mobility, in
calico-printing, 159–60, 174–6, 208, in
cloth production, 48–9, among labour
force, 176
Soler, Francesc, *fabricant* of *indianas*, resides
in Canals/Canet manufacture, 170
Soler, Gaspar, dry-salter: manufacture of,
ceases, 283, foundation of, 152; origins of,
152
Soler, Ramon, silk-braider: manufacture of,
150, 188, 191; origins of, 152
Solsona (Cervera), 126

Index

345

sources, 20–1, 186–7, 193; for 1787–1830, 276–80; on markets, 123
Spanish Succession, War of, 68, 102, 108; and commercial links with Britain, 122n
spinning, 204–5; figures relating to, employment in, 241, in Barcelona, (in 1823) 291–3, 303, (in 1829) 303, in Catalonia, (in 1814) 303, (in 1830s) 309; government and, effects of tariffs on, 236–9, interest of in promoting, 241–2; organization of, eludes the manufacture, 247, growth in scale, 266–7; progress in Canaleta's, 236–8, Glòria's, 236, late incorporation of, 235–6, others', 238–9, Royal Spinning Company's, 240–3, halt in, in 1770s, 243–4, from 1783, 246–7, 255–7, after 1802, 260–1, 295; see also hydraulic power; roller-spinning; steam engines; technical change
spinning jenny, 248–9; advantages of, 255–7, 258–9, 304–5; improvements of Haley and Highs to, 253–4
spinning machinery: adaptability of and industrial structure, 304–5; Arkwright's roller-spinning, 249–53, 257, 262–3; the Catalan version of the improved jenny, 255, 305; Crompton's mule, 262–4; energy sources used for, 305–6; Hargreaves's jenny, 248–9; import of from 1836, 310; the improved jenny, 253–4; low cost of, 305; modernization of after 1814, 303, 304; secrecy about, 248–9, 252–3; steam-power for, 264–6
spinning mule: flexibility of, 306; introduction of, 263–4; name of, 263; numbers of, 304; and the small-scale unit, 306–7
state, the: contracts with as source of enrichment, 103–4, 108, 111–13, 119; links of Catalan bourgeoisie with, 21, 91–2; pressure exercised on by printers, 134–5, 136–7, 240–1; see also political authority
state intervention, 11, 18–19; the Bonaplata privilege, 308; effectiveness of, 20–1, 187; and fluctuations in commercial investment in industry, 314, 316, 319; founding cotton manufactures, 200, 249, 260; and printed calicoes, liquidation of stocks of, 53–9, 71–2, privileges granted for, 74–5, 77, 82–4, 99n, 110, 134, 157, 303; and size of manufactures, 87–8; and spinning, impact of on, 237–9, 240–1, 247–8, and machinery in, 249, 250–1, 252–3, 254–5, privilege for, 254; and

technological diffusion, 205–6, 222; in the woollen industry, 29–30, 32–3, 41, 42, 44; see also economic policy; Junta de Comercio
steam engines, 2; accelerated diffusion of, 309; advantages of, 265; in Bonaplata mill, 307–8; introduction of, 264–6; numbers of in 1846, 310; symbolic importance of, 266
Súria (Cervera), spinning in, 303

Talarn (Pallars), calico stocks in, 58
Taradell (Vic), cloth industry of, 35, 36
Tarragona: calico stocks in, 58, 60, 64; cloth industry of, 30
Tàrrega (Lérida): calico stocks in, 60; cloth industry in, 30
Taula de Canvi, 315
tax-farming, 103
technical change: benefits for from French Revolution, 249, 259; in calico-printing, copper-plate printing, 166, cylindrical printing in, 303, lack of mechanical progress in, 181, resist process, 179–80, 223; diffusion of, 46, means of, 255; introduction of spinning machinery, 248–60, use of foreign expertise for (from England) 249–54, (from France) 249, 263–4, 287 (from Switzerland) 237; machine-making, 307–8; mechanical looms, 306, 307; and merchant investment, 43, 146, 315, 316, 319; and science, 265–6; secrecy concerning, 46, 249, 252–3; see also spinning machinery; techniques
techniques: disputes over, 142–4; the madder process, 50, 64–6, 84–5; manuals about, 206; ownership of, 141, 181; the production process, 171; resist process, 66; secrecy about, 82, 84, 138–9, 140–1, 146, 176, 180, 205–6
Terrassa (Mataró), 9; cotton industry at, 236, 246, 303; woollen industry in, 28
Thorndike and Carroll, American spinners: proposal of to set up manufacture, 272–3
Toledo: foundation of Royal Company at, 136; as market, 127
Tomàs, Francesc, ribbon-maker, 192; founds manufactures, with Capelino, 154, with Olsina, 192; origins of, 192
Tomàs and Pi, successor to Olsina's manufacture, 288
Tomba, Antoni, silk-braider, associated in manufacture, 192

Printed in the United States
By Bookmasters